The Structure of Biblical Myths

The Ontogenesis of the Psyche

Heinz Westman

Spring Publications, Inc.

© 1983 by Heinz Westman. All rights reserved.

Printed in the United States of America by Gannett Graphics, 274 Western Ave., Augusta, Maine 04330. Published by Spring Publications, Inc., P.O. Box 222069, Dallas, Texas 75222.

International distributors:
Spring, Postfach, 8800 Thalwil, Switzerland
Japan Spring Sha, Inc.; 31, Shichiku-Momonomoto-Cho;
    Kitaku, Kyoto, 603 Japan
Element Books Ltd.; The Old Brewery Tisbury Salisbury;
    Wiltshire SP3 6NH; England

cover design by Anne Kilham

Library of Congress Cataloging in Publication Data

Westman, Heinz, 1902-
    Structure of biblical myths.

    (Seminar series ; 16)
    Includes bibliographical references.
    1. Bible — Psychology. 2. Psychology, Religious.
I. Title.   II. Series: Seminar series (Spring Publi-
cations) ; 16.
BS645.W453   1983   220.6′8   83-19132
ISBN 0-88214-116-3

To My Wife

Acknowledgments

I AM INDEBTED for their so helpful suggestions to Rev. R. Ash, Ms. Jutta Etzler, Prof. Th. H. Gaster, Prof. Natalie Harris, Dr. Gareth Jones, Thorkild Jacobsen, Prof. M. Lutz, Prof. W. J. Peck, Dr. N. Rehagen, Mrs. Elena Schmidt, the late Prof. Gershom Scholem and Mrs. Joyce Sutherland. Ms. S. A. Kaubris-Kowalzyk was particularly helpful as librarian, and Ms. Joni Caldwell as copy editor.

I am very grateful to Ms. Mary Irvine and Ms. Edith Hary. Last and not least Ms. Murray Jamison deserves special acknowledgment; her indefatigable efforts contributed greatly to the growth of this book.

Contents

Chapter I
Modern Man's Problem

Chapter II
The Bible As Structural Hermeneutic

Chapter III
Self-Determination

Chapter IV

Awareness

Chapter V

Change

Chapter VI
Wholeness

Chapter VII
Integration

Illustrations

xi

Preface

"Composition" and "decomposition" are the terms used by J. Hillis Miller, a Yale literary critic, to describe writing and reading. That writing is composition is a commonplace. Everyone also can see without difficulty that, while reading, he or she de-composes or analyzes what the writer has com-posed. But what is less often noticed is the fact — as Miller points out — that *reading is also composition.*

Reading is that difficult art, seldom practiced well, in which a person composes his or her own meaning while at the same time de-composing the author's composition. The composition of meaning is in the decomposition. The writer, too, had already achieved the composition, which is now read, by de-composing the writings and thoughts of earlier writers and thinkers. Just as writing is a "reading" of things which had come before the writing, so reading is a sort of "writing" of what is next to be in meaning.

But we often forget all this as we read. Rather, we expect the writer to have done our "writing" for us. We want to be composed, rather than have to compose. And, of course, we resist decomposition altogether.

C. G. Jung seems to have known that reading, authentic reading, is the composition of decomposition, and that it will therefore not be easy. At the beginning of his little bombshell of a book, *Answer to Job*, he wrote a short preface to his readers. He called the preface *Lectori Benevolo*, "To the Kind Reader," and he used an epigram from the Bible: "I am distressed for thee, my brother" (II Samuel 1:26).

If Jung had sympathy for the hard task of reading when he wrote *Answer to Job* in 1952, he was of the same mind six years later when he wrote another preface to a book, this time a collection of his writing in English. Jung said: "I am afraid my works demand some patience and some thinking. I know: it is very hard on the readers who expect to be fed by informative headlines. . . . I warn the reader: this book will not be an easy pastime. Once in a while he will meet with thoughts which demand effort of concentration and careful reflection — a condition unfortunately rare in modern times. On the other hand, the times of today seem to be serious enough to cause at least uneasy dreams if nothing else."

Surely, the times and the nightmares of the eighties are as dis-eased as those of the fifties; nor is reading less difficult and less important. The composition of decomposition is crucial.

Perhaps the only things really worth reading are those works impossible to read in the way we were taught to read about Dick and Jane, or in the way we read *The Reader's Digest*. But then the only wines worth drinking are those magnificent varietals whose complexity defies description, and whose mystery is in the fact that their *spiritus* decomposes on the tongue, taking the breath away, while composing in the thirsty soul a bouquet and body which make the high cost of drinking worth the cost.

All this is as true of this work by Heinz Westman as it is of some writings by C. G. Jung — or so it seems to this "reader." Westman's book is not easy, but just for this reason it may become important for its real readers.

This book is *not* "not easy" in the way that Plato's *Laws*, Aristotle's *Metaphysics* and Aquinas' *Summa Theologica* are "not easy." It is rather like Pascal's *Pensées*, like Emerson's *Essays* and the *Meditations* of Marcus Aurelius. This work is a mosaic, like Jung's *Mysterium Coniunctionis*. It is a picture made of many aspects, and its *Gestalt* is synchronic, all-at-once, rather than causal, mechanistic or linear. It depicts a *mystery*, and therefore calls for a reading like that of T. S. Eliot or Jorge Luis Borges; it is not susceptible to *problem*-solving, in the manner of Mickey Spillane or Sherlock Holmes. The difficulty is that of mystery rather than problem, like a rose in a poem by Robert Burns rather than a rose in a seed catalogue.

The mystery in the case of Westman's book has to do with Archetypal Psychology. It is *psychological* because it cares for the desperately ailing spirituality of modern men and women. It is *archetypal* because its way of caring is to provide deep, collective images as resources for the expression of the ailment.

Westman calls this approach a "structural hermeneutic." He says: "A structural hermeneutic is based on analogical thought, and provides a system of concepts imbedded in images, depicting a synchronistic totality." This method of "interpreting" (*hermeneutic*) our cultural and personal disease likens the dis-ease analogically to whole structures of consciousness and understanding which are illuminated by way of archetypal images.

There is, of course, nothing new in this method. Freud and Jung and their followers have, for more than half a century, made illuminating comparisons between the discontent of persons and nations on the one hand, and on the other, the archetypal images from the structures of Greek mythology (e.g., Oedipus, Eros, Thanatos, Narcissus, Hermes, Dionysos, Hera, *et alia*).

But Westman adds a "new" resource to this important method: the Bible! It would hardly be surprising were Occidental men and women to discover that the deepest patterns of modern behavior and fantasy were as much like Jacob and Esau as like Eros and Psyche, as much like Cain and Abel as Narcissus and Echo, as much like David and Bathsheba as Hermes and the nymph of Dryops. We in the West are as much heir to Palestine as to Greece. And, after all, we today need all the archetypal resources we can discover for our dreary collective psyches.

Westman had already begun the important work of interpreting the Bible as archetypal psychology, as a "structural hermeneutic," in his book *The Springs Of Creativity*. But what was begun in that book in 1961, with accounts of Genesis and Job, is here amplified many times over in a survey of "the whole history of our becoming" told in Biblical imagery. As Westman himself says: "At the beginning, the history of becoming also began, and is therefore a history of salvation." The Biblical images "save" psychologically and morally, in his view, by bringing to articulate and profound expression our own personal and collective stories. "Moses and Christ," Westman writes, giving only two examples, "are both personifications of this becoming, and the Exodus and the Last Supper are historical symbols of the process."

A mythopoesis of the Bible! Only Northrop Frye has attempted this on such a grand scale. And his recent book, *The Great Code* (the Bible being the "code" to personal and cultural modes of meaning in the Western tradition), does not carry the psychological depth or the ethical edge that Westman's does.

Perhaps "boundary" would be a better term than "edge." The anthropologist Victor Turner calls it *liminal*, meaning "threshold" or "betwixt-n-between." But by whatever name, three boundary-zones become important in this work.

(1) *Religion and Psychology*. Westman situates his composition firmly between the soul of men and women, on the one hand, and, on the other, Biblical images. He refuses to treat either of these poles idolatrously: the work is neither behaviorist in the manner of an ego psychology, nor is it fundamentalistic or historicist concerning religion's symbols. Each informs and de-composes the literalism of the other, and thereby each iconoclastically and prophetically composes the other meaningfully. Modern psychology "reads" the Bible; but, also, the Bible "reads" the soul of modern times.

(2) *Psychology and Sociology* (*Morality*). A reigning imperialism unchallenged in recent times — a sort of fascism of the academic mind! — is the claim for supremacy by the

two most recent children of the Social Sciences. Psychological interpretations seem to rule out ethics. Meanwhile, from the side of sociological interpretations of cultural reality, there seems little sensitivity to dimensions of human depth. Statistical studies rule the day. Psychology has no moral sense; sociology has no soul. Westman won't have it! Such a fascism of the mind is attacked for what it is, decomposed in Westman's composition.

(3) *Science and the Bible.* In a day of renewed futilities between the proponents of Biblical literalism (Creationism) and Scientism (Evolutionism), Westman vigorously occupies a third boundary-zone. Already, Gary Zukav (*The Dancing Wu Li Masters*) and Fritjof Capra (*The Tao of Physics*) have ventured into this liminal "between." But in both of these cases only the science of physics is at issue, and far-away Oriental religion is the analogue, the "structural hermeneutic." Westman brings it all home. It is the Bible —the Scriptures of Jew and Christian — which gives image to *Western* science, as long as those Scriptures can be "read" (i.e., de-composed and composed) symbolically. And Westman accomplishes this, not only for physics, but for biology as well!

Truly a mosaic! — But we were never promised a rose garden, at least not a rose garden without mystery and bugs. Out of the compost heap of a decaying civilization, Heinz Westman's meditations provide a rich mix, a crucial composition.

DAVID L. MILLER
WATSON-LEDDEN PROFESSOR OF RELIGION
SYRACUSE UNIVERSITY

A Note To The Reader

THIS BOOK has been written after about 50 years of experience with men and women in quest for themselves. As such it represents a living process of interrelatedness not only between the different disciplines of life, but also between the vast spans of time and space. The method applied is therefore a structural hermeneutic and not a structural analysis, which tries to analyze parts of the whole. In the consideration of life as a unity and a continuum, the modern scientific search also expresses itself. The contents of this book are not therefore presented as isolated aspects within a limited frame.

Every judgment in science stands on the edge of error, and is personal. Science is a tribute to what we can know although we are fallible. In the end the words were said by Oliver Cromwell: "I beseech you, in the bowels of Christ, think it possible you may be mistaken."[1]

"In the beginning God created man. But now men create God. That is the way it is in the world — men make gods and worship their creation. It would be fitting for the gods to worship men!"

— Gospel of Philip, ca. 250 A.D.[2]

CHAPTER 1

Modern Man's Problem

Introduction

Denn jedem wird ein andrer Gott erscheinen,
bis sie erkennen, nah am Weinen,
dass durch ihr meilenweites Meinen,
durch ihr Vernehmen und Verneinen
verschieden nur in hundred Seinen
ein Gott wie eine Welle geht.
                                        —Rilke

To each a different God will appear, until,
Near to crying they recognize
That through their miles-apart supposing
Through their understanding and denying,
There goes like a wave one God,
Different only in his hundred tones.[3]

THE POLITICAL, economic, and moral condition of the world is once again in danger of collapse into primitive chaos. Today, every individual is faced with the need for undertaking the *opus magnum* of finding a personal direction. Religious dogma and the patterns of ritualistic ceremony have proved to be ineffective; they are being replaced as each person grows into an awareness of himself as a distinct and separate individual. Such an awareness can give direction not only to one's own life, but to the life of society as well. As we find the innate meaning of our own being, we are able to withdraw at least our own misunderstandings from the general pool of social confusion, and thus contribute creatively to the growth and development of life.

The method employed in our investigation throughout this book rests upon the conviction that essence is more vital than form. This essence expresses itself in the ontogenetic principle: namely, *that which guides the unique development of the individual.* In other words, ontogenesis is the essence of the *individual* experience of life.

The order of nature is not an order outside and separate from ourselves, though it is often understood as only external due to our own becoming, our own growth toward form and order. For the same reason, the ontogenesis of the individual psyche is echoed in the symbols of the phylogenetic (i.e., cultural) evolution reflected in religious and philosophical thought, in science, and in art. Abraham and Akhenaton, Moses and Christ, Plato and Spinoza, Galileo and Rembrandt, Gandhi and Einstein, Pope John XXIII and Jung, are public manifestations of ontogenesis in the life of civilization.

Evidence for the ontogenesis of the psyche will take us into several areas in this book. Religious writing, from the most ancient to contemporary, and manifestations in political life and in modern science will help to illustrate the development of the individual psyche. Frequent reference will be made to the Hebraic-Christian Bible. For our purposes, however, the Bible must be understood, not through structural analysis, but through structural hermeneutic. A structural analysis of Biblical writings rests on an assumed context of historicity which constructs an intellectual whole from bits and pieces, many of which have no basis in objective fact. On the other hand, a structural hermeneutic depends upon the "catholic" or universal unity of human growth and development which is revealed in the inner essence of the Biblical themes, and hence deals with the development of the psyche.

It is not structural analysis which is a guiding principle toward understanding and experiencing essential truth, but structural hermeneutic. It is the condition of "knowing" in its deepest sense. Biblical stories are mythological though they *may* be related to historical events. Stories which do have origins in historical facts may, nonetheless, be seen as inner and / or outer realities, and therefore are not limited to interpretation as "history." Biblical stories reveal not only the working of the human mind, but they are also vehicles of communication, and speak to individuals because of their phylogenetic truth. They are a living dialectic of our inner history, providing us with the satisfaction of our essential need to experience "consciously" a meaning for our own lives.

Despite the materiality of our bodies, we are not in our essential being, a substance, just as matter, in terms of quantum theory, is not a substance. Nothing fundamental is static. What we are doing when we talk about the essence of being human is describing levels of human experience. These levels, descriptive of human experience, take on an appropriate form in the same sense that art takes on a form that fits the idea which it seeks to express. (Etymologically the word *"art,"* derived from the Latin *ars*, means "to join, to fit, to bring together." In Greek, the root is *artunein,* meaning "to arrange.")

Consider, for example, the human response to idol-worship. The idol is presumed to be an objective reality within its physical form and gifted with power. As soon, however, as the deity is interiorized, it becomes a subjective being and cannot be described through analogy to an external object or by an abstract proper noun — rather, it becomes a living process. Ptah Hotep, an Old Kingdom Egyptian sage (ca. 2,500 B.C.) taught: "It is the heart which brings up its lord as one who hears [or] as one who does not hear."[4]

When persons become aware of themselves as distinct human beings, they realize that they are gifted with both mind and conscience. Cicero translated the Greek *syneidesis,* with the term *conscienta.* The Greek was coined by the

Stoic Chrysippos (ca. 280 B.C.) and means essentially "the gyroscope of the individual soul."[5]

Now the Greek *syneidesis* means knowledge shared with one's self, being "in the know," *con-science*. Socrates used *syneidesis* to mean "conscious of one's self." Conscience is therefore the result of one's relation to the self and to one's environment; it is not the result of education or indoctrination into the individual's world from outside. Jeremiah 2:19 says: "*Your* wickedness will chasten you and *your* apostasy will reprove you" (italics mine). Conscience would, therefore, seem to be an expression of a kind of directing and corrective activity from within the human organism itself.

Dietrich Bonhoeffer, the renowned Protestant theologian, being in the hands of the Nazis in prison, was confronted not only with himself and thus forced to ask authentic questions, but also with how to face the terror of the situation in which he found himself. He wrote:

> Religious people speak of God when human perception is (often just from laziness) at an end, or human resources fail: it is in fact always the *Deus ex machina* they call to their aid, either for the so-called solving of insoluble problems or as support in human failure — always, that is to say, helping our human weakness or on the borders of human existence. Of necessity, that can only go on until men can, by their own strength, push those borders a little further, so that God becomes superfluous as a *Deus ex machina*. I have come to be doubtful even about talking of "borders of human existence." Is even death today, since men are scarcely afraid of it any more, and sin, which they scarcely understand any more, still a genuine borderline? It always seems to me that in talking thus we are only seeking frantically to make room for God.[6]

For one thus thrown upon himself, God becomes superfluous as *Deus ex machina* and the real source of strength reveals itself, paradoxically, in weakness. The New Testament repeats Jeremiah's insight in these words: "My grace is sufficient for you, for my power is made perfect in weakness."[7]

By nature, the way to oneself is fraught with anxiety. One enters into a realm of as-yet-unknown aspects of the Self, and as these aspects begin to be manifest, there is great resentment and resistance to their discovery. One has entered a realm of powerful forces of anti-growth and inertia which trouble the equilibrium of the individual in the same way that such discoveries disturb the life of societies. The poets portray this essential human condition as basic in the development of the psyche. Chronos, in Greek mythology, attempts to destroy his children so that he can escape from the realization that he is growing old. From the perspective of the poetic imagination, it is the struggle between inertia, attempting to stabilize and maintain the existing situation, on the one hand, and the urge toward creativity and upward growth on the other. This struggle is a recognition of the power of life's inner demand for meaningful continuity.

If we are to appreciate the modern Self and to arrive at an understanding of what stirs in the depths of modern society — if we are to account for general social unrest as reflected in the doubts of students in relation to their teachers, and in the general and nearly universal rejection of authority — then we must seek to comprehend it in our eternal "becoming," in the development of the psyche which is frustrated by the structures of modern societies and their institutions. As Bonhoeffer writes:

> We are proceeding towards a time of no religion at all: men as they are simply cannot be religious any more.... What we call Christianity has always been a pattern — perhaps a true pattern — of religion. But if one day it becomes apparent that this *a priori* 'premise' simply does not exist, but was a historical

and temporary form of human self-expression, i.e., if
we reach the stage of being radically without religion
— and I think this is more or less the case already,
else how is it, for instance, that this war, unlike any of
those before it, is not calling forth any 'religious'
reaction? — what does that mean for 'Christianity'?

It means that the linchpin is removed from the
whole structure of our Christianity to date.[8]

The structural form of religion in its institutional, crystallized form is giving way to the experience of the ever-
creative principle which manifests itself not only in the inner
and outer life of the individual, but also on the larger plane
of society as a whole. Beyond the dissolution of institutional
religion there is also an awareness that the "universe" as we
have understood it, is falling apart, receding without a
center into the infinite. These developments may be seen as a
result of a deepening consciousness of the ontogenesis of the
human psyche.

To state the same theme differently, the projection of
human "compactness" and a stable universe into dogma and
theory is now dissolving into a free-flowing experience of
life in all its manifold aspects. We are bursting through the
mental and spiritual containment of the past as a chick does
through its shell.

The human tendency to project onto the universe the
containment and limitations of human thought is reflected
in Scandinavian, pre-Aryan Indian, Chinese, and Hebrew
mythology.

The aboriginal poets of pre-Aryan India thought not of a
god or gods at the beginning of these things but of a First
Man, Perusha (later, Prjapati, and later still Brahma). He
was

   . . . a personification of the all-containing life-
   matter and life-force itself, yearning to develop into
   teeming worlds. And he was impelled to create . . . by
   a two-fold principle. On the one hand, he felt lonely,

destitute, and *fearful,* and so brought forth the universe to surround himself with company; but on the other hand, he also felt a longing to let his substance overflow, wherefore he said to himself: "May I give increase; may I bring forth creatures."[9]

The ancient Chinese also imagined a cosmic man named P'an Ku *(P'an,* "shell of an egg" and *Ku,* "to make solid"). He was the offspring of the original dual powers, the Yin and Yang, and they set him the task of giving form to chaos and of making the heavens and the earth.[10]

In Scandinavian mythology the cosmic man was called Ymer.

From Ymer's flesh the earth was created
From his bones the mountains
From the skull of the ice-cold giant the Sky
From his blood the surge.[11]

In the Old Testament tradition, "Adam, the primal man, reached from one end of the earth to the other," or in a second version, from "earth to heaven." "Here," states the Talmud, "seems to be a contradiction," and answers its own question: "Both measurements are identical." "The dust from which the primal man was created came from the whole earth." To which Rashi (commentator, 1040-1105 A.D.) adds: "from the four corners of the world." And the Talmud expressively states: "Every man carries the stamp of the primal man and yet everyone is unique and not the same as the other." The body of the primal man came from Babylonia, his head from Israel and the extremities from all the other countries.[12]

The Basis of Dogmatism

THE IDEA from Genesis 1:26 that humanity is made in the likeness of the *One God* is so deeply imbedded in the human psyche that this notion has become the measure of person-hood. When, however, this symbol is projected onto a reli-gious or political structure, or onto a single person, then idolatry is established. The existential problem of *who* the individual is loses its spiritual significance, and each person is turned into a *what,* a thing for which freedom *to be* is denied. Then, persons are not allowed to become and grow according to their individual needs, or worse still, are simply not allowed to exist. They become objects to be evaluated solely on racist or other grounds, and are treated accord-ingly. The well-known German existentialist philosopher, Martin Heidegger, speaking as Chancellor of the renowned University of Freiburg in Germany, said on November 3, 1933: "Not precepts and 'ideas' are the rules of your exis-tence. The leader himself and he alone *is* today's and the German reality of the future and its *laws!*"13

When religious systems, as in Germany, refuse to accept responsibility for essential spiritual values and remain silent in the face of the demonic policies of the Nazis which by their exclusiveness represent the "Anti-Christ,"14 then one can see that as Bonhoeffer suggested, the "linchpin" is removed. Such exclusiveness is not relegated only to Hitler's monstrous behaviour against the Jews, but was reflected also in his refusal to acknowledge in 1936 the Olympic Gold Medalist, Jessie Owens, because he was black! This is only one example of many of the racial biases and the denial of human personhood perpetrated by the "master race."

Certainly there were clergy and other concerned individuals who resisted the Nazis and paid, like the theologian Dietrich Bonhoeffer, with their lives. At the same time, the "official" religious authorities, in order to ensure their survival, entered, as did the Catholics, into a concordat with Hitler, or signed, as did some Protestants, the so-called "Barmen Declaration." While both documents affirm a Christian stance toward the world in fine phrases, the really significant and effective portions of both statements tell another story.

Prof. Hannah Arendt wrote in relation to the murderous actions against the Jewish minority in Hungary:

> Horthy [the acting head of the Hungarian government] had been deluged with protests from neutral countries and from the Vatican. The Papal Nuncio, though, deemed it appropriate to explain that the Vatican's protest did not spring *'from a false sense of compassion'* — a phrase that is likely to be a lasting monument to what the continued dealings with, and the desire to compromise with, the men who preached the gospel of 'ruthless toughness' had done to the mentality of the highest dignitaries of the Church.[15]

The Concordat was concluded under the guidance of Pope Pius XI, and was already signed on July 20, 1933. It was celebrated in the Hedwigs Cathedral in Berlin with a special Te Deum of thanksgiving by the Papal Nuncio, Orsenigo, on September 17, 1933. To be fully understood, the Concordat and the Barmen Declaration need to be seen against the backdrop of Hitler's own attitude, reflecting, of course, the position of the Nazis in general. Hitler expressed his views to Albert Speer: "The Church will come round. I know that crew of black crows well enough to see that. What did they do in England? And how about Spain? All we have to do is apply pressure to them."[16]

The instruments of such pressure are found in Articles
XIV and XVI of the Concordat. Article XIV reads:

> The Bull for the appointment of Archbishops,
> Bishops, Coadjutors cum jure successiones or of a
> Praelatus nullius will not be issued until the name of
> the appointee is submitted to the representative of
> the National Government in the respective state and
> it has been ascertained that no objections of a general
> political nature exist. It is understood that when
> objections of a general political nature exist, they
> shall be presented in the shortest possible time.…
> The names of the persons in question will be held
> confidential until the announcement of the appoint-
> ment. A state veto shall not be required to assign
> reasons.

Article XVI reads:

> Before the Bishops take possession of their dio-
> cese, they are to take an oath of fealty either to the
> national representative in the states, or the president
> of the Reich, respectively, according to the following
> formula: "Before God and on the holy Gospels I
> swear and promise — as becomes a bishop, loyalty to
> the German Reich and to the … state. I swear and
> promise to honor the constitutional government and
> to cause the clergy of my diocese to honor it. In the
> performance of my spiritual office and in my solici-
> tude for the welfare and interest in the German State,
> I will try to avoid every detrimental act which
> endangers it."[17]

A minority of the Nazi-resisting Protestant ministers
signed the Barmen Declaration in 1934. The signatories of
this declaration, though affirming the sanctity of the individual, also were moved in Section 5 to refer to 1 Peter 2:17:
"Fear God. Honor the Emperor." And it goes on to read:

Scripture tells that, in the as yet unredeemed world in which the Church also exists, the State has by divine appointment the task of providing for justice and peace. [It fulfills this task] *by means of the threat and exercise of force,* according to the measure of human judgment and human ability. The Church acknowledges the benefit of the divine appointment in gratitude and reverence before him.[18]

This decisive part of the Barmen Declaration is based on Romans 13:1-3: "Let every person be subject to the governing authorities. For there is no authority except from God. . . . Therefore he who resists the authorities resists what God has appointed, and those who resist will incur judgment. For rulers are not a terror to good conduct, but to bad." The Nazi authorities made use of this saying of St. Paul's solely in their own secular sense. In Part II of "Pacem in Terris" Pope John XXIII quotes St. John Chrysostom in his explanation of St. Paul:

> *What are you saying? Is every ruler appointed by God? No, that is not what I mean,* he says, *for I am not now talking about individual rulers, but about authority as such . . .*
> *. . . and this authority, no less than society itself, has its source in nature, and consequently has God for its author.*[19]

Modern man, urged by the ontogenesis of the psyche, rejects both the doctrine that the end justifies the means taken by the state and the dogma that closes the mind. No spiritual sovereignty which tries to lay down rules can serve the human dilemma of today but rather a "living with" as exemplified in Christ's saying "give to Caesar what is Caesar's and to God what is God's." Man is standing simultaneously in both orders of reality, the external and the internal. It is here where he carries his cross, where the God in him speaks silently, by throwing him onto his own resources.

> Silence is woven into the very texture of human
> nature, but it is only the basis on which the higher
> appears.
>
> In the human mind silence is merely knowledge of
> the *Deus absconditus,* the hidden god. In the human
> spirit silence is merely the silent harmony with things
> and the audible harmony of music.[20]

It is tragic to realize that a war which cost 52 million lives
and which produced Belsen and Auschwitz, was apparently
necessary to convey to the world the human rights message
of Vatican II, which in turn was prompted through Pope
John XXIII's encyclical "Pacem in Terris."

The Great Criminal seems to have brought about the
conditions making it possible for humanity to achieve a new
consciousness. He broke into the old spiritual and secular
institutions in order to acquire their values for himself. But
his criminal action created the counterpoise. The inherent
value of the institutions became detached from the obsolete
shell which had grown dry and brittle, allowing access to the
burglar. The Judaeo-Christian message of love and the
mystery of God becoming man, the inner meaning of our
epoch, was now forced to find its realization on the plane of
a new reality. In this process the "criminal" acted as
accoucher. He tried to destroy the universal spiritual institutions of humanity and enforced an individual decision as to
the values inherent in the old structures.

It is tempting to believe that had the churches sounded the
clarion call of human rights before Hitler came to power, all
that followed might have been avoided; the atom bomb
would not have been produced; World War II could have
been averted; the shame of Belsen and Auschwitz would not
stare the world in the face; and 150 million East Europeans
would not be under Communist rule today[infra, p. 284]. In
1932 the Nazi party was in disarray, debt-ridden, and declin-
ing sharply in the local elections. Prof. David Schoenbaum
wrote: "By the end of the year 1932 the Nazi Party's disinte-

gration was a real possibility."[21] The silent adult majority still stood in awe of authority and would likely have listened had the churches spoken with united voices in spite of the political complexities. The average age of the members of the Nazi party in 1930-1933 was only about 22 years! Hitler's book *Mein Kampf* was well-known and readily available at that time; and the Nazi hordes were roaming the streets singing *Judenblut muss fliessen:* "the blood of the Jews must flow."

Based on the revelations, fifty years after the events, of a Catholic priest who became a close adviser in Church affairs to the Nazi authorities, Prof. Georg Denzler, chairman of the Department of Church History, University of Bamberg, Germany, wrote a detailed essay entitled: "How Catholic Bishops Became Accessories to the Guilt of Nazi Germany." Ending his article, Prof. Denzler quotes the Jesuit Max Pribilla: "If the Christians in Germany and in the whole of the Western World would have been more vital, there would not have been a Third Reich with all its symptoms of decay."[22]

After World War II had ended and the extent of the Nazi horror became world-wide information, there were signs of hope that a new birth of spirit was taking form in the institutions of religion. Thus the Vatican II document "Nostra Aetate," Declaration on the Relation of the Church to Non-Christian Religions, stated:

> For all peoples comprise a single community, and have a single origin, since God made the whole race of men dwell over the entire face of the earth. . . . One also is their final goal. God.[23]

The way to the common destiny changes from culture to culture and while it has its universal character, the path is nevertheless distinct in its uniqueness for every culture. In the Christian dogma sex is considered to be acceptable only conditionally, as it is judged against the background of the dogma of the original "sin" of Adam and Eve. St. Augustine in his treatise *On Original Sin* quotes Ambrose: "We men are all of us born in sin, our very origin is in sin."[24] And in the preceding chapter he writes: "... the fault of our nature remains in our offspring so deeply impressed as to make it guilty, even when the guilt of the self-same fault has been washed away in the parent by the remission of sins...."[25] The consideration of sex as "original sin" is also mirrored in Psalms 51:5 of the Old Testament: "Behold, I was shapen in iniquity; and in sin did my mother conceive me."

At the recent Bishops' synod "On Family" in Rome (Fall 1980), the African Archbishop Gabriel Wake of Khartoum maintained that:

> The Church's current marital rite is extraneous to people's lives. Instead of being encased in tribal custom and family traditions, the ritual is centered upon the priest. ... [Pope John Paul II] stressed the ideal of priestly celibacy as a model for the fidelity to their calling that should motivate a married couple. The Africans were knowingly defying the papal viewpoint.[26]

One of the most sacred Hindu symbols portrays Vajradhara in eternal sexual embrace, the *hieros gamos,* with his Shakti, his feminine aspect. As a symbol of wholeness, Vajradhara combines in his being also the five highest Buddhas representing the four corners of the world and Vairocan the sun Buddha.[27] Together they form a mandala [infra, p. 189]. This mandala is a supreme representation of the divine in its wholeness *as an inner vision* and can therefore not be apprehended as an idol. In Buddhism the symbol of Yin and Yang, the female and male in eternal interplay, represent the same mental reality.

Hence the Roman Catholic dogmas relating to sex and celibacy are of no compelling value in India or Africa nor is the dogma governing contraception. The latter is even not adhered to in the West, so it is assumed, by over 80% of even

Figure 1. Vajradhara and Shakti

Catholic women, not to speak of the rest of the populace.
The East is also free of the anxieties and guilt which, for the
West, result from these superimposed dogmas.

While the Second Vatican Council's "Nostra Aetate"
acknowledges that "other religions which are found
throughout the world attempt in their own ways to calm the
hearts of men by outlining a program of life covering doctrine, moral precepts and sacred rites,"[28] Pope John Paul II
in his encyclical "Redemptor Hominis" goes on to say:

Man as "willed" by God, as "chosen" by him from
eternity and called, destined for grace and glory —
this is "each" man, "the most concrete" man, "the
most real"; this is man in all the fullness of the
mystery in which he has become a sharer in Jesus
Christ, the mystery in which each one of the four

thousand million human beings living on our planet has become a sharer from the moment he is conceived beneath the heart of his mother.[29]

In this statement, the Encyclical moves from a universal understanding of what it means to be human to a concept limited by dogmatic considerations. It lost its *inclusive* character and became *exhaustive,* i.e., the all-embracing quality is denied in favor of the exclusion of differing religious experiences.

The way to the "common destiny" specified by Vatican II changes from culture to culture, and while it has a universal character, the path is nevertheless distinct in its uniqueness for every culture. Buddhism, Hinduism, Islam and Judaism are also expressions of, and vessels for "each man," the "most concrete man," the "most real."

The person gripped by the solemnity of the stark realities of our present-day problems in international and intranational relations loses his way in the welter of contradictions, unless he realizes that a new awareness, a heightened consciousness is a perennial problem. Apparently the spirit addresses itself anew in every aeon to this very growth, this becoming. A new *Zeitgeist* established itself around the time of Abraham and Akhenaton in Egypt, as it did at the beginning of our era with Christ. Symbolically this movement of spirit is expressed in Daniel 7:10, where out of the most ferocious beast with ten horns the "human" — "The Son of Man" — is born. In similar fashion, following the bestial horrors of the Nazis, Pope John XXIII could write a prayer shortly before his death which he intended to have read from all the pulpits the world over:

We are conscious today that many, many centuries of blindness have cloaked our eyes so that we can no longer either see the beauty of Thy Chosen People nor recognize in their faces the features of our privileged brethren. We realize that the mark of Cain stands upon our foreheads. Across the centuries our brother Abel has lain in the blood we drew or shed the tears we caused by forgetting Thy Love. Forgive us the curse we falsely attached to their name as Jews. Forgive us for crucifying Thee a second time in their flesh. For we knew not what we did.[30]

To appreciate fully the depth of this outstanding statement in all its greatness, one needs to keep in mind the attitude and policy of the church toward the Jews in particular and thus to Human Rights in general for nearly 2,000 years of its history. Pope John XXIII in his prayer refers not only to Cain's essential question: "Am I my brother's keeper?" (Genesis 8:9) but also in a deep sense to the "blinded" shepherd Polyphemus of Greek mythology [infra, p. 359].[31] The German Chancellor Helmut Schmidt, at the occasion of the 40th anniversary of the "Kristallnacht" (a full-fledged pogrom organized by the Nazis) said on November 9, 1978: "The Germans living today are mostly innocent as individuals. But we have to bear the political heritage of the guilty and accept the consequences. Here lies our responsibility."[32]

A statement by the Evangelical Church in Germany on the occasion of the 40th anniversary of the pogrom of November 9, 1938 reads,

Only Few Disagreed:
To ponder about the guilt and its consequences of the Third Reich is both for the Church and the country a perennial task. ... About 80,000 Jewish citizens were arrested and many of them pushed into concentration camps. The number of burnt synagogues is around 237 and the destroyed businesses and apartments numbered about 7,800.[33]

The New Testament in relation to the new aeon which came into being at the dawn of our era expressed in stark terms what a searching society felt then about the guardians of spirituality:

> But woe to you, scribes and Pharisees, hypocrites! because you shut the kingdom of heaven against men; for you neither enter yourselves, nor allow those who would enter to go in. Woe to you, scribes and Pharisees, hypocrites! for you traverse sea and land to make a single proselyte, and when he becomes a proselyte, you make him twice as much a child of hell as yourselves. Woe to you, blind guides, who say, "If anyone swears by the temple it is nothing; but if anyone swears by the gold of the temple, he is bound by his oath!"[34]

The holocaust was a primitive falling back into a scapegoat theology for salvation. Basic to this theology is the belief that the scapegoat "brings about the reversal from common danger to common salvation."[35] It is an age-old magical practice, as Burkert, for example, shows:

> ... the great plague of 1348 brought about the most terrible pogroms all over Europe against the outsiders, the Jews, said to be responsible for the disaster. Even in 1630, in Milan, during an epidemic disease some persons were put to death in an extraordinarily cruel way because they were suspected of having artificially spread the plague. It is safe to say that nobody could wage bacteriological warfare at the time; hence they were innocent; but the group reflex at the peak of anxiety found its compulsive outlet.[36]

St. Sebastian, the saint of the pest, became sanctified as a scapegoat. The stories surrounding him speak of terrible brutalities and he is displayed, shot to death by arrows, as a most prominent figure on Mathias Grünewald's famous Isenheimer Altar at Colmar, France.[37]

Man torn between heaven and earth stands alone amidst

the torrents of the apparent contradictions of Life. He is called to make his own decisions, thus to be the responsible agent for his own becoming and in this way to attest to the truth of Christ's or the psalmist's reminder: "I say, 'You are gods.' "[38]

Even in the midst of the holocaust there were some who were not dead to the inner voice. Facing his so-called "judges" at the trial for the attempt to assassinate Hitler on July 20, 1944, Ewald von Kleist-Schmenzin, one of the conspirators, said:

> "Yes I committed high treason, always and with all my possibilities since January 30, 1933. [The day the Nazis came to power] I never hid my fight against Hitler and National Socialism. I consider the fight as a duty ordained by God. God alone will be my judge."[39]

In explaining the parable of the sower, Jesus said of the seed which fell on rocky ground:

> As for what was sown on rocky ground, this is he who hears the word and immediately receives it with joy; *yet he has no root in himself,* but endures for a while, and when tribulation or persecution arises on account of the word, immediately he falls away.[40]

Von Kleist had heard the word, had roots in himself, and when tribulation or persecution arose he did not fall away, precisely because he did not follow the travesty of the Barmen Declaration granting that the state has the privilege by the use of threat and force to impose its inhumanity as a right. On July 20, 1979, commemorating in a television broadcast the heroic deed of the "traitors" of July 20, 1944, the Chancellor of the Federal Republic of Germany said: "The deeds of these men are the moral base of the republic."

It is significant to note that the civil activists who protested in the United States against the war in Vietnam and its horrors were not led by religious institutions. Ordinary citizens and some clergy acted out of their own inner moral recognition. For this inner moral foundation is the essence of personhood — the essence of our humanity which ties us to both the secular and the spiritual realities and which has reasserted itself time and again as a given in human history. It is this expression of the ontogenesis of the psyche that in our time demythologizes belief in dogmas and refuses blind obedience to authority. Dogmatic authority, whether it be political or religious, keeps the human essence imprisoned. Salvation, in the end, means the freedom to experience one's own self-fulfillment and self-realization, and in turn, this is only truly valid if it is related responsibly to society as a whole and to life as a whole. Dogma needs to be seen in relation to its spiritual function as it assists or deters the individual in the process of becoming more "human." To be sure, particular experiences of the individual often become models which take the place of emotional, unconscious dogmas; as such they are either followed or resented and thus condition the life of the person unbeknownst to him. Such mental fixtures need to be viewed in a wider context so that the individual may be released from the mental bondage which originates often from parents or from the surrounding society.

Moral Recognition
As Basis Of Personhood

TERRORISTS reflect the "dark" side of the spirit in revolt. In the use of murder to establish a new order in society, they are driven by their own dogmas to perform criminal deeds which, if successful, could only lead to another form of slavery. Their actions do not contribute to the establishment of an ethical, responsible society, but rather strengthen the malaise of an exploitative social order by adding to the widespread feeling of helplessness, depression, and a mood of gloom.

Moral man in the midst of an immoral society is not a new awareness which reaches the consciousness of man in our times. There is preserved in the British Museum an Egyptian text, a copy of which stems from the 18th Dynasty (1562-1308 B.C.). The text itself is possibly much older and may have been composed as early as the period presumed to be that of the Old Testament Patriarchs. A priest of Heliopolis named Khekhe-perre-soneb expressed for his times a salient feature of our own in the following lines:

> I have spoken this in accordance with what I have seen. . . . Righteousness is cast out, iniquity is in the midst of the council-hall. The plans of the gods are violated, their dispositions are disregarded. The land is in distress, mourning is in every place, towns and districts are in lamentation. All men alike are under wrongs; as for respect, an end is made of it. . . .
>
> When I would speak thereof, my limbs are heavy laden. I am distressed because of my heart, it is suffering to hold my peace concerning it. Another

heart would bow down, [but] a brave heart in distress is the companion of its lord. Would that I had a heart able to suffer. Then I would rest in it. . . . Come then, my heart, that I may speak to thee and that thou mayest answer for me my sayings and mayest explain to me that which is in the land. . . . I am meditating on what has happened. Calamities come to pass today, tomorrow afflictions are not past. All men are silent concerning it, [although] the whole land is in great disturbance. Nobody is free from evil; all men alike do it. Hearts are sorrowful. He who gives commands is as he to whom commands are given; the heart of both of them is content. Men awake to it in the morning daily, [but] hearts thrust it not away. The fashion of yesterday therein is like today. . . . There is none so wise that he perceives, and none so angry that he speaks. Men awake in the morning to suffer every day. Long and heavy is my malady. *The poor man has no strength to save himself from him that is stronger than he.* It is painful to keep silent concerning the things heard, [but] it is suffering to reply to the ignorant man.[41]

Modern man is experiencing a shift from faith in tradition and blind obedience to authority to a reasoned attitude toward life, and with it, new confidence in the human potential for moral responsibility. He realizes that there is no universal scale to measure the divine impulse. It creates its own standard as it finds expression in the quality of the individual. This quality is a unique response to given circumstances according to the unique spiritual nature of the individual. The consciousness of this spiritual state has profoundly influenced modern man. For consummation lies in surrendering himself to whatever composes his unique spirituality. He can achieve fulfillment only by relating his own spiritual nature to the universal.

Before he became the dogmatizing head of the Roman

Catholic Church, Karol Wojtyla, Pope John Paul II, wrote in 1969:

> Self-determination ... is that becoming of the person which both has its own specific nature which may be disclosed in a phenomenological way, and indicates its own, separate ontic identity, while in morality it stands out as an existential fact characteristic of man. ... Self-determination, which is the proper dynamic basis for the development of the person, presupposes a special complexity in the structure of the person. ... In a different order of things the person as a creature may be seen as '*belonging to God,*' but this relation *does not eliminate or over-shadow that inner relation of self-possession* or self-ownership which is essential for the person. It is not without reason then that medieval philosophers expressed this relationship in the phrase, *persona est sui iuris.*[42]

Again, the future Pope could write:

> The dignity proper to man, the dignity that is held out to him both as a gift and as something to be striven for, is inextricably bound up with truth. Truthful thinking and truthful living are the indispensable and essential components of that dignity. In a way the Council [Vatican II] spoke even more profoundly on this subject in the Declaration *Dignitatis Humanae* on religious freedom: "Because of their dignity all human beings, inasmuch as they are persons, have inherent in their nature a moral obligation to seek the truth, to adhere to the truth and to make the whole of their lives respond to truth's demands. *They are in no position to meet that obligation unless they enjoy both psychological freedom and immunity from external coercion.*"[43]

In the Talmud there is a most charming and remarkable story, which though written about 1800 years ago, goes to the root of our situation today. Like a poetic dream, deep in its symbolism, it illuminates the spiritual meaning of man's eternal problem of becoming human. The story portrays the Divine as favoring the individual in opposition to the corporate. The "miracles" in the story — events which seem *contra naturam,* "against the laws of nature," and which in fact are unscientific — depict presumably that the fixed "laws" as given in the Bible can also be subject to change. The frame of the story is the question of whether a human relationship which had broken down and been repaired, like a broken but repaired vessel, is ritualistically clean or unclean. The force holding it together is depicted as a snake, like the snake in the Garden of Eden, which after all made Adam and Eve conscious of relationship. Awareness of the true value of a relationship is what keeps marriages alive. But this symbol may also mean, according to the text, that they encompassed the repaired object "with arguments as a snake and proved it [therefore] unclean." The whole procedure we may call today "an ecclesiastical tribunal for judgment regarding the marriage's validity,"[44] which tries by clever arguments and dogma to enforce "togetherness."

The story in the Talmud enlightens the meaning of this passage about marriage and deals with strife in the home, for "if the barley is out of the storage tank, tension and argument arise." Marriage is seen, as in modern times, as a contractual arrangement, open to argument in terms of materialistic values. Marriage, in these situations, is not experienced essentially as a meeting of mind with mind. According to the contractual view, *wants* are expected to be met and if they are not, the marriage breaks down; while from the point of view of marriage as a meeting, spiritual *needs* complement each other. The clarification of such needs certainly cannot be laid down by impersonal tribunals, but can only be truly answered by the concerned individuals. Therefore, from the point of view of the ontogenesis of the psyche, the sages of the past made one rabbi, Rabbi Eliezer, declare the situation as clean; while the other side, the collective, represented by Rabbi Joshua, declared the solution as unclean. It is in such a dramatic clash of opposites that the human mind establishes its conditions for human rights. And as we shall see, the Divine is on the side of Rabbi Eliezer, yet in the end, as in our time, the collective exercises its power. So, the story goes like this:

> It has been taught that on that day Rabbi Eliezer brought forward every imaginable argument, but they did not accept them. Rabbi Eliezer said to them, "If the Halakha [i.e., interpretation] agrees with me, let this carob tree prove it." Therefore the carob tree was torn a hundred cubits out of its place — others affirm 400 cubits. "No proof can be brought from a carob tree," they retorted. Again he said to them, "If the Halakha agrees with me, let the stream of water prove it." Thereupon the stream of water flowed backwards. "No proof can be brought from a stream of water," they rejoined. Again he urged, "If the Halakha agrees with me, let the walls of the schoolhouse prove it." Thereupon the walls inclined to fall. But Rabbi Jehosua [the opponent to Rabbi Eliezer] rebuked them saying, "When scholars are engaged in Halakha dispute, what have you [meaning the heaven] to interfere?" They didn't fall in completely in honour of Rabbi Jehosua nor did they resume the upright in honour of Rabbi Eliezer, and they are still standing thus inclined; said he to them, "If the Halakha agrees with me, let it be proved from heaven." Thereupon a heavenly voice cried out: "Why do you dispute with Rabbi Eliezer seeing that in all matters the Halakha agrees with him?" But Rabbi Jehosua arose and claimed, "It is not in heaven." "What did he mean by this?" said Rabbi Jeremiah: "That the Torah had already been given

on Mt. Sinai, *we pay no attention to the heavenly voice,* for already on Mt. Sinai it has been written in the Torah: after the majority must one decide." Rabbi Nathan met Elija and asked him, "What did the Holy One, blessed be He, do in that hour?" — "He laughed with joy." He replied saying, "My sons have defeated me. My sons have defeated me." It was said on that day all objects which Rabbi Eliezer had declared clean, were brought and burned in fire; and they took a vote and excommunicated him. Said they, "Who shall go and inform him?" "I will go," answered Rabbi Aqiba, "Lest an unsuitable person go and inform him and thus destroy the whole world." What did Rabbi Aqiba do? He donned black garments and wrapped himself in black and sat at a distance of 4 cubits from him. Eliezer said to Rabbi Aqiba, "What has particularly happened today?" "Master," he replied, "It appears to me that thy companions hold aloof from thee." Thereupon he, too, rent his garments, put off his shoes, removed his seat and sat on the earth whilst tears streamed from his eyes.[45]

This remarkable legendary story not only shows the independence of human thought and reasoning — the divine even laughed with joy! — but also the enormous energy the psyche spent on its journey to self-fulfillment. The group, the collective, tried to keep the individual embraced within its own dogma just as the corporate structure of Judaism refused to allow the Master of Justice of the Essene monastery to follow his own path.

In the 23rd Chapter of the Book of Exodus there is an injunction which reads: *"You shall not follow a multitude to do evil!"*

Just as the bureaucrats of the past did not accept the teachings of Jesus' forerunner, the Master of Justice of the Essene monastery, so the office-holders of today, whether political, scientific, or religious, refuse to accept the world-wide social changes which reflect the ontogenesis of the psyche. Man is, after all, the medium through which Being comes to consciousness of itself.

We are fortunate today through the discoveries of both the Dead Sea Scrolls and the remains of the Essene monastery, in particular the *Nag Hammadi Library,* to study the ontogenesis of the psyche as an historical manifestation, and not merely through abstract formulations. Dupont-Sommer's important survey of these documents finds that

> ... the revelation of the Jewish 'New Covenant,' which has just been brought to us in such detail by the Dead Sea discoveries, enriches very substantially our knowledge of Essenism. In the last two centuries B.C. and the first century A.D. this represented a movement in Judaism as widespread as it was deep, both inside and outside Palestine. It is from the womb of this religious ferment that Christianity, the Christian 'New Covenant,' emerged. In history there are scarcely any absolute beginnings, and Christianity is no exception to the rule. Already eminent historians have recognized in Essenism a "foretaste of Christianity." This expression is one of Renan's, as also is: "Christianity is an Essenism which has largely succeeded." That scholar, at all events, hesitated to affirm a "direct connection" between Essenism and Christianity despite their deep resemblances. It was a wise and prudent attitude, in the light of the sources available in his time; but today, thanks to the new texts, the problem presents itself in an entirely new way.
>
> Everything in the Jewish New Covenant heralds and prepares the way for the Christian New Covenant. The Galilean Master, as He is presented to us in the writings of the New Testament, appears in many respects as an astonishing reincarnation of the Mas-

ter of Justice. Like the latter He preached penitence,
poverty, humility, love of one's neighbor, chastity.
Like him, He prescribed the observance of the Law
of Moses, the whole Law, but the Law finished and
perfected, thanks to His own revelations. Like him
He was the Elect and the Messiah of God, the Messiah redeemer of the world. Like him He was the
object of the hostility of the priests, the party of the
Sadducees. Like him He was condemned and put to
death. Like him He pronounced judgment on Jerusalem, which was taken and destroyed by the Romans
for having put Him to death. Like him, at the end of
time, He will be the supreme judge. Like him He
founded a Church whose adherents fervently
awaited His glorious return. In the Christian Church,
just as in the Essene Church, the essential rite is the
sacred meal, whose ministers are the priests. Here
and there at the head of each community there is the
overseer, the "bishop." And the ideal of both
Churches is essentially that of unity, communion in
love — even going so far as the sharing of common
property.

All these similarities — and here I only touch upon
the subject — together constitute a very impressive
whole. The question at once arises, to which of the
two sects, the Jewish or the Christian, does the prior-
ity belong? Which of the two was able to influence
the other? The reply leaves no room for doubt. The
Master of Justice died about 65-63 B.C.; Jesus the
Nazarene died about A.D. 30. In every case where
the resemblance compels or invites us to think of a
borrowing, this was on the part of Christianity. But
on the other hand, the appearance of faith in Jesus —
the foundation of the New Church — can scarcely be
explained without the real historic activity of a new

Prophet, a new Messiah, who rekindled the flame and concentrated on himself the adoration of men.*

Of the Master of Justice, whose career preceded that of the Galilean Rabbi by about a century, we knew practically nothing until now. The *Damascus Document* [discovered by Dr. Solomon Schechter fifty years before the actual Dead Sea Scrolls were found by some Bedouins at Qumran] remained too obscure for us to define with any precision the figure of the great Teacher, the date of his ministry or the significance of his work. Everything is now changed, and all the problems relative to primitive Christianity — problems earnestly examined for so many centuries — all these problems henceforth find themselves placed in a new light, which forces us to reconsider them completely.

It goes without saying that I cannot here offer even an outline of so vast a work. I only wish to stress for the present that the contribution of the new texts is in reality most constructive. Many problems in primitive Christian texts, which baffled the historian and could incline him to denials — in the first place the denial even of the historical existence of Jesus — will at last find a clear and positive explanation; since the historical milieu is better known, Jesus and the nascent Christian church will find themselves more firmly rooted in history. Certainly many obscurities

*This is not the place to discuss the actual career and work of this new Messiah. It is scarcely necessary to say that the author in no way wishes to deny the originality of the Christian religion. He has here noted the resemblances, but differences also clearly exist. Specialists in the history of Early Christianity will not fail to point these out. But Christianity is grafted on to the tree of Judaism; it is the point where this grafting is effected that interests the author.

will remain, but never has such a wealth of light been offered to the Christian historian."[46]

Prof. Bultman says:

> Now it is true that in the predictions of the passion the Jewish concept Messiah-Son-of-Man is re-interpreted — or better, singularly enriched — insofar as the idea of a suffering, dying, rising Messiah or Son of Man was unknown to Judaism. But this re-interpretation of the concept was done not by Jesus himself but by the Church *ex eventu*. Of course, the attempt is made to carry the idea of the suffering Son of Man back into Jesus' own outlook by assuming that Jesus regarded himself as Deutero-Isaiah's Servant of God who suffers and dies for the sinner, and fused together the two ideas Son of Man and Servant of God into the single figure of the suffering, dying and rising Son of Man.[47]

In this context it is of importance to remember that Josephus mentions twelve persons called Jesus. The name of Jesus, therefore, *may* be a symbolic crystallization for prevalent ideas just as that of Abraham, Jacob or Moses. The voluminous writings of the renowned historian Flavius Josephus carry special weight because he lived during the first century A.D.

Today, after nearly 2,000 years, the traditional collective redemptive vision is being superceded. Western Civilization *talks* about human values and rights and the respect of man-as-man on a completely abstract level. Modern society, computerized as an attempt to cope with its overgrown size, has in fact depersonalized humanity to a high degree and only strenuous mental efforts can keep anyone alive as a distinct person. The expectation of a Messiah to provide both mental and material food activates masses under Communism, though in actuality, history has shown Communism to be a "god that failed." There is a definite threat in our time that general adherence to dogma may assist in a fusion of dogmatically ruled societies and institutions. At the same time, a counter-process is at work, called by Bonhoeffer "man's coming of age,"[48] as dogmas begin to lose their power over the human mind. The ontogenesis of the psyche, expressing itself in man's coming of age, presupposes an agent in man which is acting from within, as it were, prompting millions of people to leave the church, tens of thousands of nuns and priests to leave their orders; and only through "iron curtains" can people be prevented from defecting to a different form of secular society.

Correlative to this political situation is the development in the sciences. The evolution of scientific thought is particularly evident in the field of biology where instincts have become respectable again. The awareness of the reality of an inborn agent of motivation has superceded the dogma of the past which denied its existence, and permitted only external causal agents.

Noam Chomsky, in his book *Problems of Knowledge and Freedom*, quotes Bertrand Russell: "We need certain principles of inference that 'cannot be logically deduced from facts of experience. Either, therefore, we know something independently of experience, or science is moonshine.' " To be sure, Russell's statement may be startling to the empiricists of our time, who in their own turn are predisposed to classify the Bible as moonshine. However, Russell concludes that "what can be retained of empiricism is only the condition that the verifiable consequences of the principles that constitute our knowledge 'are such as experience will confirm.' " Chomsky also writes: "The notion that there may be innate principles of mind that on the one hand make possible the acquisition of knowledge and belief, and on the other, determine and limit its scope suggests nothing that could surprise a biologist so far as I can see."[49]

Just as every child at a very early age knows how to construct sentences, so very early in human development the psyche gave expression of its own evolution, and the poets subsequently made this manifest in the symbolic images and tales which are included in the Bible. The artifacts and paintings of great antiquity speak essentially the same symbolic language. Writing specifically of postulated innate principles of language structure characteristic of the species, Jacques Monod observes:

> This conception has scandalized certain philosophers or anthropologists who see in it a return to Cartesian metaphysics. But if we accept its implicit biological content, this conception does not shock me at all.[50]

Chomsky's basic approach to language finds its justification also in the Greek assertion of *archetypoi* as underlying, determining factors; in Jung's ideas about the archetypes, and in Heisenberg's concurrence with the psychological belief that the inborn archetypes are "subconscious patterns in our mind . . . which in some way reflect the internal structure of the world."[51] The scientist's, the philosopher's and the theologian's positions coincide.

Archetypes and Wholeness

THE WORD *archetype* was used by the Early Church Fathers Tertullian and Ambrose. St. Augustine's *principales formae* is also a rendering of the Greek *archetypoi*. Augustine writes:

> They themselves neither come into being nor pass away, nevertheless . . . everything which does come into being and passes away is said to be formed in accord with these ideas. . . . They are themselves true because they are eternal and because they remain ever the same and unchangeable. It is by participation in these that whatever is exists in whatever manner it does exist.[52]

Etymologically the word *archetype* is derived from the Greek word *archē* meaning "first," "foremost" or "chief"; and *typos* meaning a "blow" or the "mark" left by a blow, and "impress" or "mold." We are familiar with the first element in such words as archipelago, architect, archbishop; and with the second in words such as type, typical and so on. Archetypes are patterns of behavior through which human actions are unconsciously conditioned, and may therefore be regarded as *a priori* categories of the mind reaching back into the levels of experience which the conscious mind neither knows nor remembers.

As Chomsky described:

> Words would have the meaning given to them by the organism, to be sure, though there would be no necessity to suppose that this 'giving of meaning' is conscious or accessible to introspection, or that the organism is at all capable of explaining the system of concepts it uses or describing the characteristics of particular items with any accuracy. In the case of humans, there is every reason to suppose that the semantic system of language is given largely by a power independent of conscious choice; the operative principles of mental organization are presumably inaccessible to introspection, but there is no reason why they should in principle be more immune to investigation than the principles that determine the physical arrangement of limbs and organs.[53]

In his prophetic lines from "Ode on a Grecian Urn," Keats anticipates the new development in science which, as it were, begins to recognize that art seems to be an intrinsic factor in the appreciation of knowledge.

> When old age shall this generation waste,
>   Thou shalt remain, in midst of other woe
> Than ours, a friend to man, to whom thou
>   say'st,

'Beauty is truth, truth beauty,' — that is all
Ye know on earth, and all ye need to
know.[54]

Heisenberg in an important lecture on *Natural Law and the Structure of Matter* ends by saying that if we are to arrive at the underlying principle behind phenomena, then "the language of the poets may be more important than that of the scientists."[55]

Dirac, proposing his quantum theory, says: "The scheme ... to be acceptable must be neat and beautiful."[56] Significantly, he did not say that it must be "true."

Watson writes in *The Double Helix:* ...

... we only wished to establish that at least one specific two-chain complementary helix was stereo-chemically possible. Until this was clear, the objection could be raised that, although our idea was *aesthetically elegant,* the shape of the sugar-phosphate backbone might not permit its existence. Happily, now we knew that this was not true, and so we had lunch, telling each other that *a structure this pretty just had to exist.*[57]

Since after all the laws of physics are explanations of man-made understanding, they presuppose that these laws contain the creative principle, namely art, as an essential ingredient. There is a growing realization today that explanations are only acceptable if they are aesthetically pleasing as well. To be sure the next step in the scientific process is experimental testing; but that also is made, constructed, and envisaged by the human mind, which arranges "objective" tests out of the very nature and structure of the human mind wherein is contained the creative and the artistic awareness. If this very truth could find its way into the lower levels of contemporary education, society might, through the readmittance of the meaningfulness of the imagery and the non-material aspects of reality, experience a renaissance.

The human race would not then die from spiritual isolation; life would be no longer empty and barren of meaning.

Fred Hoyle, writing in *Ten Faces of the Universe,* reflects the same point:

> [Miss C. S. Wu's] experiment was widely repeated in many laboratories throughout the world, always with the result that the parity-conserving theories were wrong. It followed that either Fermi's original concept was at fault, or one or more of the earlier experiments was wrong.
>
> At this point several physicists decided on quite a new approach. Rejecting the parity-conserving theories, they looked to see which parity non-conserving possibility appeared to have the simplest and most *elegant* mathematical structure — a criterion based on aesthetics rather than on an empirical comparison with experiment. The outcome was a certain explicit formulation of the weak interaction, a formulation that still contradicted certain earlier experiments. Were these earlier experiments right? Here was an interesting clash between the human concept of mathematical structure and the harsh reality of practical experiment. Which side would win when the experiments were repeated? The answer turned out to be the intellectual concept of elegance and structure. The earlier experiments had been wrong.[58]

This account of a scientific dilemma and its solution reflects the dilemma of contemporary education as well. A truly scien*tific* attitude of mind is exhaustive, i.e., it includes, or is open at least, to the manifold aspects of reality, while a scien*tistic* attitude is exclusive, i.e., it excludes, through its dogmatism, other vital parts of reality, particularly aesthetic considerations. Specialization is indeed necessary in the midst of the "knowledge explosion" of our time, but it makes all the difference if the teacher, and the student through the teacher, are mentally open, rather than confined by the narrowness of specialization. Lack of openness excludes the dire human need for communication between people as human beings, as well as between specialists. The limited vision of specialization leads to seeing man as *what* he is, but not *who* he is.

The mind in its creative apprehension transcends the intellect in the concept of elegance and structure; after all, the whole is greater than the sum of its parts. If we are leaving the aesthetic out of our comprehension of reality, we are excluding some dimension of reality; our minds are not exhausting the possibilities. When we exclude Keats' dictum that "Truth is Beauty" we are depriving ourselves also of the recognition that Life seems to be inherently beautiful. Niels Bohr said to Heisenberg:

> When it comes to atoms, language can be used only as in poetry. The poet, too, is not nearly so concerned with describing facts as with creating images.[59]

The archaeologist may speak the same language as the most advanced modern scientist. Alexander Marshack has said:

> Neanderthal men disappear and modern men appear in Europe, and we begin to find the first evidence of true carving and art. But the seemingly sudden appearance of this art poses a problem, for it is not all 'primitive.' From the beginning, the work is surprisingly sophisticated. It may have, therefore, begun earlier in some still unknown area. From the moment that art appeared in Europe, a flood of images ensued. Man, in fact, had begun to interpret the real world around him through his images, and he also began marking the real world symbolically: he put images on rock faces and deep in caves, he coloured and decorated his habitation sites, he set up symbolic poles and statues, and he decorated himself

and his dead. These images give us the earliest record of human perception of the real world, and the human relation to that world.[60]

In the same vein also, Bart Jordan writes:

One of the more revealing items in the collection with regard to art as an expression of science is the renowned meander bracelet of ivory from Mezin in the Ukraine. The bracelet has often been cited solely for the artistic value of its elegant patterning. However, the significance of the meander symbol which underlies the bracelet's geometrical ornamentation elevates this Mezin masterpiece to a plane far beyond the realm of art alone. The meander itself is a mathematically ordered symbol: a compressed shorthand way of diagramming a year....

Cro-Magnon artisans were also scientists and mathematicians capable of performing, at the very least, basic arithmetical manipulations; that they were fully cognizant of fundamental biological and astronomical cycles and of their mathematical relationships; and they had developed a complex and sophisticated graphic and sculptural tradition to symbolize these cycles.[61]

The Mind's Unfolding

W HAT we have been pleased to call 'primitive man' established as early as 70,000 years ago insights which modern science has only now begun to realize; namely that there is no absolute outside and no absolute inside, because man himself is involved. This realization is basically a demonstration of the ontogenesis of the psyche, which re-experiences itself on different levels. The higher this level reaches, the more organization one experiences within oneself and the universe.

In unison with the idea of an ever-expanding universe, we find the human mind expanding as well, as it seeks also to understand man's position in the universe.

It was only about 300 years ago that James Usher, Archbishop of Armagh, declared that the world was created in 4004 B.C., on a Wednesday afternoon at 3:30, I believe. Pope Julius I arbitrarily fixed the date of the birth of Christ to coincide with the rebirth of nature at the winter solstice on December 22nd, as Jesus' historical existence could not be subjected to scientific proof. Orthodox rabbis believe that the world is 5,741 years old, calculating that date in accordance with the Bible. The mental structures of the men who conceived these dates were confined within a dogmatic framework claiming absolute knowledge through Revelation. In our day there is a growing recognition that ideas which claim absolute knowledge through the dogmas of science, politics, or theology, only create the way to tragedy. The Principle of Uncertainty according to Schrödinger and Heisenberg gives ample evidence that with the means available to us today, certainty is unattainable. While Bishop Usher based his conclusions on the fixed date of creation on "certainty," Dirac puts the moment of the "Big Bang" when our universe began at 16 billions of years in the past. Heisenberg, on the other hand, says: "I believe the Big Bang happened 18 billion years ago." What does it matter — 2 billion years!!

Hoyle, in his reflections about the origin of the universe, believes that "the world of our experience sprang into existence 15 billion years ago in a sudden transition from another existence out of another world." This is clearly an archetypal thought about rebirth couched in scientific terms. It bridges the gap between the dogmatic rejection of evolution by some religionists, and their static conception of the universe.

The modern awareness about the expanding universe, on

the one hand, and the new theories about the distance in time of its beginning, on the other, seems to express the unfolding of man's mind in our time. In a different way the second line of the ancient Gloria Patri expresses the same insight: "As it was in the beginning, is now, and ever shall be, world without end. Amen." Participating in the unfolding of man's mind, modern science holds that an understanding of the whole universe is necessary to refine the simplistic notions of cause and effect. For now it is recognized that the earlier laws stated by the physical sciences are no longer adequate to deal with reality. They are simply too narrow. As Hoyle writes,

> Taking the local laws to be formulated with time-symmetry — i.e., without any *ad hoc* assumption of the time-sequence of cause and effect — it turns out that not even statistical predictions can be made unless the response of the universe is included in the equivalence . . . —It is an interesting speculation that consciousness itself may arise from this interaction of our mental processes with the universe in the large — not the usual cause-and-effect interaction . . . but the interaction with the future. . . . This speculation appears, almost inevitably, when we seek to relate local physics to the structure of the whole universe. Our experience then contains a major environmental component by means of which the phenomenon of consciousness may well arise.[62]

The depth of experience to which modern cosmology invites man is awesome in its dimensions, and at the same time, it not only spells hope, but it also provides profound meaning. Philip Morrison remarks: ". . . the microwave measurements (of motion) from balloon and U2 aircraft have found a remarkable result. . . . We never expected we could find a single measurement that would give us this which is the closest thing to *absolute* motion that we can think of measuring."[63]

Is science reaching out in its way to new "Absolutes" which, in time, may provide a new meaning to our existence?

Morrison, feeling his way for signs indicating how the universe of homogeneous radiation came to form galaxies and stars, wrote:

> The idea that out of a bland, homogeneous back-ground, all the complexity of the world could arise, is not an idea new to microwave astronomy. It is an idea as old as the Sanskrit philosophers. For long ago, in part of the creation myth, they told how Vishnu, the preserver, with a mighty churn made of a mountain, churned the ocean of milk, and out of the bland nourishing material came the divine cow, first nourisher of mankind, an 8-headed steed, the moon itself and other such wonders. I think you can see what is going on here. This is a *logical similarity* between the mythmakers and ourselves, who make, if you like, a grand myth out of the substance of science. We're looking for how to make the complex from the simple.[64]

Until very recently, the religious interpretation of the universe was considered to be a factual account. Today, the functional breakdown of religious systems is a direct result of the failure of those systems to interpret the universe in a way consistent with modern knowledge. Both the religious breakdown and the changing understanding of the universe are evidence for the ontogenesis of the psyche.

This vital and new approach in science may in the future create a solid basis on which not only to build a sense of security in the midst of change, but also human hope. One such approach is the "Collective Ansatz," a modern theory accepted by many scientists as a means to deal with many body events in physics. Formerly isolated events were the basis from which solutions were sought by simple deduction. The complexity of nature in its infinite varieties made this approach inadequate. A new symbolic model has been suggested in the figure of a human pyramid at a circus. One member of the pyramid suddenly jumps, say, to the top, leading to the normal expectation that the pyramid will totter. But that is not necessarily the case: ". . . if he is initially intermeshed with others in the bulk of the structure, the feat is not so much one man's leap to the top as the coordinated motions of all the artists to restore stability in the structure. We find much the same situations in atoms."[65]

The more things change, the more they remain the same. If human mentality is not fettered by fixed dogmas, but open to change, it is possible to maintain hope in the essential soundness of both the structure of life and the underlying process of life's own efforts to relate to change as of the essence of itself. Thus there is revealed an inherent process of an ever-new and continuing creation. In this process, the actual experience of a living being is involved — not merely an abstract notion: "For you have died, and your life is hid with Christ in God."[66]

The interrelatedness of events, the experience of events as "whole," is not an esoteric postulate of scientific specialists, or modes of abstract theological or philosophical thoughts; it is clearly visible in the material domain of the physical sciences. Economic interdependence as manifested by global efforts to keep the economic world from tottering, as well as attempts to arrive at a "Universal State" are manifestations of the same essence. What is catholic, i.e., "universal" for the human race, is what it has always been: meeting the material needs of food, shelter, etc. The human physical structure is also "catholic," being made up of molecules which are universal or uniform in nature. On the other hand, human spiritual or non-corporeal needs are individual, hence the eternal demand both for Freedom and Justice. These demands are drives which cannot be understood by ordinary notions of physics or chemistry. They are manifestations of the "self-organizing and self-correcting" nature of the ontogenesis of the psyche.

The word *catholic* derives from Latin *catholicus,* "universal," "general," and Greek *katholikos, keta,* "down," "completely" and *holos,* "whole." As Sir Francis Crick says:

> A biological system can be regarded as a hierarchy of levels of organization, the 'wholes' of one level being the parts of the next. Thus cells are the 'wholes' of cellular biology, but the parts of the tissue biology, and so on. In my view a simultaneous attack at more than one level will, in the long run, pay off better than an attack at a single level. . . .[67]

Much the same is approached by Karl Pribram's theory of the hologram.

> The hologram yields a new way of looking at consciousness that is very different from the old behaviorist and phenomenological approaches. The behaviorist looks for cause and effect; the phenomenologist for reasons and intentions. In holography however one looks for the transformation involved in moving from one domain to another. . . . The brain is a very particular kind of holographic instrument. . . . The holograms within the visual systems are . . . *patch* holograms. The total image is composed much as it is in an insect eye that has hundreds of little lenses instead of one single big lens; the insect eye gets a composite image that's just as good as if there were a single lens.[68]

The holographic model seemed to Pribram the best way of explaining the peculiar nature of human memory. Brain researchers had originally thought that memories were stored in specific parts of the brain, e.g., visual memories were in the temporal lobes of the brain. This turned out not to be the case: neurosurgeons noticed that massive injuries to different sections of the brain did not, as expected, destroy the memories that were supposed to be stored there. The nature of memory in relation to the brain made no sense, inasmuch as it appeared that memories seemed to be stored everywhere in general but nowhere in particular.

The model that could best account for this curious situation was that of the hologram. It appeared that the brain functioned in the same way as a hologram, not storing information in one place, but distributing it out of focus throughout the organism — when one remembers an event or scene, the distributed information is refocused and the information clearly recalled. Karl Pribram suggests the hologram not only for human memory but also for human perception; and further proposes the startling idea that the orderly world we see is not necessarily "out there," because brain research suggests that the human brain has a tendency to create the experience of objective order even where there is no objective order "out there." For example, from random noises certain sensory cells respond as if a single line of sound is being perceived — not merely a random jumble of sounds.[69]

It was Leibniz's idea that beneath all things material and mental were bundles of energy called monads. He believed that both material particles and mental ideas had their common roots in underlying monads of energy which, in themselves, were neither physical nor mental, neither in space or time — rather, they were the ultimate units from which both space and time derived.

Bertrand Russell describes Leibniz (1646-1716) as "one of the supreme intellects of all time":

> Leibniz held that extension cannot be an attribute of a substance. His reason was that extension involves plurality, and can therefore only belong to an aggregate of substances; each single substance must be unextended. He believed consequently, in an infinite number of substances which he called 'monads.' Each of these would have some of the properties of a

physical point but only when viewed abstractly; in fact each monad is a soul.[70]

This represents, in Aristotle's sense, essence. Here science, art, psychology and theology find a common root, each using its own language and expressing essentially the same truth.

It was human beings, after all, who poetically conceived creation stories the world over; likewise it is human beings who conduct experiments to fathom the secrets of the origin of life and the universe. The same creative reality inspires both the poet and the scientist.

The problem of evolution versus creation is a man-made dogmatic construction and as such lacks the essential element which can see both aspects of reality as manifestations of creativity revealed in each dimension. The human mind at its present stage of development is experiencing a revolutionary change in that its "tribal" consciousness has taken on global proportions. Man, however, in his parochial, confined characteristics remains caught in a limited mental awareness of specialized fields of knowledge, thereby producing unreal, or artificial problems. The mechanistic evolutionary argument, for example, is exclusive and not exhaustive. Therefore it may be justly said that it is "untrue" in relation to true scientific thought which endeavors to be "catholic" or all-embracing.

John Keorian has suggested that according to strict deterministic evolutionary theory, the progression of life could never have taken place because of the "fierce competition from the organisms already present and adjusted to the environment. . . . [However] as long as it is conceivable that a newly arisen organism may be compatible or symbiotic with the existing organisms in its environment, the argument is invalid."[71]

This hypothesis of compatibility has found in the language of biology a most significant name: *biopoesis*! This term means to indicate a "harmonious correlation of separate chemical processes." The formulation, proposed by the Russian biologist Oparin, introduces a value judgment into the ice-cold Darwinian theory and thus admits, albeit unconsciously, a pre-existing "meaningful" agent: ". . . modern biological molecules may have had a-biological origins in the past. In fact, this basic idea was promulgated in its present incarnation by J. B. S. Haldane in 1928 and by A. I. Oparin at about the same time."[72]

Psychophylogenesis

ANOTHER important contribution stems from Bernhard Rensch who wrote:

> Besides, it seems to be rather unlikely that psychic components and psychic laws, being fundamentally different from causal laws, originated suddenly. And it is still more improbable that in our universe, which is governed by causal laws, psychic components were developed only in the relatively short period since living beings have been in existence.
>
> Such reasons and some epistemological considerations led some well-known philosophers, psychologists, and biologists to the conclusion that even plants could be endowed with psychic components. It may be sufficient to mention G. Th. Fechner, F. Paulsen, B. Erdmann, W. Wundt, Th. Ziehen, E. Haeckel, and R. H. France. Of course, in plants as well as in Protozoa such psychic phenomena could be presumed only in the sense of more or less connected sensations (a little like those of our sensations to which we do not pay attention; for example, sensations in the periphery of our visual field). (Ziechen, 1921.)

The main epistemological reasons for presuming a more general distribution of awareness in its broadest sense (not in the sense of self-awareness) are the following ones. We get the idea of matter by reducing certain characters of our phenomena that originate only in our body. Hence, we conclude that color, taste, smell, hardness and the like are sensory characters that need not be attributed to matter itself. But in all these processes of elimination of certain characters we do not reduce from awareness as such. Hence, on principle there is no real difference between mind and matter. All matter is supposed to have "protopsychic" characters. Awareness originates when matter comes in a certain complicated connection realized in nervous systems (compare Rensch 1961). Such a hylopsychic and identistic interpretation is especially fit for understanding a gradual development of living beings from non-living matter, and it avoids many difficulties of dualistic theories.

The individual development, too, supports this interpretation. Although it seems to be unusual to reflect about such relations, the characters transmitted by heredity are basically only characters of certain chemical substances, such as DNA and proteins. During ontogeny these substances cause the development of all organs and also of the psychophysical substances in the brain (and perhaps also in the sense organs). To the physiological processes of this substance, psychological phenomena run parallel. As there is no possibility to conceive those phenomena as something that have been originated from the totally different causal processes, we must presume that already *DNA and proteins have protopsychical characters.* . . .The conclusions are supported by two more theoretical statements. Higher animals gradually developed from lower animals, possibly originally from non-living matter. It seems probable that parallel psychic components, being totally different from causal ones, appeared in the course of animal evolution. Epistemological arguments also speak in favor of psychic or 'protopsychic' components of living matter. It is impossible to prove that lower animals or plants have *no* psychic phenomena. This theoretical introduction should show that psycho-phylogenesis is a legitimate scientific problem.[73]

Kirlian photography proves experimentally this vital point in relation to both man, plants and non-living matter.[74] The use of Red Ochre, as we shall see later, gives further proof of "psychophylogenesis" leading back to the very origin of animate life.

The earth originated some five billion years ago, either as a part broken off from the sun, or by the gradual condensation of interstellar dust. Most authorities now agree that the earth was very hot and molten when it was first formed and that conditions consistent with life appeared on the earth only perhaps three billion years ago. Twenty-two different amino acids were isolated recently from Precambrian rocks from South Africa that are at least 3.1 billion years old. At that time the earth's atmosphere contained essentially no free oxygen — all the oxygen atoms were combined as water, or as oxides. . . .

The details of the chemical reactions that could give rise, without the intervention of living things, to carbohydrates, fats and amino acids have been worked out by Oparin and extended by Calvin and others. Most, if not all, of the reactions by which the more complex organic substances were formed probably occurred in the sea in which the inorganic precursors and the organic products of the reaction were dissolved and mixed. The sea became a sort of dilute broth in which these molecules collided, reacted and aggregated to form new molecules of increasing size and complexity (this might be called the 'chicken soup' theory of evolution). . . .

The first living organisms, having arisen in a sea of organic molecules and in contact with an atmosphere lacking oxygen, presumably obtained energy by the fermentation of certain of these organic substances. The first organisms were almost certainly *heterotrophs,* and they could survive only as long as the supply of organic molecules that had been accumulated in the sea broth in the past lasted. Before the supply was exhausted, however, some of the heterotrophs evolved further and became *autotrophs,* able to make their own organic molecules by chemosynthesis or photosynthesis.[75]

Through the introduction of terms like *biopoesis* or "harmonious correlation," the science of biology begins, as did physics, to answer the vexing question "why is there anything at all rather than just nothing?" To be sure, the strictly rationalistic mind, narrow in its essential attitude toward life, rejects the universal. Emotionally it resists the fundamental significance of "art" (*artunein* — "to fit"), that which is inherent in poetry and harmony. The theories of the origin of life are therefore a vital manifestation of the creative impulse. What has been viewed as chance may now be seen to be art. Its biological correlative is the admission of axioms such as the development from heterotrophs and autotrophs. The efficacious principle, in other words, the One God, is the dynamic reality creatively active within the living process of the world at large, as well as in the individual. As such, He is omnipresent and omnipotent. That is, as he experiences the ontogenesis of the psyche — as an individual becomes *autonomous* — he also experiences God as a person in the sense that one addresses Him within oneself. Yet at the same time, He is a non-person, a principle which is effective in the process of becoming.

Not only is the ontogenesis of the psyche revealed through the work of modern scientists, but in a rather overpowering way the same reality was depicted symbolically 4,000 years ago as the birth of the "Son of Man." In anticipation of the present development of the psyche, the figure of the "Son of Man" was portrayed as "reaching from one end of the universe to the other"; so the human mind today replaces the ancient fantasy of the physical extension of the "Son of Man." Today our minds reach back into the past perhaps 15 billion years, and at the same time leap forward into infinite space. The notion of the "Son of Man" curiously correlates with the results of modern quantum theory which replaces the materialistic approach to life with one which is non-materialistic. It is a veritable revolution through which modern man is passing, in which the old dogmatic authorities, be they religious, scientific, or political, have been overthrown. Now, man in his despair of finding his place in the ever-widening area of knowledge and experience, in the ever-widening, endless universe, is without direction.

IN NO DIRECTION
by Robert Graves:

To go in no direction
  Surely as carelessly,
Walking on the hills alone,
  I never found easy.

Either I sent leaf or stick
  Twirling in the air,
Whose fall may be prophetic,
  Pointing 'there',

Or in superstition
  Edged somewhat away
From a sure direction,
  Yet could not stray,

Or undertook the climb
  That I had avoided
Directionless some other time,
  Or had not avoided

Or called as companion
  Some eyeless ghost
And held his no direction
  Till my feet were lost.[76]

The despair of modern man is fed by the lack of humility in not allowing the process of becoming, the ontogenesis of the world and of his own psyche to happen; he is helplessly resisting this creative process. But man did not go to the moon before he had entered into a different dimension. However, in spite of this advance, sinister forces which politically usurp demonic power in the presumption of knowledge and the arrogant, dogmatic belief that they are right, today threaten the world with extinction because they do not have the humility to allow any other point of view. So man has "called as companion some eyeless ghost," instead of undertaking the "climb I had avoided," namely, to find himself. Instead, he has consented to a hedonistic, materialistic philosophy which he now sees crumbling before his eyes: inflation, unemployment, and the shortages of essential raw materials are but a few of the indicators.

CHAPTER 2

The Bible as Structural Hermeneutic

The World of Science

THE BASIC assumption of a materialistic philosophy was that physics was an "exact science." Today we have come to realize that even physics cannot be an exact science because every fundamental theory is a form of art, and as such cannot fit perfectly. In the materialistic world of physics we have looked for security by assuming to know certain criteria by which we believe to be able to judge what physics really is. But today's accepted philosophy about physics is that any attempt to introduce the criteria of certainty would be the death of the discipline itself because life and the universe are in process and not static. Modern physics knows that all properties of a natural event are not manifest at the same time — some remain hidden. Therefore, only by being open to life as a process and not being fettered to preconceived dogmas and ideas of what constitutes security can we arrive at an experience of wholeness as a basis for our security.

The realm of music demonstrates this need for openness to process. In one particular experiment, a single tone was released in an empty room. As it bounced off four walls, it unleashed at the same time a whole range of other tones. What, therefore, appears to be explicit — namely that a single tone is equivalent to a single idea — prohibits us from hearing the nuances of other tones because our attention is solely fixed upon what we have assumed to be explicit, namely, the single tone.

As David Bohm says:

> Physics is not primarily concerned with unambiguous communication, but rather all concepts are ambiguous; and there are certain unambiguous abstractions that can be made from ambiguous concepts; and those are the things we use for tests. But I think people get it upside down when they say the unambiguous is the reality, and the ambiguous is merely uncertainty of what is really unambiguous. Well, let's turn it around the other way. Ambiguous is the reality, and unambiguous is merely a special case of it, where we finally manage to pin down some very special aspect.[1]

Just as in the poetic language of the Book of Genesis, creation is the ordering of chaos, so out of the chaos of unknowing, the world of science develops. But the process of growth — of becoming — is inhibited so long as this human endeavor insists on projecting preconceived notions of the unambiguous onto every event. For then, quite naturally, that which will be discovered by the individual will be only the projection of a fixed and static state of mind.

It has been pointed out time and again that the data revealed in the most advanced physical experiments are limited by the preconceived ideas of the investigators, and by the available instruments as well. The instruments of modern science are most complex and exceedingly expensive. Therefore the instruments also dictate limitations because the building of new machinery to test new ideas is hampered by the need for greater support and money.

Just as in the physical sciences, so in mental science, no Archimedian point exists outside its own system. Man is the observer of himself in both orders. Both orders finally derive their meaning through their relationship to the whole of which they are a part and not in isolation by themselves.

Science has proceeded essentially by a discursive process of reasoning, excluding intuition. Thus at its very base it has been exclusive. To be sure the discursive method is vital as far as particulars are concerned. It lends itself as an invaluable tool for situational or logical analysis. But where man's whole being and life as a whole is concerned, a hermeneutical approach, which by its very nature is not exclusive, is the means to awareness. This method illuminates not only the whole, but particularly, the interrelatedness with the vital, distinctive parts of life.

In our time this process of de-materialization expresses itself scientifically in quantum mechanics on the level of physics and in the corresponding philosophy of "physics and beyond" as stated by Heisenberg, Niels Bohr, and Hoyle, to name only a few. This process has resulted in the enormity of man's ability to free energies which hitherto had been hidden in mass, and above all to deal with these energies effectively through both fission in the atomic world and fusion, changing hydrogen into helium, and using lasers. And in this change, man participates and interrelates with the universe, and it appears that the Universe participates also in this process of becoming.

> Truth must be consistent with our experience, and our experience . . . . is in final analysis an experience of personality. . . . In various forms of religious belief truth is represented as a revelation from without at some particular time and place, and not as something the nature of which is revealed in personal experience and which is constantly being revealed more adequately.[2]

Nature contains within herself the ontogenetic power to create life as we know it. The oldest trace of the origin of life is believed to be a blue-green algae which has been found in fossil form in various parts of the world. This cell belongs to the oldest organisms which were capable of producing out of themselves the oxygen on which all further life depended. In the early atmosphere of about 3 billion years ago, there was no free oxygen. Free oxygen is necessary for the oxidation of iron and the formation of iron oxides. This oxygen was produced by the earliest living organisms, which were photosynthetic, and no deposits of iron oxides are found earlier than evidence of the existence of these oxygen-producing algae. Along with the formation of so-called "red beds," the new atmospheric oxygen permitted the appearance of oxygen-consuming organisms, beginning with the more complex single-cell types and continuing with the evolution of the entire animal kingdom. As Kenneth Miller explains it:

> The earth is a planet bathed in light. It is therefore not surprising that many of the living organisms that have evolved on the earth have developed the capacity to trap light energy. Of all the ways in which life interacts with light the most fundamental is photosynthesis, the biological conversion of light energy into chemical energy. In an energetic sense all living things are ultimately dependent on photosynthesis, which is the source of all forms of food and even of the oxygen in the earth's atmosphere. The vast majority of living cells, from simple algae to large and complex terrestrial plants, are photosynthetic. Much has recently been learned about the design and function of biological structure in which light is initially trapped: the photosynthetic membrane.
>
> The overall chemistry of photosynthesis can be expressed in a deceptively simple equation. Six molecules of carbon dioxide are taken up from the

environment together with six molecules of water. In the presence of light these molecules are converted into a single molecule of the six-carbon sugar glucose and six molecules of oxygen are released. The products of the reaction hold more chemical energy than the reactants do, and so in a sense the energy of sunlight is captured in the glucose and oxygen that are produced in the process.[3]

All seawater is considered to be the primal environment of animated life. The essential chemical elements of seawater, though in different concentrations, are contained in the human blood. It is this very environmental condition that man is, so to speak, carrying with him in his blood and body. And the human foetus undergoes in the womb the mutations from an "amphibian" to a mammalian creature. It is therefore "reasonable" to hypostasize that the protopsychical expression of the experience of man's origins manifests itself archetypally in the use of red ochre, which, after all, has also the color of blood. One writer puts it this way:

> Paleontological evidence implies that until then all organisms were procaryotes, [i.e., blue-green algae and bacteria] having no nuclear wall or clearly structured chromosomes, and being incapable, therefore, of mitotic cell division and sexual reproduction in the usual sense. The presence of free oxygen, even in small quantities, was presumably followed by the evolution of the eucaryotic cell, with nuclear wall, well defined chromosomes, mitotic cell division and the capacity for sexual reproduction.[4]

The formation of these Red Beds — sediments in which the grains are coated with ferric oxides — is, therefore, the physical correlative to the ontogeny of life.

It is no wonder that the red iron oxides played a very important role also for human development in the evolution of life. A great many sources contribute to the data indicating that red ochre has played a central part in the cultural unfolding of man. The number of citations which follow give considerable weight to its importance.

Important experiments which have been conducted by NASA's Ames Research Center project that:

> . . . man may yet employ a natural converter to get energy directly from sunlight. Last week Cell Biologist Walther Stoeckenius, 54, with colleagues at the University of California at San Francisco and a team from NASA's Ames Research Center, announced that a purple pigment found in red bacteria from the Dead Sea and salt flats round the world also directly converts sunlight into energy. . . .[5]

There is evidence of red ochre in the Terra Amata Cave in layers attributed to the Early Acheulian, about 300,000 years ago. In Oldowai Bed II ochre has been found which, according to observations, is a foreign element, not occurring naturally in the vicinity of the site. Should the collecting have been intentional, which some scholars however doubt, the Australopithines would be the likely cause for it, and would accordingly move the man-ochre relationship far into the dawn of man's early history (Australopithecus is supposed to have lived about 3 million years ago).[6] Wreschner presents the following view in his 1975 study:

> During the Aurignacian, the sprinkling of red ochre on the dead spreads in France, Italy, Germany and Tchechoslovakia. In the following phase of the Upper Paleolithic this custom gains widespread acceptance and moves eastwards into Russia, from the Crimea to Siberia. . . . From the Epipalaeolithic to the Neolithic, from Chalcolithic to the East European Copper Age and to modern times there is abundant evidence for its similar or variated practice in Europe, Asia, Africa, and so far as Alaska. Red

> Ochre as the magic life-symbolizing substance gains in importance not only in the ritual use in burial, but spreads and finds expression in an ever widening range in the symbolism of prehistoric and primitive societies.[7]

> Red ochre as a 'Magical giver of Life' is used in illness and at marriage and mutilation ceremonies in Modern India. . . . If a man or woman of the Arunta tribe (Africa) feels ill, the body is rubbed and smeared with red ochre; they tell a story of a woman who, after descending to the underworld, is restored to life after obtaining a jar with red ochre and by eating the ochre becomes strong again.[8]

Red seems to be more universally used than any other color, its significance varying among different peoples; it "was anciently and generally connected with divinity and power both priestly and royal. The tabernacle of the Israelites was covered with skins dyed red and the gods and images [including the sphinx] of Egypt and Chaldea were noticeably of that color, which to this day is the one distinguishing the Roman Pontiff and the cardinals."[9]

Dr. Solecki found that about 60,000 B.C. "several split and broken mammal bones concentrated in the Shanidar II locus may have been the remains of a funeral feast. It looks as though the hearth had been covered with soil while the fire was still burning. At least, there is a layer of red soil lying over the ashes."[10] Mellaart notes that "in a grave at Shanidar a flexed burial of a young woman was accompanied by red ochre, a grinding stone and a necklace of small beads."[11] And that "most of the graves at Eynan contained red ochre."[12]

"Usually," write Hawkes and Woolley, "the Neanderthalers [died out about 35-40,000 years ago] were buried in the attitude of sleep, gently flexed and lying on one side; several were accompanied by red ochre, generally supposed to represent the life-giving properties of blood."[13]

At Shanidar, a remote part of the mountains in Iraq, a cave was discovered which contained the skeletal remains of nine Stone Age people, who had lived there more than forty thousand years ago. One skeleton was found which had been buried on a bed of flowers. Examination of pollen grains preserved in this site indicate that seven of the varieties are still in existence, and that they continue to be used because of their medical properties. It is the assumption of Dr. Solecki that the body may have belonged to a Medicine Man — a Shaman buried with his own medicinal plants in the hope that they might revive him.[14]

Not only red ochre, but also special plants were seen by our remote ancestors as life-giving agents. The archaeological discovery of Shanidar has a parallel in Greek mythology. King Minos had lost his son Glaucus; a snake spied the dead body, but before it could do any harm, Polyeidos killed the snake. A second snake with an herb in its mouth appeared on the scene, touched the body of the dead snake with the plant, and it was resurrected. Whereupon Polyeidos, quick-witted, touched the dead Glaucus with the herb; and Glaucus was also resurrected.[15]

Both the snake and a magic plant also played a vital role in the Babylonian myth of Gilgamesh. Gilgamesh wished to acquire eternal life; he was led into the depths of the sea, found the plant, but it was snatched away by a snake whilst he was asleep.[16]

In Southeast Australian initiation rituals,

> ... the teeth knocked out are put in a bag with kangaroo teeth and Red Ochre and sent away by the medicine man who extracted them. ... We all went up to the camp, and standing by the Talmura fire, the boys were invested with the man's belt. A long cord of oppossum-fur string, folded a number of times, was wound round the waist and fastened by the end being tucked under the folds. The belt is coloured with Red Ochre.[17]

In looking for the origins of trade, our starting point should be the obtaining of goods from a distance, as in a hunt. The Central Australian Dieri every year, in July or August, make an expedition to the south to obtain the red ochre used by them for painting their bodies. . . . Their neighbors, the Yantruwunta, organized similar enterprises for fetching red ochre . . . 800 kilometers distant.[18]

Twenty billion years ago the universe as we know it came into being. About four and a half billion years ago, the conditions necessary to life evolved. About three billion years ago, the first algae, *out of its own self,* created free oxygen, and through photosynthesis produced the necessary potential for all further development of life. Iron oxide was one of the results of this development, and became used as the red ochre which served the human race as a symbol of life-giving substance the world over.

Profs. Manfred Eigen and Peter Schuster received the Nobel Prize for their work which has been hailed as belonging to the greatest scientific accomplishments of this century. Their contribution is called "The Hypercycle: A Principle of Natural Self-Organization." In addition to Darwin's theories, what they have proved, both mathematically and experimentally, is that the underlying code permeating all life is dependent on a fundamental principle active from the beginning; namely the Hypercycle, the principle of *natural self-organization.* They write:

The competing molecular structures must have the inherent ability of instructing their own synthesis. Such an inherent autocatalytic function can be shown to be necessary for any mechanism of selection involving the destabilization of a population in the presence of a single copy of a newly occurring advantageous mutant.[19]

Profs. Eigen and Schuster showed,

> ... first that the breakthrough in molecular evolu-
> tion must have been brought about by an integration
> of several self-reproducing units to a cooperative
> system and second, that a mechanism capable of
> such an integration can be provided only by the class
> of hypercycles. This conclusion again can be drawn
> from logical inferences. ... If we are asked "What is
> particular to hypercycles?" our answer is "They are
> the analogue to Darwinian systems at the next higher
> level of organization." Darwinian behaviour was
> recognized to be the basis of generation of informa-
> tion. Its prerequisite is integration of self-productive
> *symbols* into self-productive *units* which are able to
> stabilize themselves against the accumulation of
> errors. The same requirement holds for the integra-
> tion of self-reproductive and selectively stable
> behaviour. Only this cyclic linkage as an equivalent
> to autocatalytic reinforcement at this level is able to
> achieve this goal.[20]

The so exciting and vital work of Dr. Barbara McClintock,
for which she received the Nobel prize, proved that genes are
capable of moving and are not fixed on chromosomes, is a
further important scientific proof of animation of "inanimate
matter."

There exists an interesting anticipation of Profs. Eigen's
and Schuster's work in alchemy. Jung writes:

> And by whatever names the philosophers have
> called their stone they always mean and refer to this
> one substance, i.e., to the water from which every-
> thing [originates] and in which everything [is con-
> tained], which rules everything, *in which errors are
> made and in which the error is itself corrected.*[21]

Modern physical science is much concerned with the invisible fine structure of matter, and that is first opened by the sharp instrument of fire. Although that mode of analysis begins several thousand years ago in practical processes ... it was surely set going by the air of magic that boils out of the fire: the alchemical feeling that substances can be changed in unpredictable ways. This is the numinous quality that seems to make fire a source of life. ...

Many ancient recipes express it.

> Now the substance of cinnabar is such that the more it is heated, the more exquisite are its sublimations. Cinnabar will become mercury, and passing through a series of other sublimations, it is again turned into cinnabar, and thus it enables man to enjoy eternal life.

This is the classic experiment with which the alchemists in the Middle Ages inspired awe in those who watched them, all the way from China to Spain. They took the red pigment, cinnabar, which is a sulphide of mercury, and heated it. The heat drives off the sulphur and leaves behind an exquisite pearl of the mysterious silvery metal mercury ...

When the mercury is heated in air it is oxidized and becomes ... an oxide of mercury that is also red. [22]

While alchemy was a precursor of modern science, it was also a projection of mental events onto matter in an effort to transmute one thing into another. As Bronowski's text, quoted above, shows, alchemical science at least contained the *idea* of self-correction, now proved by modern science to guide the evolution of life. But even here in the most complex realms of modern science, the Bible reveals itself as a progenitor in the area of the mind, revealing the ontogenetic nature of the psyche and the psyche's inherent power for self-correction.

> *Your* wickedness will chasten you, and *your* apostasy will reprove you. Know and see that it is evil and bitter for you to forsake the Lord your God; *the fear of me is not in you.*[23]

The sages of the Talmud said: "Everything is in the hands of God except the fear of God" (Berakoth 33b).

In other words, human error will provide its own correction without the "fear of the Lord." Human anxiety is the result of error, and the revealing symptom of this is the feeling that one has failed oneself, and thus failed also the Lord.

Following the "Big Bang," the Hypercycle together with the green algae and oxidation provide the possibilities for Life and thus for the appearance of man; the principles of *self*-organization and *self*-correction are givens. For modern man, the maker of tools and gadgets, and the prospective creator of an artificial mini-universe in space, it is difficult to accept the idea that what is essential to his creativity is already a "given." But because of its own inner logic, all rational, discursive thinking ends "naturally" with the rationalistically unanswerable question "What or who is the agent outside the universe which provided this 'given' in the first place?"

Red Ochre as Basis for the Biological Archetype

As EARLY AS 30,000 years ago, man was already an accomplished artist, as evidenced in figurines and paintings from that period now available to sight and touch. But even further back, 300,000 years earlier, long before what we understand as "consciousness" had developed, the custom of making use of red ochre had begun. In the use of red ochre we see the physical correlative to the inner, self-creative aspect of life, parallel to the creation of oxygen. Here we see the master pattern of self-creativity permeating all life, and here *we find the biological roots for the basic archetype of life itself.*

From people to people, from culture to culture, from continent to continent, the ritualistic use of red ochre was a custom, even in Australia which, as far as we know today, was not in any land contact with another continent. Even so red ochre was used. This fact is the more remarkable as some forty-five million years ago the continental rift is supposed to have taken place, and Australia was severed from the African continent. Australia's first settlers reached the continent about 40,000 to 50,000 years ago. They probably came from Asia by way of New Guinea; in the late 1700's about 300,000 Aborigines lived in Australia.[24] The ritualistic custom varied in its application; but it was always related to life-creating or life-sustaining rituals.

In the life-sustaining rituals, red ochre was also used as magic to ward off evil, and thus red became associated with the idea of evil. In the Old Testament the Prophet Isaiah says: "... though your sins are like scarlet, they shall be as white as snow; though they are red like crimson, they shall become like wool."[25] In the New Testament, the symbolism is used in the scarlet robe in which the soldiers dressed the Christ to mock him. Here it has the double meaning of evil and the symbol of power. "And they stripped him and put a scarlet robe upon him, and plaiting a crown of thorns they put it on his head ... And when they had mocked him, they stripped him of the robe, and put his own clothes on him, and led him away to crucify him."[26] The dramatic description of this tragic event touches the human heart at the very depths of its being.

The corrective principle is experienced in dreams as symbolic manifestations of the deeper layers of the psyche. The dream often complements our conscious attitudes, which may be contrary to the best interest of the whole personality. That is why in all cultures the dream in its guiding and warning aspect is experienced as authentic. A group of people living today in caves as if they were still in the Stone Age were asked: "Do the Tasadays have souls? We do not know. All we know outside our daily life comes from the dreams we have, but we do not know what dreams are."[27]

Precisely as our cellular energies are directed toward the orderly and harmonious realization and functioning of the physical organism, precisely as cosmic energies seem to work toward the harmony of the universe, so do the energies of the psyche in its ontogenesis work toward harmony and order and the goal of wholeness. "The psyche is a complex of energies and inertia not only potentially harmonious, balanced and whole, but actually in its ontogenesis *determined upon* the achievement of harmony, balance and wholeness."[28] To which Sir Herbert Read added: "There should be no difficulty in supposing that a tendency of this kind is built into the human organism; that in this respect the human organism does not differ from a sea shell, a flower or a crystal."[29]

This goal of wholeness has with "earlier" man been tried to be achieved through magic means. And also here the archetypal *red* played a central role. In the Old Testament, "Tell the people of Israel to bring you a red heifer without defect, in which there is no blemish, and upon which a yoke has never come."[30] The whole of Numbers Chapter 19 deals with the use of the ashes of the red heifer. They "shall be kept for the congregation of the people of Israel for the water for impurity, for the removal of sin."[31] Not only a knowing in the deepest sense is here portrayed, the ritualistic use of the living waters is also the "knowing" of the interrelatedness of life and death. The ashes of the red heifer have a double effect. On the one hand they purify things and man, who have come into contact with death and have thus become impure, but they make, on the other hand, priests and men who had been pure, impure through touching the ashes. The homeopathic principle, in minute doses, creates health out of the ill-making factor; as life is a balanced whole, so do the ashes of the red heifer call forth impurity out of purity, death as a counterpart to life.

Plutarch writes in his *Moralia:*

> The Egyptians, because of their belief that Typhon was of a red complexion, also dedicate to sacrifice such of their neat cattle as are of red colour, but they conduct the examination of these so scrupulously that, if an animal has only one hair black or white, they think it wrong to sacrifice it; for they regard as suitable for sacrifice not what is dear to the gods but the reverse, namely, such animals as have incarnate in them souls of unholy and unrighteous men who have been transformed into other bodies.[32]

Diodorus of Sicily writes:

> The sacred bulls — I refer to the Apis and the Mnevis — are honored like the gods, as Osiris commanded, both because of their use in farming and also because the fame of those who discovered the fruits of the earth is handed down by the labours of

these animals to succeeding generations for all time. Red oxen, however, may be sacrificed, because it is thought that this was the color of Typhon, who plotted against Osiris and was then punished by Isis for the death of her husband. Men also, if they were of the same color as Typhon, were sacrificed, they say, in ancient times at the tomb of Osiris. . . .[33]

Both in Egyptian beliefs and in the writings of the Old Testament, death is related to life as life is to death. The self-correcting principle is reflected in magical rites, which in turn define some of the moral and ethical issues of human behavior, and thereby reveal their true nature as demonstrations of the ontogenesis of the psyche. As we shall see later, this is most poignantly demonstrated in the Jacob and Esau story.

Meaning as the Ontogenesis of the Psyche

THE BIBLE as a structural hermeneutic derives its meaning from the ontogenesis of the psyche. Its interrelatedness is shown in that it makes use of historical, political events, and mental constructs which depict the whole structure of human existence. In this sense, what the Bible reveals is divine Truth.

In the history of religions we find an example of self-development equally as persuasive as that we have seen in the development of the sciences. It is assumed by most scholars that the time of Abraham was roughly coincident with that of Hammurabi, King of Babylon: about 1800 B.C. Hammurabi dethroned the moon goddess Sin and replaced her with the sun god Marduk. Here we see an example of the manipulation of an existing religious institution which is coincident with a rising consciousness in the spiritual realm. *Monotheism was born.* Abraham personified that vital, growing spirit. As a patriarch, Abraham became the symbolic basis for the monotheistic beliefs of Judaism, Christainity, and Islam. The Pharaoh Akhenaton tried to institutionalize monotheism in Egypt about 300 years later, but failed to accomplish his aims due to the inertia and resistance of the existing religious and political institutions.

Beginning with Abraham, the Hebrew experience has resulted in the evolutionary unfolding of the human psyche. *The Bible is the living record of this development,* and therefore it has maintained its validity throughout the ages, up to and including the technological age of our own time.

What in the Old Testament was an inner authentic experience and found its expression in "concrete" reality evolves in the New Testament into an act of faith. "By faith Abraham obeyed when he was called to go to a place which he was to receive as an inheritance."[34]

Abraham was the symbolic nucleus around which the poets crystallized the monotheistic mood as an expression of the *Zeitgeist* and which they dramatically embodied in written texts about a thousand years after the historical period of which they wrote. The name "Abram" is well attested in ancient texts as that of a merchant and warrior. This "reality" was the backdrop used by the poets to address a spiritual dimension just as real as though they were writing about a specific historical person. Abram seems to have belonged to the highly sophisticated Amarna age. Hurrian as well as Ugaritic texts, and the newly discovered vocabulary as school text in the recent archaeological finds at Ebla (ca. 2,500 B.C.) are a further substantiation. Bermant and Weitzman write in *Ebla*:

> The tablets cover a period of a thousand years before Abraham, and a thousand years, even in the fourth millennium before Christ, was a very, very long time. They tell us much, but what they don't tell

us . . . is whether the Bible is true or not. They have
nothing to do with the Bible, at least not directly, and
what we have here is not a Biblical expedition. If we
have tablets with legends similar to those of the Bible
it means only that such legends existed around here
long before the Bible.[35]

Two recent studies based on literary background and
archaeological findings have led their authors to doubt
whether the patriarchs lived at all.[36] Van Seters concluded,
after an analysis of the extra-biblical, archaeologically re-
covered parallels that Genesis 14 "cannot possibly have historical significance." Some scholars have likened Abraham
to the figure of Arthur in the Arthurian legends, and the
legendary material to the original King.

The legends prove again here the abiding richness
of the original image. It is, in fact, the image itself
which continues its own development, being re-
experienced, expanded, deepened by the poet
according to his time and disposition. It is not a
matter of fanciful elaboration but rather that the
image as archetype continues to stir the forces of the
inner world to the degree that it still holds something
of the truth of the human condition.[37]

In both the Egyptian and Old Testament traditions, the
Zeitgeist expressed itself in the evolution toward integration
and creativity. It revealed itself as well in the fact that
Akhenaton removed the multitude of Egyptian gods and
put in their place a monotheism. Hammurabi in Babylonia
displaced the moon god Sin and put in her place the sun god
Marduk likewise.

Akhenaton's belief in monism resulted in failure, and
details about this event have come down to us in two important records: (1) The Papyrus Harris, 12th Century B.C.,
refers also to the time of Akhenaton, 13th Century B.C.,
saying: ". . . they had made the gods like humans. No

sacrifices were performed anymore in the inner of the temples. The gods had been torn down to rest on the floor."[38] (2) Donald B. Redford reports about the archaeological findings in excavating Akhenaton's temple at Karnak and writes: "Our work has enabled us to reconstruct with some certainty just how the temple was destroyed. *First the statues were thrown down on their faces.* Then the piers of the colonnade were dismantled almost to ground level."[39] After 3,500 years archaeology confirms in exact details the writings of that time!

This then is the political background for the poetic setting by which the poets, through the symbol of Abram, demonstrated most dramatically the process of man's becoming in the significant message: "Go from your country" — i.e., "go forth into the land of your own becoming."

In the drama of the ontogenesis of the psyche the poets made Abram the first political or religious dissenter and refugee. As *dramatis persona* he removed himself from the scene realizing that it is neither the sun nor the moon which is the decisive deity. The decisive deity was believed to be the principle behind the sun and the moon which made them shine.

This vision pointing behind the phenomena is that principle of pure creativity which is part of all of us and reveals itself in the utterances of the poets. The realization of the inner development is expressed in the vision of Abram in which he is told to "go forth." Genesis 12:1 reads: "Now the Lord said to Abram 'Go from your country and your kindred and your father's house to the land that I will show you.'"

In a most profound and powerful picture the poets conveyed Abraham's resolve:

And he said, Lord God, whereby shall I know that I shall inherit it?
And he said unto him, Take me an heifer of *three* years old, and a she-goat of *three* years old, and a

ram of *three* years old, and a turtledove and a young
pigeon.
And he took unto him all these and divided them in
the midst, and laid each piece one against the other,
but the birds divided he not.
And when the fowls came down upon the carcasses,
Abram drove them away.
And when the sun was going down, a deep sleep fell
upon Abram, and lo, an horror of great darkness fell
upon him. . . . And it came to pass, that, when the sun
went down, and it was dark, behold a smoking furnace, and a burning lamp that passed between those
pieces. In the same day the Lord made a covenant
with Abram, saying, Unto thy seed have I given this
land. . . .[40]

This deep authentic vision of the night is all the more real
because it is related to the tangible — that is, the land
promised as an inheritance, expressing the close interrelationship of man's becoming and his environment. Following
his vision Abram went to Egypt where Akhenaton introduced monism in his quest for the Unknown God, the
Agnostos Theos of the Greek. Thus, monotheism was born
in the inner development of the prototype of the individual;
it was expressed in terms of a personal experience, rather
than as a dogma coming as a revelation from outside.

All moral culture springs solely and immediately
from the inner life of the soul. It can only be stimulated in human nature and never produced by external and artificial contrivances. Whatever does not
spring from man's free choice was only the result of
instruction and guidance and does not enter his very
being, but remains alien to its true nature. It does not
perform it with truly human energies, but is merely
mechanical exactness.[41]

The ontogenesis of the psyche expresses itself on different

levels, yet the principle remains essentially the same. The New Testament also addresses itself to this essential theme of each person becoming a self. "Unless you hate your father and mother you cannot follow me" is the "go forth" expressed in another way.[42] The parallel between the Old and New Testaments is found in the fundamentals of both: in the Christian tradition the abstract construct of the Trinity becomes fundamental. While the Old Testament tradition speaks of three personal experiences of God — the God of Abraham, the God of Isaac and the God of Jacob, each depicting a particular stage in the ontogenesis of the psyche — it is the God of Jacob which in the New Testament plays an ever-recurring and vital role. The reason for this seems to lie in the image of Jacob given us by the poets who saw him as prototypical of man's "existential" problem — that of being human with a potential for growth and becoming.

On the other hand, Abraham's hallmark is the Akedah, his willingness to sacrifice Isaac, who became the father of Jacob and Esau [infra, p. 98].

Jacob's significance is revealed in the epic story of his receiving the new name of Israel. His new name was given precisely at the moment when he became the progenitor of man's integration toward wholeness, and thus for each person's fulfillment as a distinct personality. It was at this point also that Jahweh became the God of people. In the encounter of Jacob and Esau at the ford of Jabbok, Jacob receives Esau's blessing.[43] Everything depends on this encounter for the further development of the psyche.

The Christian Church of the third and fourth centuries A.D. found in the New Testament texts which led to the tradition of God being expressed as a Trinity. Augustine, Bishop of Hippo (b. 354 A.D.) wrote a major work entitled *On the Trinity* in which he relates the concept Trinity to the perfection of the senary number [meaning six]:

> The perfection of the senary number is commended
> in the scriptures. . . . Now this ratio of the single to

the double arises, no doubt, from the ternary number [meaning three], since one added to two makes three; but the whole which these make reaches to the senary, for one and two and three make six. And this number is on that account called perfect, because it is completed in its own parts....[44]

In a Gnostic text which was in existence in the third century C. E. Allogenes writes: "I was seeking the ineffable and Unknown God —whom if one should know completely one would be ignorant of him —the Mediator of the *Triple* Power who subsists in stillness and silence and is unknown."[45]

Surely in the symbolism of numbers the principle of becoming on a rational plane also expresses itself. The concept of the Trinity represents on an abstract level a higher degree of differentiation of mental awareness and is therefore seen as a manifestation of the divine.

The concept of the Trinity has its antecedent in primitive art. A Neolithic cave painting depicts a stylized, three-horned man, and the Daunian stela, seventh century B.C. (?) portrays the same archaic motif as the three-horned Heracles and Iolaus fighting monsters.[46] In our time the concept of the Trinity seems to undergo a change to the experience of Life as a quaternity. The four-dimensional approach of science, three in space one in time, as the essence and the latest Roman Catholic dogma of the ascension of Mary, are significant signs for this development. Politically it expresses itself in the demand by women to be recognized as full partners also in religious services.

The Leiden hymns to Ammon, the Egyptian god, sing: "All gods are three: Amon, Re and Ptah and there is no second to them. 'Hidden' is his name as Amon, he is Re in face, and in his body he is Ptah."[47] Atum the god of creation in Egypt at Heliopolis "brought forth Shu and Tefnut when he was one, but then he became three."[48] Atum masturbated and brought forth from his mouth Shu and Tefnut, male

and female.[49] Brother and sister related and the result of the
relationship was mankind. The brother-sister relationship
was therefore sanctified and became quite a normal practice
in the Egyptian royal palace.

The principle of growth, the ontogenesis of the psyche,
reveals itself in two major events of the Bible which were
decisive for the development of Western culture. "And God
said to Abraham 'As for Sarai your wife, you shall not call
her name Sarai, but Sarah shall be her name. I will bless her,
and moreover I will give you a son by her.'"[50] "And the Lord
appeared to him. . . . He lifted up his eyes and looked, and
behold, *three* men stood in front of him. . . . They said to
him, 'Where is Sarah your wife?' . . . He said 'I will surely
return to you in the spring, and Sarah your wife will have a
son.'"[51]

Figure 2.   Heracles and Iolaus Fighting Monsters. Daunian stela,
seventh century (?) B.C.

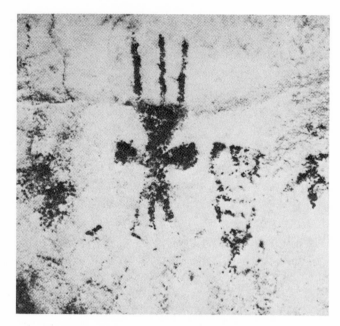

Figure 3. Stylized Man, Three-Horned (?); Stag Below. Neolithic cave paintings, near Porto Badisco.

Figure 4. Three-Horned Heracles-Trecaranus. Daunian stela.

... an angel of the Lord appeared to him in a dream, saying, "Joseph, son of David, do not fear to take Mary your wife, for that which is conceived in her is of the Holy Spirit; she will bear a son". . . . When Joseph woke from sleep, he did as the angel of the Lord commanded. . . .[52]

In both of these instances, the annunciation comes out of the depth of Being, and though both are *contra naturam*, both are authentic experiences. Sarah and Abraham were advanced in age — "it had ceased with Sarah after the manner of women." And Mary was made pregnant by the Holy Ghost.

This archetypal experience of growth and becoming manifests itself time and again in dreams of modern men and women in which either sex may give birth to a child, their "son of man" being miraculously conceived. And in both of the Biblical instances, the writers also refer to dreams.

The dream experiences of our contemporaries show such a child in a vast variety of gradations: from the radiant, all-knowing, wise infant, who, like Hermes and Herakles in Greek mythology, already as children had attained their full powers, to the other end of the spectrum of under-developed, retarded little creatures. In every case, such a child elicits care and concern, either as love or awe, and at the very least as a call for assistance to the newly born. In the Biblical story of Moses who was a foundling adopted and cared for, we have further amplification because his continued existence was decisive for further development.[53] In such situations the symbol of the child reveals something new — something not hitherto recognized in the existing situation. For the individual person, this is a process of realization reflecting participation in the widening of personal outlook, and in the process of integration toward wholeness. Even a personal refusal to participate is in itself revealing, for it confronts the subject with some aspect of the "unknown" within the self. In such experiences, the field of awareness is enriched either by the acceptance of the "new" or by the realization that one has refused to accept it. The ontogenesis of the psyche in this relation becomes the ethical yardstick relative to which the living situation becomes meaningful.

This ethical principle expressing itself in acceptance or rejection of this "new," the child, is an inborn quality of man. It is the very basis upon which man can build his humanness. To be able to do so freely is considered by Pope John XXIII as a natural *right* as this very quality is seen by him in his encyclical "Pacem in Terris" as a natural *law*. To offend this "law" is, then, the real basis of guilt and not the non-adherence to doctrinal dogmas.[54]

In much the same way an outstanding scientist considered justice to be a "part of the biological equipment of man."[55]

Maat, the Egyptian god personifying law and righteousness, Melchizedek, Christ, and the Paraclete, as we shall see later, are the spiritual correlatives to man's natural existence, which like his biological life is *given* and not made by man. The theological and psychological techniques for "making" ethical attitudes are, therefore, contradictions in terms. The realization of this "givenness" is one of the major reasons why modern man is inclined to reject the external imposition of intellectually conceived dogmas, political or otherwise. Abraham's authentic experience of the ontogenesis of the psyche describes the inner motivation for his move. And the Covenant, promising an enrichment and widening of experience to new areas of the mind is expressed by the poets as "the land I will show you." The Covenant is sealed by the symbols of the fire and the smoking furnace or oven. Essentially the same symbol is expressed by Jesus' saying: "I am the fire and the light" and unless you leave your parents' home "you cannot follow me."

The cynics of our time will say that if we look at the "real" world out there where bribery, corruption and crime are ever-present, we will see that the world has not been redeemed. There is a partial truth, to be sure, in such a view.

The assumption, however, that man remains unchanged is contradicted on many levels: by going to the moon man has transcended his "natural" habitat; the fact that slavery has been largely abolished; the fact that society increasingly permits self-expression and individual development; the fact that the weaker nations are now less suppressed by the more powerful; all these social factors show movement in a teleological direction. The shifts in scientific thought from a rigid determinism to broader freedom reflect the same direction of movement.

The contemporary sense of being lost like an atom in an ever-expanding universe is due basically to holding onto a state of mind dominated by dying, static signs. Resistance against life experienced as a flowing stream creates despair and gloom, as though demons were assailing man in order to subdue him. The tumult of our times is witness to the basic flow of life, and witness to the eternal becoming, ever-expanding, changing central Being. Life as a process of becoming through change is expressed in Chinese philosophy in the figures of Yin and Yang, embraced not only by modern youth, but by serious scientific thinkers and theologians.[56] Consider Dietrich Bonhoeffer who writes:

> The "beyond" of God is not the beyond of our perceptive faculties.... God is the "beyond" in the midst of our life. The Church stands not where human powers give out, on the borders, but in the centre of the village. That is the way it is in the Old Testament, and in this sense we still read the New Testament far too little on the basis of the Old. The outward aspect of this religionless Christianity, the form it takes, is something to which I am giving much thought.... It may be that on us in particular, midway between East and West, there will fall an important responsibility.[57]

CHAPTER 3

Self-Determination

Justice As Part of the Biological Equipment of Man

IT IS A curious paradox that the more "real" man becomes in the material world, the more "unreal" or abstract the old "hard realities" seem to become. For example, mathematical models and abstractions are used increasingly to deal with economic theories and the problems of productivity, thus dehumanizing material production and concrete existence. Speaking of the relationship between spiritual and material or economic values, Pope John Paul II said in his address to the United Nations:

> It is the spiritual values that are pre-eminent both on account of the nature of these values and also for reasons concerning the good of man.
>
> It is easy to see that *material goods* do not have unlimited capacity for satisfying the needs of man. They are not in themselves easily distributed and in the relationship between those who possess and enjoy them and those who are without them, they give rise to tension, dissension and division that will often even turn into open conflict. *Spiritual goods,*

on the other hand, are open to unlimited enjoyment
by many at the same time without diminution of the
goods themselves.[1]

Material goods can be dealt with mathematically because
they are, in essence, universal, subject to natural laws formulated by science. But spiritual experiences, on the other
hand, are as unique as the individuals who have them, and
therefore to equate spiritual experience with material goods
becomes a most potent source for cynicism. Dogma, economic or spiritual, has proved to be of diminishing value,
and yet continued adherence to dogma may easily engulf
civilization in a holocaust which guarantees wholesale
destruction. The logical outcome of continued neglect of the
psyche is its projection into "isms" and to continue this trend
is only to increase our peril.

Two messianic dogmatic political systems, the Communism of the Kremlin and the Communism of Peking, are
repeating the Nazi holocaust in Cambodia, while to a lesser
degree, in Ireland the Catholic and Protestant Christian
brothers and sisters are killing each other for the sake of
power. The Cain and Abel story is repeating itself!

The meaning of individual spirituality which expresses
itself in symbols is discernible only through amplification in
relation to the context in which they are experienced. These
symbols are authentic, and as such, have transforming
power. On the other hand, signs, as we use the term, denote
abstractions of known contents which may have universal
application. These signs, however, have *no transforming
power* on the mind, for they are only intellectually conceived. Is this not why, in spite of a high degree of verbal
education, people and the societies they form do not change?
What real meaning, for example, has the word "Zeus" to
contemporary man? It has become an abstraction and therefore has lost its dynamically moving character. In our Western tradition, because of the lack of authentic, individual
experience, the word God has become for many just a phrase

covering up selfish desires. As in ages past, so today persons in their aloneness suffer the dire consequences.

The Old Testament prophet Micah raises his voice:

> The godly man has perished from the
>   earth,
> and there is none upright among men;
> they all lie in wait for blood,
> and each hunts his brother with a net.
> Their hands are upon what is evil,
> to do it diligently;
> the prince and the judge ask for a bribe,
> and the great man utters the evil desire of
>   his soul;
> thus they weave it together.
> The best of them is like a brier,
> the most upright of them a thorn
>   hedge. . . .
> Put no trust in a neighbor,
> have no confidence in a friend;
> guard the doors of your mouth
> from her who lies in your bosom;
> for the son treats the father with
>   contempt,
> the daughter rises up against her mother,
> the daughter-in-law against her mother-
>   in-law;
> a man's enemies are the men of his own
>   house.[2]

About 1500 B.C. an Egyptian scribe Neferrohu copied an old text whose papyrus is preserved in the Leningrad Museum and speaks to our situation.

> Give heed, my heart and weep for this land. . . .
> Ruined is this land, while none is concerned for it,
> none speaks, and none sheds tears. . . . All good
> things have passed away, and the land is prostrate in

wretchedness. . . . I will show thee a son as an enemy,
a brother as a foe and a man slaying his own father.
Every mouth is filled with "Love me" . . . and all good
things have passed away. . . . The land is diminished
while its rulers are multiplied. . . .[3]

Neferrohu in the following remarkable words proclaims
the coming of the king who is to save it:

The people of this time shall rejoice, the son of
man shall make his name forever and ever. . . .
Righteousness (Maat) shall return to its place,
unrighteousness shall be cast out. Let him rejoice
who shall see it and who shall be serving the king.[4]

"Serving the King" within our own four walls is a specific
and concrete contribution to society because it creates ripples which spread outward to the world at large.

According to age-old Egyptian texts, the principle of
justice, Maat, is a given from the beginning of human existence. The same thing is reflected in the symbol of Melchizedek who, as a balancing principle of peace, blessed
Abraham when he came back from making war.[5] This "mysterious" blessing of Melchizedek reflects the ontogenesis of
the psyche as man emerges from his mystic participation
with nature. Good and evil, here symbolized as peace and
war, now become ethical principles. At this point, mankind
reached the "Abrahamic" stage of development in his journey to self-becoming. Continued differentiation today has
resulted in his "coming of age" as he tries to comprehend the
meaning of his life through experiencing what is truly real,
and to come to a knowledge of the value of values. In our
time the symbol of transubstantiation cannot authentically
become mental reality because the Messianic idea has not
been transmuted after thousands of years of promise. For
contemporary man, the God who is not experienced, but
merely conveyed as an intellectual abstraction, is dead.

"Don't offer me religion as an escape; that doesn't satisfy me" is the cry of modern man in need.

> These are the secret sayings which the living Jesus spoke and which Didymos Judas Thomas wrote down.
> (1) And he said, "Whoever finds the interpretation of these sayings will not experience death."
> (2) Jesus said, "Let him who seeks continue seeking until he finds. When he finds, he will become troubled. When he becomes troubled, he will be astonished, and he will rule over the All."
> (3) Jesus said, "If those who lead you say to you, 'See, the Kingdom is in the sky,' then the birds of the sky will precede you. If they say to you, 'It is in the sea,' then the fish will precede you. Rather, the Kingdom is inside of you, and it is outside of you. When you come to know yourselves, then you will become known, and you will realize that it is you who are the sons of the living Father. But if you will not know yourselves, you dwell in poverty and it is you who are that poverty.[6]

The place of belief has been taken today by the desire for *knowledge through authentic individual experience*. An objective experience of reality is, however, only possible if the material and spiritual planes are equally well apprehended. While the discovery of natural law on the material plane is the task of science, modern man gathers around its temples expecting to find salvation, as if scientific planning of economic and social life alone could provide it. The modern religious problem is therefore dictated by a paradox. The development of science makes it ideally possible to effect the necessary planning for a universally healthy economic and social life. It appears to be possible on the material level to establish a truly universal plan. The material necessities for human life and the preconditions necessary to provide them are indeed universal. But at the same time, we must recognize that there is no "universal man." Only individuals are real. The notion of a "universal man" is an abstraction from individual spiritual qualities. Modern humanity seeks to experience the meaning of life through the unique individual experience of each person's spiritual being, and not by means of abstractions.

This paradox constitutes the modern religious problem because it reflects a reversal in the *Weltanschauung* of the past. On the material and economic side, the individual standard has been hitherto the directing and decisive factor, while on the spiritual side, the ruling principle has been the universal. Now, however, the universal principle is becoming the standard of value for the material side of life, while the standard for spiritual values is an individual experience. What was once relegated to Providence has become a problem to be solved by technology and science, and the lone individual now becomes responsible for shaping his spiritual life.

In myths, the poets have illuminated the difficulties and anxieties of man's voyage to self-awareness. The word *myth* is etymologically derived from the Greek *mythos,* meaning a "legend," "story," "word" or "speech"; it is an expression of the creative imagination of the psyche itself. It is art in its truest sense in that it fits man both aesthetically and emotionally. Myth is an art form and appears when the psyche in its ontogenesis has reached a level of readiness both to express and receive it. Epistemological grounds are a sure guide for a voyage through the "enlightening" world of myth and an authentic experience of art.

In this sense myths are as real as any "reality" can be. They are manifestations of activating and directive forces of the "inner reality." This "inside" loses its separateness, however, from the general flow of Life just as modern atomic physics did, by losing its concrete factualness. David Bohm describes this flow as the dissolution of atoms into a deeper structure that ultimately merges with the field of the whole universe. As the instruments which observe that field are composed of the same atoms and finer particles as our own brains and nervous systems, so Bohm reflects for modern physics the mythic awareness that we in our act of observation are like that which we observe.

The efforts of the psyche to fulfill itself have been depicted in mythopoetic representations. Oedipus, as a child, was exposed or doomed to die, threatened by a decree of a king; so was Sagan I, King of Assyria (ca. 2350 B.C.), who like Moses was cast by his mother into a river in a basket of rushes sealed with pitch.[7] And when Abraham was born, Nimrod's courtiers wanted to put him to death; thus he was kept in a hiding place beneath the ground for 13 years, during which time he did not see the sun or the moon.[8] "Now when they had departed, behold, an angel of the Lord appeared to Joseph in a dream and said, 'rise, and take the child and his mother, and flee to Egypt, and remain there till I tell you; for Herod is about to search for the child, to destroy him.'"[9] According to the Koran, Ishmael, Abraham's son with Hagar, his servant, was left by Abraham in a desolate valley with scarcely any food.[10] When asked by Hagar: "Has your Lord instructed you to leave us here alone?" Abraham answered affirmatively; but Hagar said, "God will not abandon us." Isaac was also exposed to die upon the altar of sacrifice,[11] but became the father of the two most important figures in the ontogenesis of the psyche, namely Jacob and Esau.

In each of these stories from widely divergent cultures and epochs, the common theme is the exposure motif. What is here symbolically expressed is the conflict between the inner urge for personal growth and development and the counterforce of anxiety at the prospect of being exposed to the vicissitudes of life. In Greek mythology, Zeus was in danger of being devoured as was Dionysos in danger of being destroyed as a child. The destructive forces of mythology are often personified as "gods" reflecting the individual's inner rejection of the new and the unknown.

In *Enuma Elish*, the Babylonian creation myth, the father Apsu speaks to the mother Tiamat in this way:

> Apsu opened his mouth
> And said to Tiamat in a loud voice:
> ". . . By day I cannot rest, by night I cannot
>   sleep;
> I will destroy (them [our children]) and put an
>   end to their way,
> That silence be established, and then let us
>   sleep.[12]

The *Atrahasis Epic*, roughly contemporary with *Enuma Elish*, 16th Century B.C., says with a sound familiar to our "Malthusian age":

> The land became wide, the people became
>   numerous,
> The land hummed like a Lyre [?]
> The God was depressed by their uproar.
> [Enli] heard their clamour
> [And] said to the great gods
> "The clamour of mankind has become
>   oppressive.
> By their uproar I miss sleep
> I will (cut) off the supply of flour for man,
> In their bellies let the greens be too few.[13]

The eternal struggle between creativity and inertia, between acceptance and rejection of the new, expresses itself most dramatically in Ezekiel: "And because of all your abominations I will do with you what I have never yet done, and the like of which I will never do again. Therefore fathers shall eat their sons in the midst of you, and sons shall eat their fathers. . . ."[14]

Does this Biblical quotation not depict an ever-recurring human, all too human, theme of anger due to unfulfilled

Figure 5. The King as *Prima Materia*, Devouring his Son.

expectations when broken promises have become an abomination?

The alarmingly high rate of adolescent suicides, of child abuse, divorce and armed violence in family relations are the modern equivalent of the psyche's persistent urge to retreat into a state of mindlessness. Such acts of violence erupt despite repeated conscious promises to reform, and again and again, the "father eats the son." The same is symbolically depicted in Matthew's Gospel:

And the brother shall deliver up the brother to death, and the father the child: and the children shall rise up against their parents, and cause them to be put to death. . . . But he that endureth to the end shall be saved.[15]

These Biblical and mythological poetic utterances both demonstrate the psyche's persistent urge to return to the mindless state of non-being in the "Garden of Eden." In such symbols, man's interrelatedness with the universe as "we know it" is expressed.

The awareness of it arises from the depth of the unconsciousness of our "origin," which through the process of becoming created our consciousness and expressed itself in symbols of ever-greater complexity. The means for the apprehension of this process is the psyche itself.

In the biological discipline the same is essentially expressed in its idiom. In an essay on "The Origin of Genetic Information," Prof. Manfred Eigen, Prof. Peter Schuster, et. al., write:

> . . . functional molecules may have been important in the chemistry of a prebiotic soup. They could not evolve, however. Their accidental efficiency rested on non-accidental structural constraints, such as *favorable interactions with neighboring molecules.* . . . If their efficiency was to improve, and if more functional variants were to be favored over less functional ones, they would have to escape such structural constraints. Only self-replicative, information-conserving molecules could do so.[16]

In nature, the self-correcting principle takes many, many years to make its influence felt. Man, in his awareness as the carrier of this principle, is of relatively late date. The difficulty in exercising this principle without some knowledge and understanding of the working of one's own inner mind is poignantly expressed by St. Paul:

The good that I would I do not:
But the evil I would not, that I do.[17]

The fact that most individuals lack awareness of their own potential for making choices is widely accepted as a natural condition, and is one of the main reasons that societies remain relatively static. It is assumed that the "evil I would not, that I do" of St. Paul is simply a description of "the way things are." There is, however, a transforming and transmuting agent — the "Christ within." But the potential of this power is counteracted by dogmas of social institutions which try to control man from the outside. Externally imposed dogma, in fact, prevents the development of personality, and the natural consequence is that society necessarily continues to cater to the lowest common denominator.

Balaam—The Speaking Ass

As A structural hermeneutic of the ontogenesis of the psyche, the Biblical narrative contains a significant symbol of the self-correcting principle and its difficulties. The account of Balaam and his ass reveals the tendency of the psyche to move toward wholeness by integrating what is regarded as detrimental to further growth.[18] According to the story, the Israelites had been victorious in a battle, and the defeated king sought to obtain revenge through a curse imposed by the seer, Balaam. It is possible that the story springs from an actual historical event, but the circumstances become a symbolic backdrop to illustrate the much deeper problem of man's coming to terms with himself.

Balaam, here the symbol of the individual in quest of wholeness, is urged by King Balak to curse Israel. The problem arises in Balaam's reluctance to accept this task. This is a problem not only for Balaam and for the poets who wrote the story, but a universal problem for the human race.

Balaam knows that he may not contradict the word of the Lord "to do either good or bad of my own will, what the Lord speaks, that I will speak."[19] Here the poets raise the supreme issue:

> Balaam rose in the morning, and saddled his ass, and went with the princes of Moab. But God's anger was kindled because he went; and the angel of the Lord took his stand in the way as his adversary.[20]

Accordingly, Balaam's ass turned aside and refused to go further. Balaam strikes the ass. The scene repeats itself three times, and in the end:

> The Lord opened the mouth of the ass, and she said to Balaam "What have I done to you, that you have struck me these three times?" . . . . Then the Lord opened the eyes of Balaam, and he saw the angel of the Lord standing in the way. . . . "Why have you struck your ass these three times? Behold I have come forth to withstand you, because your way is perverse before me. . . ."[21]

The Hebrew word *Shatan*, the angel of the Lord, as it is usually translated, means, in fact, "to obstruct, oppose." It is in this passage that the word *Shatan* appears for the first time in the Old Testament. "Nowhere in the Old Testament does Satan appear as a distinctive demonic figure, opposed to God and responsible for all evil. . . . It is only in the Deutero-canonical scriptures that Satan begins to emerge as a distinctive personality."[22]

The obstructing, correcting agent we have come to consider as "the devil." The answer to the poet's question is given supremely in Matthew: "Then Jesus was led up by the Spirit into the wilderness to be tempted by the devil."[23] Jesus confronted the devil and "out of his own will" withstood the temptations. Balaam, at a lesser level of development of the psyche, did not understand — could not "act out of his own will." It was only after beating his ass *three* times that a higher consciousness ignites, and then the ass speaks symbolically to make Balaam aware of his personal situation. The Unknown God, the *Agnostos Theos*, confronts him directly in the symbol of *Shatan* as a symbolic means for his own becoming, his own growth to be himself. Significantly it is in this very passage that the words "Son of Man" appear for the first time in the Bible:

> God is not man, that he should lie,
> or a *Son of Man*, that he should
> repent.[24]

In Nietzsche's *Zarathustra* the same theme is sounded:

> "But speak what are you seeking here in *my* woods and rocks? And lying down on *my* path, how did you want to try me? In what way were you seeking to test *me*?" Thus spoke Zarathustra, and his eyes flashed. The old magician remained silent for a while, then said, "Did I seek to test you? I — merely seek. O Zarathustra, I seek one who is genuine, right, simple, unequivocal, a man of all honesty, a vessel of wisdom, a saint of knowledge, a great human being. Do you not know it, Zarathustra? *I seek Zarathustra*."[25]

Here is man in search of himself. In the Akedah, God tempted Abraham to sacrifice his son, and yet the poets tell us that "the angel" (Abraham's own inner voice) spoke to Abraham telling him to stay his hand. In Matthew 4:1 Christ is driven into the wilderness of unknowing and there the devil tempts him. God and Devil, the irreconcilable opposites and antagonists in the human psyche, are in an eternal struggle depicting man's encounter with himself.

An important and recurring symbol in the ontogenesis of the psyche involves the number three — often "three days." As Abraham journeyed to Mount Moriah he was wrapped in silence for three days. So also with Jonah, whose refusal to

speak out against the evil of Nineveh resulted in a deep
depression leading, as with Balaam, to a deepened insight.
Jonah rose to flee to Tarshish from the presence of the Lord;
he was thrown into the "raging waters" of the inner struggle,
and:

> The waters closed in over me,
> the deep was round about me;
> weeds were wrapped about my head
> at the roots of the mountains.[26]

Jonah, however, comes out of his depression at the very
moment he remembers that those "that observe lying vanities, forsake their own mercy,"[27] which is to say that those
who adhere to idols of whatever kind forsake their own
forgiveness and are forever haunted by guilt. Dogmas,
indoctrinations from without, are in this sense "lying vanities," idols. Before Jonah came to this realization he was like
Abraham coming to Mount Moriah "for three days in
silence." Awareness is also symbolized by Christ "rising."
Before the resurrection, Christ spent three days in Sheol —
the Underworld. Saul, after being struck down on the road
to Damascus, was for "three days . . . without sight and
neither ate nor drank,"[28] and after "light from heaven
flashed about him"[29] . . . "something like scales fell from his
eyes."[30]

Abraham, Jonah, Christ, and Paul at important junctions
pregnant with meaning, repeat the same archetypal motif in
the process of the ontogenesis of the psyche, reflecting the
psyche's inborn quality for self-correction, and for freeing
itself from adherence to idols. For Saul, a new enlightenment was revealed through his own inner experience and
resulted in a change of name. Saul became Paul, as Abram
had become Abraham, Sarai, Sarah and Jacob, Israel. As
Paul, no longer Saul, he came to Athens to find an altar
dedicated *To An Unknown God* — the *Agnostos Theos*.[31]
"What therefore you worship as unknown, this I proclaim to
you."[32]

. . . yet he is not far from each one of us,
for in him we live and move and have our being.[33]

Paul rejected an idolatrous understanding of Law, as had Moses. Moses said, "Cursed be the man who makes a graven or molten image."[34] "For this commandment which I command you this day is not too hard for you, neither is it far off. It is not in heaven, that you should say, 'Who will go up for us to heaven, and bring it to us, that we may hear it and do it?' Neither is it beyond the sea, that you should say, 'Who will go over the sea for us, and bring it to us, that we may hear it and do it?' but *the word is very near you*; it is in your mouth and in your *heart*, so that you can do it,"[35] thus enabling man to command himself morally.

Essential and basic revelations in man's search for himself fall like lightning into man's unknowing and have their roots in Genesis as the poets have it: "And God said let there be light; and there was light."[36] Theologizing, spiritualizing or psychologizing these essential experiences into constructs transforms them into idols, for the deity is seen and expressed then as a being external to the self. Man, in his search for God and for himself is led astray by positing an exterior God, for in such a case, the individual ceases to be instructed by his own inner experience of "stations along the way," and fails to find the altar of the divine within himself — the *Agnostos Theos*.

In idolatry, the deity has a presumed objective existence. As soon, however, as it is transformed into a subjective reality, the deity can no longer be expressed as an analogy of things nor as names of things. Rather, it then becomes a living process. Isaiah 48:9-12 says:

For my *name's* sake I defer my anger, for
the sake of my praise I restrain it for you,
that I may not cut you off.
Behold, I have refined you, but not like silver;
I have tried you in the furnace of affliction.
For my own sake, for my own sake, I do it,

for how should *my name* be profaned?
My glory I will not give to another.
Hearken to me, O Jacob, and Israel, whom I
   called!
I am he, I am the first, and I am the last. (Italics
mine)

The above quotation in conjunction with Isaiah 2:3 is then
the rock, the Peter's rock, upon which the Church built its
own church.

Come, let us go up to the mountain of the Lord, to
the house of the God of Jacob; that he may teach us
his ways and that we may walk in his paths. . . .

With St. Paul, the realization is more problematical.[37]
Paul writes:

". . . I found also an altar with this inscription, *To
The Unknown God.* What therefore you ignorantly
worship as unknown, this I proclaim to you . . . 'In
him we live and move and have our being'; as even
some of your poets have said, 'For we are indeed his
offspring.' "[38]

On the one hand, Paul speaks about an altar he had seen
dedicated to an unknown god. (To date, no such altar has
been unearthed in Athens, though altars to unknown *gods*
have been found.[39] On the other hand, in Romans, Paul
writes:

Let every person be subject to the governing authorities. For there is no authority except from God, and
those that exist have been instituted by God. Therefore he who resists the authorities resists what God
has appointed, and those who resist will incur
judgment.[40]

In our experience, the existing authorities arrogate to

themselves the messianic aspects of man's inner existence and therefore stand in opposition to individual conscience. Men in this stage of development are like Balaam, without a will of their own. Karl Barth wrote: "We must not give to the word 'God' the value of a clearly defined, metaphysical entity. What will it profit us if a formal fidelity to the meaning of the word is purchased at the cost of complete infidelity to the Word? He of whom the *power* is and by whom the every existing authority is ordained is the God the Lord, The Unknown, Hidden God, Creator and Redeemer, the God who elects and rejects."[41] In Germany St. Paul's epistle was followed to the letter. The inability of the ordinary citizen in Germany to respond to the outrageous claims of the Nazis by maintaining silence, has religious roots wherein the "word" was mistaken as the "Word," and the letter became the spirit and the Spirit became the letter.

Through the rumblings of the awesome events of destruction and innovation in our twentieth century there echoes the cry: "*Eli, Eli, lama sabachthani?*" — that is, "My God, my God, why has thou forsaken me?"[42]

The Old and New Testaments are the records of man's heroic efforts to come to terms with his human condition through the ontogenesis of his psyche. Judaism, Christianity and Islam all claim their historical roots in the figure of Abraham. Most Biblical scholars have agreed to date the patriarch's sojourns about 1,800 B.C. The latest discoveries in 1975 at Ebla, a town in Northern Syria, however, make the date of the origin of Abraham's saga much more likely to be at least as early as 2,300 B.C. Though only a few of the 15,000 or so tablets have been deciphered, those few include the name of Abraham (Ab-ra-um). The poets have made use of a possible historical background as they tell the epic story of man's becoming. Some 1,500 years later they depict Abraham's coming home from a successful war and being met by Melchizedek who anoints him by serving him bread and wine.[43] Melchizedek's name reappears in the Old Testament only once, in a Psalm:

The Lord has sworn and will not change his mind,
You are a priest for ever after the order of
Melchizedek.[44]

The whole tenor of the Old Testament is permeated by
this archetypal personification of the principles of justice,
balance, and wholeness. In particular, the Old Testament
describes the defeat of idols in any manner or form.
Through the symbolic act of Melchizedek anointing Abraham, the poets complement the still war-minded psyche
which Abraham personifies, by balancing it with righteousness and peace. In turn, the poets tell us that Abraham
acknowledges this reality by paying a tithe to Melchizedek.

Abraham's Sacrifice of Isaac — The Establishment of Personality

THE SUPREME test of whether the symbolic anointing
had become a psychic reality — that is, whether the ontogenesis of the psyche had, so to speak, taken root — is the
Akedah, a poem of the most awesome archetypal dimensions: "After these things God tested Abraham.... 'Take
your son...and offer him...as a burnt offering.'"[45]
Abraham out of his own inner "knowing" does not fail in
this gruesome test, but emerges as a personality, making his
own decisions out of the depths of his own being. God
accepted the sacrifice, accounting it as though it had been
Isaac, and said, "It was manifest to Me and I foreknew that
thou wouldst withhold *not even thy soul* from me!"[46]

Abraham, in his faith and irony, proves to have been
right: God does provide Himself with His own victim.
Because He foresaw the Akedah, He prepared for it by
creating the ram in the twilight of the sixth day of Creation

and left him to graze under the tree of life until an angel brought him out of Eden to Mount Moriah. The ram, according to the legend, is a *knowing* victim; Satan restrains him because the time is not yet ripe. It comes to its fullness when Abraham lifts the knife, and then it is as though his brutality leaps forth and takes the ram's shape, and he can *see* it and see the possibility of choosing a different way. He has no reason to believe the sacrifice will be acceptable, that the blood of the ram will be taken in place of the blood of his son, but he takes the risk, the 'existential leap' beyond all certainty, and in doing so poses and answers a crucial question about the nature of God and the nature of man. Taken inwardly, as a distillation in symbolic action of a discovery about the inner world, about the nature of the psyche itself, the event, the question and the answer are momentous. The psyche proves to hold *within itself* the means with which to confront and transform its own blind and brutal forces. In the lightning flash of this insight, the inner world appears radically changed.

There is a great deal of lore about Mount Moriah. It is said that at the end of his three-day journey, when he first lifted his eyes,

> [Abraham] noticed upon the mountain a pillar of fire reaching from earth to heaven, and a heavy cloud in which the glory of God was seen. Abraham said to Isaac: "My son, dost thou see on that mountain which we perceive at a distance that which I see upon it?" And Isaac answered, and said unto his father: "I see, and lo, a pillar of fire and a cloud, and the glory of God seen upon the cloud." Abraham knew then that Isaac was accepted before the Lord for an offering. He asked Ishmael and Eliezer: "Do you also see that which we see upon the mountain?" They answered: "We see nothing more than like other mountains," and Abraham knew that they were not accepted before the Lord to go with them.[47]

The place on which Abraham had erected the altar was the same whereon Adam had brought the first sacrifice, and Cain and Abel had offered their gifts to God — the same whereon Noah raised the altar to God after he left the ark.[48]

The place is also said to be the same as Golgotha, which may be seen as a region of the psyche, a sacred precinct to be arrived at by choice, through that silence that is like dying. The need to make the journey, springing out of the psyche's urge toward wholeness, is what brings so many people to psychotherapy; what makes it so difficult is that the way necessarily leads through the primitive, subrational and dark in man's nature.

Thou shalt love the Lord thy God with *all thine heart,* with *all thy soul* and with *all thy strength.*[49]

All is the crucial word: it encompasses the soul's evil along with its good. In the legend, Satan's presence on Mount Moriah is as necessary as God's. Abraham enters the sacred precinct driven by what we would call the 'demonic,' by those forces of his inner world that deny life and would destroy it, but there is a duality, an opposition, within the demonic itself (it was his God who tempted him); in other words, he moves into a direct experience of the dualities of man's nature, and the instant he lifts the slaughtering knife, those opposites collide and out of the resounding crash comes awareness of the possibility of choice. In really seeing his own brutality, he can see his relationship with it and thus its power over him; the eternal round is broken. The war of opposites ends and the opposites are revealed as harmonious: God and Satan stand together in the sacred precinct; Abraham, the man, stands between them. Man as *man,* an individual distinct within, and vitally related with, the forces of his being, becomes an actuality. *Personality* is established.

In Genesis, Melchizedek blesses Abraham and "brought

out bread and wine,"[50] ritualistically anticipating the Last Supper. The poets clearly characterize Melchizedek as the King of Salem. In Hebrews 7:1-3, a further amplification is clearly stated:

> For this Melchizedek, king of Salem, priest of the most high God, met Abraham returning from the slaughters of the kings and blessed him; and to him Abraham apportioned a tenth part of everything. He is first, by translation of his name, king of righteousness, and then he is also king of Salem, that is, king of peace. He is without father or mother or genealogy and has neither beginning of days nor end of life, but resembling the *Son of God* he continues a priest forever.[51]

The Bible is a supreme work of art, and true to the epistemological meaning of *art* — that is, "to join, to fit" — the Bible relates the above quotation to a Psalm of David:

> The Lord sends forth from Zion
> your mighty scepter. Rule in the midst of your
>   foes!
> Your people will offer themselves freely
> on the day you lead your host upon the holy
>   mountains.
> From the womb of the morning like dew
> your youth will come to you.
> The Lord has sworn and will not change his
>   mind
> You are a priest forever after the order of
>   Melchizedek.[52]

The king of Salem, King David, and Christ the King lose their individual identity when fused symbolically by virtue of the ontogenetic principle into the messianic promise of daily rebirth:

> From the womb of the morning like dew
> your youth will come to you.

There is an experience of the same archetypal order expressed in Egyptian lore. *Maat*, the fundamental criterion of every action, was established by God at the creation. The word *Maat* is one of the first tangible ideas preserved as a noun in human speech.[53] *Maat* as "balance, righteousness, justice and peace" endured for about a thousand years (3,500 - 2,500 B.C.) Personified as Melchizedek, this same principle, true to its intrinsic nature, balances war with peace. It is therefore basically a principle of integration toward wholeness and thus, toward monotheism.

> In Egyptian there was no word for 'state,' for what we understand by that term was embodied, especially in the early period, wholly in the person of the king, i.e., the institution of the monarchy. . . .
>
> Maat . . . is brought into being by the primordial God and then constantly refreshed or restored by the king.[54]

In the New Testament tradition, Melchizedek played a very important role, particularly in the Letter to the Hebrews:

> For when God made a promise to Abraham. . . . "We have this as a sure and steadfast anchor of the soul, a hope that enters into the inner shrine behind the curtain, where Jesus has gone as a forerunner on our behalf, having become a high priest forever after the order of Melchizedek."[55]

And at this point in the New Testament there follows the passage quoted in which Melchizedek is seen as "resembling the Son of God." In the tradition of the Old Testament the figure of Melchizedek is highlighted in the texts found at Qumram in 1956:

> How beautiful upon the mountains are the
> feet of him that bringeth good tidings, that
> publisheth peace, that bringeth good tidings

of good, that publisheth salvation, that saith
unto Zion: Thy heavenly one is King.[56]

... through him the Name of God had first
been made known among men.[57]

... king and priest shall be in the place ... in
the middle of the earth where Adam was
created . . .[58]

... and there shall be (Melchizedek's) grave.[59]

The symbolic figures and tales of both the Old and New
Testaments reveal the self-organizing principle — the ontogenesis of the psyche in stark significance. Of central importance for this symbolic, poetic reality is the experience of
Jerusalem as the center of the earth, and of Melchizedek as
both king and priest of Jerusalem. Thus the messianic promise that peace will balance conflict unfolds in ever-renewed
cycles around the still point of Melchizedek/Maat.

Modern humanity yearns to experience life with meaning
beyond that provided by the rationalism of a scientistic
approach. Modern art strongly expresses this yearning, particularly in Barnett Newman's powerful but "imageless"
unicolored paintings, which present a fine line as an
entrance to their depth. Barnett Newman's 12 Stations have
a distinctly religious theme. For him, God seems to be
Depth and Silence. He wrote: "I do *not* come with dogmatic
beliefs for others, I take full and single responsibility for my
work, thoughts, acts."[60] For Newman, essence is more vital
than form; and the message is the essence, not the medium.
Barnett Newman, as a sensitive artist, expressed in both his
work and words the ontogenesis of the psyche. Newman
stands in stark contrast to a 17th century Russian patriarch:

Russian icons portrayed the spirit and spoke to the
soul in a language determined by the Church centuries ago. Russian painters could never display invention or worldliness. A 17th Century patriarch,

Nikon, condemned and excommunicated all who painted in the Western manner, which was considered too carnal. According to one warning: "He that shall paint an icon from his own imagination shall suffer endless torment."[61]

The dogmatic orthodoxy of Hitler's Nazi Germany and Stalin's Communist Russia had its antecedents. Some of the Christian writings of New Testament times, later called apocryphal, received the same repressive treatment. The Seventh Ecumenical Council of the Church met in Nicea in 787 A.D. and on the Acts of John pronounced the following: "No one is to copy (this book): not only so, but we consider that it deserves to be consigned to the fire." Three hundred years earlier Pope Leo the Great had given a similar verdict on the entire body of apocryphal works named after the Apostles. "The apocryphal writings, however, which under the names of the Apostles contain a hotbed of manifold perversity, should not only be forbidden but altogether removed and burnt with fire."[62]

These apocryphal writings are, in fact, the strenuous effort of the psyche to come to terms with itself in its manifold aspects. In one of these apocryphal accounts, "Encounter with a Parricide," a son murders his father. The father is revived by the Apostle John, who then confronts the son who had in mind to kill a woman with whom he had had an adulterous affair, and then to kill her husband as well as himself. But, confronted by John and his father's resurrection, he cut off his private parts instead. John says to him: "It is not those organs which are harmful to man, but the unseen springs through which every shameful emotion is stirred up and comes to light."[63]

In another account from the Acts of Thomas we are told of a woman who had abstained from having sex with her betrothed, and whom she also declined to marry. But then "a demon" came and had intercourse with her night after night for five years. She prayed to the Apostle: "drive out the demon that continually vexes me . . ." The apostle said: "O evil not to be restrained! . . . O thou of many forms — he appears as he may wish, but his essence cannot be altered." And when the apostle had said this, the enemy stood before him, no one seeing him except the woman and the apostle, and with a very loud voice said in the hearing of all: *"What have we to do with thee, apostle of the Most High?* [referring to Mark 5:7] What have we to do with thee, servant of Jesus Christ? . . . Thou hast authority in thine own [sphere] and we in ours. Why dost thou wish to exercise despotic rule against us, especially since thyself dost teach others not to act despotically? . . ." "And when he had said this, the demon vanished; only as he departed fire and smoke were seen there, and all who stood by were astounded. When the apostle saw it, he said to them: 'That demon showed nothing strange or alien, but his own nature, in which also he shall be burned up.' "[64]

Since the advent of depth psychology, we now describe the same psychic situations and their resolutions in different terms, reflecting a higher level on the spiral of becoming. The Apocryphal Acts of the Apostles were written on one level of description, to free the enslaved psyche from its own bondage and to help the psyche achieve the freedom necessary to partake in the processes of life. Both of these stories are expressions of instinctual desires; the woman's demon is a personification of her sexual libido, and in the case of the young man, we are dealing with incestual fantasies couched in oedipal terms.

Today through our extended awareness, we have gained a kind of Archimedian point outside the system of our previous history which allows us to realize that in order to "know" we need to confront life with the whole of our being and not only to gauge it from a superficial and partial approach. The history of a system is only part of an explanation. An exegetical approach focuses either on the overt and actual process, as in the case of ritual, or on an intellectual system built upon that which is presumed to be historical fact. But in either case, today such an approach has become bankrupt.

"It must never be forgotten," writes Nahum Sarna, "that the Biblical stories are not 'historiography' as we understand the term, but rather 'historiosophy,' that is, the didactic use of historical material. Exclusive concentration on the criterion of historicity obscures the intent, meaning and message of the narrative which, after all, are its enduring qualities."[65]

A more meaningful way seems to lie in the attempt to discover in the various systems an underlying essence, which we are calling the ontogenesis of the psyche. This approach links the biological evolution with a spiritual ontogenesis in a vital way. It is here that we find universality. Neither the contents of the various systems nor their source are of prime importance. The contents are but the symbolic medium which embodies the universality of the self.

The achievement of our time lies precisely in the fact that man has begun to confront the "Unknown God." Modern man does not see the "Unknown God" as transcendent, nor in terms of the Greek Hades, which is an endless dying, but rather in terms of eternal daily rebirth. "From the womb of the morning like dew your youth will come to you. . . . You are a priest forever after the order of Melchizedek." The ontogenesis of the psyche is the very source of the need of man for religion. Yes, the ontogenesis is religion itself.

This growing awareness may give contemporary man the strength and hope to survive with patience the dismal signs of impending doom. From the most unexpected source, namely science, comes the proof that there is a balancing and self-correcting power active in life. This power, perceived however unscientifically, in the past was symbolized in the figure of Justitia, blind-folded and holding the scales of justice. In mythology it is represented by the Maat-Melchizedek-Dike-Christ image. These poetic expressions from the inmost center of persons of widely different times and cultures, reveal the same essential message.

"The first point to make about Maat (the Egyptian goddess of justice)," writes Morenz, "is that it originates with the creation: it is brought into being by the primordial god and then constantly refreshed or restored by the king."[66]

In Greek mythology, Dike the daughter of Zeus is the goddess of Justice. "Justice . . . is the daughter of Power and Good Counsel, and the sister of Peace . . ." "The issue of Dike is ultimately serenity, for Dike gave *virgin birth* to one daughter, Hesychia, goddess of 'stillness resting in itself.' "[67] Dike originally meant the "indication" of the requirement of the divine law, Themis. *Themis* derives from *tithemi*, "I place" or "lay down."[68]

"The supreme god of the universe is Zeus. . . . He is the champion of Dike, *the order of the universe,"*[69] i.e., balance and wholeness. In *The Iliad* Zeus' justice may be performed, as in Egypt or in the Old Testament "through the judgments of kings who are his agents, but may be manifest [also] in the actual workings of events."[70] "For Protagoras, the concept of justice . . . [was] a norm, a concept created by the human mind . . . the power to establish such a norm is implanted in men by Zeus himself."[71] Man, apparently, alone among the animals believes in gods, because they are akin to him.

". . . In Greek thought in its early manifestations a true and specific definition of justice will be sought in vain." "From the union of Zeus and Themis is born Dike." Both Themis and Dike are "mythical images"; Themis was originally seen as the "counsellor" of Zeus.[72]

The slow dawning of this balancing principle in the psyche and its ethical implications is clearly stressed by Hesiod.

> Justice herself is a young maiden
> She is Zeus' daughter
> The man who does evil to another
> does evil to himself
> and the evil counsel is most evil
> for him who counsels it.
> Athene is the equal of her father in wise
> council

> and strength; but then a son to be King
> over gods and mortals
> was to be born of her, and his heart
> would be overmastering;
> but before this, Zeus put her away
> inside his own belly
> so that this goddess should think for
>   him
> for good and for evil.[73]

Just as charming, humorous and profound at the same time as the Talmudic story where the rabbis argue about a just and right decision [supra, p. 25] is the Greek legend about the psyche's birth to itself from itself.

> But Athene's own priests tell the following story of her birth. Zeus lusted after Metis the Titaness, who turned into many shapes to escape him until she was caught at last and got with child. An oracle of Mother Earth then declared that this would be a girl-child and that, if Metis conceived again, she would bear a son who was fated to depose Zeus, just as Zeus had deposed Cronus, and Cronus had deposed Uranus. Therefore, having coaxed Metis to a couch with honeyed words, Zeus suddenly opened his mouth and swallowed her, and that was the end of Metis, though he claimed afterwards that she gave him counsel from inside his belly. In due process of time, he was seized by a raging headache as he walked by the shores of Lake Triton, so that his skull seemed about to burst, and he howled for rage until the whole firmament echoed. Up ran Hermes, who at once divined the cause of Zeus's discomfort. He persuaded Hephaestus, or some say Prometheus, to fetch his wedge and beetle and make a breach in Zeus's skull, from which Athene sprang, fully armed, with a mighty shout.[74]

In the Old Testament, Melchizedek, the King of Salem, the King of Peace "brought out bread and wine;" he was the priest of the God Most High. And he blessed [Abraham]"[75] and thus laid the foundation to Justice or Balance. Around 2,000 years later at the beginning of our era, the New Testament lifts this vital mental quality, "which has neither beginning of days nor end of life" on the spiral of becoming to its very height.

> Christ did not exalt himself to be made a high priest, but was appointed by him who said to him, "Thou art my Son, today I have begotten thee"; as he says also in another place, "Thou art a priest forever after the order of Melchizedek."[76]

Again, after 2,000 years, as a new aeon is about to begin in our own time, Justice is being considered as "part of the biological equipment of man" [supra, p. 78]. In the preface to *The Self and Its Brain,* Karl R. Popper and John C. Eccles quote C. S. Sherrington:

> Each day is a stage dominated for good or ill, in comedy, farce or tragedy by a *dramatis persona,* the 'self,' and so it will be until the curtain drops.

And Sir John Eccles remarks:

> I would like to say that man has lost his way these days — what we may call the predicament of mankind. He needs some new message whereby he may live with hope and meaning. I think that science has gone too far in breaking down man's belief in his spiritual greatness and in giving him the idea that he is merely an insignificant material being in the frigid cosmic immensity. Now this strong dualistic-interactionist hypothesis we are here putting forward certainly implies that man is much more than is given by this purely materialistic explanation. I think there is mystery in man, and I am sure that at least it is

wonderful for man to get the feeling that he isn't just a hastily made-over ape, and that there is something much more wonderful in his nature and in his destiny.[77]

The whole of sacred scripture revolves around the hub of Maat-Melchizedek-Christ, trying to assist the individual to bring his vital center into a living contact with the periphery of the wheel of life. Collective or universal laws can, as we have learned from science, at best be approximations, and are not valid accounts of the unique individual. To be meaningful and therefore supportive for the individual in the daily encounter with life, personal experience needs to be individually *authenticated*. It is *only* in this context that the person is real and can find his or her real*ization* — or be actual and experience actual*ization*. Mere adherence to dogma is at best an attitude of imitation and is not, therefore, true, real or actual.

As long as persons are prejudged in accordance with intellectually conceived schemes, and their individual actuality is not taken seriously, so long will society be unable to change. The effect this has on ethical values is that it creates revolution and/or terrorism because society is then ruled by inhuman demons and inertia rather than by justice.

The Apocalypse of Peter addresses "the predicament of mankind" of today, mirroring Matthew 23:13-15:

> And still others of them who suffer think that they will perfect the wisdom of the brotherhood which really exists, which is the spiritual fellowship with those united in communion, through which the wedding of incorruptibility shall be revealed. The kindred race of the sisterhood will appear as an *imitation*. These are the ones who oppress their brothers, saying to them, "Through this our God has pity, since salvation comes to us through this . . ."[78]

They will cleave to the name of a dead man, thinking

that they will become pure. But they will become greatly defiled and they will fall into a name of error and into the hand of an evil, cunning man and a manifold dogma, and they will be ruled heretically.[79]

And there shall be others of those who are outside our numbers who name themselves bishop and also deacons, as if they have received their authority from God. They bend themselves under the judgment of the leaders. Those people are dry canals.[80]

Gnosis, as an early Christian development, upheld the legitimacy of the individual's unique experience as at least on a par with the dogmatic formulations evolving in the life of the Church. The roots of Gnosis go back to Jewish mysticism as well as to Babylonian and Persian sources, and the Gnostics expounded the Gospels from a perspective far different from the dogmatic position of the "official" Church.

The writings of the Gnostics can only be understood in themselves, and in the context in which they were written. Etymologically, *gnosis* means "knowledge," from the Greek *gignoskein* — "to know." In relation to a growing body of Church dogma, these "knowers" were judged to be heretics because of their experiential orientation and their divergent interpretation of scripture. Fortunately, through the discovery by some peasants in 1946, a whole Gnostic library came to light at Nag Hammadi in Egypt. Now we can know directly that which formerly could only be gleaned from the writings of those "orthodox" opponents of Gnosis who attacked it in the name of the Church.

The Gnostic writings, like dreams, can only be apprehended in their complexity out of their self-revealing character. One cannot interpret them by projecting assumed meanings derived from intellectually constructed systems. The intrinsic characteristic of a dream becomes mental reality if one listens silently and patiently to what the *dream* itself tries to convey to the individual. The importance of dreams has now been proved even to scient*istic*ally-minded positivists with the aid of mechanical devices. Further, the intrinsic value of dreaming to the whole system, physical and mental, has been demonstrated through the use of encephalographs and electrodes, which monitor the eye movements which accompany dream activity. By waking the experimental subject as soon as the indicators signal a dream, the dream activity is prevented. In such experiments, animals which are prevented from dreaming become uncontrollably ferocious. Human subjects undergoing the same treatment demonstrate near psychotic outbreaks and deep emotional disturbance. The often weird language of dreams is like the language of atomic science which also understands itself through itself.

As Niels Bohr said to Heisenberg: "When it comes to atoms, language can be used only as in poetry. The poet, too, is not nearly so concerned with describing facts as with creating images."[81]

There is an important Gnostic text in the Nag Hammadi Library which addresses our contemporary situation in the search for meaning and truth. Here the whole question as to the validity and meaning of the approach to sacred scripture is touched at its deepest point. In the following text, the Gnostics were warning against second-hand knowledge — a knowledge not derived from authentic experience, but through imitation.

> It is not possible for anyone to see anything of the things that actually exist unless he becomes like them. This is not the way with man in the world: he sees the sun without being a sun; and he sees the heaven and the earth and all other things, but he is not these things. This is quite in keeping with the truth. But you saw something of that place and you became those things. You saw the Spirit, you became spirit. You saw Christ, you became Christ. You saw

[the Father, you] shall become Father. So [in this place] you see everything and [do] not [see] yourself, but [in that place] you do see yourself — and what you see you shall [become]."[82]

[But] all the natures [and all the . . .] will say [these things] while they are *receiving from* [*you*] *yourself,* O [Melchizedek], Holy One, [High Priest], *the perfect hope* [*and*] *the* [*gifts of*] *life.*"[83]

From the Melchizedek-Christ symbol *as an experience* of inner, genuine balance, one not only receives oneself as an authentic personality, but also "the perfect hope and the gifts of Life." Man, in quest for himself, disappointed as he is, and doubting as he does today, asks "What does it all mean?" In the Gospel of Thomas, the Gnostic answers this question:

These are the secret sayings which the living Jesus spoke and which Didymos Judas Thomas wrote down:

(1) And he said, "Whoever finds the interpretation of these sayings will not experience death."

(2) Jesus said, "Let him who seeks continue seeking until he finds. When he finds, he will become troubled. When he becomes troubled, he will be astonished, and he will rule over the All."

(3) Jesus said, "If those who lead you say to you, 'See, the Kingdom is in the sky,' then the birds of the sky will precede you. If they say to you, 'It is in the sea,' then the fish will precede you. Rather, the Kingdom is *inside of you,* and it is outside of you. When you come to know yourselves, then you will become known, and you will realize that it is you who are the sons of the living Father. But if you will not know yourselves, you dwell in poverty and it is you who are that poverty."[84]

Though these Gnostic Gospels were written many hundreds of years after the exhortations of Moses to Israel were committed to writing, they are not only an example of the continuing Judeo-Christian tradition, but they are also an expression of the psyche establishing itself through authentic experience, and not by means of imitation. Having discovered that one cannot "become Christ" by mere believing, and that the world is not redeemed, disappointment and doubt are born of this bitter experience.

In the Old Testament, Deuteronomy 30:11-14, Moses speaks:

> For this commandment which I command you this day is not too hard for you, neither is it far off. It is not in heaven, that you should say, "Who will go up for us to heaven, and bring it to us, that we may hear it and do it?" Neither is it beyond the sea that you should say, "Who will go over the sea for us, and bring it to us, that we may hear it and do it?" But the word is very near you; it is in your mouth and in your heart, so that you can do it.

By balancing the Melchizedek principle of peace with the Cain-like attitude of human aggression, the poets gave expression to a new awareness. Cain looms as a vital figure against the vision of the duality of existence, peace and aggression, good and evil. He stands in an essential relation with it; in him, the symbol of the psyche's potential wholeness begins to be infused with meaning. Here the poets of Genesis, being wholly one with their theme, are led to save the brutal and unredeemed in human nature, the better to explore the possibilities of the individual's relation with it and its eventual redemption.

The Old and New Testaments As A Record of the Ontogenesis of the Psyche

With A fine sense of evolutionary sequence, the poets bestowed on Abraham the Melchizedek experience after he had left "his home and kindred" and was truly embarked on the voyage of self-discovery. Abraham, in true human fashion, doubted the validity of the Melchizedek experience, but proved to himself through an awe-inspiring dream in authentic terms the validity of his mental integration. Let me repeat part of this all important passage.

> As the sun was going down, a deep sleep fell on Abram; and lo, a dread and a great darkness fell upon him.[85]

> When the sun had gone down and it was dark, behold, a smoking fire pot and a flaming torch passed between these pieces. On that day the Lord made a covenant with Abram. . . .[86]

The Covenant which the Lord made with Abraham is the symbol of integration in that on a higher level of awareness the oneness of unknowing is separated, and later finds its apparent symbiosis on a higher level of awareness in wholeness. The great importance of the Melchizedek story for the Old Testament tradition is expressed in a legend which describes in symbolic language the very center of personality, the Self:

And this high priest instructed Abraham in the laws of priesthood and in the Torah, and to prove his friendship for him he blessed him, and called him partner of God in the possession of the world, seeing that through him the Name of God had first been made known among men.[87]

The king and Priest shall be in the place of Ahuzan (i.e., Jerusalem), that is to say in the middle of earth where Adam was created. Jerusalem is the centre of the earth, and Melchizedek was both king and priest of Jerusalem.[88]

Due to its fateful location and history, Jerusalem is a sacred city for Judaism, Christianity, and Islam. By virtue of its history, and its spiritual legacy, it is the very hub around which Western civilization turns. It is therefore a symbol of the Self, both for the individual personality and for Western society as a whole.

Abraham's way is the mythopoetic prototype of man's way to himself as a distinct individual. Hence this "archetype" has become the patriarchal root of the three great Western religions. To reach the authenticity of individual spirituality the psyche had to make determined efforts to attain that goal. A very painful step towards a heightened awareness had to be realized. Melchizedek was the bringer and representative of peace; in Matthew Jesus is purported to have said:

Do not think I have come to bring peace on earth; I have not come to bring peace, but a sword. For I have come to set a man against his father, and a daughter against her mother, and a daughter-in-law against her mother-in-law, and a man's foe will be those of his household. He who loves father or mother more than me is not worthy of me; and he who loves son or daughter more than me is not worthy of me; and he who does not take his cross and follow me is not worthy of me. He who finds his life will lose it, and he who loses his life for my sake will find it.[89]

These are strange sayings to be found at the very center of Christianity which understands one of its main functions to be that of helping to maintain the family structure. In contemporary culture, the family is precisely the point at which enormous change is taking place. It is as though the sayings of Jesus were being taken literally by an unconscious society. Families *are* disintegrating! The search for self-actualization, self-realization, extracts an enormous price in following the teachings of the New Testament. In the fluid movement of life in general and in the flowing, living waters of the spirit there seems to be lurking a strange paradox which presents itself to a heightened consciousness in modern man, who has learned how to read. It is also very difficult for the conservative, literal-minded fundamentalist to keep his eyes closed to the actuality of the words presented to him in Holy Scriptures. Luke 14:26-27 reads:

> If any one comes to me and does not hate his own father and mother and wife and children and brothers and sisters, yes, and even his own life, he cannot be my disciple. Whoever does not bear his own cross and come after me, cannot be my disciple.

The early Christians, in their Gnostic writings, went even a step further in the direction of extreme radicalism. A Gnostic passage, similar to Luke 14:26 is found in the *Gospel According to Thomas:*

> Jesus said: "Whoever does not hate his father and his mother will not be able to be a disciple . . . to Me, and [whoever does not] hate his brethren and his sisters and [does not] take up his cross in My way will not be worthy of me.

Jesus said: "Whoever has come to understand the world has found a corpse, and whoever has found a corpse . . . of him the world is not worthy."[90]

Because the parental images of mother and/or father buried in unconsciousness can maintain a dogmatic rule over individual behavior, authentic life is only possible when these factors have been brought to consciousness. Until such a realization can be incorporated emotionally, there is no true recognition that we have been held in unconscious incestuous bondage with father or mother, sister or brother.

The Gnostic text does not speak about the relations of husband and wife, while Luke does: "If any one comes to me and does not hate his father and mother *and wife* and children. . . ."

Often we are not motivated by the living stream of ever-renewed life; rather, our motivations come from corpses, the dead of the underworld, the Hades of Greek mythology which was peopled by all sorts of punishing creatures: Nemesis, the Erinnyes, etc. It is these dogmatic "gods" which keep us in the bondage of our own unconscious and compel us to actions which are not born authentically from ourselves. In Greek mythology these demons were the gods and goddesses of Hades, the underworld, and in the parlance of modern depth-psychology they are called autonomous complexes. "The gods grab us, and we play out their stories."[50] The Gnostic Gospel of Philip extols "God is a man-eater,"[51] and about people in the grip of a particular idea or set of ideas we say: "they are eaten up by them." But the one who has seen through the illusions, the Maya of Indian philosophy or the Hades-like character of autonomous complexes, to use the language of modern depth psychology, is certainly out of reach of these "ghosts" and is "superior to the world." Such a one is able to "carry his own cross" of becoming and thus is able to follow his own inner Christ.

In the sayings of Oxyrhynchus, which are attributed to

Jesus, vitally important statements have come to light. Oxyrhynchus is a place near Cairo where the ancient texts were found at the turn of this century, 1897. These papyri go back to the first century A.D., some of them confirming both Luke and Matthew. However, close to Matthew 18:20, which runs: "For where *two or three* are gathered in my name, there am I in the midst of them"; yet significantly different from the canonically fixed authoritative expression of faith, is the following text:

> Jesus saith:
> Wheresoever there be two, they are not
>   without God,
> And where there is one alone, I say, I am with
>   him.
> Lift up the stone, and there thou shalt find
>   me;
> Cleave the wood, and there I am.[91]

The canon does not mention the lone individual at all and excludes Irenaeus who said: ". . . the spirit is in us all . . . there is one father above all things and in all things" [infra, p. 305; n. 43]; while the papyrus includes both.

St. Augustine wrote in his *Book of True Religion*:

> Noli foras ire, inteipsum redi;
> in interiore homine habitat veritas.
>
> Go not outside, *return* into thyself:
> *Truth dwells in the inward man.*[92]

The Gnostics anticipated St. Augustine in their basic attitude toward both authentic religion and truth:

> Seek Him "God" from out thyself, and learn who it is
> that has taken possession of everything in thee, say-
> ing my god, my spirit, my understanding, my soul,
> my body; and learn whence is sorrow and joy, and
> love and hate, and walking though one would not,

and getting angry though one would not, and sleeping though one would not, and if thou shouldst closely investigate these things, thou will find him in thyself, the One and the many like to that little point, for it is from thee that he has his origin.[93]

The ontogenesis of the psyche parallels the evolution of religion. The Gnostic sayings which have at their center "Know Thyself" are of particular interest in our time. Here is to be found the alchemy of the soul which modern depth psychology has revealed to us.

Beginning with the blissful unconsciousness of the Garden of Eden, and moving to the differentiation of the mind in the stories of Adam and Eve, Cain and Abel, the essential theme is spun into further differentiated organization in the Abraham legend. When "a dread and great darkness" fell upon Abraham, out of the deep of unknowing, a process of transformation began. In the fire, as an agent of transformation pictured by the poets as a smoking furnace, and enlightenment symbolized as a flaming torch, this process of change became psychic reality. The ensuing "genesis" of the mind leads, as a further vital step in its growth toward awareness, to the realization of the "laws" of conduct on a conscious level at Mt. Sinai. From there a further "exodus" — the crossing into another state of mind — is symbolized by the crossing of the river Jordan. This time, the "exodus" is a withdrawal of the Law as projected onto an external power and delivered from on high (Mt. Sinai). The shift from external to internal is unmistakably marked by Moses' exhortation in Deuteronomy 30:14: the law is "in your mouth and in your heart."

This is also the basic position of some of the Gnostics, and so it would seem, of some moderns for whom the time of dogmatic religion is past (e.g., Bonhoeffer). The seat of the Godhead is no longer felt to reside in the heavens of fantasy external to man, but in the reality of experiencing the ever-flowing stream of life in the very center of personal being.

The Gnostic Gospel of Thomas, log. 70, reads: "Jesus said: 'If you bring forth that within yourselves, that which you have will save you. If you do not have that within yourselves, that which you do not have within you will kill you.' "94

Abraham, as the symbol of the psyche, found in the Covenant a kind of proof that the "promise" will be kept, and that the personality will be enriched by new dimensions. This promise is fulfilled in the Biblical story by a symbol of ultimate concreteness — namely, the acquisition of land, additional space in which to live. The poets tell us that for Abraham, this was an authentic experience because it came from his own dream, and thereby provided a powerful motivation for the psyche. At the same time, this development takes place within the context of a very human tension: Abraham was in doubt, and asked the perennial question: 'Will I really benefit by all that is happening to me?' ". . . He said, 'O Lord God, how am I to know that I shall possess it?' "95

This is the same question the pragmatic man of today asks himself, the answer to which he finds most difficult to accept. "What good," he says, "can come to me, insecure as I am, living in this 'age of anxiety.' " We are told that if we are faithful and keep up our end of the covenant, our business will flourish and our enemies will be overcome." Through our scientistic education, the essential error is perpetuated: the inner man is disregarded.

The promise of a reward in the Hereafter is unacceptable to those living in the atomic age. In the end, the modern is like the Wabanaki Indian tribes of Nova Scotia, New Brunswick and Northern Maine, who have given the name "Glooskap" to the Great Spirit. *Glooskap* means "*Liar*, because it is said that when he left earth . . . he promised to return, and has never done so."96

The Great Spirit, seen as a liar and unfaithful, is not unlike the greater and lesser Messiahs of our own time; Messiahs like Stalin and Hitler who promised the redemption of the world, would the world but follow their dogmatic insights. Yet the world remains unredeemed. The human race may easily be destroyed through human error such as that of the Three Mile Island nuclear reactor incident, or the false alarm of a nuclear attack on the United States, November 10, 1979. And since that date two more "errors" were committed. Such errors as these may destroy the human race physically, just as surely as the scientistic attitude which creates a computerized society, can destroy man on a mental level.

Practically speaking, the individuation process is primarily of value to the psyche, and not necessarily of material use. The individual, however, who through his own becoming refrains from projecting his own problems into the world at large, is able to deal with outside reality more realistically, and will therefore be able to handle practical affairs more successfully on the whole.

The Covenant

THE RELATIONSHIP with oneself, to "the truth(which) dwells in the inward man" is a kind of *covenant*, which, if not adhered to, often produces dire consequences. The *conscience*, the "knowing with," "the gyroscope of the individual soul" [supra, p. 4] cannot function properly. Today we call this state of affairs neurosis, which not only affects individuals, but through them society as a whole.

In Hebrew, the word for *covenant* is *berith*, the equivalent of the Assyrian *beritu*, meaning "bond" or "fetter." The word *covenant* permeates both the Old and New Testaments. In the New Testament (I Corinthians 11:25): "This cup is the new covenant in my blood. Do this, as often as you drink it, in remembrance of me," and in the context of the Last Supper the word is used as equivalent to *new testament*: This is my blood of the new testament which is shed for many" (Mark 14:24). As the ontogenesis of the psyche moves upward on the spiral of becoming, the "bonding" of covenant is lifted upward to the level of spirit. Isaiah 59:21 reads:

> And as for me, this is my covenant with them, says the Lord: my spirit which is upon you, and my words which I have put in your mouth, shall not depart out of your mouth, or out of the mouth of your children, or out of the mouth of your children's children, says the Lord, from this time forth and for evermore.

From Melchizedek to Abraham, thence to Moses, Isaiah and Christ, the psyche relentlessly urges forward to its own self-actualization. Christ the prince of peace and harmony, and Melchizedek the priest of peace and justice, are psychically the personifications of the "covenant" — the "bond" to the ultimate reality of being.

The covenant with Abraham reflects the teleological meaning of change as symbolized by the passing of the smoking furnace and the flaming torch between the portions of the sacrificial animal. The smoking furnace changes matter into energy, and the flaming torch provides "enlightenment" — i.e., light by which to see. But as the word *covenant* (from the Latin *convenire*, "to come together"; so also the Hebrew word *berith*, "the bond") indicates, there must be *two* parties contributing to the meaning of the whole.

This is a correlative move, so to speak, in which circumcision, for the first time introduced in the Old Testament, is also introduced in this chapter. Circumcision is the human contribution to the significance of this fundamental drama of man's becoming. As long as the deity is seen as an agent outside, the circumcision is a ritual with limited efficacy. To circumcise the heart is a poetic expression which presents a teaching from the inside. To "know" the meaning of circumcision is an intensely personal experience directly related to the process of becoming which alone enables one to choose. Circumcision is a visible sign that the covenant is essentially a symbol of justice — a balanced process. As such, it precludes expectations which have been born of our lack of authenticity. Surely the problem of grace is closely connected with man's expectations, depriving him of the experience of being a free agent. On the other hand, acceptance of the responsibility to be a co-worker with the divine, is the essence of being a free agent.

In the end, this is the enormity of the problem of Job in which the great poem provides a powerful answer to the problem it poses.

> . . . the immediate conflict is that of a deeply individual mind and heart. From the psychological point of view, the story of Job may be seen as remarkable poetic exposition of man's struggle to achieve personality, a sound means of relations with experience.[97]

The epic drama of Job starts with Job 2:9:

> Then his wife said to him, "Do you still hold fast your integrity? Curse God, and die." But he said to her, "You speak as one of the foolish women would speak. Shall we receive good at the hand of God, and *shall we not receive evil?*" In all this Job did not sin with his lips.[98]

The poem reaches its climax in 40:15: "Behold Behemoth, which I made as I made you."

Behemoth is etymologically the plural of *behemah*, "the beast." "The verbs used with the noun in this passage are third person masculine singular thus indicating that a single beast is intended and that the plural form here must be the so-called intensive plural, or plural of majesty, the Beast *par excellence.*"[99]

> Confronting Behemoth, Job really confronts the unnamed stuff of life, all that will forever remain beyond the reach of righteousness; the tempestuous, brutal, violent, the mindless which man fears in him-

self and in the world outside because he is not mindful of it. God tells Job to look, by *seeing* to bring this unnamed stuff of life into the light of his awareness, *to accept it as a part of himself and to achieve a human relation with it.* Behemoth is a natural inhabitant of the inner world, and though he may be beyond the reach of righteousness, he is not beyond the reach of rightness. The vast energies of Being that he symbolizes may drive man, rule him, overthrow him and destroy him as a man, or when, as a man, he experiences them rightly, they may do the opposite. Behemoth is the source of individual woe or the source of the energies of human creativity.[100]

Job said:

I put on righteousness, and it clothed me:
my justice was as a robe and a diadem.[101]

"Here, unaware, he goes to the roots of his troubles. . . . He *sins* in his belief that he *is* his own righteousness, that it sums him up completely, and in cursing a creation that no longer testifies to that fact."[102]

In the Book of Job as well as in Abraham's experience of the covenant, justice is revealed as a two-way process. Thus, the archetype of justice became the basis for the three great religions of the West. In Buddhism the same is expressed in their archetypal symbol of Justice, the Taigitu, where the Yin and Yang, female and male, light and darkness are in an eternal balanced process, depicting Life as it really is.

A Jewish legend asserts that Adam, Seth and Melchizedek were born with the sign of the covenant upon them. Seth the fruit of the reunion of Adam and Eve was destined to become the ancestor of the Messiah![103] Adam and Eve perpetrated the Fall; and yet, the poetic seers of the past unleash the archetypal symbol that out of the "original sin" the Messiah is destined to be born. Deuteronomy 6:5 says: "you shall love the Lord your God with all your heart, and with all your might." Rashi, the commentator of the 11th century A.D. explains: with all your heart — with both your impulses!

The custom of circumcision is age-old and world-wide; and although it was no doubt partly introduced for hygienic reasons, it became a powerful initiation ritual giving a sign to the community that it belonged together. But this obvious approach does not begin to reach the depths of its meaning. Karl Barth comments on Romans 3:1-2:   ′

> Do Judaism and circumcision then have no value at all; do they have no real and permanent distinction? Paul replies that to think that would be the greatest possible mistake. The Jews are and remain the nation entrusted with the words, the revelations of God up to and including the person of Jesus Christ. The Gentiles, when they attain to faith, can in a way only be their guests. It must rest at this: "Salvation comes from the Jews" (John 4:22).[104]

As Frazer points out, the Hebrew word for making a covenant "is literally to 'cut a covenant', and the inference is confirmed by analogies in the Greek language and ritual; for the Greeks used similar phrases and practiced similar rites. Thus they spoke of *cutting* oaths in the sense of swearing them, and of *cutting* a treaty instead of making one."[105]

In Jeremiah 34:18 it is said: "the covenant which they made before me, I will make like the calf which they cut into two and passed between its parts. . . ." The Old Testament's basic attitude toward the inherent meaning of the ritual of circumcision could not be more dramatically displayed than in the consideration of the first covenant and the last covenant as sure signs of the history of the ontogenesis of the psyche and the slow birth of the son of man. In the first covenant not only an oven and a flaming torch the poets made passing through the "cut" animals, but also in the circumcision man is "cutting" the foreskin of the penis. In the last covenant in the Old Testament,[106] as in Joshua 8:30-33 where the Israelites face Mount Gerizim, the mountain of blessing, and Mount Ebal, the mountain of curse, was a "covenantal ceremony." *In this ceremony man himself is passing through the halves* formed by these two mountains; they pass through them before they can enter the "promised land." And, significantly, facing each other, the ark stood between them.[107] While in the first covenant the law is given to man, in the last, in the words of Moses, man is becoming aware "that the law is written upon their hearts" and the "words have been put into their mouths" and above all, *man is becoming the chooser*: "I have set before you life and death, blessing and curse; *therefore choose life.*"[108]

With these words Moses exhorts the Israelites before they pass over the Jordan, the land of freedom of choice as an authentic experience. And fully in keeping with the ontogenesis of the psyche the poets in Deuteronomy jubilantly declare: "And the Lord your God will circumcise your heart and the heart of your offspring, so that you will love the Lord your God with all your heart and with all your soul, that you may live."[109] "Circumcise therefore the foreskin of your heart, and be no more stiffnecked."[110] This, the essence of the Old Testament, is then lifted on the spiral of man's becoming aware of himself as a responsible being; "circumcision is that of the heart, in the spirit and not in the letter," echoes the New Testament.[111]

Christ's saying I have not come to destroy the law but to fulfill it reveals itself in awesome dimensions. The new covenant, the new testament, echoes majestically in John: "I am the vine, ye are the branches: He that abideth in me *and I in him*, the same bringeth forth much fruit: for without me you can do nothing."[112] The awareness of the covenant as a two-way process, the awareness of the complementarity of God's needs of man and of man's needs of God could not have been more beautifully expressed and hence: "Ye have not chosen me, but I have chosen you, and ordained you, that ye should go and bring forth fruit and that your fruit should remain: that whatsoever ye shall ask of the father in my name, he may give it to you."[113]

The ritual of circumcision according to Jewish tradition is that the father should perform the operation and if he is unable to do so another Israelite can act as his agent. "The father should place his son upon the knees of the God-father and hand the knife to the operator."[114] This rather gruesome ritual depicts the ultimate of committal; by committing his son the father commits himself, fulfilling the supreme sacrifice asked of Abraham to sacrifice Isaac, his son. The Akedah, Abraham's sacrifice of Isaac, in its essence establishes personality by overcoming the child sacrifice.[115] Man chooses and thus embarks on the long journey through the darkness of his own becoming to the rhythm and light of life. It is not the admonition by dogma nor fear which brings about real change and new life, but man's own choosing as a responsible partner in the covenant. The Akedah is in its truest sense a "pass-over" from one state of being to another.

The symbol of "passing through," that is, from one state of being to another, is repeated in the passage of the host of Israel through the Red Sea signaling their entrance into new areas of spiritual experience. Note that in order for the Israelites to make this passage, the Red Sea had to be divided — i.e., "cut in two."

"Cutting in half" as a symbol of creating a higher consciousness is depicted in a dramatic manner in the oldest existing creation myth. In *Enuma Elish*, the Babylonian Genesis, Marduk, the hero, has subdued Tiamat, the primal monster, the *prima materia*; and "He split her open like a mussel (?) into two (parts); Half of her he set in place and formed the sky (therewith) as a roof."[116] Basic reality thus established, the poem then describes how the primal gods [men] attempted to create order out of chaos. In contemporary terminology, we would say that they were striving to realize the complementarity of values of heaven and earth, of God and man. They were attempting to establish "the harmony of the spheres," or the harmony of interrelatedness, just as modern physics in parallel fashion strains to achieve a unified field theory.

It is here in these wide swings of the mind that the evolution of the psyche expresses basic truth about the wholeness of life. Poetically on one level and mathematically on a more sophisticated plane, the self influences the conscious brain.

As Sir Charles Popper says:

> I have called this section "The Self and its Brain," because I intend here to suggest that the brain is owned by the self, rather than the other way around. The self is almost always active. The activity of selves is, I suggest, the only genuine activity we know. The active, psycho-physical self is the active programmer of the brain (which is the computer), it is the executant whose instrument is the brain. The mind is, as Plato said, the pilot. . . . Like a pilot, it observes and takes action at the same time. It is acting and suffering, recalling the past and planning and programming the future; expecting and disposing. It contains, in quick succession, or all at once, wishes, plans, hopes, decisions to act, and a vivid consciousness of being an active self, a centre of action.[117]

Grammatically also, the covenant is a two-way process. The Hebrew word for covenant, *berith*, is feminine; on the other hand the *sign* of the covenant *oth berith* is masculine. The masculine member on which the sign of the covenant appears is the symbolic representation of the creative forces of life. "The Hebrew word for bow is *Kesheth* which means, in the Hebrew literature, not only the 'rainbow' [the sign of the covenant after the flood] but also the 'penis.' "[118]

In Genesis 24:2 and 9 Abraham makes his servant swear not to find a wife for Isaac from other than among Abraham's own people, telling the servant, "put your hand under my thigh." In the same manner, Jacob insisted that his son Joseph swear not to bury him in Egypt, saying: "Put your

hand under my thigh and promise to deal loyally and truly
with me. Do not bury me in Egypt" (Genesis 47:29). Egypt is
the symbol of bondage and Jacob's demand archetypally
demonstrates the move toward freedom. The circumcised
penis is in the Old Testament tradition of the same significance as in our days the Bible upon which oaths are also
sworn, by putting the hand onto it.[119] In Latin *testis* means
both "scrotum" and "witness." In German the word for
"witness" is *Zeuge* and the verb *zeugen* means "sexual intercourse" [infra, p. 321].

Circumcision is also symbolic of the Passover, the passover from one state of mind to the other. According to
Exodus 12:43-49 a stranger or slave, once he is circumcised,
may be "considered a native of the land" and is allowed to
participate in the passover meal. This custom not only links
the circumcision with its world-wide ritualistic use, but in
the tradition of the Old Testament it also lifts man's bondage to nature onto a symbolically higher level of psychic
organization into the realm of spiritual freedom. It is like the
spring rebirth of nature where creativity rekindles itself in all
its glory and promise, or where, in the actuality of living
experience, the mind presents itself to itself with its own
characteristics. No wonder then that the ontogenetic principle is displayed in all its wonder in the Bible.

In the New Testament tradition participants in the ritual
of the Holy Mass need to have been baptized, as a symbol of
rebirth. On Mt. Moriah the supreme sacrifice is asked of
Abraham, which had its antecedents in the covenant and the
circumcision. On Mt. Golgotha the drama repeats itself in
the "scandal of the cross," wherein the creatureliness of man
is supposed to have cried out: *Eli, Eli, lama sabachthani?*
— "My God, my God, why hast thou forsaken me?"

In our time, man has cut himself off from his roots in the
past, and has thus lost the relation to himself, or more
poignantly expressed, to his *Self.* The Old Testament tradition showed man is a living relation to his ethnic roots,
which modern man painfully tries to re-establish. It was

dramatically shown to Abraham, the doubting man, that things can change. The same essential message, that change from one state of being to another is possible, was also shown to the doubting Moses:

> Then Moses answered, But behold, they will not believe me or listen to my voice, for they will say, "The Lord did not appear to you." The Lord said to him, "What is that in your hand?" He said, "A rod." And he said, "Cast it on the ground." So he cast it on the ground, and it became a serpent; and Moses fled from it. But the Lord said to Moses, "Put out your hand, and take it by the tail" — so he put out his hand, and caught it, and it became a rod in his hand — "that they may believe that the Lord, the God of their fathers, the God of Abraham, the God of Isaac, and the God of Jacob, has appeared to you."[120]

In this dream-like account, we see a transformation of symbols, as the rod is transformed into a serpent and reversed again. This is analogous to the modern scientific transformation of matter into energy. As a result of this remarkable development in science, the older theories of objective materialism have undergone a decisive change. The interpretation of life as a material phenomenon has given way to interpreting life as energy, no longer a concrete reality, but now understood abstractly. Man now recognizes energy as a reality internal to himself as well as an outside force. This new recognition becomes a counterpoise to exploitative materialism in a growing concern for ecological considerations, and for a humanistic economy. Values once thought to be primarily external to man are now seen to have their primary reference within.

Furthermore, we believe today that we have recaptured the past by splitting the atom, thus relating to the primal act of creation where condensed matter appears to have exploded into energy at the beginning.

In the magic world of the "primitive" man, virility and fertility as manifestations of energy were also felt to be conditioned through a relationship to the distant past. In primitive societies the ritual of circumcision often takes place where the spirits of the ancestors are thought to dwell. It was understood that to fulfill its purpose, the initiation had to spill the sacrifical blood of circumcision on the ground where the ancestors could be thus contacted. This sacrifice was felt to be a prerogative of the gods, the *jus prima noctis.* The apparent need for man to establish contact with his historical past creates an enormous interest in archaeology today. It is as if man, through widening his horizon, experiences a kind of contact with his vital past. For the Self, archaeology establishes, in addition to its historical implications, a vehicle for the satisfaction of a deep-seated need, namely, to be in contact with "creation" and, through it, with the creator.

In the same chapter in which Moses, discoursing with the Creator, is shown the symbol of the potential act of transformation, the poets were moved to include another symbol of vital significance. It is a strange paradox that God should have threatened to kill the man he had chosen to lead mankind into the realm of a new spiritual freedom. Nonetheless, in Exodus 4:24-26 we read:

> At a lodging place on the way the Lord met him and sought to kill him. Then Zipporah took a flint and cut off her son's foreskin, and touched Moses' feet with it, and said, "Surely you are a bridegroom of blood to me!" So he let him alone.

As with Abraham and the convenant, the mind was expanded to new areas of experience, so with Moses in his decisive exodus, circumcision is a vital part of the mythopoetic drama. Only through the interference of Moses' wife, Zipporah, who as a stranger knew instinctively the mythic ways of the past, Yahweh was satisfied. Yahweh is also a dynamic symbol of the past which itself demands to be related to the present as an expression of the two-way process of Life. The Self acts within the psyche, rooting it, as it were, and establishing thus a whole situation in the very moment it is developing to reach out to a further differentiation. Zipporah circumcises her son, a ritual symbolizing relatedness, which Moses had overlooked.

From a structural hermeneutical point of view, it is of interest to note that the euphemism for penis, "foot," has a parallel where a brother is obliged to sleep with his brother's widow so that she may not be barren. But if he refuses, saying: "I do not wish to take her," then "his brother's wife shall go up to him in the presence of the elders, and pull his sandal off his foot and spit into his face."[121]

In spite of the fact that these stories were written down at least a thousand years after the presumed events, they seem to stem from an historical context. In the temple at Medinet Habu in Egypt there exist two reliefs depicting the signs of victory of Ramses III over his enemies. On these reliefs scribes are counting not only the bearded heads of the vanquished, but also the cut-off penises and foreskins. Exact figures are even given:

Total of foreskins 12,535
Total of heads   12,535
Total of phalli   12,758[122]

In Isaiah 7:20 the same theme is sounded as euphemism, or poetically as synonym:

In that day the Lord will shave with a razor . . .
the head and the hair of the feet, and he will sweep
away the beard also.

To be sure these dark sayings of the Bible are reminders to modern man that the poets must have felt themselves to be in the same creative stillness which every serious artist experiences in his work. The essence of any creative act will be readily attested by any serious artist that out of the silence of his unknowing, however turbulent, his work creates itself. The artist knows that he is the medium for his art which demands his full committal. And so it must have been with the narrators of the past to whom we owe the trenchant record of the ontogenesis of the psyche.

The Word

THE DEPENDENCY of the mind on the innate springs of creativity and the man being the medium for their manifestations, is most poignantly expressed in Exodus:

> But Moses said to the Lord, "Oh my Lord, I am not eloquent, either heretofore or since thou hast spoken to thy servant; but I am slow of speech and tongue." Then the Lord said to him: "Who has made man's mouth? Who makes him dumb, or deaf, or seeing or blind? Is it not I, the Lord? Now therefore go, and I will be with your mouth and teach you what you shall speak" .... "He shall speak for you to the people; and he shall be a mouth for you, and you shall be to him as God."[123]

Here is the echo of Abraham's experience, when his rational doubts did not allow him to trust his inner voice until a dream had spoken to him most convincingly [supra, p. 115].[124]

Moses, the great law-giver, who was so brilliantly capable of rationalizing and formulating the laws which maintained the structure of his people, failed, however, to read the signs of mythic thinking. Like Abraham, he doubted whether the new level on the spiral of the psyche's growth could be achieved, and even if it were possible, he could not see how. Because of his rationality, Moses failed to trust in the potential for the new reality which lay before him. Overly rational modern man faces exactly the same problem. In our time, too, there is doubt and fear of the new reality offered by human potential.

It was Moses' confrontation with the Burning Bush on Mt. Horeb which opened these new dimensions for the ontogenesis of the psyche. A most significant passage which reveals the import of this development has been placed by the poets after the experience of the Burning Bush. In Numbers 20:8, the Lord says to Moses:

> "Take the rod, and assemble the congregation, you and Aaron your brother, and *tell* the rock before their eyes to yield its water; so you shall bring water out of the rock for them. . . ." And Moses lifted up his hand and *struck* the rock with his rod twice; and water came forth abundantly, and the congregation drank, and their cattle. And the Lord said to Moses and Aaron, "Because you did not believe in me, to sanctify me in the eyes of the people of Israel, therefore you shall not bring this assembly into the land I have given them."[125]

It was, after all, the creative word which fashioned the world. "God *said* let there be light and there was light." God had commanded Moses to *speak* to the rock, but instead, Moses chose to strike the rock with his rod. The command to speak to the rock was placed by the poets significantly *after* the events of Sinai. This vital change demonstrates the new in the development of the psyche.

The symbolic power of the word deserves careful examination. Marduk, in the *Enuma Elish*, proved his power through the power of the word:

> "By the word of thy mouth, let the garment be destroyed;
> Command again, and let the garment be whole!"

He commanded with his mouth, and the garment
was destroyed.
He commanded again, and the garment was
restored.[126]

In Egypt the god Ptah by the power of thought and
commanding word brings into being the fundamental elements of the universe. The *word* used here in these vital
contexts is therefore closely related to energy — power. The
noun *energy* stems from the Greek *en,* "in," and *ergon,*
"work." It means therefore literally "to work within." Both
the quantum mechanics of physics and the Hypercycle in
biology describe life essentially in terms of energy in movement. It works within the atoms, within the elementary
particles, within the cells and organs, and ultimately merges
with the universe as a field of movement. The same creative
power works within the artist, and basically in every human
being. The artist demonstrates for us the organizing of the
movement of energy most visibly in his creations.

> ... in the ancient Orient the divine word pos-
> sesses peerlessly a dynamic force; as examples of this,
> several predictions from the great bidding prayer to
> Marduk-Ellil may be cited:
> His word, which proceeds like a storm . . .
> The word which destroys the heavens above
> The word which shakes the earth beneath
> His word is a rushing torrent against which there is
> no resistance.
> His word destroys the mother with child like a reed
> The word of Marduk is a flood that breaches the dam
> His word breaks off great mesu-trees
> His word is a storm bringing everything to
> destruction
> His word, when it goes about gently, destroys the
> land.[127]

The Gnostic Markos says that "in the beginning was the first being who had no father, of whom one cannot think, who had no substance, and who was neither male nor female, which cannot be [rationally] understood. He opened his mouth and produced the *Word*."[128]

A Samoan creation myth says:

> Then Tangaloa *said* to the rock: "Split yourself open," and out came mythic figures. Then Tangaloa . . . *hit* the rock with his right hand and it split again and out came the parents of all the nations of the earth, and the sea came also. . . .
>
> And again Tangaloa *spoke* . . . Then man came forth, and then came the spirit *(Anga-nga),* then the heart *(loto),* then the will *(fingalo),* and finally thought *(masalo).*[129]

In Psalms it is said: "The voice of the Lord is upon the waters . . . The voice of the Lord is full of majesty . . . "[130]

The New Testament in Matthew 8:26 says: "'Why are you afraid, O men of little faith?' Then he rose and rebuked the winds and the sea; and there was a great calm."

The creative word, however, does not only belong to the physical but in particular to the spiritual, mental sphere:

> Let the prophet who has a dream tell the dream,
> but let him who has my word speak my word faithfully . . .
> Is not my word like fire, says the Lord, and like a hammer
> which breaks the rock in pieces?[131]
>
> . . . so shall be my word that goes forth from my mouth;
> it shall not return to me empty, but it shall accomplish
> that which I *purpose.*[132]

A most *outspoken* example is the dialogue in Job 40:

> And the Lord said to Job: "Shall a fault finder contend with the Almighty? He who argues with God let him answer it." (1)

> Then the Lord answered Job out of the whirlwind: . . . "Will you even put me in the wrong? Will you condemn me that you may be justified?" (38)

> "Behold Behemoth, which I made as I made you . . ."(15)

> "He is the first of the works of God . . ." (19)

In Hebrew *dabar* is "dynamic both objectively and linguistically; it comes from the verb *dabar,* ordinarily used in the Pi'el form, *dibber,* both forms meaning simply 'speak.' The basic meaning is 'to be behind and drive forward,' hence 'to let the words follow one another,' or even better 'to drive forward that which is behind.'"[133]

The creative word exists because man exists. Animals and birds of all kinds communicate through the sounds which they create. We do not understand these sounds as language, but the sounds we call "words" convey meaning to us. F. L. Moriarty asserts that,

> . . . at this [earlier] stage of man's thinking, the word appears to be apprehended as a unit of power which has its own independent and fixed existence. The word's function as a term of signification does not seem to have emerged clearly; the line between concept and the thing is blurred. Instead of pointing to some objective content, the word itself sets itself in place of this content, becoming a power which exercises its own proper influence upon events.[134]

For the Hebrews, Boman writes, "*dabar* — 'the word in spoken form,' hence 'efficacious fact,' is . . . the great reality of existence . . . When the Hebrews represent *dabar*

Figure 6.   Dabar — The Word.

as the great reality of existence, they show their dynamic conception of reality."[135] The essence is more important than the medium. Above all, the revelation in Israel takes place within the context of the covenant *and* a strictly monotheistic framework, absolutely unique in the ancient world.

In the Egyptian view, the word and the object were identical.[136] From the mouth of Atum came everything forth. ". . . we have arrived at the quintessence of the doctrine of creation through the word. 'It is the mouth which pronounced the name of everything. . . .' "[137]

In Genesis 2:19: "the Lord . . . brought them [the animals] to the man to see what he would call them; and whatever the man called every living creature that was its name."

In India,

> . . . the primeval God transformed himself into a golden egg which was shining like the sun and in which he himself, Brahman, the father of all the worlds, was born. He rested a whole year in this egg and he then *parted it into two parts* through a mere word.[138]

In the Old Testament the vitality of the word is most visibly displayed in Art in Hebrew Bibles illustrated by Jewish artists, a fact which may surprise many readers.[139]

The British Museum Bible has a magnificent plate [supra, p. 139] showing the word *dabar* surrounded by four figures depicting man's emergence from the beast and in the Kennicott Bible the artist's signature is written in Hebrew characters composed of men and beasts.[140] Both these examples, painted in the 13th - 14th Century, show in a most impressive way the essence not only of the word as "a dynamic expression of reality," but also of the ontogenesis of the psyche. These drawings illustrate in art what the most scrutinizing etymological studies have confirmed.

To portray the "word" as the creative agent in its manifold

Figure 7. The Artist's Signature: "I Joseph and Ham drew and completed this book." The Hebrew characters are composed of men and beasts.

manifestations within the quasi-historical and historical records of the world religions was certainly not the intention of the poets and authors who compiled the writings. The "word" rather speaks through these creative persons, and is the self-representation of the creative psyche.

Today we have begun to understand the language of the images which have come to us from long before even the Ice Age. The replacement of image language with the written word was a vital step in the ontogenesis of the psyche. For primitive man, the image was the essence, and not the creative word, for with the invention of writing, the "word" moved upward on the spiral of man's becoming.

For example, the Samoan myth [supra, p. 137] is an autonomous product, despite its similarity to the story of Moses striking the rock to bring forth water. The "artist" is truly the psyche finding verbal expression through the poets, who are, in Boman's terms, "driven forward from behind."

The Book of Exodus is certainly not the intentional construction of a drama based on historical configurations and contexts, but an instance of the genuine creativity of the psyche. Because it is genuine, the Biblical account reflects in symbolic form, not historical events, but the ontogenesis of the psyche. So insistent was the pressure of the psyche in its phylogenetic development that the compilers and scribes were impelled to record the story a thousand years or more after the events of which they spoke. It is for this reason that the Biblical narrative continues to speak even to our own time of doubt and over-rationalization. We are in the fortunate position, however, of having the recent developments in science to assist our understanding, and we need not rely solely on belief or faith. One such development has been recorded very recently by Ralph Cohen, who writes:

> . . . I am suggesting that at the very least the traditions incorporated into the Exodus account may have a very ancient inspiration reaching back to the MBI period. [2,200 B.C. to about 2,000 B.C.] The migration of the MBI population from the southwest and their conquest of the Early Bronze civilization evidently made a very deep impression, and the memory of these events was preserved from one generation to the next. . . .
>
> The similarity between the course of the MBI migration and the route of the Exodus seems too close to be coincidental and a comparable process

may have operated here. "The late Bronze Age (1550 - 1200 B.C.) — the period usually associated with the Israelites' flight from Egypt — is archeologically unattested in the Kadesh-Barnea area ... but MBI remains abound and seem to provide a concrete background for the traditions of settlement."[141]

We are now approaching the high drama of the Mt. Horeb/Mt. Sinai experience. But before we reach that point, we must heighten the tension further by reference to some important historical and archaeological data. It is simply a fact that of the thousands upon thousands of documents, inscriptions, and tablets reflecting the social life of Egypt from the period presumed to be the date of the Exodus, there is not a single mention of Hebrews as such. There is a single mention of the name Israel on the famous Merneptah stele. This monument "set up at Thebes [Luxor] by Merneptah, son of Ramses II, a decade or two before 1200 B.C. preserves for us a hymn of victory in which is included the boast: "Israel is wasted; his seed is not."[142]

Hab/Piru

WHAT IS WELL PRESERVED, however, is the name Hab/'piru. The most diligent efforts by scholars and their painstaking work to relate Hab/'piru to Hebrews is admirably summarized by Moshe Greenberg. He comes to the conclusion that "the Hab/'piru = Hebrew equation is improbable." "What remains is the possibility — which must be considered — that the beginnings of Israelite history were bound up with a 'wandering Aramean' whose social status and mode of life mark him as an 'Apiru." There is evidence that the Hab/'piru were the "restive ones" or "those provided for." In other words, in terms of today's dissenters, they were those who did not accept the prevailing power structure:

The only definition which does justice to all the evidence is "free-booters" (*Freischaren*) who manage themselves independently in disorganized conditions, but who can exist under state control in organized lands. Since individuals may also be called [Hab/'piru] it may be assumed that the [Hab/'piru] bands were so called because they were composed of persons of the [Hab/'piru] class.[143]

Edward Campbell concurs:

Often the term *'Apiru* in the Amarna letters is used with a form of the Akkadian verb meaning "to do" or "to make," the verb appearing in a passive form with a variety of Canaanite affixes. The phrase has to mean something like "to be made 'Apiru or simply to become 'Apiru . . ." 'Apiru is seen to be a label simply meaning "outlaw" or "rebellious" in this context, it is at least possible, and to me very probable, that "to become 'Apiru" means "to defy the authority of the crowd.'[144]

And George Mendenhall:

The code of Hammurapi already must make provision for the situation in which a person states, whether overtly or in effect, "I hate my king and my city." By this hatred, he has renounced any obligation to the society in which he formerly had some standing (if not status), and has in turn deprived himself of its protection. This is all that is meant by the term "Hebrew," *Hab/'piru, 'Apiru,* which recurs in many sources from 2000 B.C. to its last occurrences in the Hebrew Bible about the time of David, who was himself a Hebrew in this sense when he was fleeing from King Saul — not through choice, but through necessity of self-preservation . . . In other words, no one could be born a "Hebrew"; he became so only by his own action.[145]

For our considerations here, these "scientific finds" are of great importance. As we have shown, Abraham seems to have been "a restive One" whose inner development urged him to leave "his home and kindred,"[146] anticipating, as it were, the archetypal situation from which the New Testament as well formed its images: "He who loves his father or mother more than me . . . he who does not take his cross and follow me is not worthy of me."[147]

W. F. Albright and C. S. Mann in their introduction to Matthew in *The Anchor Bible* write: "This Gospel presupposes and grows out of the Old Testament, and there is no understanding of the books of the New Testament without the books of the Old." And further: "Without the Covenant of Sinai and the election of Israel there is no understanding of the Gospel."[148] Therefore, these considerations about Abraham as well as those about the Hab/'piru lift the Exodus legend to a profound level of the psyche's own becoming, and all these matters are but the entrance to the depth and height of the "covenant of Sinai."

Moses, the representative of the questioning mind, after he, like Abraham, had heard the *WORD*, asked for still stronger evidence: "How shall I know? What is your Name?" This is the same question Jacob had asked at the ford of Jabbok after wrestling all the night with an unknown antagonist.[149] When Jacob asked for his name, instead of revealing it, he in turn called Jacob by a new name: Israel. Here Jacob's wrestling with himself, the Christ within, is depicted as the archetype of becoming, of integration.[150] The poets have presented Jacob as a man with all of the human frailties and shortcomings that are characteristic of the human race; yet it was this mere man who rose to the height of wholeness by an act of integration within himself. Jacob had become whole. "Whole," "healthy," "holy" all have the same etymological root which is *hāle*. Jacob acquired, through his own commitment, both the qualities of the human and the divine.

The story of Jacob tells us how recognition of the "natural" in himself led to the integration of his "other side," thus balancing the psyche. This is a parallel to the story of Abraham in which balance comes through the blessing of Melchizedek. As a mythopoetic reflection of the central law in man's becoming, the covenant at Sinai embraces manifold inner realities and gives expression to its complexity, and therefore has become of central importance for the spiritual development of the Western world. It is the very basis of the spiritual background to Justice.

W. F. Albright in his introduction to Matthew says:

> The (miscalled) Sermon on the Mount, or Great Instruction — which was private instruction for the inner circle of the disciples — with its strong emphasis on the law underscores the unique character of Israel's law, represents Jesus as compelling the errant community to return to the fundamentals of all law. So far, conceding the degree of authority attributed to Jesus and also incidental assertions of his relationship with God which close the instruction, there is nothing which marks off the ministry as being more than largely a recapitulation of Israel's history, though admittedly in high relief.[151]

Dominating the whole poetic narrative on Mt. Sinai is the response to Moses' doubts as he asks for a name he can tell to the people: "What is his name? What shall I say to them?"[152] This doubt leads to a symbolic demonstration of the essential meaning of "the name" as a partial answer to the vital question. Moses' rod, which had the appearance of material stability, was transformed into an animate creature, as if to say that the central law of life is the capacity for change. Modern atomic science proves such to be the case. The concept of Ansatz [supra, p. 40] is today a scientific model for continuity in change. The symbol of Ansatz, for the scientific mind, has as much motive power and mystique as the Burning Bush has for the poetic mind.

The Burning Bush

THE MYTHOPOETIC symbol of the Burning Bush is awesome in depth, providing in us an awareness of that which is eternally the same and yet always becoming.

> . . . and he looked, and lo, the bush was
> burning, yet it was not consumed.[153]

The scientist in our time expresses the same truth couched in different words: "Fire is a process of transformation and change, by which material elements are rejoined into new combinations. The nature of chemical processes was only understood when fire itself came to be understood as a process."[154]

> . . . mathematics becomes a dynamic mode of
> thought, and that is a major step in the ascent of
> man. . . .
>   The laws of nature had always been made of
> numbers since Pythagoras said that was the language
> of nature. But now the language of nature had to
> include numbers which described time. The laws of
> nature become laws of motion, and nature herself
> becomes not a series of static frames but a moving
> process.[155]

The description of the Burning Bush is found in Exodus 3:2-6:

> And the angel of the Lord appeared to him in a flame
> of fire out of the midst of a bush, and he looked and
> lo, the bush was burning, yet it was not consumed.

... God called to him out of the bush ... and he said, "I
am the God of your father, the God of Abraham, the
God of Isaac, and the God of Jacob. ..." And Moses
hid his face, for he was afraid to look at God.

It is a fact that on Mt. Horeb/Sinai, there is a bush which,
when struck by the rays of the sun, appears to be on fire.
This phenomenon may well have inspired the poetic fancy to
create the symbolic Burning Bush. "... The bush is described
as '*the* thornbush,' that is, the specific bush which is known
to grow upon Sinai."[156]

At the traditional site of the Burning Bush on Mt. Horeb, St.
Catherine's Monastery was built in the 6th Century A.D.,
and there a lovely mosaic of the Transfiguration of Christ
has been preserved.

The mosaic is all the more precious because so few
mosaics of the Age of Justinian have survived any-
where. The same edict which in 726 forbade the
making of holy images also ordered all existing ones
destroyed. The work of the iconoclasts (who
regarded images as idols) was so thorough that in
Constantinople not a single mosaic escaped their
furor.[157]

The importance of this mosaic, however, as an expression of
the ontogenesis of the psyche, lies in the fact that "in the Old
Testament. . . . neither Moses nor Elijah were permitted to
look upon the Lord face to face, but only to hear his voice
(Exodus 3:4, 33, 20), whereas on Mount Tabor the two
prophets do see the Lord in the manifestation of Christ
(Mark 9:2)."[158]

The central theme around which both the Old and New
Testaments are woven is the covenant of Sinai. And yet,
apart from the Bible itself, there is no confirmation of the
historicity of Moses. The authenticity of Moses is like that
of Abraham — it resides in the activity of the human psyche,

of which the Biblical story is the record. The drama in its majestic dimensions reverberates throughout history.

"Without the Law there would have been no Gospel: *ex nihilo nihil fit* is valid today as it was in the Middle Ages: without the Covenant of Sinai and the election of Israel there is no understanding of the Gospel."[159]

It is in the few lines about the Burning Bush that the drama of Sinai approaches its climax. The Self, symbolized as the Burning Bush, however, is not limited thereby. The Self is a symbolic manifestation of the psyche as a whole; it is felt to have constancy at the moment of experience, but then moves on as a changing expression of the kernel of life itself. In modern science this experience is expressed, as we have seen, as life being essentially ambiguous in all its complexity, reaching out to a fusion with the Universe. What we are able to conceive *rationally* is the unambiguous, which is naturally only a part of the whole. The Burning Bush is a poetic model corresponding to the innate need of man's urge towards wholeness expressed in terms of our aesthetic sensibility. As such, it speaks to us, addresses us in terms of continuity.

When Moses asked, "What is your name?" the answer was rung from the depth of Being itself: *Eheyeh asher Eheyeh* — "I Am That I Am!"

> Then Moses said to God, "If I come to the people of Israel and say to them, 'The God of your fathers has sent me to you,' and they ask me 'What is his name?' what shall I say to them?" God said to Moses, "I am who I am." And he said, "Say this to the people of Israel, 'I AM has sent me to you.' "[160]

In these three words, *Eheyeh asher Eheyeh,* "I Am That I Am," is couched the grandeur and the very zenith of the Bible. Jacob could say "I have seen God face to face"; Moses was "afraid to look"; and Jesus said, "I am the way, and the truth, and the life; no one comes to the Father, but by me."[161] The "I am who I am" is the *hayah* in the ontogenesis of the psyche. Etymologically the verb *hayah,* meaning "to be" (*eheye,* "I am," is a derivative) has three principle meanings: "to become," "to be," and "to effect."

> *Hayah* signifies *real becoming,* what is more either an arising or passage from one condition to another.[162]

The poets of the Old Testament are also referring to the "Lord" as the *living* God. This experience is innate to the mind in the sense that Descartes held that the idea of a true triangle is innate: "because we already possess within us the idea of a true triangle, and it can be more easily conceived by our mind than the more complex figure of a triangle drawn on paper, we, therefore, when we see that composite figure, apprehend not itself, but rather the authentic triangle."[163]

Prof. Noam Chomsky writes:

> The notion that there may be innate principles of mind that on the one hand make possible the acquisition of knowledge and belief, and on the other, determine and limit its scope, suggests nothing that should surprise a biologist, so far as I can see.

> Words would have the meaning given to them by the organism, to be sure, though there would be no necessity to suppose that this "giving of meaning" is conscious or accessible to introspection, or that the organism is at all capable of explaining the system of concepts it uses or describing the characteristics of particular items with any accuracy. In the case of humans, there is every reason to suppose that the semantic system of language is given largely by a power independent of conscious choice; the operative principles of mental organization are presumably inaccessible to introspection, but there is no reason why they should in principle be more immune to investigation than the principles that determine the physical arrangement of limbs and organs.[164]

An essential principle of science is, after all, that science itself constantly changes and grows and that it expresses beliefs which while being couched in static concepts, nevertheless portray a living experience. The law of Entropy predicts that mass which exploded in the moment of the Big Bang will in the end fall together again and then another Big Bang will happen and another universe will be born. Now this experience is expressed already in the burial customs of the so-called savages, by using red ochre, which is, after all, the physical correlative to the experience by the organism of birth and the use of it in burial rituals symbolizes the hope of rebirth. Thus basic scientific laws were already in prehistory expressed symbolically, and basic scientific laws are often expressions not only of empirical facts but also of innate ideas, e.g., the complementarity of light or the complementarity of values.

> Eichrodt is of the opinion that Jahweh is an expanded form of . . . the archaic (*qal*) of the Hebrew verb "to be." The meaning of the word, if this derivation be accepted, is "he that is," not in the metaphysical sense of absolute existence, but in the sense of "he that is present," and thus ready to manifest himself as helper. This account of the history of the divine name Jahweh, Eichrodt connects with, and believes to be supported by, the story of the commission which Moses received from God in Exodus 3:14.[165]

> "I shall be there" . . . gives exact expression to the personal "existence" of God (not to his abstract "being"), and expression even to his living presence, which most directly of all his attributes touches the man to whom he manifests himself. The speaker's self-designation as the God of Abraham, God of Isaac, and God of Jacob (Exodus 3:15) is indissolubly united with that manifestation of "I shall be there," and he cannot be reduced to a God of the philosophers.[166]

The archaeological findings of Ebla which are dated 2,500 B.C., i.e., about 1,000 years before the presumed date of Abraham and/or Moses, confirm to an astonishing degree the findings of the scholars. Alfonso Archi writes:

> As A. Finet has shown, Mari names of the Ya(h)wi-ON type derive their forms from the root *hwy* and probably mean 'Dagan//Addu/etc. is/shows himself.
>
> Even if the Amorite gods included one named Yahweh, he was not the same as the Yahweh of Israel, for no such god is included in the onomasticon or in the offering lists at Ebla.[167]

And Giovanni Pettinato adds: "As regards the general interpretation of theophoric names ending in -*il* or -*yà*, I am now convinced that both elements are generic terms for 'God' and do not indicate, at least not always, a particular divinity."[168]

As an illustration of *hayah*'s dynamic sense of effecting, Boman in his authoritative and exhaustive study of the verb mentions the verb "lighten," which means "not only to be bright or become bright but also to make light effective, i.e., illuminate,"[169] and goes on to say:

> It is correct to say ... that "being" (e.g., the being contained in stative verbs) represents an inner activity which is best to be grasped by means of psychological analogies with human psychic life. ... In the full Old Testament sense "being" is pre-eminently *personal being* (Person-Sein). What does it mean that a person *is*? .... The person ... is in movement and activity, which encompasses "being" as well as "becoming" and "acting," i.e., *he lives*. ...
>
> The *hayah* designates existence; only that to which one can contribute a *hayah* is effective. ... Jahveh ... is the sum of all the dynamic existence and the source and the creator of it. This lies in the embattled verse: *'eheyeh 'asher 'eheyeh* — "I am who I am". ...

> The . . . unity inherent in *hayah* of "becoming,"
> "being" and "effecting" is curious to us because our
> thinking takes its orientation from visible things.
> However, if thinking is oriented psychologically, the
> synthesis is quite comprehensible, for the person is
> an active being who is perpetually engaged in becom-
> ing and yet remains identical with himself.[170]

And so it is in the life of a nation whose ethnic roots are the
determining factor for its characteristics. Boman quotes
W. F. Otto saying: "The most significant event in the life of a
people . . . is the emergence of a mode of thought that is
peculiar to it, *as if designed for it from the beginning of time,*
by which it is henceforward distinguishable in the world's
history."[171]

The Revised Standard Version of the Bible translates
Eheye asher eheye as "I Am Who I Am," but significantly, it
has a footnote "I shall be that I shall be," expressing a state
of becoming — after all, "to be" is an imperfect verb. *Hayah*
reveals its meaning fully if it is not seen in isolation, but in
relation to the three central events of the covenant of Sinai:
the Burning Bush, the Golden Calf, and the Tablets of the
Law.

Just as Boman's analysis of *hayah* came to the conclusion
that "the person is an active being who is perpetually
engaged in becoming and yet remains identical with himself," so the Burning Bush remained the same; and in the
context of the Golden Calf story Aaron said: ". . . then I
threw it [the gold] into the fire and there came out this
calf."[172] The rendering of Rashi, the commentator, reads: "I
cast it into the fire, I did not know that the calf would come
out, it fashioned itself!" In the same chapter of Exodus,
however, there is a second version which portrays Aaron as
a technician: ". . . because they *made* the calf which Aaron
made . . ."[173] The two versions depict two different states of
mind. In the one, the calf came out by itself, and in the other,
it was fashioned. The first version is a mythopoetic demon-

stration, the second, a more conscious, rational account. But both are expressions of the *hayah*, the "I Am." God was not only active on the mountain top, but also on the plain, and in both places with a teleological purpose. The Golden Calf legend is another but still more dramatic version of man's encounter with himself, depicted so poignantly in the Jacob-Esau story.[174]

The find of an Israelite cult bull provides further substance for the view of the Bible being a true record of the ontogenesis of the psyche.[175] "And he took the calf which they had made, and burnt it with fire, and ground it to powder, and scattered it upon the water, *and made the people of Israel drink it*" (Exodus 32:20). The mythopoetic description of the autonomous happening — "I threw it into the fire and there came out this calf" (Exodus 32:24) — as well as the cultic idolatrous rationalization, display the same essential symbolic meaning.

Jacob "integrated his opposite side" symbolized by his brother Esau.[176] The Israelites drinking the ashes of the Golden Calf is another symbol of integration. So also are the stories of Job ending with the integration of Behemoth, and at the Last Supper: ". . . take, eat, this is my body; this is my blood, all of you, drink of it." All these important integrative events are preparations for still another vital step in the ontogenesis of the psyche, Moses' concise statement that "the word is in your heart."[177] This all-important text is concluded by addressing the dignity of man: "I call heaven and earth to witness against you this day, that I have set before you life and death, blessing and curse; *therefore choose life*."[178] With these ringing words, as an application of *hayah* in its essence, Moses puts the responsibility of choice and its consequences on the shoulders of the individual.

I Am That I Am

THE GREATNESS of *Eheyeh asher eheyeh*, "I Am Who I Am," lies precisely in the fact that it is not a static image of perfection, but a process of becoming which never ends. The "I Am Who I Am" is the essence of "moral man commands himself," and expression of *dignitatis humanae*, and the *hayah*, a demonstration of the inner workings of the divine. As a mythopoetic thought it embraces manifold inner realities and gathers in a monotheistic sense the complexity of them into "they shall be gathered all in one" [infra, p. 306].[179] The second commandment: "You shall not make yourself a graven image, or any likeness of anything that is in heaven above, or that is in the earth beneath, or that is in the water under the earth,"[180] centers the divine as a creative process in the person. The Bible as a whole is, as it were, demonstrating this centering process in order to free man from the demonic compulsion to see God outside fixed into materialism.

The Burning Bush, the Tablets of the Law, and the Golden Calf are all aspects of a whole, manifestations of the equal psychic value of the *hayah*. And again, the poets' creation was not a conscious intention of a rationalizing intellect, but a true, genuine piece of art where the whole is greater than the sum of its parts, the essence revealing itself through itself.

The laws of Sinai written upon the tablets of stone have an antecedent in the famous Hammurabi stele. It is a "pillar of dark stone, some eight feet high and two feet across, and now stands in the Museum of the Louvre, in Paris. It was discovered in 1902 at Susa, near the Persian gulf. . . ." "Its first special interest lies, of course, in the fact that it is the oldest known code of laws. . . . This Code of Hammurabi is known to date from 2270 B.C."[181]

The laws of Sinai were not committed to writing earlier than 700 B.C. and scholars are in no way in agreement as to the authenticity of Moses. However, "he represents in germinal form the whole future life of Israel. Condensed into this one man are the figures of prophet, priest, judge . . . lawgiver, intercessor, victor, exile, fugitive, shepherd, guide, healer, miracle-worker, man of God, and rebel."

> He looms large in the Pentateuch [the five books of Moses], but perhaps the dominant position there results from the piety of later generations of Israelites. If they have not actually created the figure as the nation's founder, perhaps they have magnified his importance and pictured him in such a way as to derive sanction for their own practices and values."[182]

The Code of Hammurabi is dominated by the so-called *lex talionis*, which is also to be found in the Old Testament: "Eye for eye, tooth for tooth," etc.[183] In the Code of Hammurabi Section 197 it is stated, for example, "If any one breaks a man's bone, one shall break his bone."[184] The Sermon on the Mount lifts this age-old law as an expression of the ontogenesis of the psyche into man's heart and mouth, asking him to *face fully the "evil" in himself in order to learn its nature.* "You have heard that it was said, 'An eye for an eye and a tooth for a tooth.' But I say unto you, do not resist one who is evil."[185] "Think not that I have come to abolish the law and the prophets; I have not come to abolish them but to fulfill them."[186]

The Code of Hammurabi shows that injustice, bribery and corruption were part of society's life then, as they are today; but it also underlines through its very existence, as does that of the Sermon on the Mount, that the realization of its content is a major part of the individual's way to his self-actualization, and a guide for the individual to help to establish a responsible society. The Code of Hammurabi as an early law is interesting also in that it shows that basically society has not changed much in central respects from the past. One law, e.g., the malpractice law, as we would call it today, shows also the very structure of the upper, middle, and lower class society of about 2,500 B.C. The law says:

> If a physician treat a man for a severe wound with a bronze knife and heal the man . . . he shall receive ten shekels of silver. If he [the patient] be a freedman, he shall receive five shekels. If it be a man's slave, his owner shall pay the physician two shekels of silver. If a physician treat a man for a severe wound with a bronze knife and kill him, or if he open an abscess [near the eye] and destroy the eye, one shall cut off his hands. [Insurance companies today guard the doctor against such contingencies.] If a physician treat the slave of a freeman for a severe wound with a bronze knife and kill him, he must replace the slave with another [of course of equal value]. If he open an abscess [near the eye] with a bronze knife, and destroy the eye, he shall pay one-half what the slave was worth.[187]

The essence of both the Old and New Testaments and the development of modern scientific theory is enshrined in the *I Am That I Am* as a living process. The covenant of Sinai, the Burning Bush, the Law and its complement, the assimilation of the Golden Calf, the Sermon on the Mount and its symbolical exhortation, "don't resist evil," are the sure guides for the satisfaction of man's yearning to become himself and to gain the dignity of his manhood.

Self-Determination

Self-determination is only possible on the ground of
self-possession. Every authentically human "I will" is
an act of self-determination; it is so not an abstraction and isolation from the dynamic personal structure but, on the contrary, as the deep-rooted content
of this structural whole.[188]

IN GENESIS, the poets amplify the same essential theme:
"the Lord appeared to Abram and said to him: 'I am El
Shaddai; walk before me and be blameless.'"[189] El Shaddai
is given as the name for the deity in places. The King James
Version of the Bible and the Revised Standard, in these
instances, translates it as "God Almighty." Originally, however, the name may have meant "God, the one of the mountains." The poets unleashed and established archetypal
reality: Mt. Olympus, Mt. Moria, Mt. Sinai, Mt. Golgotha
are ever-recurring symbolic manifestations of a *heightened*
awareness. And, as if to justify the poets' insights, "God said
to Moses [on Mt. Sinai]: 'I am the Lord. I appeared to
Abraham, to Isaac and to Jacob as El Shaddai, but by my
name Lord I did not make known myself to them.'"[190]
    At this time, the guiding principle was still, to a large
degree, from behind. With Moses, however, it had reached a
level of formal structure and law, which, as a self-organizing
principle for life has permeated human existence ever since.
The traditional translation of Shaddai as "Almighty" goes
back to an early rabbinic etymology: Self-sufficient! The
ontogenesis of the psyche had reached, at this point, a new

and heightened awareness of the nature of itself, and revealed to itself the laws by which it needed to be governed. In rabbinic tradition, El Shaddai is highlighted as "When I wait with longsuffering patience . . . my name is El Shaddai."[191] God, as El Shaddai behind man ("walk before me"), moves as a guiding principle to the fore in the later development of the psyche, differentiating light and darkness, each complementing the other.

Prof. David Biale established in his essay, "The God With Breasts, El Shaddai in the Bible," that "fertility notions [are] connected to the image of an androgynous God" and wrote that ". . . the possibility that God reflects the whole human condition — and not just its masculine aspect — was already evident to some Biblical authors."[192]

Biale's scholarly analysis lends weight to the depth-psychological approach of our thesis, as does the existence of the four-faced Babylonian god and his four-faced consort [infra, p. 254]. Emanating spontaneously from the depth of unconsciousness the same motif was drawn by a patient — a figure with multiple breasts and a penis — as an autonomous expression of the ontogenesis of the psyche [infra, p. 160]. "The hermaphrodite is a collective symbol found in all cultures, and it stands for a *natural activity of the psyche*, an insistent urge toward structure and form through which opposed energies and inertias are reconciled."[193]

> And the Lord went before them by day in a pillar of cloud to lead them along the way, and by night in a pillar of fire to give them light, that they might travel by day and by night; the pillar of cloud by day and the pillar of fire by night did not depart from before the people.[194]

As El Shaddai in the back of man, "walk before me," moves as a guiding principle to the front and appears as light and darkness, truly a most significant symbol — light and darkness are standing in relation to each other, the light

Figure 8.   Hermaphrodite, from "The Case of Joan," in H. Westman,
The Springs of Creativity, plate 22.

complements the darkness and the cloud or smoke, the light — so Christ steps in front as a guide to man's development as man.

"If any one comes to me and does not hate his own father and mother and wife and children and brothers and sisters, yes, and even his own life, he cannot be my disciple."[195] These stark and somber words raise the issue of man's whole existence. "Walk before me and be blameless"[196] rings in our minds as does the exhortation of the Sermon on the Mount: "You, therefore, must be perfect, as your heavenly Father is perfect"[197] or "Say to all the congregation of the people of Israel, You shall be holy; for I the Lord your God am holy. Every one of you shall revere his mother and father. . . ."[198] "For every one who curses his father or his mother shall be put to death; he has cursed his father or his mother, his blood is upon him."[199]

There seems to be an insoluble problem in the human soul, buffeted as it is between a need to bring peace to the warring claims of one's own becoming and the conflict with the biological history of the race which leads back to time immemorial. In the First Letter of Peter, there is a possible answer, which modern man, however, feels to be incongruous.

> Therefore gird up your minds, be sober, set your hope fully upon the grace that is coming to you at the revelation of Jesus Christ. As obedient children, do not be conformed to the passions of your former ignorance, but as he who called you is holy, be holy yourselves in all your conduct; since it is written "You shall be holy for I am holy."[200]

The enormity of the conflict in man's mind between science and religion, between his own becoming and his escape from freedom, expresses itself in two traditional sayings, the first of which is the Lord's prayer:

Our Father who art in heaven,
Hallowed be thy name.
Thy kingdom come,
Thy will be done,
On earth as it is in heaven.
Give us this day our daily bread;
And forgive us our debts,
As we also have forgiven our debtors;
And lead us not into temptation,
But deliver us from evil.[201]

And in Pirke Abbot, a collection of traditional Jewish sayings:

The ones who are borne are to die.
Against thy will thou are formed.
Against thy will dost thou learn.
Against thy will dost thou live.
Against thy will dost thou die.[202]

The great political and economic events of our time are the reflections of such inner conflicts and of changes now occurring in the innermost depths of society. These changes so affect Western man that he finds himself in the midst of a struggle for a new conception of value thereby influencing existing ideals, and consequently, the religious outlook of society.

Modern man wishes to know! His surrender to the as-yet unknown is superstition to him. Things which are obscure because of his ignorance today might be revealed to him by his science of tomorrow. He sees his fulfillment through the experience of real realities, in a knowledge of the value of values. For him the God who is not experienced, but only conveyed as an abstract message, is dead. "I don't want religion as an escape. It's too unsatisfying for me," is the cry of modern man in need.

The place of faith has been taken today as the desire for knowledge through individual experience. An objective experience of reality is, however, only possible if the material and spiritual planes are equally well apprehended. The discovery of life's laws on the material plane is the task of science. Modern men gathering around temples of science expect their salvation from it, as if scientific planning of economic and social life could alone deliver a message of salvation.

The modern religious problem is therefore dictated by a paradox. The development of science makes it ideally possible to effect the necessary planning of economic life. It is realized that it might be possible on a material plane to arrive at a universal scale of measurement. Man's material necessities for life and his physical condition are basically universal. But it is also realized that there is no "Universal Man"; that there are only individuals. The idea of "Universal Man" is an abstraction of the spiritual qualities of man. Modern man desires to experience the meaning of his life through the uniqueness of his spiritual being and not in accord with an abstraction. The individual becomes responsible for shaping his life on a spiritual plane.

The ever-growing awareness of the world's material interdependence and the consequent search for a new international monetary system is the physical correlative to the spiritual problem of modern man, creating the danger of a tyrannical "golden" oligarchy, if not recognized as such.

The need by the multi-national corporations for international currencies compels them to manipulate the international currency markets and to try to govern governments. The enormous size of their office buildings, be they in New York or Singapore, bear witness to the confluence of material values which dwarf, at this point in time, the person, reducing him to an ineffective and impotent isolated unit. Hitler said to his architect Speer: ". . . our great Movement buildings in Berlin and Nuremberg will make the cathedrals ridiculously small. Just imagine some little peasant coming into our great domed hall in Berlin. That will do more than take his breath away. From then on the man will know where he belongs.[203]

The slow, but ever-growing ethnological movement is beginning to balance the monolithic structure of political dogma. Man's attempt to find his identity and individuality expresses itself in the numerous ethnic moves toward separateness. Consider, for example, the Poles, the French-speaking Canadians, the Walloons and Flemings in Belgium, the Welsh, Scots and English in the British Isles, the various separatist tendencies in Spain and the U.S.S.R., and even the fact that a new Canton has been voted approval in Switzerland.

A most striking example for the vitality and importance of ethnic roots as tenets of identity is the Balkans. Having been released from tutelage under the Turks after 400 years at the end of World War I, the different ethnic groups surfaced without any loss of time and established themselves again. It is a moot point as to whether Yugoslavia, as a political entity, will survive now that President Tito has passed away. At the end of World War II, only a limited number of national states belonged to the United Nations; this number has at least trebled in the course of a few years because of the yearning for ethnic independence.

The ethnological movement, global in character, differentiates itself from mere nationalism because the latter cannot satisfy the need for spiritual roots, as the rise of Islam demonstrates. Western man, awakening to himself, does not accept nationalistic or religious dogma as a substitute for roots. Dogma, by its very nature, is exclusive and not universal, and hence fails in justice. The demand for justice manifests itself, therefore, on ever so many different levels of relationship to intrinsic values.

CHAPTER 4

Awareness

A Biblical Account Of Man's Development As A Social Being

THIS NEED OF MAN expressed itself with "primitive" man in the mythic belief in spirits of the soil. Through the growth of mindful awareness, this belief was lifted in the Old Testament to a more differentiated level. Both the realization of the need for social justice and adherence to incestuous taboos are expressed in stark emotive language; also expressed succinctly is man's deep and abiding closeness to the soil, the land. After having related the "abominations" of incestuous sexual conduct which inhibits the growth of an individual as a person, the Old Testament (Leviticus 19:9) reaches out to justice, from whence it proceeds to the centre and heart of what both the Old and New Testaments express as moral integrity and wholeness: *Love Thy Neighbor As Thyself.* Here is the relevant text of the Revised Standard Version:

> None of you shall approach any one near of kin to him to uncover nakedness. I am the Lord. You shall not uncover the nakedness of your father, which is the nakedness of your mother; she is your mother;

you shall not uncover her nakedness. You shall not uncover the nakedness of your father's wife; it is your father's nakedness. You shall not uncover the nakedness of your sister, the daughter of your father or the daughter of your mother, whether born at home or born abroad. (Leviticus 18:6-9)

Do not defile yourselves by any of these things, for by all these the nations I am casting out before you defiled themselves; and the land became defiled, so that I punished its iniquity, and *the land vomited out its inhabitants.* (Leviticus 18:24-25)

When you reap the harvest of your land, you shall not reap your field to its very border, neither shall you gather the gleanings after your harvest. And you shall not strip your vineyard bare, neither shall you gather the fallen grapes of your vineyard; you shall leave them for the poor and for the sojourner: I am the Lord your God. (Leviticus 19:9-10)

You shall not hate your brother in your heart, but you shall reason with your neighbor, lest you bear sin because of him. *You shall not take vengeance or bear any grudge against the sons of your own people, but YOU SHALL LOVE YOUR NEIGHBOR AS YOURSELF: I am the Lord.* (Leviticus 19:17-18) (Italics mine)

Matthew 5:43-44 of the New Testament says: "You have heard that it was said: 'You shall love your neighbor and hate your enemy.' But I say to you, Love your enemies and pray for those who persecute you." 'Hate your enemy' is an addition which is extraneous to the Old Testament's teaching. Leviticus 19:17 stresses: "You shall not hate your brother . . . but reason with your neighbor."

W. F. Albright and C. S. Mann in their commentary to Matthew 5:43 write:

You shall love your neighbor. This is a quotation from Leviticus 19:18, but the remainder of the verse is oral commentary inferred from the distinction drawn in the post-Exilic period between dealings with Jews on the one hand and dealings with Gentiles on the other. All such distinction is here made impossible for the disciples. All men are neighbors to the man who has assumed the responsibilities of discipleship.[1]

It is of significance to note that Albright translates *teleios* in Matthew 5:48 as "You therefore must be *true*, as your heavenly father is *true*" and not as *perfect* as it is normally done [infra, p. 396, see also n. 5].

The ancient law of *lex talionis*, "an eye for an eye," is a juridical expression [supra, p. 156] and is lifted both in Leviticus 19:17 and Matthew 5:39 into the inner realm of man's need to become aware of "primitive," unreflected reactions. The passage reads: "You have heard that it was said, 'An eye for an eye and a tooth for a tooth.' But I say to you do not resist one who is evil." Through man's becoming aware *of his* potential "evil," through this process of integrating these forces into his consciousness, he is able to choose.

The same essential theme of choice, as in Leviticus 18:25 "... lest the land vomit you out," is sounded on a higher level of the psyche's awareness in Revelation 3:15-16 and 20-22:

I know your works: you are neither cold nor hot. Would that you were cold or hot! So, because you are lukewarm and neither cold nor hot, I will *spew you out of my mouth.* . . . Behold, I stand at the door and knock; If any one hears my voice and opens the door, I will come in to him and eat with him and he with me. He who conquers, I will grant him to sit with me on my throne, as I myself conquered [Temptations, Matthew 4:7-11] and sat down with my

Father on his throne. He who has an ear, let him hear
what the Spirit says to the Churches. (Italics mine)

The poets express the way to salvation, i.e., the psyche's
urge to grow and to become as *hayah,* or in Jesus' sayings:

I have not come to bring peace, but a sword. For I
have come to set a man against his father, and a
daughter against her mother.... He who loves father
or mother more than me is not worthy of me; and he
who does not take his cross and follow me is not
worthy of me. (Matthew 10:34)

Both Leviticus 18:28 and Revelation 3:16 say essentially
the same: unless your incestuous attitude cease, you cannot
be my disciple, i.e., you cannot really become yourself and
grow as a person. Therefore "the land will vomit you out"
(Leviticus 18:28) and "I will spew you out of my mouth"
(Revelation 3:16) express the freeing of the psyche's containment in Hades — the underworld of unconsciousness with
all uncertainties.

If taken literally, the saying "If any one comes to me and
does not hate his own father and mother and wife and
children and brothers and sisters, and even his own life, he
cannot be my disciple" (Luke 14:26) is impossible to square
with Matthew 19:19: "Honor your father and mother, and,
You shall love your neighbor as yourself." However,
approached not in a fundamentalist sense or rationally or
analytically, but from a structural hermeneutical point of
view, the darkness lifts and reveals itself as stages in the
ontogenesis of the psyche, anticipating all modern psychological theories. The answer to the Freudian father, mother,
sister or brother complexes was anticipated by the Bible's
poets by more than 2,000 and by the Babylonian's "knowers" by about 4,500 years in their epic drama *Enuma Elish*.[2]

The security once felt by the masses through belonging to
a universal spiritual principle no longer exists. Security once
found its expression in the idea of an all-embracing Church,

an institution which today no longer casts its spell over a great majority.

In our time, the ideal is to obtain security through the realization of a universal economic structure which will exercise humanitarian principles, and establish it on the plane of material reality. Security, however, cannot be achieved by solely material factors. There remains the as yet unresolved problem of spiritual security, which has now become essentially an individual problem.

Today it is more and more clearly realized that social morality differs from that appropriate to the individual. Social morality is basically opportunist, while the morality of an individual is conditioned by his quality. It was formerly the chief task of the Church to provide the universal principle through which the individual could deal with his "sins." The rise of the awareness that the spirituality of each individual is unique confronts modern man with the necessity of finding a new solution to this problem by himself. To do so may become an integral part of modern religion, as it recognizes the importance of each individual's relationship to his own inner law.

As long as no consciousness of the "divine" in man existed, it was reasonable that the divine law should be represented by projection (mythology), or based upon group experience (taboo). The divine impulse was felt to be extraneous to the individual. God's abode was in heaven. Modern man's development, however, which made the creation of science possible, in turn deprived the phenomena of the external world of their divine character. The divine impulse is therefore now no longer seen as external to man. It has now become enshrined in the inner life, or more accurately, its real seat has now come properly within human awareness. "Christ within us" was once simply an article of faith. Now, this conception has become a *necessary experience* for those to whom a spiritual life is to have any meaning at all, and who will accept the responsibility which this new awareness places on their shoulders.

Where modern man feels that responsibility and submits himself to this experience, he realizes that there is no universal scale of measurement for the divine impulse within him. It lays down its own standard inasmuch as it expresses itself in the quality of the individual. The surrender to this individual quality is consummation, since modern spiritual life derives its value from the quality inherent in each person.

Spiritual reality is no longer conditioned by the commandments or abstractions of an external God. Modern man has reached a level where redemption is possible in so far as he can fulfill the quality of his individual being.

On the other hand, the failure of the universal standards of redemption are painfully demonstrated in wars, tyrannies, and the manifold evils of our time. Redemption for modern man is redemption in order to live — redemption from dogmatic constraints and frustrations, whether they be political or religious, and which hinder the realization of the manifold possibilities of life.

A new ethos awakes to the extent that the individual surrenders to the powers of the inner demand, wherein his redemption lies. This ethos leads to the discovery of the laws of his own person. Not the universal but his own inner code becomes the standard. Violation of the inner law not only means the loss of a genuine and natural relationship to the Self, but it is also a loss which leads to unhappiness, and brings about an unsatisfactory relationship to life in general. The fulfillment of individual quality, however, gives birth to a meaningful life, even when renunciation and consequent grief are involved. This sacrifice is basically a voluntary one, as it is related to the individual's own inner sense, and not to an external postulate.

The danger of "God identification" is counteracted by the new consciousness which makes each person recognize not only his own personality, but also his limitations. It permits him to discover that his personality is the result of the confrontation of the uniqueness of his being with the impersonal or archetypal aspects of his spiritual inheritance.

To make acquaintance with one's Self may become a rich part of life if one feels inclined to participate in the responsible creation of a new approach to life. The realization of Self differs from neurotic narcissism, as it is essentially a cultural task and not an escape from life. Its inner meaning is to give expression to the spiritual development of modern times as well as to attain a fuller life. Individuation is far from being an unworldly mysticism, for it is related to the actual facts of the individual's being and not to the theoretical abstractions of impersonal ideas.

The more mature the individual becomes — that is, the more one's own latent possibilities become differentiated and developed — the more independent one becomes of a mythology reaching out into extra-human, metaphysical realms. The mature personality is able to carry his own God and give expression to his inner divine quality in the actuality of his daily life. His values have the quality of reality and are not lost in a maze of abstractions.

Escapism from the Self was encouraged unconsciously by the religious institutions of the past because one of their aims was to bring about redemption through the establishment of universal principles. Consequently, straying into universal metaphysical worlds followed. The actual experience of the Self, as a religious experience, is inexpressible. It is formed of a quality which cannot be comprehended by the intellectual function alone. Therefore, to intellectualize it in verbal forms is most inadequate. The rational aspect is merely a part of the totality of human perception and is therefore unable to express the whole of which it is itself only a part. Feeling and intuition, being integral parts of the experience, cannot be "thought."

To experience the divine within himself provides for modern man a sense of security, a sense of being embedded in a meaningful existence. To relate his individual spirituality to the universal becomes a fulfillment. This development of modern man, and with it, that of his individual religion, enables him to experience the value of values relative to himself as well as to the impersonal, archetypal background of his being. For modern man, to fail means not to be guilty in relation to the assumption of "original sin," but rather to be divided within and against one's self.

The chaos and anarchism of our time is not the result of individuals who, following their own inner law, reject the social and religious dogmas of the past. On the contrary, participation in the spirit of our time seems to be the only directive which will call to man's attention the hedonistic and narcissistic expectations which have led to the emptiness and meaninglessness of existence and thence to anarchism.

The spiritual development of modern man which has led him into new knowledge and an awareness of the freedom of the Self, has confronted him, therefore, with the basic issue presented by formalized religion. "Our Father which art in heaven . . . thy will be done," reflects the problem. It has been assumed that dogmatic religion represents the divine will, and that the religious impulse is fulfilled in response to the externals of religious teachings. To be sure, the old forms envelop and graciously receive those who are still able to completely efface themselves in following what they conceive to be the will of God. Those, however, for whom the impact of our time has created new religious forms, experience the external manifestations of the divine impulse as projections.

Through this immense advance, the fulfillment of the "Father's word by the Son" is lifted, in the dissolution of these projections, into the sphere of intrinsic legality as the individual becomes mature. The reversal of the old standards of value is a manifestation of human growth toward personal responsibility and self-determination for the spiritual life, and is therefore, an answer to the perplexities of our time. The individual's acceptance of his cultural task is his personal fulfillment as he becomes his own authority. Thus, one earns the dignity of personhood, fulfilling "The Word of the Lord" and imparting the ultimate, responsible, ethical meaning of the "son" becoming "man." The universal spiritual principle, having become intensely personal, now loses its character as "the Unknown God."

"Set your affections on things above and not on things on earth. For ye are dead and your life is hid with Christ in God," is a text which no longer inspires modern man. The knowledge of his individual value with regard to the spiritual plane animates him today, as does his science on the material plane. As the New Testament developed from the Old, so belief finds its evolution in the desire for knowledge and for the most intimate individual experience of the divine impulse. Life is experienced in ever-renewed cycles. While appearing to change, the new reveals itself as an aspect of the old.

The essence of both the Old and the New Testaments is expressed in a poem attributed to Isaiah who lived about 700 B.C. Spiraling upwards around the ontogenesis of the psyche as its core, and reaching out toward an infinite past as well as an infinite future, Isaiah proclaims:

> It shall come to pass in the latter days
> that the mountain of the house of the Lord
> shall be established as the highest of the mountains,
> and shall be raised above the hills;
> and all the nations shall flow to it,
> and many peoples shall come, and say:
> "Come, let us go up to the mountain of the Lord,
> to the house of the God of Jacob;
> that he may teach us his ways
> and that we may walk in his paths . . ."
> He shall judge between the nations,
> and shall decide for many peoples;
> *and they shall beat their swords into plowshares,*
> and their spears into pruning hooks;
> nation shall not lift up sword against nation,
> neither shall they learn war any more.
> O house of Jacob, come,
> let us walk in the light of the Lord.[3]

It is of significance to note that Pope John Paul I used this passage in his homily at the time of his installation.

The principle of Maat and Melchizedek crowns this message as an essential hope: "And they shall beat their swords into plowshares. . . ." Lifted to a heightened awareness, the temple of insight is placed symbolically on a mountain. But most important is its specific relationship to the figure of Jacob: "O house of Jacob, come, let us walk in the light of the Lord . . . that he may teach us his ways and that we may walk in his paths."

The Jacob-Esau Story

THE JACOB-ESAU epic underlying the Isaiah poem is of the greatest significance, depicting as it does the ontogenetic principle in its most rarified dimensions. The story is an experiential truth of greatest significance. Just as modern science has added the poetic, aesthetic dimension in its efforts to understand the phenomena of life, so the Jacob-Esau legend reveals its nature when it is approached with the tools of research developed by modern science and applies it to its own self-understanding. Approached only analytically, the epic at best reveals its composite nature. Scholars generally agree that the stories were originally separate legends, later combined into a coherent opus by the sages of the past.

At the beginning, the various stories were most probably popular in various districts, such as Bethel or Haran. A structural analysis reveals that perhaps Genesis 25:21-27, 32:4 and 33:17 are the real center of the Jacob tradition. Jacob's name is most probably originally theophorous, i.e., a combination, and not only as it is etymologically understood in the Bible itself. "Afterward his brother came forth, and his hand had taken hold of Esau's heel; so his name was called Jacob."[4] (That is, "he takes by the heel," or "he supplants.") The name Jacob was common in Palestine and in Mesopotamia. Graves and Patai give this account:

> The explanation of the name *Israel* in Genesis 32:29 is popular etymology. In theophorous titles, the element containing the deity's name is the subject, not the object. Israel therefore means "El strives," rather than "He strove with El"; just as the original form of Jacob, Ya-qobel, means "El protects" . . . and just as the original meaning of Jerubbaal was not "He fights against Baal" (Judges 6:32), but "Baal fights." The intention of names such as these was to enlist divine help for those who bore them. *Israel* thus meant "El strives against my enemies." The prime enemy to be faced by Jacob upon crossing the Jabbok was his twin Esau, from whose just anger he had fled twenty years before.[5]

Experienced in terms of a structural hermeneutic, however, the story reveals why it has become the ground of, and one of the most central events for, both the Old and New Testaments. The epic demonstrates the underlying problems of man's voyage to himself —his inner conflicts and their resolution.

The psyche in its ever-renewed upward and downward spiraling creativity produced the Isaiah poem, which on a different level of becoming, also integrated the warring parts of the human psyche as does the Jacob-Esau story. In the poetic phrase ". . . they shall beat their swords into plowshares," the very basis for war, narrowness of outlook and greed, are being transformed from the depth of being itself. The lengthy part of this story, the motivation of Jacob's flight to Laban, and the subsequent interaction of Jacob and Laban, is all too human a story. Jacob is described as a deceived deceiver, one who lied and was lied to, one who cheated and was cheated. And in all this, he was not acting out of his own direction, but out of dependency upon his mother.

This is not a very pretty picture, to be sure, but it is a true symbiosis of man's nature in action and reaction. Poetically expressed, Jacob's awareness was born of a dream which showed him the interrelatedness between heaven and earth, the above and the below. "He dreamed that there was a ladder set up on the earth, and the top of it reached to heaven; and behold, the angels of God were ascending and descending on it!" When Jacob awoke, he said: "'Surely the Lord is in this place; and I did not know it.' And he was afraid, and said, 'How awesome is this place! This is none other than the House of God, and this is the gate of heaven.'"[6]

Just as Kingu in the *Enuma Elish* is dependent upon the mother,[7] symbolizing a stage in the development of man, so does Jacob symbolize the same. Tiamat took her son, Kingu, as her husband.

> She gave him the tablet of destinies,
>   she fastened (it) upon his breast, (saying):
> "As for thee, thy command shall not be changed,
>   (the word of thy mouth) shall be dependable!"[8]

The psyche, in its upward-spiraling creativity, expresses the same truth on a higher level of development, reflected in Luke as earlier demonstrated: "If anyone comes to me and does not hate his own father and mother and wife and children and brothers and sisters, yes, and even his own life, he cannot be my disciple. Whoever does not bear his own cross and come after me, cannot be my disciple."[9]

But even more than the multi-dimensionality of the story, the most vital link with the beginning of animated life, as far as we know it today, is the very center of the epic.

"Once when Jacob was boiling pottage, Esau came in from the field, and he was famished. And Esau said to Jacob, 'Let me eat some of that red pottage, for I am famished!' ... Jacob said, 'First sell me your birthright.' Esau said, '*I am about to die*; of what use is a birthright to me?'"[10] The Hebrew word for *pottage* used here is *haadam*,

literally "the red fruitful earth." Esau, specifically and point-
edly, is prepared to exchange his birthright for that *red,*
because *"I am about to die."* With this all-important statement, the relation between death, birthright, and the *red* is
clearly established.

Pointing back to the very beginnings of animated life, the
red — red earth, red ochre — has been a symbol from time
immemorial reflecting, as we have indicated earlier, the
eternal renewal of life. Lacking the data of modern science
and anthropology, and prompted only by archetypal
insights, the poets and Hebrew sages who composed the
original epic referred to the interrelatedness of the *red* with
death and rebirth. According to Ginzberg: "The reason they
are used for the mourners' meal is that the round lentil
symbolizes death: as the lentil rolls, so death, sorrow, and
mourning constantly roll about among men, from one to the
other."[11]

Only recently, an ancient Jewish burial place was discovered in the hills of Jericho. The ossuaries and coffins stem
from the 1st century B.C. to the 6th A.D. On the ossuaries,
in which the bones of the dead were buried after the body
had decomposed, "red paint was often added to the decoration." The decoration consisted of "two or three rosettes
within a frame."[12]

The rosette is a symbol of wholeness, and is particularly
evident in the Sassoon Bible, one of the rare examples of a
Hebrew Bible illustrated by Jews. The British Museum
Bible from the 15th century A.D. contains exactly the same
kind of rosettes, formed by Hebrew letters!

The Jacob-Esau story in its dense symbolism overarches
life in its essence — beginning with the birth of an essential
duality of character, moving through the experience of
becoming as an integration of the duality, and then on to
life's finality, we see both death and the hope for rebirth.

This hope for rebirth is expressed in the Old Testament in
Daniel 12:2: "And many of those who sleep in the dust of the
earth shall awake, some to everlasting life . . ." Through the

Figure 9.   Limestone Ossuary, Jericho, 100 B.C.-600 A.D., from *The Biblical Archaeology Review,* July-August 1979, p. 31.

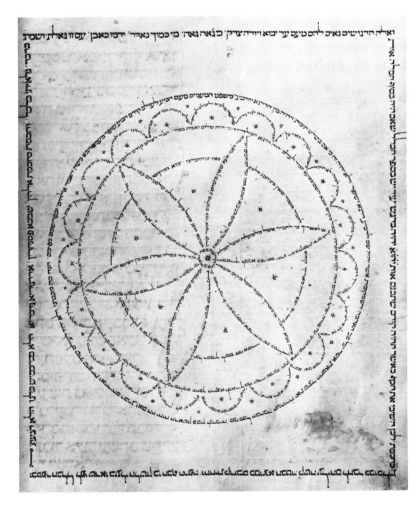

Figure 10. 15th century Rosette, formed by Hebrew letters.

Pharisees, "belief in a personal and physical resurrection eventually evolved into a fundamental principle of Jewish faith."[13]

Archaelogical findings show that in burial places of early Cananites (3,100 - 2,900 B.C.) *"the bones seemed to have been covered with red ochre* . . . In these burials the bones may have been painted red in order to return to them some life-force . . ."[14]

At Aby Hureyra, a pre-Neolithic farmer's village on the Euphrates, (20,000 - 8,500 B.C.) artifacts were found which the Mesolithic occupants had used.

> Prominent among the artifacts were stone pestles, rubbing stones and milling stones. Many of them were stained with red ochre, evidence that they had been used for crushing this decorative pigment into powder. The presence of the milling implements in the pit dwellings and hollows suggests that they were also used to process plant foods.[15]

A further proof of the actuality of the age-old archetypal belief of rebirth, are the apparent fertility goddesses of pre-Ice Age art, about 25,000 B.C.

> Similar images that date from the Ice Age have been found in Italy, Austria, Czechoslovakia and the Ukraine. Images of naked females in a somewhat different style have been found at Ice Age sites in Siberia. The images often show the polish of long use and, at times, the remains of *red ochre* which indicates that they were often symbolically painted.[16]

"For the primitive world, the sacred means not only everything that we now understand by religion, but also the whole body of the tribe's mythological and cultural tradition." Initiation rituals mean therefore not only the separation from the mother, but also "to introduce the candidate to the cultural mode, i.e., to spiritual values." In an Australian ritual "the novices are seized by their guardians and carried off to the forest, where they are daubed with *red ochre.*"[17]

Clearly the Australian ritual differentiates the source of life from the mother and refers it to the initiate; while in the Ice Age art this differentiation had not yet taken place.

As far back as it is possible for us to see today, man as a participant in the annual renewal of nature held a hope for personal rebirth. As the growth of conciousness is dependent upon linguistic expression, so is mythological awareness expressed in symbols and ritual actions appropriate to the level of experiential development.

In a remarkable find in El Juyo, Spain, a sanctuary was unearthed, which is dated 12,000 B.C., a date confirmed by Carbon 14 tests. This sanctuary not only shows isolated aspects of a practiced religion, but a religious system as a whole. "The complex was constructed to impress an audience of living people." There was discovered a head which showed two distinct halves in his face: ". . . . half wild beast, half man . . . . The admirably harmonic fusion of these two natures in a single figure would be a graphic representation of their integration during the individuation process."[18] Eliade has observed that the reconciliation of opposed principles is among the oldest and most widely diffused symbols of "the paradoxical state of the totality, the perfection, and consequently, the sacredness of God."[19]

John Canady in his essay "The Greek Who Bore Gifts To All Mankind" wrote that El Greco, in his superb art succeeded in,

> . . . separat[ing the earthly and heavenly units] spiritually by dividing a single picture into two contrasting styles — while maintaining the picture's unity. Supernatural bursts of light and *weightlessness* that allowed heavenly figures to levitate or sit upon clouds were considered sufficient differentiation between the two worlds. Otherwise, the two halves were painted with the same degree of realism."[20]

Figure 11.   Sculpted face, El Juyo sanctuary.

Figure 12. Unicorn in the Lap of a Lady.

In Plato's *Republic* the theme of justice, i.e., balance and harmony like a distant song from the depth of becoming human, is sounded. The apparent harmony of the El Juyo face is lifted onto still another level of integration as an expression of the *hayah,* the ontogenesis of the psyche. The quotation runs:

> Since we are at this point in the argument, let's take up again the first things said, those thanks to which we have come here. It was, I believe, said that doing injustice is profitable for the man who is perfectly unjust but has the reputation of being just. Or isn't that the way it was said?
>
> "Yes, it was."
>
> "Now then," I said, "let's discuss with him, since we have agreed about the respective powers of doing injustice and doing just things."
>
> "How?" he said.
>
> "By molding an image of the soul in speech so that the man who says these things will see just what he has been saying."
>
> "What sort of image?" he said.
>
> "One of those natures such as the tales say used to come into being in olden times — the Chimera, Scylla, Cerberus, and certain others, a throng of them, which are said to have been many *ideas* grown naturally together in one."
>
> "Yes," he said, "they do tell of such things."
>
> "Well then, mold a single *idea* for a many-colored, many-headed beast that has a ring of heads of tame and savage beasts and can change them and make all of them grow from itself."
>
> "That's a job for a clever molder," he said. "But, nevertheless, since speech is more easily molded than wax and the like, consider it as molded."
>
> "Now, then, mold another single *idea* for a lion, and a single one for a human being. Let the first be by

far the greatest and the second, second in size."

"That's easier," he said, "and the molding is done."

"Well then, join them — they are three-in-one, so that in some way they grow naturally together with each other."

"They are joined," he said.

"Then mold about them on the outside an image of one — that of the human being — so that to the man who's not able to see what's inside, but sees only the outer shell, it looks like one animal, a human being."

"The outer mold is in place," he said.

"Then let's say to the one who says that it's profitable for this human being to do injustice, and that it's not advantageous for him to do just things, that he's affirming nothing other than that it is profitable for him to feast and make strong the manifold beast and the lion and what's connected with the lion, while starving the human being and making him weak so that he can be drawn wherever either of the others leads and does not habituate them to one another or make them friends but lets them bite and devour each other."[21]

In Plato not only the awareness of man's interrelatedness with his biological past is indicated, but also the past, the animal in him as the "conditioner" for his unjust actions. The integration as anticipated in the face of El Juyo as a process of perfecting, is also the "mythological" theme of the Bible. In El Juyo we are finding the essential theme more than 11,000 years before Plato wrote his *Republic* and about 12,000 years before the Book of Revelation saw the "beast rising out of the sea with ten horns and seven heads." And "men worshipped the dragon . . . saying 'Who is like the beast, and who can fight against it?'"[22] In the Book of Daniel, which is roughly contemporaneous with Plato, it is said:

> After this I saw in the night visions, and behold, a fourth beast, terrible and dreadful and exceedingly strong; and it had great iron teeth; it devoured and broke in pieces, and stamped the residue with its feet. ... it had ten horns. I considered the horns, and behold, there came up among them another horn, a little one, before which three of the first horns were plucked up by the roots; and behold, in this horn were eyes like the eyes of a man, and a mouth speaking great things ... I saw in the night visions, and behold, with the clouds of heaven *there came one like a son of man.*[23]

In Plato's "Dialogue," significantly, the *hayah* as the principle of choice, of self-correction, the "Hypercycle" is at work in the deepest recesses of the human soul. "Well then, mold a single idea for a many-colored, many-headed beast that has a ring of heads of tame and savage beasts and *can change them* and make all of them grow from itself."

The artist with his imagination and acute insight [supra, p.177] provided in 1472 A.D. with his images at the frontispiece of the Bible its essence: the *hayah,* the ontogenesis of the psyche, its growth toward maturity.

The symbol of rejuvenation, of rebirth, heads the page: the deer which, like the snake changing its skin, sheds its antlers and renews them yearly. The second illustration shows Adam and Eve, who by eating the apple, *"you will be like God,* knowing good and evil,"[24] have acquired the discerning power of differentiation. Through this assimilation something new has entered the field of experience of the psyche. The artist conveys this "new" through the snake's head — it is a child's face and not a vicious stare. The third illumination at the bottom of the page, as if it were the foundation of the Bible's teaching, shows a unicorn in the lap of a lady [infra, p. 436]: the irreconcilable has become reconciled; the ferocity of untameable nature has become a peaceful complement and together they portray a symbol of wholeness.

Important details of the archetypal theme of development have been found in El Juyo, just as they are present in both the Old and New Testaments. Remnants of a *red* deer and a roe deer were discovered. They are reminiscent of the *red* animals which were used in purification rites both in the Old Testament, in Greece and elsewhere. For the Huichol Indians, Sierra Madre, Mexico:

> The deer [are] *the* most sacred beings in the animal world . . . no ceremony or major agricultural act could commence without a prior ceremonial deer hunt. . . . [The Huichol believe] that life resides in the bones and that the deer will be reborn from its skeletal parts . . . that the bones are the seat of life, and that rebirth proceeds as much from one's bones as the life of a tree springs from the hard seed — universally called "bone" in Mesoamerica — contained within the flesh of a fruit. These concepts of the bone soul and rebirth from one's skeletal parts are characteristics of shamanic ideology the world over."[25]

Colloquially we say: 'I feel it in my bones'; the bones are therefore also "besouled" [infra, p. 381].

The Huichol Indians portray in their sacred art, still today, the symbol of the red deer. "All sacred things are symbols to primitive man, and the Huichols have literally no end of them. Religion to them is a personal matter, not an institution, and therefore their life is religious — from the cradle to the grave wrapped up in symbolism."[26]

Eliade writes: "The ambivalence of the divinity is a theme constant to the whole religious history of humanity. . . . The gods reveal themselves as at once benevolent and terrible."[27] As we shall see later, the Greek goddess Artemis of Ephesus, for example, is portrayed with both the symbols of: (a) the benevolence of creative giving — the multiple breasts, and of (b) terrible, fierce beasts adorning her figure [infra, p. 438]. The Christian abstraction of God as the *summum bonum,* the sum of all good, is not upheld in the other great religions of mankind. Awareness of being in the world results in the consciousness of duality, i.e., we can realize light only through the existence of darkness or vice versa, and the male through the existence of the female.

The Bible, true to its basic significance as a way of becoming, exemplifies Jesus as the unifier of irreconcilables, e.g., fire and water. In Matthew 17:15 and Mark 9:22 Jesus heals an epileptic who "suffers terribly; for often he falls into the fire, and often into the water." The significance of this essential theme of the reconciliation of opposed principles is an expression of the *hayah,* the becoming through change. As an inner, mental reality it is superbly expressed in Matthew 3:11: "I baptize you with water for repentance, but he who is coming after me . . . will baptize you with the Holy Spirit and with fire," i.e., the fire as a principle of change and not of destruction. Etymologically expressed, the healing process is that of becoming healthy: whole, healthy and holy have the same root: *hale!*

The Old Testament expresses the divine also in complementarities: in Genesis 1:1 it is said that "God *created* the heavens and the earth" and in Deuteronomy 4:24, "The Lord your God is a *devouring* fire."

"The reconciliation of opposed principles" has found a supreme expression some 15,000 years after the creation of the El Juyo sanctuary in the Buddhist temple at Borobudur, Java, built around 750 A.D. As in modern physics opposites are experienced as complementarities, each mirroring the other, so in Borobudur the apprehending of the essence of life is seen as "mirrorlike knowledge."

> The ability to view reality in terms of mental phenomena [is expressed in mandalas]. They are diagrams with a supreme deity . . . at the center, secondary deities on the *four* [!] sides . . . [W]hen mandalas began to be used as meditational aids . . . it was realized . . . that the pictured deities merely

Figure 13. Temple at Borobudur, Java, ca. 750 A.D.

stood for certain mental qualities, like "mirror-like Knowledge," and had no real existence outside the mind.

In Shingon Buddism [a Japanese sect] there are two mandalas. . . . One of the Shingon mandalas is called the womb mandala, the other the diamond mandala.

The womb mandala stands for the real world, the diamond mandala for the ideal world.

There is a unity behind this duality, and it can be found at Borobudur. The enlightened know that the two mandalas cannot exist independently. Their ultimate nature is that of Mahāvairocana, the name of the supreme cosmic Buddha of the Shingon Buddhists.[28]

Thus the Borobudur sanctuary is held to be an architectural structure mirroring that of the mind. Heinrich Zimmer writes: ". . . one is entitled to call Borobudur the greatest mandala which the art of Buddhism ever achieved to present to the world as an image of its truth.[29]

The basic complementarities of Existence, Life and Death, inner and outer reality, and the essence of life's *hayah,* its becoming, are expressed in these dynamic symbols. The resurrection idea, seen in this context, is then an expression of the mental effort to find a reconciliation of the contraries in the hope of the continuance of Life.

The archetypal belief in rebirth and resurrection was in the past symbolized by the use of red ochre. In modern times this ritual has found a different form, yet with the same essential meaning.

> Perhaps the most telling indication of the failure of Soviet religious restrictions comes in a statistical detail. The Patriarchate annually prints and distributes over 1 million 'garlands and prayers,' paper strips inscribed with religious pictures and text that are placed in the coffin during Orthodox funerals. Since that is roughly 60% of the annual U.S.S.R. mortality rate, such a large-scale printing can only mean that however irreligious they are supposed to be in life, Russians still are drawn to the church in death.[30]

The impressive Buddhist temple of Borobudur, Zen Buddhistic theology, the Chinese symbol of Yin and Yang, symbolizing the female and male principles of the inner life, portray the message of the integration of complementarities as an eternal dance of daily rebirth. The Chinese symbol is of particular significance in that the half in white is separated by a waved line from the other half in black. These halves contain each their own opposite within themselves — the white a black dot and black a white one.

Whether it is the Eastern approach or the face of El Juyo,

Yin and Yang

each in its own way demonstrates the essential message of the integration of complementarities, of change. But so also do Christian teachings. According to the Coptic Gospel of Thomas:

> They said to Him: Shall we then, being children, enter the Kingdom? Jesus said to them: When you make the two one, and when you make the inner as the outer and the outer as the inner and the above as the below, and when you make the male and the female into a single one so that the male will not be male and the female [not] be female . . . then you shall enter [the Kingdom].[31]

By "Kingdom" seems to be meant the knowledge of the workings and participation in the inner life. In Matthew 18:3 the same motif of change is alluded to: "Truly I say to you, unless you *turn* and become like children, you will never enter the Kingdom of heaven" (italics mine).

This turning, this change, is then stressed as a vital motif in both the Old and New Testaments, as the record of the ontogenesis of the psyche:

> Jesus said: Whoever is near to me is near to the fire, and whoever is far from me is far from the Kingdom.[32]

And fire, says Bronowski, is a "process of transformation and change, by which material elements are rejoined into new combinations. The nature of the chemical process was only understood when fire itself came to be understood as a process."[33]

Thomas the seer and Bronowski the scientist record within the context of their respective fields of awareness the ontogenesis of the psyche and demonstrate the efficacy of the *hayah*, the "to be," the becoming a human being in the fullest sense.

> And the angel of the Lord appeared to him in a flame
> of fire out of the midst of a bush; and he looked, and
> lo, the bush was burning, yet it was not consumed.[34]

This "mirrorlike knowledge" of transubstantiation found its supreme example in the twins of Jacob and Esau.

> Esau accosted Jacob thus, "Why art thou preparing
> lentils?" Jacob: "Because our grandfather has passed
> away; they shall be a sign of my grief and mourning,
> that he may love me in the days to come." Esau:
> "Thou fool! Dost thou really think it possible that
> man should come to life again after he has been dead
> and has mouldered in the grave?"[35]

This legend expresses the kernel of deepest religiosity: Death and Resurrection, Reality and Belief. It has been held that on such a cornerstone, the turning point of world history hinges, based on I Corinthians 15:13-19:

> ... if there is no resurrection of the dead, then Christ
> has not been raised; if Christ has not been raised,
> then our preaching is in vain and your faith is in vain.
> We are even found to be misrepresenting God,
> because we testified of God that he raised Christ,
> whom he did not raise if it is true that the dead are
> not raised. For if the dead are not raised, then Christ
> has not been raised. If Christ has not been raised,

your faith is futile and you are still in your sins. Then those also who have fallen asleep in Christ have perished. If in this life we who are in Christ have only hope, we are of all men most to be pitied.

In the supreme doubt expressed by these words of Paul, the searching mind transcends the mythological inheritance. Many scholars are convinced that the outline of Christ's life as mirrored in the Gospel stories has its roots in Babylonian legends, i.e., the Gilgamesh Epic, the Marduk mythologies and in particular Tammuz, the Babylonian god of the renewal of vegetation and the fertility of the herds (e.g., Christ as shepherd).[36]

The question of evidence occupies not only the minds of scholars of comparative religion, but, naturally, the minds of theologians as well.

It was the appearances which, according to our evidence, transformed the apostles. If we do not accept that the appearances produced the belief, then we have to postulate that the belief produced the appearances. They then become, if not pure hallucinations, at any rate the projections, objectivizations, of an already formed conviction that Jesus was alive and sovereign: the disciples believed themselves into seeing. But this still leaves unexplained where they derived the idea that he could be alive — nothing, on the face of it, seems to have been further from their minds. Moreover, the accounts of the appearances betray no trace of mass suggestion, but (except in the case of the five hundred brethren at once) speak of separate manifestations to persons and other groups who show no signs of suggestibility or hysteria; . . . In contrast with the empty tomb, the resurrection appearances look far less tangible as evidence. It can never be proved that they were seen except by those who were previously prepared to believe.[37]

In the statement above, so typical of theologians, there is an ignorance of the way the mind experiences and functions. In particular, it portrays "the misunderstandings of the Church." In a book by that title, Prof. Emil Brunner writes:

> The Holy Ghost seizes the heart, not merely the *nous* (Gr. nous, *noos*, mind, intelligence, perception): it pierces the heart until it reaches the depths of the unconscious and even the physical constituents of personality. Theology is not the instrument best adapted to elucidate just *this* aspect of pneumatic manifestations. For theo-*logy* has to do with the Logos and therefore is only qualified to deal with matters which are in some way logical, not with the dynamic in its a-logical characteristics. Therefore the Holy Ghost has always been more or less the step-child of theology and the dynamism of the Spirit a bugbear for theologians; on the other hand, theology through its unconscious intellectualism has often proved a significant restrictive influence, stifling the operations of the Holy Ghost, or at least their full creative manifestation.[38]

A dependency on rationality alone fixes the mind on the material dimension — the physical body — and results in projecting "the living God" thereon. It provides the basis for a completely materialistic philosophy. *Hence the strained effort of the psyche to satisfy its vital need for its own transubstantiation.* The unique individual experience of spirituality becomes imprisoned in a universal doctrine of belief. "Universal," however, refers only to the material aspect of his being. Man's bondage to this dogma disallows him to experience his "daily renewal" and to be open for change. "Set your mind on things that are above, not on things that are on earth. For you have died and your life is hid with Christ in God" does not describe any actual experience.[39] St. Paul also wrote in the same letter to the Colossians (2:12): ". . . and you were buried with him in baptism, in which you were also raised with him through faith in the working of God, who raised him from the dead."

Baptism is a symbolic ritual act which derives whatever meaning it may have only from an intensely personal experience of change and growth, in the context of a uniquely individual mental state. As a mere ritual, it is not efficacious; if it were, the Western world would long since have become an ethically different place than we see it today. On the other hand, in Mark 12:26-27, Jesus says:

> And as for the dead being raised, have you not read in the book of Moses, in the passage about the bush, how God said to him, "I am the God of Abraham, and the God of Isaac, and the God of Jacob?" *He is not God of the dead, but of the living* . . . (Italics mine)

Spiritual experiences are only meaningful in terms of personal symbolism, which in turn derives its meaning from the context in which the experience takes place. Religious teachings are regarded with doubt in our time precisely because they are based on abstractions, i.e., the accounts of experiences for which there is no "proof" apart from the testimony of a tradition which has heaped interpretation on interpretation of what was a presumption in the first instance. And ultimately, the interpretations are dogmatically presented as factual.

In order to help solve this conundrum of rebirth in our time of tranquilizers, an hypothesis has been put forward:

> His [Jesus'] whole ministry was purposeful, masterful and practical . . . it is difficult to credit that he had neglected to do anything about the supreme crisis of his career, when it was imperative that he should outwit the forces arrayed against him and wrest victory from the very jaws of death. . . . Two things, however, were indispensable to the success of a rescue operation. The first was to administer a drug

to Jesus on the cross to give the impression of prema-
ture death, and the second was to obtain the speedy
delivery of the body to Joseph. . . . If what he
received had been the normal wine vinegar diluted
with water the effect would have been stimulating. In
this case it was exactly the opposite. Jesus lapsed
quickly into complete unconsciousness. His body
sagged. His head lolled on his breast, and to all
intents and purposes he was a dead man. . . . As
arranged Jesus was conveyed carefully to the nearby
tomb. . . . in the darkness of Saturday night when
Jesus was brought out of the tomb by those concerned in the plan he regained consciousness tempo-
rarily, but finally succumbed. . . . Before dawn the
mortal remains of Jesus were quickly yet reverently
interred, leaving the puzzle of the empty tomb.[40]

In order to prove Jesus' historicity Schonfield constructs
a plot and uses in it chemotherapy, a drug. Dr. Morton
Smith, in his book *Jesus the Magician,* sees Jesus as a
magician. He writes:

. . . the Gospels were written not merely to record
events, but also to produce and confirm Jesus the
Messiah (that is Christ), the son of God — not a
historical figure, but a mythological one. . . . Jesus'
exorcism and cures "have resulted from a sudden
cessation of hysterical symptoms and cognate psychological disorders!"[41]

Magic tricks have a long history as precursors of man's
later developments in his dealings with nature. Jacob, for
example, used "genetic tricks":

Then Jacob took fresh rods of poplar and almond
and plane, and peeled white streaks in them, expos-
ing the white of the rods. He set the rods which he
had peeled in front of the flocks in the runnels, that

is, the watering troughs, where the flocks came to drink. . . . The flocks bred in front of the rods, and so the flocks brought forth striped, speckled and spotted.[42]

Another Biblical example is:

Aaron cast down his rod before Pharaoh and his servants, and it became a serpent. Then Pharaoh summoned the wise men and the sorcerers; and they also, the magicians of Egypt, did the same by their secret art. For every man cast down his rod, and they became serpents. But Aaron's rod swallowed up their rods.[43]

Man's outgrowing of magic as a means for trying to control nature reveals another aspect of the ontogenesis of the psyche. The significance of Jesus as a magician surely lies in the fact that Jesus related himself directly to the needs of individual human beings.

There is an Islamic belief, the idea of the Ahmadiyya, which holds that Jesus escaped to India, where he taught and was buried in Srinagar, Kashmir.[44] The, for scholars, so important *Q* material — which is a hypothetical source for Matthew and Luke *(Q =Quelle,* "source"), does not contain any reference to the death and resurrection of Jesus, in spite of its being dated 50 A.D.

Our ancestors, feeling in them an unconscious pull from the beginning of animated life, went to great lengths to get hold of the magic substance which psychically promised them not only renewal, but also the experience of the universality of life. As a kind of food, it not only accompanied the dead on their journey through the netherland, but it also promised an eternal return, and the ritual was performed to keep the *memory* of the departed alive as well.[45]

The birthright of materialism of mundane life is of no import in relation to the assimilation of the potentiality of renewal. This is the hub around which the poetic messages of both the Old and New Testaments turn in ever-changing, kaleidoscopic images as colorful and rich as life itself. It is at one and the same time the most intimate human life, and the life of the Cosmos as well, including its material aspects. It reaches to the endless infinity of the stars, ever-searching, ever-growing, ever-dying and ever-reborn in the eternal dance of "the dew of the morning." The poets of the Old Testament have succinctly described this process of growth and becoming: "Come, let us go up to the mountain of the Lord, to the house of Jacob; that he may teach us his ways."[46] "The Lord has sent a word against Jacob, and it will light upon Israel"[47] . . . the pregnant word which created the Light at the beginning of Being.

> The people who walked in darkness
> have seen a great light;
> those who dwelt in a land of deep darkness,
> on them has light shined.[48]

> For to us a child is born,
> to us a son is given;
> and the government will be upon his shoulder,
> and his name will be called
> "Wonderful Counselor, Mighty God,
> Everlasting Father, Prince of Peace."[49]

This "child," this new awareness, is meaningful because it can be realized in the life of the individual as a spiritual experience. It is enlightenment — realization of the inter-relatedness of action and reaction, of deceit and being deceived. It is "the light," making experiential the interconnections of things below with those above.

The Jacob-Esau story is thus the archetype of growth par excellence, spiraling upward, revealing the ontogenesis of the psyche in Isaiah, and finding its culmination in the New Testament. It is the archetype par excellence because it depicts both biological and mental interrelatedness, the Alpha and the Omega, as a symbol of the creative, self-organizing and self-correcting faculties in man, leading back into the infinite past and forward into the infinite future. This central story depicts not only the ontogeny of the psyche, but also the phylogeny of the race as a living being.

The poem finds its sublime apex when Jacob meets "a man" at the ford of Jabbok. Everything else in this most significant poem has been a preparation, stages in a drama, for this supreme moment.[50] But as everything else in this great book, the Bible needs to be seen as emanating from a core of multiple dimensions, so this encounter of the psyche with itself needs to be approached hermeneutically, as it depicts essentially the problems of relationship to the "other," whoever or whatever "the other" may be, inclusive of good or evil.

Closely parallel to Jacob's preparation for crossing the ford of the river Jabbok and the Christian ritual of baptism is the Indian term for pilgrimages to sacred places: *tīrtha*. A study by Prof. Eck of the ancient and modern implications of this term shows it to have:

> dynamic and transitive connotations more accurately conveyed by "ford" or "crossing place". *Tīrtha* in Sanskrit means crossover. The root verb *tī* includes subsidiary meanings — to master . . . to fulfill, to be saved — as well as its primary meaning, to cross. . . . It refers not to the goal, but to the way, the path one travels.[51]

This trenchant study reveals the archetypal character of the Biblical motif of Jacob's meeting with Esau and the Christian baptism:

> The act of crossing in the Upaniṣads is a spiritual transition and transformation from this world to what is called the world of Brahman, the world illumined by the light of knowledge. It is a crossing which must be made with the aid of a guide, a guru, and by means of the knowledge he imparts.[52]

A ... group of *tīrtha* meanings emphasizes the
nature of the *tīrtha* as limens: the threshold, betwixt
and between ... The liminal nature of the *tīrtha* is
made clear in one hymn which compares time's thresh-
olds — the twin twilights of dawn and dusk — with
tīrthas.[53]

The same time-limited motif is found in the story of
Jacob: "The same night he arose ... a man wrestled with
him until the breaking of the day."[54] Prof. Eck elaborates
further: "In the thousands of particular tales which attach to
tīrthas everywhere ... one finds repeatedly the theme of the
appearance of the divine."[55] This is reflected in Genesis
32:28 which reads: "You have striven with God and with
men, and have prevailed." Prof. Eck continues: "Every
tīrtha's tale is of hierophany, the residents of heaven breaking
in upon the earth," and describes a further correspondence
with the Jacob story:

> ... it is commonly said of *tīrtha* that they are places
> for "crossing beyond" sins. The destruction of sins,
> perhaps the sins of a lifetime or of many lifetimes, is
> ascribed to *tīrthas* great and small, calling to mind
> some of the Vedic and Brahmanic association of the
> word *tīrtha* with purification. The purifying waters
> of a *tīrtha* wash away one's sins, or the very dust of
> the place may be purifying.[56]

To be in contact with the origin of man, the dust and / or
the primal waters is essentially a rebirth and thus an act of
purification:

> In India, where the pure *(pavitr)* is the closest equiv-
> alent of what we call the "sacred," the purifying
> power of the *tīrtha* is very significant indeed.
>
> ... the Indian tradition balances the pilgrim's faith in
> the sheer transforming power of the place itself with
> a persistent reminder that the *tīrtha* is an internal as

well as an external crossing and that the *tīrtha* to which one journeys is also close within ... we begin to glimpse the way in which India's great *tīrthas* inherit the wisdom traditions of crossing: crossing beyond birth and death, crossing from darkness to light, crossing from ignorance to knowledge.[57]

The following reaffirms from Indian culture the essential meaning for both the Old and the New Testament of Jacob's encounter on the ford of Jabbok: "As Yudhisthira once said to the wise Vidura, who had returned from a *tīrtha-yātra,* 'Devotees like you, who have become *tīrthas (tīrthabhūtāh)* themselves, are the ones who make the *tīrthas* into *tīrthas (tīrthīkurvantī tirthāni)* by embodying the presence of God there! ...'[58] This passage sheds a bright illumination on the following lines of Rilke as well:

> To each a different God will appear, until
> Near to crying they recognize
> That through their miles apart supposing
> Through their understanding and denying,
> There goes like a wave one God,
> Different only in his hundred tones.

Focusing the responsibility upon the individual and his actions, Confucius spells out his way for man. His Ta Hsüeh, the Sermon on the Mount, and Jacob's Way show essentially the same road to salvation:

> Everything has its roots and branches. Affairs have their end and beginning. To know what comes first and what comes last is to be near to the *Tao.*
> The ancients who wished clearly to manifest illustrious virtue throughout the world would first govern their own states well. Wishing to govern their states well, they would first regulate their families. Wishing to regulate their families, they would first cultivate their own persons. Wishing to cultivate their own persons, they would first rectify their

hearts. Wishing to rectify their hearts, they would first seek sincerity in their thoughts. Wishing for sincerity in their thoughts, they would first extend their knowledge. The extension of knowledge lay in the investigation of things.

Only when many things are investigated is knowledge extended; only when knowledge is extended are thoughts sincere; only when thoughts are sincere are hearts rectified; only when hearts are rectified are our persons cultivated; only when our persons are cultivated are our families regulated; only when our families are regulated are states well governed; only when states are well governed can the world be at peace.

From the Son of Heaven down to the common people, all must consider the cultivation of the person as the root. When the root is in disorder, the branches cannot grow in order. To treat the important as unimportant and to treat the unimportant as important — this should never be.

This is called knowing the root; this is called the perfection of knowledge.[59]

Commenting on Confucius' teaching in Ta Hsüeh, the Chinese editors bring this archetypal way of becoming, Jacob's and Jesus' way, into relation with baptism.

On the bathtub of the Emperor T'ang[T'ang Dynasty 618-906 A.D.] the following inscription was engraved: "Be sincere in renewing yourself every day, and do so day after day. Yes, let yourself be renewed always!" ... In the announcement to K'ang [1662-1722 A.D.] it is said: "To urge the people to renew themselves."[60]

Christian baptism has its roots in Judaism, which also used water for the purpose of religious purification.

Starting at the beginning of the voyage of man's psyche to

its own fulfillment stands Adam's encounter with the *other,* Eve. This relationship to the *other* brought into the awareness of the psyche also the realization that man's mere reaching out for the "tree of life," without making the personal effort would mean to fall into the hands of inertia, into mindlessness.

> And the Lord God said, Behold, the man is become as one of us, to know good and evil; and now, lest he put forth his hand, and take also of the tree of life, and eat and live forever: *therefore* the Lord God sent him forth from the garden of Eden, to till the ground from whence he was taken.[61]

The dynamic birth of the awareness of relationship to the *other* reveals itself in all its grandeur and majesty as the *hayah,* the inborn urge to become. It is seen to be the *fall,* "Original Sin."

> Was not the whole point of the Garden story the presumptuous rebellion of man against God? And how can we see this event as anything but wrong, wrong, wrong, and therefore unproductive?
>
> It would appear to this reviewer that we are here dealing with a momentous spiritual issue: the question whether obedience even to God — and certainly to lesser authorities — can have any spiritual meaning apart from preparation for revolt. Can any basis of obedience less than the ground of discovered autonomy be a total, and therefore totally loyal, commitment of the self?[62]

The fact of man's achievement through his own efforts is exemplified by the poets through the drama on Mt. Moria in the story of Abraham's sacrifice of Isaac.[63] The Akedah demonstrates not only the psyche's essential step toward the establishment of personality, but Abraham's choice not to kill his son also revealed a result of vital importance. Isaac could then father Jacob and Esau as archetypal symbols of man's becoming, and the drama could thus continue. (The name Esau appears in the findings of Ebla some 1,800 years before the Biblical narrative supposedly was written.)

Again, the barrenness of Sarah is a symbol of non-creativity as was also Rebekah, the mother of Isaac. Both experienced, as did Mary, the mother of Jesus, an annunciation in which they were told that, *contra naturam,* they would be with child. Rebekah gave birth to twins; to man in his shortcomings and misunderstandings — man as he really is. Jacob and Esau are not single personalities, but together they form a composite symbol of man's potentialities, torn as he is between heaven and earth, between good and evil. Isaiah said that man was formed from the dust from all over the world and its four corners, and many legends amplify this essential insight. "The dimensions of his body were gigantic, reaching from heaven to earth, or what amounts to the same, from east to west.[64]

The echo of this teaching is also heard in Paul: "And as we have borne the image of the earthly, we shall also bear the image of the heavenly."[65] Thus primal man became the archetype for all living human beings, who in turn participate essentially in the epic drama of becoming — precisely that which is depicted in the Jacob and Esau legend. The Zohar, apparently relating the decisive psychological encounter between Jacob and Esau to Jacob's dream with the ladder reaching from heaven to earth says: ". . . until Jacob was at peace with the chieftain of Esau, Esau was not at peace with Jacob. For in all cases power below depends on the corresponding power above."[66]

The Growth of Awareness

JUST AS the psyche symbolized in Adam experiences a heightened awareness as a result of Adam's actions, so also does the psyche symbolized in Jacob and his actions. As Adam broke out of the entanglement with inertia of mindless unconsciousness, so also did Jacob. By selling the *red,* he broke the unconscious unity with nature and the psyche entered the realm of awareness and of action begetting reaction.

Jacob's way reflects a universal experience and is not a private mystery. While Jacob's way as a prototype is a universal way, the experience of it is private and unique for every individual. The private symbol is the understandable reality for the person because it is uniquely his most personal experience and is not lost in impersonal constructs, such as Ego or Archetype — that is, Ego and Archetype are general descriptive nouns and therefore do not in themselves convey the way of salvation for an individual.

Just as unanimated life created animated life, so action results in reaction. There reverberates through the silence of the universe, the sound which both figuratively and actually is related to the beginning of all things. And as primitive man was haunted by fears of unknown reactions to his behavior, so modern man lives in an "age of anxiety," unable, despite the "knowledge explosion," to predict the results of the actions which he has initiated.

The poets of old described Adam as "reaching from one end of the universe to the other," and today the mind of man reaches from an imagined beginning to the furthest reaches of unfathomable space. Cosmologists believe they have established a beginning for the universe, and the scientists who have formulated the theory of the "Big Bang" postulate that there may have been another universe even before the present one was formed. Were we to have lived in some other historical epoch, it is conceivable that we might have described "the beginnings" as a song emanating from the deity.

The sound which modern science hears far out in distant space might have been understood to be the reverberating music and harmony of the spheres. After all, sounds of certain frequencies can shatter material substance, as was claimed for the sound of the trumpets which caused the fall of the Walls of Jericho.[67] Archaeology has found no physical evidence to substantiate this claim.

And further, modern cosmology believes to know that everything in the universe is essentially of the same physical and chemical composition, inclusive of man. The interrelatedness of man's mind with the endless multifariousness of the cosmos and Life is both awesome and humbling. Here in the deepest recess, as far as we know today, both science and religion coincide.

The participating psyche not only expresses itself in science as a structural analysis of events, but also in a structural hermeneutic revealing values which the analytically-oriented mind by its very exclusiveness does not reach. 3,800 years ago, the poetic mind conceived of meaningful relations between events in human and cosmic history. About a thousand years later, these relationships were committed to writing in dramatic form. Whether we ascribe to this historical process a discernible purpose or the workings of blind chance, the human experience of relationship to the universe in its manifold manifestations provides the basic axiom of both science and religion.

Science expresses itself basically in mathematics and experimentation; experiments are constructed on the very basis of mathematics. Wittgenstein expressed this by saying: "What a mathematical proposition says is always what its proof proves. That is to say, it never says more than its proof proves."[68] Mathematics is essentially a pattern of relationships between numbers and symbols. And significantly for Einstein, God was a mathematician — he did not play dice. (Etymologically, the word *religion* is derived from the Latin *re-ligare* = "to relate," "to bind together.")

As the psyche has moved upward into awareness of relationship among all things, it has had to contend with the power of inertia. In the story of Adam and Eve, the overcoming of inertia was called "original sin," demonstrating the natural inclination to resist change and a new concept. The response of the Church to Galileo was a reflection of the same inertia in the assumption that a stable universe demanded that the earth be the center of creation. And so was man supposed to be in his state of mindlessness.

Today the upward movement of the psyche to a new level on the spiral of becoming is demonstrated not only in political and economic affairs, but more particularly in the area of human relationships. The individual person has now become the sole arbiter of value as reflected in personal choice. Rejected today are the postulates of institutions, the impersonality of social mores, and the reduction of human dignity through statistical computerization of personality, which is thus deadened.

The social results of the failure of society to produce both individual freedom *and* responsibility are tragic. Nearly 50% of all marriages in the United States end in divorce as people change spouses according to their narcissistically imagined needs. In a small school with a total attendance of 95 pupils, more than 50% of the children do not carry the same surname as their mothers. In one instance, an eleven-year-old girl asked her father when he would be getting a divorce. He answered: "Darling, you know I love mother, she loves me, and we both love you; there is no thought of divorce." Whereupon the girl said, "You know, Daddy, then I would be the only one in my class whose parents are not divorced." A strange turn of events, when being the odd girl out results from having parents who are not divorced!

Teenagers and young adults are both the victims and

culprits in much of our present social malaise. At a school which was administering innoculations against measles, it was necessary to ask each teenage girl if she were pregnant or had had sexual intercourse since her last period, in order to avoid possible danger to an unborn foetus. It is common in the teenage generation and among young adults to indulge excessively in drugs and alcohol to avoid meaningful relationships which result from a free-flowing being together.

Society, after all, is an amalgamation of individuals, and it can easily revert to a state of mindlessness. This was the state of Adam and Eve before they symbolically differentiated and experienced relationship, i.e., "the Fall." The mindless oneness lived by Adam and Eve before their differentiation was considered to be "The Garden of Eden." Despite the fact that the ontogenesis of the psyche brought about a vital corrective, freeing Adam and Eve from their "mindless oneness," it is still considered to be "the Fall" rather than an elevation to a higher state. "And the eyes of both were opened, and they knew that they were naked."[69] Modern society reacts to this experience in all sorts of "liberation" movements, from workers' strikes to women's lib, revolting, as it were, against containment in preconceived dogmas and the failure to recognize persons, seeing them as "objects to be counted."

The awareness of distinct personalities is depicted in the earliest art which archaeology has discovered to date. Whether we look at the female figurines, possibly fertility idols, of pre-Ice Age art from about 30,000 years ago,[70] or at the findings at Catal Hüjük, the human experience of relationship is portrayed in these remarkable statuettes. In the statuette of Catal Hüjük, a human couple is depicted in close sexual embrace, and attached to this stone statuette is a mother embracing a child. Mellaart writes: "This may be one of the earliest representations of the *hieros gamos*, the 'sacred marriage,'"[71] similar to the Indian figure of Vajradhara and Shakti [supra, p. 15].

Figure 14. Catal Hüjük, statuette, 7000 B.C.

Any attempt to control human behavior by indoctrination — political, religious, or otherwise — puts the subject into a straightjacket of artificially conceived codes. Such codes are inimical to the creative spirit which needs freedom of personal development in order to find its expression. Dogma then comes between the person and the inner Self, and results in unproductive guilt.

We have seen in the case of Jacob, how the denied and rejected aspects of personality (symbolized by Esau, the red, hairy one) can be assimilated to produce reconciliation and peace. A lack of trust in the Son of Man within the human psyche has left generations of humanity in perplexity and doubt. Through the lack of integration of the rejected part of the personality, there is tension instead of peace. The rejection is expressed in "Can anything good come out of

Nazareth?"[72] and in the lack of harmony that "the Son of man has nowhere to lay his head."[73] Simply to follow a dogma is not enough.

> A scribe came up and said to him,
> "Teacher, I will follow you wherever you go."
> And Jesus said to him, "Foxes have holes,
> and birds of the air have nests;
> but the Son of man has nowhere to lay his head."[74]

The human race is left thus in confusion, crying out for messiahs to solve the problems of coming to maturity on their behalf, to calm the emotional storms, and to deal with the obsessions, compulsions, and the autonomous complexes which rule, as though they were demons, from the depths of the psyche.

> And when he got into the boat, his disciples followed him. And behold, there arose a great storm on the sea, so that the boat was being swamped by the waves; but he was asleep. And they went and woke him up, saying, "Save us, Lord, we are perishing." And he said to them, "Why are you afraid, O men of little faith?"[75]

In a most dramatic way the poets describe the resolution of this human predicament as a process:

> And when he came to the other side . . . two demoniacs met him, coming out of the tombs, so fierce that no one could pass that way. . . . And the demons begged him, "If you cast us out, send us away into the herd of swine." And he said to them, "Go." So they came out and went into the swine.[76]

Jacob's way led him to the confrontation at the ford of Jabbok, and Jesus' way led him to the encounter with his devil in the wilderness, both being supreme examples of the way an individual becomes whole within himself. Paul, writing to the Philippians, points the same direction:

Therefore, my beloved, as you have always obeyed, so now, not only as in my presence but much more in my absence, *work out your own salvation* with fear and trembling; *for God is at work in you* . . .[77]

"The Son of man has nowhere to lay his head" says Jesus. Artificially conceived dogmas are a hindrance to the voyage of man to himself, and thus to peace. Essentially they deny the workings of the divine in man, and portray a lack of faith in the *Self*.

As it was 2,000 years ago, so it is today. A dogmatic, one-sided materialism has led us into experimentation with the foundations of life itself. Gene-splitting, test-tube babies and human sperm banks are a reflection of our willingness to manipulate the material order without regard for the consequences for other dimensions of life. If it should come to pass that these efforts achieve technical "success," it would not mean that the results are of positive value in the universal sense. We have indeed achieved technical "success" in unleashing the power of the atom, but to what end?

These modern scientific designs to tamper with the basic structures of living matter open the door to dangerous and arrogant social engineering. It is argued from a materialistic point of view that it is in the genes themselves that a justification is to be found for further experimentation and interference with the life-process.[78] But how can these social engineers be sure that it is not also in the genes that the profound opposition and reaction to mindless experimentations may be found?

J. B. Haldane said:

If materialism is true, it seems to be that we cannot know that it is true. If my opinions are the result of chemical processes going on in my brain they are determined by laws of chemistry and not logic.[79]

And Sir Karl Popper wrote: ". . . in the present Darwinian climate, a consistent materialist view of the world is only possible if it is combined with a denial of the existence of consciousness."[80] Interference with the ontogeny of cells is one thing, but it is quite another thing to interfere with the non-materialistic dynamics inherent in life from the moment of creation. In the end, these dynamics have been responsible for the creation of consciousness, which in turn has made science and religion possible.

About 150 years ago, Goethe described the successful creation of an artificial man in a test tube, a remarkable poetic anticipation of our time of gene-cloning and electronic education. In Act II, Part II of *Faust* in the scene entitled "Laboratory," Wagner appears and says:

> What man conceived in nature as mysterious,
> We dare today to test with reason.
> And what nature organized by herself
> We bid now artificially to crystallize.

Mephistopheles:

> Whoever lived long experienced much
> Nothing new can happen for him in this world.
> I have seen in my wanderings
> Many a mortal who was crystallized.

Wagner:

> A great design at first seemed mad,
> We, however, in the future will laugh at chance
> A brain that thinks correctly,
> Will soon be created by rational man.
> . . . .
> What more can we or the world desire
> The mystery is now within our reach.

The artificially created human being, Homunculus, speaks now to Wagner out of the test tube:

> Now old man! How are things now? It was no jest.
> Come hold me tenderly to your breast

But not too strongly, the glass might shatter.
Such is the essence of Life:
For the natural is the universe just big enough
The artificial demands boundaries!

Concepts, dogmas, like machines are contained within limited frames of reference, boundaries; therefore, Goethe assigns to the protagonist Mephistopheles at the close of the scene to say:

In the end we depend on creatures
we ourselves created.

The Gnostics, according to the Gospel of Philip, said: "That is the way in the world — men make gods and worship their creation" [supra, p. xxi]. The result is that man has grown humanly torpid and is mentally crystallized. The text in German reads:

Wagner:

Was man an der Natur Geheinmisvolles pries,
Das wagen wir verständig zu probieren,
Und was sie sonst organisieren liess,
Das lassen wir krystallisieren.

Mephistopheles:

Wer lange lebt, hat viel erfahren,
Nichts Neues kann für ihn auf dieser Welt geschehn.
Ich habe schon in meinen Wanderjahren
Kristallisiertes Menschenvolk gesehn.

Wagner:

Ein grosser Vorsatz scheint im Anfang toll;
Doch wollen wir des Zufalls künftig lachen,
Und so ein Hirn, das trefflich denken soll,
Wird küntfig auch ein Denker machen.
Was wollen wir, was will die Welt nun mehr?
Denn das Geheimnis liegt am Tage.

Homunculus:

> Nun Väterchen! wie steht's? es war kein Scherz.
> Komm, drücke mich recht zärtlich and dein Herz!
> Doch nicht zu fest, damit das Glas nicht springe.
> Das ist die Eingenschaft der Dinge:
> *Natürlichem genügt das Weltall kaum,*
> *Was künstlich ist. Verlangt geschlossenen Raum.*

Mephistopheles:

> Am Ende hängen wir doch ab
> Von Kreaturen, die wir machten.[81]

Against these boundaries, artificially created, man is in constant revolt in one form or another. However, the Bible gives a hint pointing in a different direction from the "normal" dogmatic education.

> Come, let us go up the mountain of the Lord,
> to the house of the God of Jacob,
> *that he may teach us his ways*
> *and that we may walk in his paths.*

Jacob, the human, all-too-human figure, is full of "sin"; he lies and cheats; yet Esau is depicted solely by the poets as hairy, red, a man of the field — the natural man. The eternal conflict in man's psyche between two opposing tendencies and their possible reconciliation is already depicted in Genesis with the birth of Jacob and Esau:

> The children struggled together within her; and she
>   said,
> "If it is thus, why do I live?" So she went to
> inquire of the Lord. And the Lord said to her,
> "Two nations are in your womb,
> and two peoples, born of you, *shall be divided;*
> the one shall be stronger than the other,
> the elder shall serve the younger.[82]

It is of signal importance that the poets used the normal sibling rivalry as a symbol, saying: "the elder shall serve the younger." According to Biblical law the first fruits and the first born belong to God. "You shall set apart to the Lord all that first opens the womb."[83] "All that opens the womb is mine."[84] The poets use the old law of primogeniture and sibling rivalry as the focal point of the drama of becoming.[85] According to the law of primogeniture the first son becomes the heir to the estate, a law still practiced in parts of Europe.

By a vivid description in the Jacob-Esau legend of a deeply human situation, the Bible, true to its prime vocation as a record of the ontogenesis of the psyche, is thus a guide to salvation. In the Jacob-Esau story, as in the Abraham-Isaac drama, not an abolition of the law but its fulfillment gets expressed. In the Akedah, Isaac the first born was to be sacrificed, but at the instant of the sacrifice it is God Himself who thwarts His own purpose. In the Jacob-Esau story it is Jacob who has to earn his maturity through his own efforts, and to establish it as mental reality through the reconciliation of the opposites within himself.

Tradition heaped upon Esau all evil because he hated his brother, a most natural reaction, while in fact according to the narrative, it was Jacob who, if anyone, was evil. And yet "he may teach us his ways"! It is the integration of the two sides of man's nature which is the essence of the Biblical drama.

We have followed the psyche's means of becoming aware that action creates reaction, the entering into the "knowing" of the essences of relationship, up to the supreme moment in the Biblical poem where "the elder shall serve the younger" becomes a reality in a psychic sense. Everything else in this very significant story has been a preparation, as stages in a drama, for this supreme moment. But as everything else in this great book, the Bible, this apex needs to be seen as emanating from a core of multiple dimensions.

> The same night he arose and took his two wives,
> his two maids, and his eleven children, and crossed
> the ford of the Jabbok.... And Jacob was left alone;
> and a man wrestled with him until the breaking of the
> day. When the man saw that he did not prevail
> against Jacob, he touched the hollow of his thigh....
> Then he said, "Let me go, for the day is breaking."
> But Jacob said, "I will not let you go, unless you bless
> me." And he said to him, "What is your name?" And
> he said, "Jacob." Then he said, "Your name shall no
> more be called Jacob, but Israel, for *you have striven
> with God and with men, and have prevailed.*" Then
> Jacob asked him, "Tell me, I pray, your name." But
> he said, *"Why is it that you ask my name?"* And there
> he blessed him.[86]

In the Biblical narrative, starting at the beginning of the
voyage of man's psyche to its own fulfillment, stands
Adam's encounter with Eve. In Jacob's struggle with a man
at the ford of Jabbok, the alienation and estrangement of
man from himself is symbolically overcome. Jacob earns his
new name Israel and none is the victor. However, the
unknown man reveals himself in not revealing his name:
Jacob could not have recognized him since the man was also
himself, his inner twin. If it would have been "God" or an
"angel" as the compilers have it, the poets of the Bible, to be
sure, would have felt free enough to say so. They did not do
that, and neither god nor angel struck Jacob with a little
finger. Jacob prevailed, as Christ prevailed in the desert.
What the poets do say is: "I have seen God face to face, and
yet my life is preserved"[87] and "I have seen thy face, as
though I had seen the face of God."[88]

We shall return to the Jacob-Esau story in several different contexts. The legend contains the essential elements
portraying the psyche's becoming: from man's shortcomings to genuine love and to the valiant struggle to integrate
the complementarities of human existence. And we shall

have occasion to show that the essence of this fundamental legend is not confined to the cultures which are represented by either the New or Old Testaments.[89]

In the Exodus account, Moses speaks to God, saying: "I pray thee, show me thy glory."[90] Appropriately, the poets, out of the depths of their insight about man's growth to himself, created this profound answer: ". . . I will be gracious to whom I will be gracious, and will show mercy on whom I will show mercy. And he said, 'You cannot see my face; for man shall not see my face and live.'"[91] To be alive is to become, and this process has no static face and gives no guarantee nor promise of reward or redemption.

Christ's encounter with the devil, Jacob's with Esau, and Moses' experience on Mt. Sinai are vitally related stages in the ontogenesis of the psyche. In the symbolic event at the ford of Jabbok, the poets portray an integration and relatedness to the natural: "And the elder shall serve the younger." This integration leads back to the very beginning, as it were, of animated life, where the green algae created out of itself the Red, for which Esau is the symbol. Let me repeat: that his name is derived from *adama*, "the red earth," and *E-ea-um*, is attested in the discoveries at Ebla, and hence is of great antiquity.

On Mt. Sinai, as a result of conscious relation to empirical facts, laws are formulated; and yet these laws only become final after the "natural" — the Golden Calf — had been assimilated. As Esau ate the "Red," so the Israelites had to drink the ashes of the Golden Calf.[92] The existentiality of these symbolic events is the essence of both Old and New Testament guidance, expressed in the Law of the Old Testament as:

> You shall not hate your brother in your heart, but you shall reason with your neighbor, lest you bear sin because of him. You shall not take vengeance or bear any grudge against the sons of your own people, *but you shall love your neighbor as yourself.*[93]

and, expressively:

> You shall not abhor an Edomite [Esau's dependents], *for he is your brother.*[94]

and:

> And thou shalt love the Lord thy God with *all* thine heart, and with *all* thy soul and with *all* thy might.[95]

The New Testament *repeats* this vital theme:

> You shall love the Lord your God with all your heart, and with all your soul, and with all your mind. This is the great and first commandment. And a second is like it, *You shall love your neighbor as yourself.*[96]

These essential sayings are then on the upward moving spiral of man's mental evolution expressed in the Sermon on the Mount, which succinctly states: "But I say unto you, that ye resist not evil. . . . Be ye therefore perfect, even as your Father which is in heaven is perfect."[97] To be perfect means, as we have seen, to be whole, healthy, holy, etymologically derived from the root *hāle*.

The corruption of the world, deadly wars between brothers of the same nation, e.g., Belsen and Auschwitz, make the exhortation of the Sermon on the Mount seem very strange if it is literally applied to the secular world. Seen in the light of the ontogenesis of the psyche, however, both the Old and New Testament sayings are the most powerful guides for the *individual's* own becoming. It is from this context that the sayings of the Sermon on the Mount derive their dynamic meaning; namely, "resist not evil" *within yourself,* so as to learn the ultimate character of it ". . . whosoever shall compel thee to go a mile, go with him twain . . . whosoever shall smite thee on thy right cheek, turn to him the other also. . . ."[98] Thus not laws nor dogmatic indoctrination, but the awareness of "thine own wickedness shall correct thee."[99] In this way, the "Son of Man" assists the immature son to become mature, enabling him to bear the stark truth: "I form the light, and create darkness: I make peace, and create evil: I the Lord do all these things."[100] And ". . . shall there be evil in a city, and the Lord hath not done it?"[101]

After the bombing of Hiroshima, the use of Napalm in Vietnam, the entry of tanks from Russia into Hungary, Czechoslovakia and Afghanistan, after Belsen and Auschwitz and the threat of the super-powers to annihilate each other, and the whole world, the enormity of the ethical demand as a burden too heavy to carry, now rests on the shoulders of individual man. The modern problem is basically the same as that addressed by the poets in the Book of Job.

> Shall we receive good at the hand of God,
> and shall we not receive evil? In all this
> Job did not sin with his lips.[102]

The burden lifts when:

> Yahweh answered Job and said:
> "Will the contender with Shaddai yield?
> He who reproves God, let him answer for it."[103]

and God confesses to Job, the man:

> Then will I also acknowledge to you,
> *That your own right hand can give you victory.*
> *Behold, Behemoth.*[104]

Now, *Behemoth* is the plural of *behemah*, "the beast," and Marvin Pope says:

> An apparent plural of the common noun *běhēmāh,*
> "beast, cattle." The verbs used with the noun in this
> passage are third masculine singular thus indicating
> that a single beast is intended and that the plural

form must be so-called intensive plural or plural of majesty, The Beast, par excellence.[105]

The single isolated beast is made to stand for all the blind forces of creation, for the *natural* in the inner as well as the outer order of experience. Now, as Job's eyes meet the eyes of the beast, as it were, and his ears hear the voice of his God, Job himself comes to stand for all men who, in their confusion about man's true nature and about the ways of God, aspire to an unnatural distinction *from* the orders of experience, and intimacy with *their* God which would in effect rule out nature.

Confronting Behemoth, Job really confronts the unnamed stuff of life, all that will forever remain beyond the reach of righteousness —the tempestuous, brutal, violent, the mindless which man fears in himself and in the world outside because he is not mindful of it. God tells Job to look, by *seeing* to bring this unnamed stuff of life into the light of his awareness, *to accept it as a part of himself and to achieve a human relation with it.* Behemoth is a natural inhabitant of the inner world, and though he may be beyond the reach of righteousness, he is not beyond the reach of rightness. The vast energies of Being that he symbolizes may drive man, rule him, overthrow him and destroy him as a man, or when as a man he experiences them rightly, they may do the opposite. Behemoth is the source of individual woe or the source of the energies of human creativity.[106]

CHAPTER 5

Change

*Wolle die Wandlung. O sei
für die Flamme begeistert,
drin sich ein Ding Dir
entzieht, das mit Verwand-
lungen prunkt;
jener entwerfende Geist, wel-
cher das Irdische meistert,
liebt in dem Schwung der
Figur nichts wie den
wendenden Punkt.*

*Be open to change, O be
enraptured with fire
In it a configuration escapes
you which is
glittering with transformation
The creative mind, which is
mastering the universe
loves in the dance of the
formed nothing better
than the turning point.*[1]

The Process of Change

THE BRIDGE between the essence of the Jacob-Esau legend with the events on Mt. Sinai and the Last Supper is a statement of Paul in his First Letter to the Corinthians: "Let a man examine himself, and so eat of the bread and drink of the cup."[2] The "I Am That I Am" and the "Burning Bush" are symbolic revelations to man of the human capacity for change and transformation. Likewise the Last Supper is a symbol for transformation. Man in his need for becoming, man in his capacity for change and his propensity for choice, is himself the bridge between the complementarities within himself and those of life's duality. The very nature of life is expressed in its perpetual evolution as a process of change. St. Paul's reference to man's need to know himself is a reference to a process of change and transformation, for which the Bread and Wine of the Last Supper are supreme symbols. Awareness of the capacity for transformation enlightens man's way to himself, and in so doing sheds light upon the mystery of the Cross. As long as it remains a mystery, man remains in a state of unknowing about himself — he remains a mystery to himself.

Whether one calls life's capacity for change and transformation by the name of "evolution" or by some other word, it comes into being as a manifestation of energy, which in turn may be named "chemistry" or whatever. And whether these reactions are brought about by a grand design from the beginning, or by the "ghost in the machine" or "vitalism" or "life blood," it is essentially the experience of man's keeping pace with the ontogenesis of life itself. Is it not the fact that the scientist's ignorance of his own being is at the root of the assumption that life came about simply by chance? And does not man's partaking in the still partial knowledge of his own development over the last three million years represent a heightened awareness of the ontogenesis of the psyche itself?

Biological "facts" are the physical correlative to mental experiences of a directed activity from within the organism itself. Some thirty years ago, the use of the term "instinct" meant to be dubbed "unscientific" and to be sent straight into the scientists' hell. Since the publications of Tinbergen, Lorenz and others, the former attitude to the idea of instincts has been largely dissipated. Tinbergen in his book *The Study of Instincts* cites a large number of responses to image releasing stimuli.[3]

One of Tinbergen's experiments was conducted with herring gulls. In this experiment, he drew a crude effigy of a beak over the nest of young seagulls. The mother bird of this species has a red dot on her beak. Tinbergen found that in proportion to the accuracy with which the spot was placed on the effigy of the beak, or the nearer the color value of the spot to the actual color, the higher the response of the young birds opening their beaks, though the mother bird was completely absent. The birds' reaction was an image reaction, which a response to a *gestalt* with a complete bird-image would signify.

Or consider the killdeer birds I observed on my driveway where the birds were nesting. About two hours after hatching, the newborn birds were out pecking in the driveway — no feeding by the parents. Some sixteen hours later, the parents left the young to their own devices without having taught them to fly!

Sir Alister Hardy in his book *The Living Stream* writes:

> *Marsipella spiralis* makes a long cylindrical case, but here the spongespicules, in a single layer, are always built into the wall in a spiral, giving added strength to the structure. To my mind these various

astrorhizid Foraminifera (protozoa) present one of the greatest challenges to the exponents of a purely mechanistic view of life. Here are minute animals, apparently as simple in nature as amoeba, without definite sense-organs as eyes, and appearing as mere flowing masses of protoplasm, yet endowed with extraordinary powers; not only do they *select* and pick up one type of object from all the jumble of fragments of other sorts on the sea-bed, but they build them into a design involving a comparison of size. They build as if to a plan. Here is another mystery worth looking into. There must be an instinct of how to build and some sort of "memory" as to how far they have filled in the spaces and what sizes of spaces remain to be picked up to complete a section. Of course the whole activity of the animal is performed according to the physics and chemistry of the living material; we may be sure that none of these laws are broken, but are we so sure that this intricate physico-chemical machine has not been evolved as much by a selection of variations made by the animal's behavioural pattern as by the environment? The mystery surely concerns the relation of the "psychic" life of the animal to its mechanical body, and indeed is just as much a mystery as our own body-mind relationship.[4]

Hardy continues:

My "vitalism" is a belief that there is a psychic side of the animal which, apart from inherited instinctive behaviour may be independent of the DNA code that governs the form of the physical frame, but that it may interact with a physical system in the evolutionary process through organic selection.[5]

The great insights of biological science today were symbolically anticipated in the Babylonian epic of Atrahasis, where "on the advice of Enki the gods decided to create a substitute to do the work of the gods; and Enki and the mother goddess created man from clay and from the flesh and blood of the slain god 'We-ilu, a god who has sense,' from whom man was to gain rationality."[6]

The story of Zeus eating the Goddess of Justice whom he had created and putting her back into his belly so that there she could think for him, is but another mythological motif anticipating our understanding of the biological theories of today. In Egyptian religion:

> It has been well said that originally *ba* was not a part of anything (and therefore not a 'soul' either), 'but on the contrary a concept of totality . . . designed to differentiate a divine being from human subjection to form.' The analysis we have made corroborates this, for the *ba* is in fact the vitality and divine substance which either gives life to inanimate material or elevates from within living earthly creatures.[7]

Another example, more easily understood than the *Marcipella spiralis,* is that of the blind termites, a genus of African termites, which despite their blindness, build the most perfect arches. They demonstrate

> a true civilization and its architecture. I think it's an extraordinary if not awesome statement. — Notice that it is an affair without symmetry, without plan, with no blueprint, with no fixed outcome. The outcome is purely functional. There will be no Palladian school. The situation will have about it a curiously effective and yet to the human eyes and minds a curiously random pattern. The blueprint exists nowhere. It arises out of the interaction of the insects with some cues admittedly we don't know, some inbuilt instructions that we don't know, but with several other important cues that come from the structure itself upon which they are working. And

that is enough to put together the arch which will function well on the average. Truly, an extraordinary outcome. . . . Insects like this, termites, learn little individually. All they know is coded deep within . . . it is an organic whole that we are looking at.[8]

The essences, according to Aristotle, are inherent in the physical things. "In the case of organisms, they may be said to live in the organism, as its principle of life. The irrational souls or the essences of Aristotle may be said to be anticipations of modern gene theory: like DNA they plan the actions of the organism and steer it to its *telos*, to its perfection."[9]

From the vantage point of modern evolutionary theory, there appears to be a relationship between the development of the human brain and man's use of tools. Though it is possible to assume that a more complex and developed brain has led to the creation and use of tools, the examples of the *Marcipella spiralis* and the blind termites suggest that we need to be open to the possibility of the reverse. That is to say, perhaps an innate and unconscious capacity for using tools has led to the development of a more complex brain structure.

In modern technology, repeated errors in the use of tools eventually enforces a more extensive training of the brain. Therefore it would not seem unreasonable to assume that interrelatedness with the universe is causally antecedent to the development of the modern brain — a proposition consistent with theories of modern physics. The shift away from interpreting the universe through a mechanistic materialism and toward an interpretation based on the concept of energy would seem to preclude an exclusive approach.

Fred Hoyle, as mentioned earlier, says: ". . . it turns out that not even statistical predictions can be made unless the response of the universe is included in the equivalence." This vital realization is a step toward wholeness in which the essence of man in its immateriality is in close contact with the self-organizing and self-correcting movements of energy. While being fully "rational" within the context of specificity it is nevertheless not graspable with the means of an excluding mind, which by its very nature must doubt even the possibility of a linkage to Life's earliest beginnings, as modern biology dares to assume it, by accepting the idea of models as innate characteristics.

The word *invention* is derived from *invenire,* "to come upon." A hundred and fifty years before the time of Galileo, Leonardo da Vinci "came upon" the flying machine, and in so doing, lifted man in essence out of the narrowness of his earthbound existence into the vastness of the universe. A century and a half later, Galileo achieved the same effect from another direction.

Da Vinci's *Mona Lisa* demonstrates artistically and abstractly the "vastness" of the dimensions of his soul, which his engineering mind expressed in his mechanical "inventions." Human ability to deal with symbols differentiates us from the purely natural evolutionary process, which may utilize aeons of time to accomplish a very small change. The basic tools for engineering are the wheel, a very early development, and the lever, a paleolithic development. These two items are so fundamental that man has yet to add anything essentially new. Only the time has been immensely shortened which natural evolution would have needed for its own specific application of these inventions. Leonardo da Vinci demonstrates these two levels of ontogeny convincingly through his creations.

According to modern theories of physics, electrons and protons ultimately merge with the universe in the form of energy, and the energy stored in constructs such as chemical molecules do the same. This free-flowing energy is then a true expression of the *hayah* — the "to be" [supra, p. 150] as a correlative to the *hayah* in man's becoming. It is here where the spiritual reality of man is essentially complementary to the reality that we experience on the chemical level of our being. These two aspects of our humanity are conjoined as an expression of ultimate reality. The process of auto-catalysis "plays a major role in molecular selection. Autocatalysis is indeed the chemical term for a self-reproducing system, a property that biologists are prone to use as one of the criteria for a living system."[10]

As a spiritual correlative to life's biological evolution, poetry evolved in the ontogenesis of the psyche. In the religion of Egypt, for example, the god Thoth who was "self-produced" represented the Divine Intelligence;[11] and what modern biology identifies as the "messenger" —DNA and DNR — was symbolically anticipated in the god Thoth who was considered the messenger of the gods and who has a function equivalent to that of Hermes in the Pantheon.[12] "I descended to earth with the secrets of 'what belongs to the horizon' ";[13] he was the interpreter of the two lands.[14]

Matthew 6:10 reads: "On earth as it is in heaven." The major role played by Thoth in Egyptian religion as messenger of the gods, was filled by Hermes for the Greeks. As Hermes Trismegistus, he revealed divine secrets of which G.R.S. Mead in *The Thrice Greatest Hermes* gives full account. Depth psychology in our time is another manifestation of the structural hermeneutic as an interpretation of the unbroken and undivided totality of the basic experience of life.

> The early Church fathers accept[ed] the Trismegistic writings as exceedingly ancient and authoritative. . . . The Church Fathers appealed to the authority of antiquity and to a tradition that had never been called in question, in order to show that they taught nothing fundamentally new . . . . they taught on main points what Hermes had taught.[15]

In the middle of the 17th century, however, an effort was made to declare these ancient writings as forgeries and fraudulently having been taken from Christianity. More recently, one might add, some Church authorities attempted at first to declare the Dead Sea Scrolls to be forgeries. An exclusive, hence dogmatic, attitude to life perceives reality only in accordance with its own order.

What is significant for our purposes is the conjunction of several ancient sources: Christ, saying: "I am the *way*" (toward becoming), anticipated by the Old Testament "I Am That I Am," and echoed again in a Hellenistic tribute to Hermes: "Thou art the great, the only God, the Soul of Becoming," and finally in Egyptian mythology: "Thoth was also Lord of Rebirth."[16] The assumption was that Hermes was a real, existing personality like Enoch or Noah and possibly prior to or contemporary to Moses.[17]

Modern science believes it is able to trace the direction of evolution for about three thousand million years, and also believes that the direction of evolution gives the appearance of a planned program. This program is seen as a selection for change, the survival of the fittest it is called, thus showing the nature of life to be one of perpetual evolution, constantly in a process of change. The inability to change ultimately leads to disaster in one form or another.

In ancient religious poetry, this scientific insight has its *Urbild* —its primal image — in the Flood. The story of the flood, as it appears in the Old Testament, has many parallels in other cultures. It is doubtful that there is any historical grounding for the various accounts of a great flood. Most of the sages, however, describe the Great Flood by relating it to the "sins" of mankind. Therefore it is worth raising the question as to whether the linking of the great deluge with the "moral" failures of men, might not be a spiritual correlative to the corrections which take place in the evolution of biological life.

Is not this interpretation another manifestation of the ontogenesis of the psyche, that "the heart of man [is] his God himself,"[18] from which follows the ancient belief that God is at work within man and determines his entire nature by way of his heart? The heart is a figure borrowed from the physical realm to refer symbolically to the mind. Does not Moses address himself directly to this inborn quality of man when he says:

> For this commandment which I command you this day is not too hard for you, neither is it far off. It is not in heaven, that you should say, "Who will go up for us to heaven, and bring it to us, that we may hear it and do it?" Neither is it beyond the sea, that you should say, "Who will go over the sea for us, and bring it to us, that we may hear it and do it?" But the word is very near you; it is in your mouth and in your heart, so that you can do it.[19]

In the flood stories of the Babylonian culture (about 2,500 B.C.), the *Gilgamesh Epic*[20] and the *Atrahasis Epic*,[21] the two central figures Uta-Napishtim and Atrahasis are depicted as "Exceedingly Wise" or "Abounding in Wisdom" and were granted the advice as to how to survive, *in a dream*: "I let Atrahasis see a dream and he perceived [lit., *heard*] the secret of the gods."[22] In the Old Testament, on the other hand, Noah is informed directly by God without the medium of a dream.

Animated life, in particular human life, is not an orderly continuum, but essentially a process of the becoming of that which is inherent in it. And part of that inherent life is depicted by the poets of these epics as a sense of justice, as if it were part of "the biological equipment of man."[23]

In Jeremiah 31 it is said: "I will put my law within them, and I will write it upon their hearts." It is a new covenant of personal responsibility: *"In those days they shall no longer say: 'The fathers have eaten sour grapes, and the children's teeth are set on edge.' But every one shall die for his own sin; each man who eats sour grapes, his teeth shall be set on edge."*[24]

The Egyptian poets expressed this quality as *Maat,* "truth, justice, righteousness"; *Maat* is one of the earliest abstract terms preserved in human speech.[25] "Great is Maat;

its dispensation endures, nor has it been overthrown since the time of its maker."[26] "Maat is the goddess of the unalterable laws of heaven," and in our over-rationalized time she might be seen as the goddess of the unalterable laws of physics!

Western culture has adoped the ancient Latin symbol for justice —*Justitia*, the blind-folded female. Like the *Marsipella Spiralis,* Justitia is blind, but "knowing." Modern man also appears to be blind, but *unknowing* in that he shirks the essential task of our time, which is to turn from the external authoritarian laws and dogma, and in their place to discover the "law written on the heart." Or, to say it another way, the task of modern man is to substitute the unique laws of personal responsibility for the impersonal, statistical laws written for a "universal man" who does not exist.

What we find, however, is that entrenched bureaucracy constantly drives society in the direction of totalitarianism in order to deal with factions of irresponsible self-interest which capitalize on the latent hedonism in all men. As governing under these circumstances becomes increasingly difficult, the tendency to blame the "governor" is likewise increased. There is an old Egyptian saying: "If the King is at fault, man eats man, and parents seil their children." Thus Diodorus wrote:

> The life which the kings of the Egyptians lived was not like that of other men who enjoy autocratic power and do in all matters exactly as they please without being held to account, but all their acts were regulated by prescriptions set forth in laws, not only their administrative acts, but also those that had to do with the way in which they spent their time from day to day. . . .[27]

The king is "at fault" when his authority has lost its spell, either because he did not fulfill the rules by which he was supposed to live, or because misfortune was laid upon his steps. The authority, however, carries the responsibility which is basically that of the individual. The "king" is only the symbol of the authority of the collective mind. Not much has changed since ancient times. Perhaps the chief difference is that now we say "dog eats dog" instead of "man eats man." It has been reported that thousands upon thousands of children between the ages of six and fourteen years are sold or rented for pornographic or commercial purposes. In Los Angeles alone there are 30,000 children so used, according to a report in *Time* magazine.[28] If these figures concerning the children are correct, what possible number can we ascribe to the adults making use of them?

The problem of "surviving the flood" is perennial. Today we are flooded with the threat of nuclear war, economic war, the computerized destruction of individual personality, where individuals have even become "objects to be counted."

The New Testament speaks of a new covenant: "not like the covenant that I made with their fathers,"[29] and repeats the text from the Old Testament: "I will put my law within them, and I will write it upon their hearts; and I will be their God, and they shall be my people. And *no longer shall each man teach* his neighbor and each his brother, saying, 'Know the Lord' . . . for I will forgive their iniquity, and I will remember their sin no more."[30] At its very center, the ontogenetic principle moves in its spiraling activity from judgment and redemption, merely promised, to personal responsibility for one's own problems, and thence to change. The messianic hope that the messiah will fulfill the existential task for the individual has been miscredited empirically now, as fruitful teaching.

Linguistic analysis of the verb "to be," so vital for the "revelation" on Mt. Sinai, reveals the same meaning as the ontogenesis of the psyche, namely, man's becoming himself through a close interrelation with the universal creator. The events of Mt. Sinai trenchantly depicted by the poets, lead them directly to the "law" as an expression of man's growth toward a conscious and moral personality.

Man's Experience of Himself

Make his will as thy will, so that he may make thy will as his will, make naught thy will before his will so that he may make naught the will of others before thy will.[31]

M AN EXPERIENCES himself in his uniqueness in a three-fold relationship to life: in his relationship to himself; in relationship to others; and in relationship to his environment, in particular to cultural propensities. The essence of this experience is abstractly expressed in the words of the sages quoted above, and at the same time, it expresses man's relationship to the living God. It is in this way that man is confronted with the positive as well as the negative aspects of his being. It is here that man meets his shortcomings, his lies and his bestial characteristics, his Behemoth. But it is also in the context of such relationships that man, suffering the discomfort of being a unique personality, can experience basic changes and transformations, as through a fire of purification. Being fearful, however, of change, man, like St. Paul, expresses change as anxiety: "It is a fearful thing to fall into the hands of the living God,"[32] an expression to which any creative artist will readily admit.

The voice of the living God spoke out of the midst of the fire: "The Lord spoke to you face to face at the mountain, out of the midst of the fire," and as the poets perceived it then, so it is today: ". . . you were afraid because of the fire, and you did not go up into the mountain."[33] The Ten Commandments and the Sermon on the Mount are guides for man's voyage into self-discovery, a lifting of the psyche to a higher level of awareness of the meaning of his relationship to life. But shy and fearful, like a deer in a clearing in the darkness of the forest, man's psyche is anxious. To allay its fears, the psyche needs the direct experience of symbols which express the uniqueness of personal being. The preconceived and static utterances of dogma which man has been taught to trust actually stand between him and the truth of his own psyche. Because dogmatic answers to the problems of the individual have not grown out of his personal encounter, they tend to produce hypocritical mouthing of opinions which are basically alien to one's true nature.

> As a hart longs
> for flowing streams,
> so longs my soul
> for thee O God.
> My soul thirsts for God,
> for the living God.
> When shall I come and behold the face of God?
> My tears have been my food
> day and night,
> while men say to me continually,
> "Where is your God?"[34]

Survival, not only in a physical but particularly in a human, moral sense, is the question which confronts us today. The stories of the Flood are a poetic dramatization of being overcome by forces over which man seems to have no control. Every year there are local floods, and boats must be sent in to rescue isolated persons. The poets of the past lifted the actuality of such minor disasters onto the height of epic drama. There is no real evidence of such a global disaster. The divine advice given to Noah and the Babylonian sages "to enter the ark" is a symbolic answer to the perennial question of the "flood" which confronts us today with the same and maybe even more powerful urgency. Not only the moral but the physical survival of this planet is at stake.

Prior to the time the psyche had developed sufficiently for the poets to recognize and express the divine essence as "I Am," the external gods were clearly in control. In the myth of Atrahasis, it is told that the gods decided to "cut off nourishment from the people, scant became the vegetables in their bellies." The gods planned to annihilate the human race completely by means of starvation — the ancient equivalent of the atomic bomb! "This device, which could not be defended against by any concentration of worship, proved deadly."[35] "Enlil had lost all patience . . . and determined on the complete annihilation of man. He bound all his fellow gods by oath to bring on a flood."[36]

In the Old Testament, the ontogenesis of the psyche made a gigantic step forward by adding a new dimension to the symbol of physical survival. To be sure, the reality of the danger of being overcome by destructive forces beyond the immediate control of the individuals still exists, but in a dramatic way the psyche created its own corrective — the *Ark*.

"In the Greek Bible, but not in the Hebrew, the same word is used for the Ark of the Covenant, the box containing Israel's sacred objects."[37] The Hebrew word for the ark of bulrushes and Noah's ark is *tebah*, meaning "chest." In Numbers 10:34-35 it is written: "And the cloud of the Lord was over them by day, whenever they set out from the camp. And whenever the ark set out, Moses said, 'Arise, O Lord . . .' " Here the ark has become, in the eyes of the poets, the embodiment of "I Am," both physically and symbolically.

In Deuteronomy 10:1 the ark is clearly stated as the container for the "law":

> At that time the Lord said to me, 'Hew two tables of stones like the first and come up to me on the mountain, and make an ark of wood. And I will write on

the tables the words that were on the first tables which you broke, and you shall put them in the ark.

In Deuteronomy 30:14 the "chest" becomes the "heart": "... the word is very near to you; it is in your mouth and in your heart"; and in Deuteronomy 10:16 the poets place the essential meaning of the covenant where it has been all along: "Circumcise therefore the foreskin of your heart. ..." It is here, in the heart, and only here, where the *hayah*, the *I Am*, has its real seat and becomes genuinely efficacious.

> I will establish my covenant with you; and you shall come into the ark, you, your sons, your wife, and your sons' wives with you. And of every living thing of all flesh, you shall bring two of every sort into the ark, to keep them alive with you; they shall be male and female.[38]

> Noah went forth, and his sons, and his wife, and his sons' wives with him: Every beast, every creeping thing, and every fowl, and whatsoever creepeth upon the earth . . . went forth out of the ark.[39]

> And God said: "This is the sign of the covenant [the rainbow] which I make between me and you and every living creature that is with you, for all future generations."[40]

> I will remember my covenant which is between me and you and every living creature of all flesh; and the waters shall never again become a flood to destroy all flesh.[41]

Only a few thousand years after these dramatic lines were written, man threatens himself with "a flood to destroy all flesh," i.e., nuclear warfare. It is as if, inexorably, in accordance with the law of entropy, the famous second law of thermodynamics, society is doomed. This "eternal" law, however, is now seen as valid only in particular situations.

Ilya Prigogine, a Belgian chemist who won a Nobel Prize in 1977, proved in the field of chemistry,

> . . . that some small systems utilize the decay of the larger system to organize the dispersing components into more complex structures, thus creating order from chaos. Each molecule knows only its immediate neighbors and its direct environment, and it acts accordingly. That is normal. But in these new structures, the interesting thing is that the molecules also exhibit a coherent behavior that goes beyond the requirements of their local situations, that makes them suit their behaviour to the organization of a parent organism, which increases in complexity and grows to something vastly different from the mere sum of its parts. This is something completely new, something that yields a new scientific intuition about the nature of our universe. It is totally against the classical thermodynamic view that information must always degrade. It is, if you will, something profoundly optimistic.[42]

In its relentless urge for continuing growth and development of the inner life of man, however, the poets of the Bible spiritually anticipated by nearly 3,000 years a "physical principle — a fundamental impetus inexorably pushing life and human beings to further evolution and complexity, for better or worse, perhaps even against his will."[43]

In a drama of unsurpassed beauty and significance, the Biblical poets recount the process of change. The Ark is first symbolic of the presence of the Lord; it then becomes a shrine in which the Tablets of the Law found their sacred abode; and finally it comes to rest in the Holy of Holies, the sacred place at the heart of the Temple which even the High Priest entered but once a year. Above the Ark in the Holy of Holies was seen in a vision of unearthly majesty: the mercy seat, the seat of forgiveness. This symbolic evolution of the

Ark as the central theme in the myth of survival finds its continuation in Jeremiah, and then moves to the New Testament.

> We have this as a sure and steadfast anchor of *the soul*, a hope that enters into the inner shrine behind the curtain, where Jesus has gone as a forerunner on our behalf, having become a high priest forever after the order of Melchizedek.[44]

In a moral sense, the problem of the flood is the same problem dealt with in two other epic stories of the Bible. In the Old Testament, the resolution of the story of Jonah hinges on a text: "They that observe lying vanities [idols] forsake their own mercy."[45] That is to say, dogmatic adherence to misunderstood or un-understood values turns them into idols and leads man to "forsake his own mercy" — his own forgiveness. Thus, man is kept in a perpetual state of guilt and is dependent on "grace." The "grace" presumably mediated by the institutional Church is invalidated by the fact that it is "institutional." Unless grace is experienced authentically, that is, as a manifestation of *hayah* within the context of the personal and unique situation, nothing is changed.

The problem of grace raises the issue of why there remains injustice in the world at large. It is presumed that through adherence to the dogmatic teachings of the Church, the moral climate for a more humane society will prevail. On the contrary, in 2,000 years of the history of the Church, Western "Christendom" has a consistent record of brutal wars, hypocrisy, and individual suppression.

Perhaps this is so because the church has not elevated to the status of "dogma" the statement quoted earlier from *Dignitatis Humanae*, issued by Vatican II:

> Because of their dignity all human beings, in as much as they are persons, have inherent in their nature a moral obligation to seek the truth, to adhere to the

truth and to make the whole of their lives respond to truth's demands. They are in no position to meet that obligation unless they enjoy both psychological freedom and immunity from external coercion.

Unfortunately, in the fall of 1980, the Roman Catholic Church seemed to take a step backward on the issue of reconciliation for those whose marriages have been broken by divorce, and have entered into a new contract in a second marriage.

> To these pleas, the curial bloc, led by the Church's chief legist, the rotund Cardinal Pericle Felici of the Segnatura [the equivalent of the Church's supreme court], turned a deaf ear, with the observation that the law and not compassion was the criterion of the Church's moral code.[46]

Thus the external law is once again imposed upon the psyche.

Significantly, the theme of the Jonah epic is the task of awareness of values, in which task Jonah refused to participate:

> Now the word of the Lord came to Jonah . . . saying: Arise go to Nineveh, that great city, and cry against it; for their wickedness has come up before me. But Jonah rose to flee to Tarshish from the presence of the Lord . . . he found a ship going to Tarshish. . . . But the Lord hurled a great wind upon the sea, and there was a mighty tempest on the sea. . . . Then [the mariners] said to him: "What shall we do to you, that the sea may quiet down for us? . . ."

> So they took up Jonah and threw him into the sea. . . . And the Lord appointed a great fish to swallow up Jonah; and Jonah was in the belly of the fish *three days and three nights*. . . . "The waters closed in over

me, the deep was round about me; weeds were
wrapped about my head at the roots of the mountains. . . . When my soul fainted within me, I remembered the Lord and my prayer came to thee, into thy
holy temple: *those who pay regard to vain idols
forsake their true loyalty."*[47]

It is the same mythopoetic motif as in the New Testament:

And a great storm of wind arose. . . .
And he [Jesus] awoke and rebuked the wind,
and said to the sea, "Peace! Be still!"
And the wind ceased, and there was a great calm.[48]

In the Old Testament it is God who creates the storm; in
the New Testament it is Jesus who calms the storm. In the
Old Testament Jonah falls into an emotional state which the
poets describe as a storm and portray in symbols of deep
depression — "the weeds were wrapped round my head" —
because he had failed himself. Again, in the New Testament
Jesus asked: "Why are you afraid? Have you no faith?"[49]

In the Old Testament it is man through his own action, his
own remembering, his own awakening, who gets rid of the
demon which refused to listen to the voice from within and
sent him into a state of despair and depression. In the New
Testament it is Jesus who drives out the demons; it is Jesus,
the personified heightened awareness and awakening. Significantly, in the chapter immediately following the stilling
of the storm, Jesus sets several people free from their demons. It is only by acting out of an awakened state that
individuals will be enabled to cast out their demons, whether
they be political, economic, or religious. Only thus can the
moral problems confronting every person be dealt with, and
the world freed from its demonic drive toward self-
destruction in an atomic flood.

In Greek mythology these demons were the gods and
goddesses of Hades, the underworld, and in the parlance of
modern depth psychology they are called autonomous com-

plexes. "The gods grab us, and we play out their stories."[50] The Gnostic Gospel of Philip extols "God is a man-eater,"[51] and about people in the grip of a particular idea or set of ideas we say "they are eaten up by them."

Jonah's problem mirrors the problem of the world, and is essentially reflected in Job's misery and complaint about the injustice of the world. The problems of both Job and Jonah are resolved the moment they realize that they have not beheld (recognized and acknowledged) some essential aspects of their own being. The ontogenesis of the psyche had reached a level in these epic stories where the duality of life's inherent qualities could be experienced as parts of the whole. Reconciliation is to be found in the sacred precinct of man's inner self, his heart. It is essentially Jacob's way.

As Noah was advised to take "the seed of man and the seed of beast" into the ark, so in Jeremiah the ontogenesis of the psyche as drama moves into a new order in which the vexing problem of evil becomes the hinge on which further development turns. In the covenantal ceremony of Erbal and Gerizim, the Ark stands in the "midst," the very center, as the hub and meaning of the ceremony.

> Thereupon I awoke and looked, and my sleep was pleasant to me. "Behold, the days are coming, says the Lord, when I will sow the house of Israel and the house of Judah with *the seed of man and the seed of beast.* And it shall come to pass that as I have watched over them to pluck up and break down, to overthrow, destroy, *and bring evil,* so I will watch over them to *build and to plant,* says the Lord. In those days they shall no longer say:
>
>> "The fathers have eaten sour grapes
>> and the children's teeth are set on edge."
>> But every one shall die for his own sin;
>> each man who eats sour groups, his teeth shall be set
>> on edge. . . .

And no longer shall each man teach his neighbor and
each his brother, saying,
"Know the Lord," for *I will forgive* their iniquity
and I will *remember their sins no more.*" (Italics
mine)[52]

The eternal theme of integration, of wholeness, rings in
impressive sounds out of this dream-like poem. Both the
human seed and the seed of the beast belong together, but
man alone becomes responsible for his actions. Thus, the
ontogenetic process can turn creative: "I will watch over
them to build and to plant." And this personal experience of
integration excludes the whole edifice of moral teaching and
of being taught, because *the effort* of reconciliation by the
individual himself of the human and the beast within him *is
in itself forgiveness.* "... I will forgive their iniquities and I
will remember their sins no more." Again, this poem
responds to the problems of Job and Jonah, who through
their own personal integrative processes grew to answer the
questions posed by their life experiences.

Doubts about the validity of external and dogmatic moral
and ethical teachings have been legitimately raised in the
face of overwhelming crime and corruption which rule the
scene and thus weaken the body social the world over.
Certainly there is little success to show when, in the face of
traditional teaching, crime reaches from top to bottom of
the social order. 4,500 years ago an Egyptian poet composed
the following lines which might well have been written
today:

To whom do I speak today?
Brothers are evil,
Friends of today are not of love.

To whom do I speak today?
Hearts are thievish,
Every man seizes his neighbors' goods.

To whom do I speak today?
The gentle man perishes,
The bold-faced goes everywhere.

To whom do I speak today?
He of the peaceful face is wretched,
The good is disregarded in every place.

To whom do I speak today?
When a man should arouse wrath by his evil
   conduct,
He stirs all men to mirth, although his iniquity is
   wicked.

To whom do I speak today?
Robbery is practiced,
Every man seizes his neighbor's goods.
  . . . .

To whom do I speak today?
There are no righteous,
The land is left to those who do iniquity.[53]

This Egyptian sage addresses the same fundamental problems which confront us today. The quality of human relationship has deteriorated as more and more people think of their neighbor as a "what" rather than a "who." The tragic result is an exploitative society, and hence there is a desperate outcry for human rights and equality.

The Scapegoat

THE STAGES of the "presence" unfold. The divine in man's being presses relentlessly toward further and further differentiation and complexity. In the 16th Chapter of Leviticus we read the following:

> And Aaron shall offer the bull as a sin offering for himself, and shall make atonement for himself and for his house. Then he shall take the two goats, and set them before the Lord at the door of the tent of meeting; and Aaron shall cast lots upon the two goats, one lot for the Lord and the other lot for Azazel. And Aaron shall present the goat on which the lot fell for the Lord, and offer it as a sin offering, but the goat on which the lot fell for Azazel shall be presented alive before the Lord to make atonement over it, that it may be sent away in the wilderness to Azazel.

Aaron is then urged to kill a bull as a sin offering for himself:

> ... and he shall take some of the blood of the bull, and sprinkle it with his finger on front of the mercy seat ...

> Then he shall kill the goat of the sin offering which is for the people ... sprinkling it [the blood] upon the mercy seat and before the mercy seat ... There shall be no man in the tent of meeting when he enters to make atonement ... for himself and for his house

and for all the assembly of Israel. Then he shall go out to the altar which is before the Lord and make atonement for it, and shall take some of the blood of the bull and of the blood of the goat, and put it on the horns of the altar round about. And he shall sprinkle some of the blood upon it with his finger *seven* times, and cleanse it and hallow it from the uncleannesses of the people of Israel. And when he has made an end of atoning for the holy place and the tent of meeting and the altar, he shall present the live goat; and Aaron shall lay both his hands upon the head of the live goat, and confess over him all the iniquities of the people of Israel, and all their transgressions, all their sins; and he shall put them upon the head of the goat, and send him away into the wilderness. . . . The goat shall bear all their iniquities upon him to a solitary land; and he shall let the goat go in the wilderness.[54]

The Greek word *pharmakos* is equivalent to scapegoat and *pharmakon* means medicine, or drug. A close linguistic relationship between the expectation of healing and its effectiveness as a medicine is indicated. Frazer in his *Golden Bough* devotes a whole volume with innumerable examples from "primitive" societies to this very problem and Burkert does so from Greece.[55]

However, the ritual of the sacrifice of a scapegoat is not efficacious, as history has shown. On the contrary, the experience of the 20th century has proved the opposite. Instead of freeing society from its entanglement with the archaic past, from its denial of human values and the non-recognition of the "the sacredness of the person," the rationalized stupefaction of religious institutions embroiled as a consequence the superpowers in the deadly process of "scapegoating," and thus hastened their own decay. Instead of giving the lead exactly 50 years ago, seriously resisting racial policies by excommunicating Hitler and his fanatic followers, the religious institutions allowed the scapegoat ritual to take place. The result is, for the opposing ideologies, to consider the opponents' "religion" to be the scapegoat, which needs to be annihilated.

As a "natural" consequence the whole world is standing on the brink of extinction — a global holocaust through atomic bombs, affecting humans, animals and plant life alike, not only for the present but for future generations as well. Is not "evolution" conceivably testing itself whether or not the principle of the Hypercycle [supra, p. 61], with its proved self-correcting faculty, tries to correct the possible error of having created the human race, if it fails to make the correct, the human, choice?

Die Zeit, on April 23, 1982, writes:

> In the last issue of *Die Zeit* we reported a case which concerned a child, who was thrown out of the ecclesiastical Roman Catholic "Rheingold" — Kindergarten [sacrificed like a scapegoat] because he suffered from Epilepsy and occasional unconsciousness. The court of Mannheim ordered the Catholic congregation to reaccept the child "so as to enable the other children to learn how to deal naturally with disabled people" (a practical application of the legend of the good samaritan). The Catholic Church appealed the decision in the meantime.

Newsweek magazine on March 29, 1982, in a scientific context, published "The Mystery of Evolution," displaying on its front cover the dinosaur Tyrannosaurus Rex with its frightful fangs. The upper fangs could easily be imagined to represent the one, and the lower the other, superpower. In between these fangs the individual and society as a whole is crushed and the result is, as the unrelated caption of the front cover indicates, "The Outcry Over Nuclear Arms." Tyrannosaurus Rex, surely, is physically extinct; but can we be so sure that its spirit is not determining the world scene today, revealing itself as a balance of tyrannical terror?

While the one superpower is basically exploitative, trying to mould its citizens to the imagined wants of a consumer society, the other denies the right of the person *to be* for the sake of its exclusive philosophy which determines its imagined wants. Both these negatives are projected onto the other as a scapegoat; and both powers are therefore scapegoats for each other. The issue today therefore is not peace or war; the issue is peace or mutual annihilation. In war, even for the defeated, survival is possible. Deuteronomy 30:19: "I call heaven and earth to witness against you this day, that I have set before you life and death, blessing and curse; therefore choose life, that you and your descendants may live. . . ."

The issue is still more complicated by the fact that while the corporate personality, the state, is responsible for government and policies, it nevertheless consists of individuals. It is the degree of integration and the level of sophistication which determines the conduct of public affairs, whether they are ruled by the corruptive forces of the lowest common denominator or the ideals of justice. The lack of authentic personhood by the leaders is often covered up under the misleading slogan of "national sovereignty" and this in a time of satellites and rockets which know of no boundaries, as well as in a time of millions of hopeless refugees.

To kill the *pharmakos,* the scapegoat, to ban him, is not the healing *pharmakon,* the medicine. Again the Bible gives a pertinent hint. Significantly, as an illuminating detail of an illustration of the dragon being cast out in the Book of Revelation, an artist shows that to attempt to kill the scapegoat only leads the arrows back against the archer [infra, p. 445]. Just as Cain is not killed at the beginning of the Biblical story of becoming, so in Revelation, which forms the last book of the Bible, the dragon is not killed either.

In the exact details of the scapegoat ritual there is a fine mode of differentiation. Aaron is asked to make a sin offering both for himself as an individual and as a priest. In a further passage it is said:

> ... and Aaron shall lay both his hands upon the head of the live goat, and confess over him all the iniquities of the people of Israel and all their transgressions and all their sins; and he shall put them upon the head of the goat and send him away into the wilderness.

While in the former context Aaron confesses his sins as an individual, in the latter it is a ritualistic act for the corporate personality of Israel. In a later stage of development, expressing a higher level of the ontogenesis of the psyche, Moses addressed not the corporate personality, but the uniqueness of the individual when he said "the word is very near you; it is in your mouth and in your heart, so that you can do it" [supra, p. 114].

In this very statment, through the process of internalization, the "corporate sin" becomes a personal problem which the poets expressed appropriately: "*Your* wickedness will chasten you, and *your* apostasy will reprove you" [supra, p.64].

The poets in writing their myths were not creating out of a cultural vacuum; their stories were always culturally interrelated. Azazel is mirrored like a serpent in appearance, having hands and feet like a man and twelve wings.[57] He is described as the chief of the fallen angels, and the symbols surrounding this figure are snakes.

> In thousands of texts, mainly on the walls of the group of temples on the island of Phila, the goddesses Baat and Sochit, the indivisible aspects of a single female primal form, are being brought into contact with fire and heat. They are spitting fire, usually in the form of snakes, on to the adversaries of Osiris and contribute to his destruction.[58]

In Egyptian mythology as in Moses' exhortation, sin and virtue are related to life and death. Osiris is ever dying and reborn like nature. However, the Old Testament gives an answer to the pagan eternal round in giving guidance as to how to deal with evil:

> ... then the Lord sent fiery serpents among the people ... so that many people of Israel died. And the people came to Moses, and said: "We have sinned, for we have spoken against the Lord and against you; pray to the Lord, that he take away the serpents from us." So Moses prayed for the people. And the Lord said to Moses, "Make a fiery serpent, and set it on a pole; and every one that is bitten, when he sees it, shall live." So Moses made a bronze serpent, and set it on a pole; and if a serpent bit any man, he would look at the bronze serpent and live.[59]

In other words, the healing process is not the transferring of "sins" onto a scapegoat, but the direct conscious relation with what assails the person.

In Arabia pieces of these "metal serpents" have been found which were a symbol for god in the old Arabic religion. The metal serpent, as an idol, was worshipped by the Hebrews; and in later times Hezekiah "broke the pillars and cut down the Asherah. And he broke in pieces the bronze serpent that Moses had made, for until those days the people of Israel had burned incense to it; it was called Nehushtan."[60]

> While normally the Hebrew word for these and other snakes is *nahas,* the name *nehustan* is old Arabic ... *Nehustan* is feminine; compare the poetic word for snake *liwjatan,* Psalms 104:26; Job 3:8; Isaiah 27:1. As one finds *nahas* as a name for a person, I Samuel 11:1; II Samuel 10:2, 17:25, 27 so is *lewi minaic. Lewi*

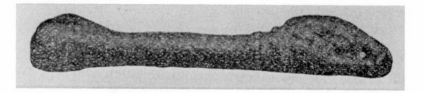

The Top Part of a Metal Serpent.

The Middle Part of a Metal Serpent.

Figure 15.   Metal Serpent.

denoting the priest, the priestess is called in *north-minaic* inscriptions *lewiatan*.[61]

In Judaism which is closely related to the old Arabic, *Lewiatan* is the symbol of evil, a primal monster like Behemoth, which if properly related to, indicates the way to salvation, as the Book of Job shows:

> Then will I also acknowledge to you, that your own right hand can give you victory.
>
> Behold, Behemoth, which I made as I made you . . . *He is the first of the works of God*.[62]

From a structural hermeneutic point of view both in old Arabic and Babylonian religion [infra, p. 262], the principle of complementarity was upheld and the feminine aspect was included in the totality, as it is so strikingly expressed in the Buddhist symbol of Yin and Yang.

A Jewish legend holds:

> Azazel persisted obdurately in his sin of leading mankind astray by means of sensual allurements. For this reason two he-goats were sacrificed in the Temple on the Day of Atonement, the one for God, that He pardon the sins of Israel, the other for Azazel, that he bear the sins of Israel.[63]

In our time through the efforts of establishing equal rights for females and males modern man is reaching into the very depth of human existence. The ontogenetic process of the psyche's becoming expresses itself in the search for equality and thus in a changed attitude toward sex itself.

Both this Jewish legend and Leviticus 16 unmistakably display God and the redemption from sin as an exterior to man. On the Day of Atonement "a memorial proclaimed with the blast of trumpets, a holy convocation shall be held." From the Day of Atonement with its expectation of forgiveness, the ritual action was carried into the realm of secular life, initiating the Jubilee year. Etymologically, the word *Jubilee* is most probably related to the Hebrew word *jobel*. *Jobel* means a "ram's horn" — a musical instrument — the *shofar,* which is still blown in the Jewish synagogue on the Day of Atonement each year. According to Leviticus 25, every fiftieth year is a Jubilee Year, when all debts are forgiven, men freed from slavery, and people are allowed to return to their property. In Leviticus 25:25, for example: "If your brother becomes poor and sells part of his property, then his next of kin shall come and redeem what his brother has sold."

The custom of extending the Jubilee to secular affairs as in the Old Testament was spiritualized and institutionalized by Pope Boniface VIII in 1300 A.D. The Jubilee Year, closely related to the description in Leviticus 25:10, is cele-

brated every seventh year in Rome, and represents seven
cycles of seven years. On the Jubilee Year, the closed and
bricked-up holy doors of *four* basilicas are opened. The
Pope opens the sealed door at St. Peter's with a silver
hammer as he chants: "Open to me the gates of justice."
Pilgrims coming to Rome for the Jubilee Year take communion, enter the confessional and visit the *four* cathedrals.

The Four-Faced Babylonian God

IT IS OF interest in this context to note that in the museum
of the Oriental Institute of Chicago a four-faced god and a
four-faced goddess are exhibited. They are of Babylonian
origin, stemming from Ishchali, and are dated 1800 B.C.
The four-faced god holds his left foot onto a ram and in his
right hand a staff. Surely, a structural analytical approach
could not see any relation between the four basilicas and
these Babylonian gods.

Burkert has written: "Structural — that is, synchronical
— methods have taken over and promise to bring about a
real science of the human mind and its creative output." And
he continues: "A myth, qua tale, is not identical with any
given text; the interpretation of myth therefore is to be
distinguished from the interpretation of a text, though both
may evolve in a hermeneutic circle and remain mutually
dependent upon each other.[64]

The four-faced god, who has not yet found a name, may
be possibly a representation of Marduk. Thorkild Jacobsen
in a private correspondence holds it possible that the four
faces may be symbolical of the four winds with which Marduk overcame the primal chaos, Tiamat, which *Enuma
Elish*, the Babylonian Genesis, Table IV, 37 states thus:

Figure 16. Bronze four-faced god, possibly Marduk, Old Babylonian Period, ca. 1800 B.C.

He took up the club and grasped [it] in his right
hand. . . .

and Tablet IV, 42-54 says:

[And] had the four winds take hold that nothing of her
might escape;
The south wind, the north wind, the east wind [and] the
west wind. . . .
The fourfold wind, the sevenfold wind, the whirlwind,
the wind incomparable. . . .
The Lord raised the rain flood, his mighty weapon.
He mounted [his] irresistible, terrible storm chariot;
He harnessed for it a team of *four* and yoked [them]
to it,
The Destructive, the Pitiless, the Trampler, the Flier.
They were sharp of tooth, bearing poison;
They knew how to destroy, they had learned to
overrun.[65]

And Tablet I, 81;93-98, says:

Within the *Apsû* [his mother] Marduk was born
. . .
Artfully arranged beyond comprehension were his
members,
Not fit for [human] understanding, hard to look
upon.
Four were his eyes, *four* were his ears.
When his lips moved, fire blazed forth.
Each of [his] four ears grew large,
And likewise his eyes, to see everything.[66]

The four-faced Babylonian god and his four-faced consort are a mythic anticipation of the four-dimensionality of
modern physics. Just as in the world of modern physics
apparent contradictory concepts are experienced to be different aspects of the same reality, so space and time are seen
to be equivalent. Appropriate to the thinking of about 4,000

years ago in the Babylonian figures equivalent concepts are also integrated into a four-dimensional continuum. In the difference between modern and mythic thinking the ontogenesis of the psyche expresses itself.

The symbolic struggle of Marduk with Tiamat is truly a gigantic step of the psyche toward freeing itself from the tumultuous darkness of unconsciousness. At the same time, the symbol dramatically integrates the multi-dimensionality of life into a single figure.

A structural analytical approach separates the world into individual parts, each of which is understood to exist as a distinct entity. And this mechanistic idea holds that something emerges mechanically from what was already present. Hence the frantic search in a so-called scientific method for local sources. This scientistic approach, however, has broken down in one field of knowledge after another.

Summing up, in a mindful scientific attitude, Niels Bohr in his speech on the occasion of his receiving the Nobel Prize in 1922 said:

> ... Sir Joseph Thompson and Sir Ernest Rutherford, who have inscribed their names in the history of science as shining examples of how imagination and acute insight are capable of looking through the multiplicity of experiences and laying bare to our eyes the simplicity of nature. On the other hand, abstract thought, which has always been one of mankind's most powerful aids in lifting the veil that conceals the laws of nature to the immediate observer, has been of decisive significance for applying the insight gained into atomic structure to explain the properties of the elements directly accessible to our senses.[67]

And some 30 years later, he says:

> A new epoch in physical science was inaugurated, however, by Planck's discovery of the *elementary*

quantum of action, which revealed a feature of *wholeness* inherent in atomic processes, going far beyond the ancient idea of the limited divisibility of matter.[68]

Not only do these penetrating remarks illuminate the profundity of Bohr's mind, but so also does the Coat of Arms he was awarded in 1947 in honor of his scientific achievements. The symbol crystallizes the mind's eternal quest to integrate apparent opposites. The age-old symbol of Yin and Yang, as exemplified also in the El Juyo face [supra, p. 182] of 12,000 B.C. illustrate this fundamental truth, as do the Biblical stories of the Golden Calf and the Jacob-Esau legend. Niels Bohr's emblem expresses it as *Contraria Sunt Complementa* — "Opposites Are Complementary."

As in the world of physics so in the mental world contraries are twins and the process of their integration is the theme of the mental drama of becoming. According to Chinese philosophy the Laws of Life "are the harmony of Movement which inhere in Life."[69] The Babylonian *Enuma Elish* "deals with universal human experiences, which it renders in familiar symbolic patterns, archetypes of individual development."[70] The four-faced Babylonian god with his attributes may be seen as a representation of this motif, anticipating mythologically what modern man experiences in his science today. Niels Bohr also writes: "We are not dealing with more or less vague analogies, but with clear examples of logical relations which, in different contexts, are met with in wider fields."[71]

The world of classical physics sees the staff, for example, that which the figure holds in his right hand, as a staff, just as Gertrude Stein says that "A rose is a rose is a rose is a rose,"[72] that is, a constant. A structural hermeneutic, on the other hand, sees the symbol of the staff in terms of interrelated discontinuity. The rod may have been experienced first as a weapon; for Moses on a level of heightened aware-

In 1947 Niels Bohr was awarded the Danish Order of the Elephant, which is normally only given to members of royal families and presidents of foreign states. On this occasion a coat-of-arms had to be designed which—according to the rules of the order—has to be placed in the church of the Frederiksborg Castle at Hillerød. Bohr chose the Chinese symbol for Yin and Yang, the two elements, which are opposite to and at the same time supplement each other. Together they form the world. The device represents the idea of complementarity: "Opposites are complementary".

Figure 17.   Niels Bohr's Coat of Arms.

ness it changes into a symbol of movement, the moving snake, but it is at the same time a weapon in the sense that it displays superiority. "Lift up your rod, and stretch out your hand over the sea and divide it, that the people of Israel may go on dry ground through the sea."[73]

Just as Marduk divided Tiamat into halves, so God separated the waters in Genesis.

> Let there be a firmament in the midst of the waters, and let it separate the waters from the waters. And God made the firmament and separated the waters which were under the firmament from the waters above the firmament. And it was so. And God called the firmament Heaven. And there was evening and there was morning, a second day.[74]

Moses also divided the sea as if the halves were like the mountains Erbal and Gerizim in Deuteronomy 27 through which the Israelites passed later on a higher level of the ontogenesis of the psyche, which allowed them to apply choice to life. The choice confronting Moses as a symbol of humanity he was not yet mentally prepared to accomplish; he used the rod instead of the Word. In Exodus 17:5-6 he is still using the rod: ". . . take in your hand the rod with which you struck the Nile. . . . I will stand before you there on the rock of Horeb; and you shall strike the rock and the water shall come out of it." The psyche, in a great play of movement of development, made the compilers of scripture fathom essential truth. Only *after* the great event on Mt. Sinai, in a most significant act, they present man in the figure of Moses with the new and decisive level, *the level of choice.* Being able to choose signifies the level of development *before* and *after* Sinai. In Numbers 20, the same motif reappears. The Israelites had no water:

> "Take the rod and assemble the congregation, you and Aaron your brother, and *tell* the rock before their eyes to yield its water. . . ." And Moses and Aaron gathered the assembly before the rock, and he said to them, "Hear now, you rebels; shall we bring forth water for you out of this rock?" And Moses lifted up his hand and *struck* the rock with his rod twice . . . And the Lord said to Moses and Aaron: "Because you did not believe in me, to sanctify me in the eyes of the people of Israel, therefore you shall not bring this assembly into the land which I have given them."[75]

The essence of life is multi-dimensional, and what is implicit is unfolded as the movement progresses. The movement itself reveals the essence; hence, dogmatic constrictions prevent the experience of a true "catholicity." The ram under the foot of the four-faced figure is a symbol we have encountered before. It plays a pivotal role in the Akedah when a ram is substituted for Isaac in the sacrifice. The ram's horn in the tradition of the Old Testament is a musical instrument which sounds at the moment of forgiveness and justice. As in the case of Jonah, forgiveness is dependent on man's own awakening to himself, on the realization that both the seed of man and the seed of the beast are part of himself, and that his own choice determines his mental aliveness or death. Above all, ". . . no longer shall each man *teach* his neighbor and each his brother, saying, 'Know the Lord' . . . for I will forgive their iniquities . . ."

In private correspondence, Thorkild Jacobsen wrote of the Ram:

> . . . the ram under his foot seems an emblem of sorts and I would connect it with a Sumerian concept that the clouds were the wool of a heavenly sheep and that snow and rain was the shearing of it. As a God of storms and rains this heavenly sheep would thus fit him [Marduk].

The ontogenetic problem of integration is superbly summed up in Psalm 147:

> He sends forth his command to the earth;
> He gives snow like wool . . .
> He makes his wind blow, and the waters flow.
> He declares his word to Jacob, his statutes and
>   ordinances to Israel.
> He has not dealt thus with any other nation; they do
>   not know his ordinances.[76]

The same motif of integration and choice as an archetype reappears in Isaiah 1:18:

> Come now, let us reason together, says the Lord:
> though your sins are like scarlet,
> they shall be as white as snow;
> though they are red like crimson,
> they shall become like wool.

The wind, the waters, the wool, the red and forgiveness are combined in this poem in a unifying symbol. A structural hermeneutical method reveals an essential psychic interrelation. The poets composing the Psalms, as well as Isaiah speaking as a prophet, give artistic expression to what is prevalent in the psyche, both at a particular moment and at a timeless point. Four, as a symbol of unification and wholeness, speaks to us with the same meaning from many different fields of knowledge and cultures.

And in Blake's magnificent painting "Ezekiel's Vision," the same archetypal theme is sounded in yet another variation:

> From the midst of [the fire] came the likeness of four living creatures. And this was their appearance: they had the form of men, but each had four faces, and each of them had four wings.[77]

The problem of accounting for the universal appearance of certain symbols clothed in manifold garbs throughout the world is sometimes thought to be solved by a theory of "migration." But even if we accept such a dubious theory, there remains the question of why a particular symbol was accepted while others were not. I hold that the unifying symbol is the essence of the heart which is expressed in the *hayah,* which stands for the "I Am" of becoming, the Tetragrammaton, the unpronounceable YHWA. In every case it comes from the same internal impetus of the psyche, but is embodied in a variety of manifestations, and yet is truly "catholic," "different only in his hundred tones," as expressed in its cultural and individual presentations.

As it is with the four-faced god, so it seems to be with the four-faced goddess. She apparently was conceived as the consort to the four-faced god, as vital in the scheme of things as her counterpart. In the Babylonian Genesis, Tiamat was considered to have, like Marduk, four eyes: "Her two right eyes are the Tigris, her two left eyes the Euphrates."[78]

Figure 18. William Blake, *Ezekiel's Vision.*

Figure 19.   Bronze four-faced goddess, consort, Old Babylonian
Period, ca. 1800 B.C.

Clearly, there is therefore a close mythological relation
between Tiamat and "life-giving waters." The four-faced
goddess holds in her hands a most significant symbol: "the
flowing vase from which life-giving water streams down on
either side."[79] According to the tradition of the Old Testament, the life-giving well which accompanied the Israelites
on their journey through the desert was called Miriam's
well. This "well dates back to the beginning of the world, for
God created it on the second day of the creation."[80]

A river flowed out of Eden to water the garden,
and there it divided and became *four* rivers.[81]

In the Old Testament, the female image becomes a decisive turning point for the further development of the
psyche.[82] Miriam, the sister of Moses, so the legend tells us,

"had hardly died when the well also disappeared. . . . She was the only woman who died during the march through the desert."[83] Miriam's well is a symbol of the life-giving waters, which existed in the "midst" of the people, and therefore symbolizes not an exterior force, but an internal reality.

At Dura Europos, a town in Syria, the oldest Christian Church and a decorated synagogue were discovered during World War I. At the west wall of the synagogue, one of the murals depicts Miriam's well, symbolically feeding the twelve tribes.

> Discovered forty years ago in what Mikhail Rostovt-zeff called "The Pompeii of the Syrian Desert," the third-century Dura-Europos synagogue has success-fully challenged stereotyped and well-established scholarly theories. Although not as well-known or as widely publicized as the Dead Sea Scrolls, the synagogue, nonetheless, has revolutionary implications of great importance to all students of ancient history, religion and art. The first major Jewish artistic monument ever to be unearthed, it contains the earliest known significant continuous cycle of biblical images. Figural decoration of similar complexity and extensiveness does not appear in Christian art until the fifth century.[84]

The very fact that the theme of Miriam's well was also chosen for representation in a mural shows the significance of the religious awareness attached to its symbolic meaning. As we shall see later, the symbol represented by the head of John the Baptist on a platter is also expressed in art. True to the monotheistic characteristic of the Old Testament, the wind and the water as distinctive features of the male and female four-faced Babylonian gods have been transferred to the one God. "He makes his wind to blow and the waters to flow,"[85] and "the Spirit of God was moving over the face of the waters."[86] The Hebrew word for *spirit* used here is *ruach*, meaning both spirit and wind. In the New Testament, Jesus becomes the master of both wind and water. Mark 4:39 tells that "the wind ceased and there was a great calm," and Matthew 14:25 tells of Jesus walking on the water.

A structural hermeneutic approach reveals a close interrelation of Numbers 20 with Matthew 14. As Numbers 20 of the Old Testament demonstrates the ontogenesis of the psyche in terms of events *before* and *after* Sinai, so Matthew 14 signifies another watershed in the psyche's development. Before Sinai, Moses is told to use his rod, while after Sinai he is directed to use "the word" — because he disobeyed this order he was not allowed to enter the promised land.

The Significance of Herod

THOUGH Herod in Matthew 14 is attested historically, scholars believe that the events of this chapter are legendary. This aspect is important in the context of religious acceptance and belief. Again, as with Abraham, the writer(s) of Matthew here make use of a historical figure around which to create their message. In Matthew 14 is the dazzling dance of Herod's granddaughter, which results in the beheading of John the Baptist. A member of the Herod dynasty is the reason that Mary and Joseph must flee with the infant Jesus:

> ... an angel of the Lord appeared to Joseph in a
> dream and said, "Rise, take the child and his mother,
> and flee to Egypt, and remain there till I tell you; for
> Herod is about to search for the child, to destroy
> him." (Matthew 2:13)

Herod is used here poetically as another representation of inertia trying to stop the growth and development of the psyche.

As a further example of this fact, the exposure motif of an

infant exists in many different versions the world over. The Sargon legend portrays the child to be endangered or abandoned, as was Moses.[87] Most of the variations upon the same theme have three motifs in common. First, the ruling principle — often symbolized as a king — feels threatened by a son, i.e., the inertia stands conservatively against the "new" and tries therefore to annihilate the infant. Secondly, the threat often reaches the awareness through the unconscious mode of a dream and thirdly the pregnancy is frequently due to "abnormal" circumstances, portrayed as an indiscretion or rape. These facts demonstrate both the universality of basic psychic themes, as well as the ontogenesis of the psyche. However, the activity of the self-regulating power of the psyche is resisted by the dogma-like, fixed, ruling position of consciousness. For life to continue to grow, the "new" needs to outgrow the old, which considers "naturally" from its position, the new as "ill-begotten." Freud built his whole theory upon this mental reality, based on the Oedipus version of the Sargon legend and provided thus a "scientific" garb for the dogma of Original Sin. On the other hand the dogma of Immaculate Conception is a spiritualization and theologizing of the natural order and therefore a particularly striking example of the persisting urge of the psyche toward a "higher order of organization."

The awesome dramatic representation of the psyche's urge to retreat and hold back is gruesomely depicted in that John the Baptist's head is served *on a platter* as if it would be food. This stark motif inspired many artists to paint their pictures, which, in their realism, touch deep springs in man. In cannibalism, our ancestors tried in an acquisitive manner, magically to *acquire* the power of the deceased through the act of eating. In Matthew 14 Salome's mother Herodias is a symbol for the negative non-giving mother who is making use of her own child to achieve her ends. She tried to destroy the imprisoned John the Baptist, whose existence symbolically confronts her with her own task of giving, of loving. Scripture, after all, portrays human relationship as the motif for John's imprisonment; and John is here the representative for the reborn, the giving, the Christ. Herod on the other hand adheres to his earlier intention, as a symbolical representation of inertia who had tried before to kill the infant. However, in this act of the drama of the ontogenesis of the psyche the head of John the Baptist is presented on a platter *as if* it would be food. This dramatic scene represents symbolically on a higher level of differentiation the needed assimilation which cannibalism on a lower level depicts. The importance of this chapter is emphasized by the fact that in Mark 16:1 it is Salome who brings spices "to anoint [Jesus]," and according to Mark 16:4, Salome is one of the women who discover the "risen Christ" and the empty tomb. The stark importance of this powerful image stimulated the imagination of artists.

In Oscar Wilde's play, "Salome," he says to her: ". . . get thee to the desert and seek out the Son of Man." Salome passionately pronounces, referring to the mouth of John: "I will bite it with my teeth as one bites ripe fruit."[88] In both versions, the New Testament and the artistic one of Oscar Wilde, there is disappointed human relationship, the hunger for love.

Most significantly, there is Donatello's relief "The Feast of Herod" — ca. 1425, the baptismal font of S. Giovanna — which depicts the serving of John's head on a platter to Herod.[89] The ontogenetic principle is expressed in this piece of art, and is of great importance when it is seen in connection with the Last Supper and with the ritual described in Colossians 2:12: "Buried with him in baptism, wherein you were also raised with him . . ." Richard Strauss also composed his opera "Salome" around the same theme. Matthew 14 in combination with Mark 16 is a superb example of the interaction of various levels of psychic experiences spun around a central theme like a symphonic poem. In this case, the theme is faith in giving, trust in love.

Equally moving is the higher level of psychic organization demonstrated significantly in the *same* chapter of the Bible

Figure 20.   Donatello, *The Feast of Herod,* ca. 1425.

in the feeding of the multitude, which Jesus accomplishes
with just five loaves and two fishes; miraculously, the more
people there were, the more there was to feed them.[90] Surely,
this is reminiscent of the manna from heaven which sus-
tained the Israelites in the Exodus account. What is depicted
here is a symbolic demonstration of that to which all can
attest — namely, that the more one is prepared to give, the
more greatly one feels the power to be able to do so. Here, as
in Numbers 20, the centering process of this "water of life" is
the essential message; it is the process of being one's own
self, the source, the well of giving.

At the same time, the dramatic movement of mental
energy is accompanied by its natural component: fear.
Immediately following the "miraculous" feeding of the multitude, the poets take us to the story of the stilling of the

storm. Having confronted man with the tremendous potential within himself, the natural and creaturely response was
to draw back in fear. Fearful and mistrustful and not believing in his own mental powers, the poets describe this insta-
bility of man in terms of the raging waters, which as the
personification of the "new," Jesus masters spiritually: *Noli
timere ego sum* — "Don't be afraid, it is I." That is to say, I
am the living representation of your own *hayah*, your own
"I Am".

As with the well of Miriam in the Old Testament, so is
Christ's walking on the waters a vital demonstration of the
inherent quality of man to make actual his propensities and
to realize them in the context of a non-material meaningful
existence. It is the preparedness for a humanistic distribution of life's generous gifts as a conscious decision born of
freedom, not coercion, which constitutes our humanity.

The drama of Matthew 14, which may be considered to be
the hub around which the motivation of genuine religion
turns, is in an artistic sense created with the same motifs as
Numbers 20. In Numbers it is the death of Miriam around
which a further differentiation of the psyche is spun; in
Matthew 14 it is the death of John the Baptist which is the
motivating agent. In Numbers 20 the question is raised by
the poets of the lifting of awareness from the level of materiality of the rod to the level of the immaterial yet efficacious
word. In Matthew 14 the acquisitive mood of eating is
transformed, symbolically, into giving. Thus basic to both
dramas is the theme of faith, of confidence, the inner confidence in the Self. In Matthew 14 this *self*-confidence is an
ever-renewed well for the potential of giving, i.e., feeding,
expressed in the symbol of five loaves and two fishes, which,
ever-renewed, fed the multitude. In Numbers 20 the waters
of life spring forth in abundance.

In Numbers 20 there is fear and high emotionality because
of the absence of the well, so it is in Matthew 14 where Jesus
is absent: "he went up into the hills by himself to pray. When
evening came he was there alone."[91] "Then he made the

disciples get into the boat . . . and the boat was tossed by the waves.[92] Both these basic dramas depict the ontogenesis of the psyche growing towards further and further differentiation in the heart of man.

In the 6th chapter of John's Gospel, we have the same story of the feeding of the multitude with a few loaves and fishes. For the New Testament writers, this "miracle" story is supremely important since it is included in all four of the Gospel accounts. In John also, the story of the stilling of the storm also follows the miracle of the loaves and fishes, the account of which is as follows:

> When Jesus therefore perceived that they would come and take him by force, to make him a king, he departed again into a mountain himself alone. And when even was now come, his disciples went down unto the sea, and entered into a ship, and went over the sea toward Capernaum. And it was now dark, and Jesus was not come to them. And the sea arose by reason of a great wind that blew. So when they had rowed about five and twenty or thirty furlongs, they see Jesus walking on the sea, and drawing nigh unto the ship: and they were afraid. But he saith unto them, It is I; be not afraid. Then they willingly received him into the ship: and *immediately the ship was at the land whither they went.*[93]

Here we have a clear-cut demonstration in poetic form of the conquering of anxieties, and the result of man's relation to himself in the context of his anxieties.

In Greek mythology the same process, but not yet on the level of psychic development as in the Gospel, seems to be indicated in Odysseus' tying himself physically to the mast of his ship. There is no freedom of movement or choice as with Christ facing his temptations in the desert. In Homer these temptations are symbolized by the Sirens. Today, people no longer entrust themselves to "the ship" which symbolizes the Church in Christianity.

Hippolytus was the first of the Fathers to express the symbolism of this idea with something like a painter's sureness of touch. As a ship leaves no trace upon the changing waters, so also the Church which traverses this world after the manner of a ship; for she has left behind her on the shore all hopes that she otherwise might have had, and has pledged her life in advance to the heavens.[94]

For modern men in their realism, this ship allowed itself to be tossed by the storms of the times and did not stand upright, and thus neither spoke to nor could calm the waves as Christ did. The Pope's blessing, e.g., of the arms and the poison gas Mussolini used in his war against helpless Abyssinia, and his silence in relation to the crimes of the Nazis, have shaken the foundation of trust in our time.

The New Testament assessed the misunderstanding of the crowd correctly, that "they would come and take him by force, to make him a king," i.e., to keep inert in their expectations to be fed, instead of growing toward an attitude of giving; the poetic symbol also revealed that as soon as the propensity for giving, for love, is integrated, "immediately the ship was at the land whither they went." The openness and preparedness for integration, for acceptance of the "new," is security itself and demonstrates the way of the ontogenesis of the psyche.

According to Jewish legend, when Moses died, "the well, the clouds of glory, and the manna disappeared forever."[95] The manna, the loaves, and the fishes are no longer gifts from the heaven "out there" but become components of the human heart, regulating and determining agents for the life of a truly human person. As with all great art, the poetry of the Bible has the power of transforming concrete images into a living symbolism. And to the degree that each person is open and willing to listen to the essence within himself, he becomes independent of those other teachers who are prone to tell him to "Know the Lord."

Rembrandt in his art brought to bear the inner light upon

the "reality" of his portraits and transformed the "It," the thingness, into a "Thou," the inner essence of man; *a* man, *a* woman, into This Man, This Woman, and allowed the inner essence to show forth. In his famous etching labeled "Faust," the artist not only enlightens the mirror with his own light, but it in turn enlightens his subject. In his painting "Jewish Bride," the reality of the heartbeat is transfigured into the beauty of love. And in the "Head of Christ," the expression is "no longer based on anecdotal gesture. It emanates like a light; it radiates like the ardor of love. For Rembrandt, the Christ is a problem of the soul, of his own inner life."[96]

In terms of the ontogenesis of the psyche we must not forget that Rembrandt's painting came after the imprisonment of the individual's mind in the Middle Ages, and breathed a breath of freedom, the freedom to experience his own depth in an unfettered way. As long as the artist served a common faith, the images became corporate idols; and therefore the individual with his unique and immediate relation with the Divine was suppressed. Corporate images had in themselves an inertia about them, because of their precise contours in form and colour which had to fit into the constructs of a common faith. Images born of our own inner experience and reflections are varied and diffused while being concrete condensations of those experiences, and as such express the individual's unique experience.

In the past, art and the artist were at the service of a common faith and that is why in antiquity there is no name of any artist preserved for us. But in the 17th century we are finding a definite change from the artist's main task of illuminating the common corporate faith; and we find it particularly expressed in Rembrandt, who gave his art the stamp of his personal sensibility and enriched the visual object through the masterful introduction of his own inner light. And that inner light was the light of the Divine in man which could be accepted unquestionably because it did not present itself in a static, fixed form of an idol.

Figure 21. Rembrandt, *Faust Watching a Magic Mirror,* 1652.

Figure 22. Rembrandt, *Head of Christ,* 1656.

It was Rembrandt's contemporary, Galileo (Galileo Galilei died in 1642; and Rembrandt died in 1669), in whom the human spirit broke the static patterns and fossilized dogma of a thousand years, opening the mind of man to the wonders of the world of science. In the same way, Teilhard de Chardin describes his experience with the inner world:

> We must try to penetrate our most secret self, and examine our being from all sides. Let us try, patiently, to perceive the ocean of forces to which we are subjected and in which our growth is, as it were, steeped. . . . And so for the first time in my life perhaps (although I am supposed to meditate every day!) I took the lamp and, leaving the zone of everyday occupations and relationships where everything seems clear, I went down into my inmost self, to the deep abyss whence I feel dimly that my power of action emanates. But as I moved further and further away from the conventional certainties by which social life is superficially illuminated, I became aware that I was losing contact with myself. At each step of the descent a new person was disclosed within me of whose name I was no longer sure, and who no longer obeyed me. And when I had to stop my exploration because the path faded from beneath my steps, I found a bottomless abyss at my feet, and out of it came — arising I know not from where — the current which I dare call *my* life. . . .
>
> At that moment, as anyone else will find who cares to make this same interior experiment, I felt the distress intrinsic to an atom lost in the universe, the distress which makes human wills founder daily under the crushing number of living things and of stars. And if something saved me, it was hearing the voice of the Gospel . . . speaking to me from the depth of the night: *ego sum, noli timere* ("It is I, be not afraid").[97]

The Four-Foldedness

THE STRUCTURAL hermeneutic method reveals another essential psychic interrelation between the *four* cathedrals and the *four* faces of the gods, and to an extent, also enlightens Teilhard de Chardin's experience of the "bottomless abyss."

To explore the psychic significance of the number four is to review much of the human apperception of reality. We can only skim the surface here, and of the multitude of instances we might cite, only a few must suffice to illustrate its archetypal significance.

To begin, it should be noted that in the field of science, this number four plays a vital role. We perceive reality in four dimensions, three in space and one in time; we find ourselves oriented in space by the four points of the compass — north, south, east and west. The unified field theory tries to find unity in four areas: gravity, the electromagnetic field, and that of the low and highly charged particles. And last, but not least,

> . . . the primeval atmosphere on the surface of the earth was, in all probability, a reducing one containing essentially the *four* elements carbon, hydrogen, nitrogen and oxygen, primarily in their reduced form, as the simplest molecules . . . the development from atom to molecule, from polymer to cell shows the four elements that are involved in the primeval atmosphere.[98]

We see the same number in the philosophical quaternity of the Greeks who named the essential elements of life as earth and air, fire and water. The early Christians chose *four* Gospels in their canon of scripture. The Egyptian pyramid stands on a square with four equal sides. The numinous symbol of the cross also points to four dimensions. Above all, the unpronounceable name of the divine, the tetragrammaton consists of four letters: *yod, he, wav, he — Yhwh — Yahweh — Lord*. There are *four* apocalyptic horses magnificently displayed over the main entrace to St. Mark's Cathedral in Venice. But,

> . . . these horses are not Christian at all. They might, at a pinch, be thought to recall the Four Horsemen of the Apocalypse; but they have no riders. In historical fact their presence commemorates one of the most unchristian acts . . . yet another crusade [the fourth crusade launched by Pope Innocent III, which reached the Bosporus in 1204]. . . .
>
> The horses are made of bronze. They were once gilded, and some of the gold remains to this day. Nobody knows their origin, but they were made about the 3rd Century B.C., and may have been in Rome before they were carried off by Constantine to his new capitol on the Bosporus. They probably drew a chariot, and they are so superbly done that they might even have been created by the Greek sculptor Lysippus.[99]

This reference is to the Four Horsemen in Revelation 6; the first was white, the second bright red, the third black and the fourth pale, representing retributive and punishing power. "By these three plagues a third of mankind was killed, by the fire and smoke and sulphur issuing from their mouths. For the power of the horses is in their mouths and in their tails; their tails are like serpents, with heads, and by means of them they wound."[100]

The number four also appears in Revelation 4:6-8:

> And round the throne, on each side of the throne, are

four living creatures, full of eyes in front and behind: the first living creature like a lion, and the second living creature like an ox, the third living creature with a face of a man, and the fourth living creature like a flying eagle. And the four living creatures, each of them with six wings, are full of eyes all round and within, and day and night they never cease to sing, "Holy, holy, holy, is the Lord God Almighty, *who was and is and is to come!*" (Italics mine)

Nor is the number four confined to the ancient world or the sphere of Indo-European culture. In North America, the figure also plays a part. In a revelatory vision, a holy man of the Oglala Sioux Indians saw a powerful spectacle — The Horse Dance:

There were four black horses to represent the west; four white horses for the north; four sorrels for the east; four buckskins for the south. For all of these, young riders had been chosen. . . . After the horse dance was over, it seemed that I was above the ground and did not touch it when I walked. I felt very happy, for I could see that my people were all happier. Many crowded around me and said that they or their relatives who had been feeling sick were well again, and these gave me gifts. Even the horses seemed to be healthier and happier after the dance.[101]

It is of interest, as well as of some curiosity, to note that the American dollar bill shows a pyramid resting on a square with four triangles conjoined in the "all seeing eye," and inscribed "In God We Trust," and "He Approves of the New World Order."

The four as a symbol of unification and wholeness speaks to us with the same meaning from ever so many divergent cultures. We hold that the symbol of unification is the essence of the heart as expressed in *hayah,* the "I Am," which all the world over stems from the same source, but embodies itself as becoming in a truly "catholic" sense, in different tones.

According to the Apocrypha "Adam's name was constructed from the initials of the four corners of the world."[102] And in some Gnostic writings, Adam's name is symbolic because he represents the four directions of the wind.[103]

Both of the above sources are more recent by at least a thousand years than the original writings in which man's creation from the dust of the earth was first recorded. Yet in these stories we can trace the ontogenesis of the psyche, ever lifting human experience to a higher level of organization — to a new and different dimension of consciousness, to a new dimension of awareness.

The four-faced Babylonian god and goddess, the four rivers flowing from the Garden of Eden and the four basilicas in Rome are all symbols of human growth and the movement toward universality of experience as each person moves toward fulfillment.

Hans Küng, a contemporary Swiss theologian of considerable stature, confirms much of our use of the structural hermeneutic in regard to the scripture when he writes: "Divine revelation and human experience are not simply antithetical. Rather, divine revelation is only accessible through human experience."[104] These experiences are not necessarily bound to history in order to express their truth. In the Bible historical events are often used only as a backdrop to express poetically and dramatically aspects on the way to salvation. Salvation for modern man is salvation from unconscious constraints and frustrations which hinder the realization of the fullness of life's manifold possibilities.

Is There A Purpose?

I asked the plum tree: is there a purpose?
Weighed down by a crop heavy as grief,
It answered, "The purpose is to be a tree.
What other purpose could there be?"
But I watched it sicken of silver-leaf.

I asked the willow warbler: is there a purpose?
Young innocent in the thorny brake,
It answered: "The purpose is to be a bird.
What other purpose could there be?"
But I saw no mercy in the eye of the snake.

I asked my blood brother: is there a purpose?
Busy at his craft in the sun-washed room,
He answered: "The purpose is to be a man,
What other purpose could there be?"
When they called him to breakfast he did not come.

I asked the Hidden One: is there a purpose?
Dear and doomed in brother, bird and tree,
He answered, "The purpose is creativity."
What other purpose could there be?
Am I not creating you — and you Me?"
                    — F. Pratt Green[105]

CHAPTER 6

Wholeness

To see a World in a Grain of Sand,
And a Heaven in a Wild Flower,
Hold Infinity in the palm of your hand
And Eternity in an hour.[1]

Jesus then said:
"You will seek me and you will not find me;
where I am you cannot come."[2]

A Lamp am I to you that perceive me. Amen.
I am a mirror to you who know me. Amen.
I am a door to you who knock on me. Amen.
I am a way to you, the traveler. Amen.

Now if you follow my dance,
see yourself
in Me who am speaking,
and when you have seen what I do,
keep silence about my mysteries. . . .

You who dance, consider
what I do, for yours is
This passion of Man
which I am to suffer.

For you could by no means
have understood what you suffer
unless to you as Logos,
I had been sent by the Father. . . .

[What I am] you shall see
when you come yourself.[3]

What I Am You Shall See When You Come To Yourself

A S AN EXPRESSION of deepest religion, albeit unconsciously, the children from the Nazi horror camp of Terezin,
through which about 15,000 passed, of which however only
around 100 came back alive, drew pictures onto the walls of
the death prison. Drawings and poems of these children
have been collected in a moving volume entitled ". . . I Never
Saw Another Butterfly . . ." One of these drawings depicts
six children holding hands and performing a dance while at
the same time expressing in their bodily forms the horror
they lived. Out of the very depth of Being they danced a
sacred dance, transcending the stench of the corpses, the
moaning and groaning of the dying, the blood of the tor-
tured. These drawings are genuine in the sense that they do
not illustrate a story of a literal dance.

The drawings give lie to the assumption that man is solely
the product of his environment, which portrays a pathetic
state of mind shared by the arrogant and dogmatic exclusiveness in the ideas held by political and religious institutions. These innocent children danced an ode to life in much
the same manner that their elders sang a messianic song as
they rode the death trains to Auschwitz or Belsen.

In *Studies in the Gospels*, Prof. Donald McKinnon says,
"The Messianic banquet remained for the Jews of Hitler's
Europe the symbol of promise."[4] The songs the elders sang
demonstrate his thesis:

> Rabbi, our Rabbi, what will be
> when the Messiahs will have come?
> There will be a big meal.

Rabbi, our Rabbi, what will one do
on this banquet?
The leviathan will be slaughtered,
on this banquet of the future.

Oh, Rabbi, our Rabbi, what will one drink
on this banquet of the future?

Sacred wines one will drink,
Meat and fish will be eaten,
On the banquet of the future.[5]

The roots of this remarkable poem about a Messianic banquet go most probably back to Psalm 74:14 and thence to the Talmud in which it is said: "In the future a banquet from the flesh of the Leviathan will be arranged for the just."[6] The Apocrypha Baruch 29:4 reads: "And Behemoth shall be revealed from his place; and Leviathan shall ascend from the sea. These two great monsters which I created on the fifth day of creation, and have kept them until that time. Then they shall be food for all that are left."

The drawing of the sacred dance by a child, and the song of the elders in the death trains to Belsen and Auschwitz, may have been symbolically expressing some reasons for the apparent apathy of the Jews not to fight back violently against the Nazis. The Jews knew themselves to be totally isolated and utterly betrayed by the professed spirituality of the religious institutions as to the eternal value of the person. In face of the most monstrous program of systematic murder the world has ever seen, the response of the Church was — silence!

The innermost feeling which condemned these innocent victims to inaction may have been also to fulfill a fate for the world at large. They seem to have assimilated the radical evil of the Nazi "Leviathan," accepting the enormity of the horror of evil's existence by symbolically eating it or transcending it in a sacred dance. In their devout acceptance of their fate, they reflect again the response of the embattled verse of the Essenes — they "offered sacrifices *within themselves.*"[7] "Any contact with impurity, either physical or moral . . . any infringement of traditional taboos, and any violation of cultic laws, was regarded by the Hebrews as entailing an impairment of the *offenders'* essential 'self' " (italics mine).[8]

Today exactly 50 years after the Church authorities should have spoken out, the faculty, staff and student body of the Harvard Divinity School in Cambridge voiced their objection against the use of nuclear weapons. They declared: "In the name of God, let us speak out now, lest our silence once again make us accomplices to holocaust, this one threatening the very existence of humankind."[9]

The depth of the enormity of what is symbolized in the words of Leviathan or Behemoth can perhaps to some degree be gauged in two related factual accounts of actual experiences, and not as abstractions, as "the Eichmann in all of us." On March 10, 1978, *Die Zeit* reports a trial which has been taking place since September 1975 and which at the date of writing these lines, May 7, 1980, has not yet found its end. *Die Zeit* stated:

> Between 1942 and 1944 in the death factory of Maidanek, a suburb of Lublin in Poland, tens of thousands of women and children were gassed, beaten, tortured and murdered. The concentration camp especially for females and children was situated on a tract of 245 acres, contained 125 barracks, 7 gas chambers and a crematorium. Confronting a defendant, a witness stated: "Yes that is her. She has been a bloody monster. She has always been present when they beat up somebody. She was nicknamed the bloody Brigitte. With her one always saw blood, always the blood of our comrades. There was nobody like her who really could give orders more beastlike, more sadistic. For us here, there was

simply nobody in the whole world who could have been worse than her." Hildegard Lechert who was at the time 20 years old, trampled her victims to pulp. She had ordered to have fixed special iron caps onto her pointed boots. The witness remembers, "One day she whipped and trampled upon somebody who had worked in the ditch. She did not stop before she had torn her to pieces, 'til she has been nothing more than a junk of a human body, a clump of flesh. Then she asked the other inmates to remove that piece of dirt" (translation mine).

An Egyptian poem of about 2,000 B.C. says:

> Death is before me today
> Like the recovery of a sick man,
> Like going forth into a garden after sickness.
>
> Death is before me today
> Like the odour of myrrh,
> Like sitting under the sail on a windy day.
>
> Death is before me today
> Like the odour of lotus flowers,
> Like sitting on the shore of drunkenness.
>
> Death is before me today
> Like the course of the freshet,
> Like the return of a man from the war-galley
>   to his house.
>
> Death is before me today
> Like the clearing of the sky,
> Like a man fowling towards that which he
>   knows not.
>
> Death is before me today
> As a man longs to see his house
> When he has spent many years in captivity.[10]

Laurens van der Post in his book, *A Bar of Shadow*, reports his experiences in a Japanese prison camp:

> It was John Lawrence, who suffered more at Hara's hands than any of us except those whom he killed, who first drew our attention to his eyes. I remember so clearly his words one day after a terrible beating in prison.
>
> "The thing you mustn't forget about Hara," he had said, "is that he is not an individual or for that matter even really a man." He had gone on to say that Hara was the living myth, the expression in human form, the personification of the intense, inner vision which, far down in their unconscious, keeps the Japanese people together and shapes and compels their thinking and behaviour.[11]

During World War II, towns like Dresden and Hamburg were destroyed without any overriding military justification. Vietnam alone was subject to more bombs than the total used in the whole of World War II. Torture and imprisonment of political dissenters is meted out today in many nations, and in turn, many of the victims become murdering terrorists. In the United States alone, after 4,000 years of the Judaeo-Christian tradition, there is sacrificed on the altar of destructive force a disproportionately high percentage of its annual available expenditures. And the Vatican, despite the pronouncements of Vatican II in *"Dignitatis Humanae,"* has reintroduced an inquisition to deal with dissenting clergy. This step has led the eminent theologian, Hans Küng, to declare: "Catholic Church, yes! Roman Inquisition, no!"[12]

The overweening power of Leviathan is the basis of Hobbe's political philosophy, in which the powers of the sovereign are unlimited. In the mythopoetic realm of the psyche, Leviathan often overrules conscious intentions as if this monster were a politically institutionalized censor. The mindless submission to an institution, be it political, religious or otherwise, and man's identification with it, denies the person the way to himself, and thus to essential truth. One is ruled by whatever the Leviathan as part of the essential self in an individual situation represents. Out of the primal soup (Genesis 1:21) the "chicken broth" of the biologists, Leviathan as part of the *prima materia*, the primal stuff, is born. The most essential task and therefore meaning of man's existence seems to be the transfiguration of this primal stuff. The ontogenetic process of the psyche expresses itself in these experiences of which alchemy is, on its philosophical level, a correlative manifestation. In alchemy the monster, the dragon, is both the transforming power and the *prima materia* to be transformed, through the alchemical process of becoming. The end product of this process is then the "pearl of highest price," the philosopher's stone, the experience of the individual's uniqueness. The brutalities of one-sided political systems, holy wars, the age-old corruption of society from the very top down to the level of the ordinary citizen are certain signs that the transformation of the Leviathan within the individual, and consequently within the sphere of corporate experience, has not taken place. Religious rituals, by the very fact that they are corporate expressions and not experiences of the individual, have proven not to be efficacious. Just as in I Corinthians 15:12-19 [supra, p. 192] supreme doubt about the reality of the resurrection is expressed, so also in the Apocrypha, though its canonical status has had a checkered history of acceptance and rejection.

II Esdras 7:62-69 says:

> O earth, what have you brought forth, if the mind is made out of the dust like other created things! For it would have been better if the dust itself had not been born, so that the mind might not have been made from it. But now the mind grows with us, and therefore we are tormented, because we perish and know

it. Let the human race lament, but let the beasts of the field be glad; let all who have been born lament, but let the four-footed beasts and the flocks rejoice! For it is much better with them than with us; for they do not look for a judgment, nor do they know of any torment or salvation promised to them after death. For what does it profit us that we shall be preserved alive but cruelly tormented? For all who have been born are involved in iniquities, and are full of sins and burdened with transgressions. And if we were not to come into judgment after death, perhaps it would have been better for us.

And answers in verses 71-73:

And now understand from your own words, for you have said that the mind grows with us. For this reason, therefore, those who dwell on earth shall be tormented, because though they had understanding they committed iniquity, and though they received the commandments they did not keep them, and though they obtained the law they dealt unfaithfully with what they received. [13]

Through the growth of the mind, comes a deeper understanding; and through greater awareness comes a greater responsibility. Copernicus and Galileo opened the door to new knowledge for us, and as a result, our minds have grown through the development of science. But with new knowledge came also a need for greater responsibility in the awesome decisions of modern man to use or not to use the tools which his new understanding has produced. In the cosmic drama of our time, we can see clearly displayed on a macrocosmic scale, the microcosm of our individual situation. Just as the laws of modern science help to overcome man's subservience to the primordial forces of nature by taming them, so in the Old Testament tradition it is said that to counteract the evil tendencies that God created in man, he gave man the Law, so that those who listen to the Law would not be delivered into the hands of brutal nature.

In Job we meet exactly the same problem where Job is told: "I will also confess unto thee that thine own right hand can save thee. Behold now Behemoth, which I made with thee . . . he is the chief of the ways of God: he that made him can make his sword to approach unto him" (Job 40:14-15, 19). The ontogenetic principle expresses itself not only in man's growing awareness of the laws of nature, but also his own being and by following his own inner laws he has the healing within himself.

Don Cupitt wrote:

> The Magisterium [the Vatican] then, protects the fundamental truths of the deposit of faith. It has, apparently, privileged access to revealed truths, of a kind not vouchsafed to mere theologians. Now, would somebody care to explain just what this privileged knowledge can consist in? I'd love to know, because we benighted theologians are not aware of any other way to religious truth than the way of hard study and sleepless nights and the struggle to give birth to something genuine and cogent out of one's own soul. It's very hard work, and it does not issue in any certainty at all.[14]

Just as the principle of the Hypercycle has proved that while the "primal stuff," the basic molecules out of which life has been formed, remains the same, there is nevertheless a process at work toward higher differentiation and self-organization. And as it is in the basic elements of nature, so it is with the human mind. Like the Burning Bush, the mind remains basically the same, but it changes in both its expressions and comprehensions. The rather disparaging Biblical concept about the creation of man from the dust is today lifted to a level of greater differentiation through the tools of science as they reveal that even plant life is animated. Not

only in Kirlean photography, which shows differing gradations of radiation in the stages of aliveness, but also in
particular chemistry which has proved that manifestations
of this energy is what we call life. Biology has proved this
fact hormonologically and / or energetically, i.e., atomically.

Man is the medium through which life becomes conscious
of itself; he is the co-worker with the divine. In this context,
Bonhoeffer's statement that only "a suffering God can help"
reveals a more profound meaning.[15] Neither ritual action
nor magical formulae for transubstantiation can bring
about the transformation which only awareness and responsible action by the individual can achieve.

The question from the Book of Esdras is a question for
our day as well; but the *hayah*, the divine "to be" in man,
gives different answers to the same essential experience of
origin. Couched in different terms, the burial rites of prehistoric man, pre-ice age art, Babylonian, Egyptian, Far
Eastern and Middle Eastern sacred writings all give the
same message, "different only in its hundred tones." Every
one of these spiritual manifestations of man's existence
shows a different stage in the ontogenesis of the psyche. And
whether it is the Egyptian Maat, the Old Testament *hayah*,
or the New Testament Christ, they all have one thing in
common: the more mature the individual becomes, i.e., the
more his latent possibilities have become differentiated and
developed, the more independent he becomes of a mythology which reaches out into extra-human and metaphysical
realms. The more mature personality is able to carry his own
God and actually give expression to the inner divine quality
in his daily life. His values have the quality of reality and are
not lost in a heaven of abstract concepts.

Salvation for modern man is salvation in order to live,
that is salvation from unconscious constraints and frustrations which hinder the realization of life's manifold
possibilities.

Although it is widely regarded as frivolously superficial to suppose that the human predicament is

remediable, nothing in reality could be more superficial than failure to realize that acquiescence in the notion of impending doom is a principal factor in helping it to come about. In spite of all its frightening groans and rattles, the great world machine can still be made to work, but not unless it comes to be accepted that the long-term welfare of human beings cannot be secured by policies that promote the interest of some people at the expense of others or even the interests of mankind at the expense of other living things. The *unity of nature* is not a slogan but a principal to the truth of which all natural processes bear witness. The lesson has been learnt too late to save some living creatures, but there may just be time to save the rest of us.[16]

There is revealed in these measured words of one of the world's leading scientists the fact that though science is usually understood to be without values, it is nevertheless permeated by a deep sense of personal value and responsibility. The uniformity of scientific concepts does not necessarily mean unity. The experience of the unity of nature is a specific human form of awareness. That awareness, in constant change and flux, expresses the ontogenesis of the psyche as an expression of authentic creativity.

Dogmatic presuppositions such as the reductionist attitude that humans are "nothing but physiochemical reflective units" is a limited and not a universal claim, and therefore cannot also lay claim to be "the truth." To fail to state the truth is *the* sin in the temples of science. In the wider context appropriate to the times in which we live, it affirms the statement of the New Testament: "If you were blind, you would have no guilt; but now that you say, 'We see,' your guilt remains."[17]

This kind of "seeing" is the human imagination. It is closely related to the process of acquiring knowledge. And through that process, real personal awareness is established.

Descartes' dictum: *Cogito ergo sum* — "I think, therefore I am," was elaborated in *Existentialism and the Modern Predicament* by F. H. Heinemann as: *Respondeo, ergo sum* —"I respond therefore I am."[18]

This principle is not offered as a truth of indubitable certainty from which otherwise indubitable propositions could be derived. Like Descartes' *Cogito ergo sum*, it is a matter-of-fact truth, and not a truth of reason. It does not intend to formulate more than a key-symbol for the co-ordination of the different spheres of our experience, a key-symbol which reveals to us some of the mysteries of human existence. I am in so far as I respond. I arise on all levels of my being (body, sense-organs, soul and mind) only by responding.[19]

Response emerges as a term connecting Nature and History, Matter and Mind and therefore exercises an important function in bridging the gulf between these realms.[20]

Man's position in the universe is unique in that he, as a responding being, becomes answerable for his actions. This is the moral aspect of his freedom. *Respondeo, ergo sum* now means that I am in so far as I accept responsibility for my actions.[21]

This existential predicament was seen and answered roughly 2,000 years ago in the Talmud (600 B.C.-400 A.D.). Made in the image of God, "Every man carries the stamp of the primal man, and yet everyone is unique and not the same as the other."[22] Uniformity does not mean in this "catholic" context a statistical unit —man is uniform only in his material, physiological aspects, being made from "the dust of the earth." Man is unique — not a statistical unit — in his creative imagination, which informs his responses. The lines:

> To see a World in a Grain of Sand,
> and a Heaven in a Wild Flower

could never have come about by chance, say by monkeys thumping typewriters; and it is very unlikely that any human being other than Blake could have written them. There is only one Blake and one Shakespeare, but there are many statisticians using the same methods of arriving at the same uniform results.

In "The Scale of Structural Units in Biopoesis," Prof. J. D. Bernal writes:

> In all discussions referring to the evolution of material systems, be they galaxies, organisms or societies, two aspects have to be kept in mind simultaneously at every stage in the discussion — the *dynamic* and the *static* — the *processes* and the *structures*. Living organisms are built from atoms and at the same time they react and change according to the laws of atomic combination. Systems of extraordinary complexity and variety are built up, maintained and modified but all repose on the same elements, that is on certain simple properties common to all actual or possible Life. These provide the given data into which all schemes of biopoesis must be fitted....
>
> One argument which has been used from the highest antiquity against any spontaneous evolution of life has been the apparent impossibility of such an arrangement coming together by chance. It was already used against the early Greek atomists, of which we catch a seventeenth century echo in John Hall's *Epicurean Ode*:

> Since that this thing we call the world
> By chance on Atomes is begot,
> Which though in dayly motions hurld,
> Yet weary not,
> How doth it prove.
> Thou art so fair and I in love?

Some have taken up this theme less poetically in

modern times and have claimed to demonstrate by mathematical arguments that even such a small part of organized nature as a molecule of ribonucleic acid would, if it had to come together by chance from a congeries of atoms, take almost infinitely more time then the presumed age of the universe. I know Professor Haldane has argued that a very unlikely thing is not an impossible thing and that the chance origin of life cannot be altogether neglected, but most of those bringing forward such arguments use them in a purely negative sense. If life could not have come together by pure chance, they argue, then its presence is either illusion or that *life was created and guided at every step by an intelligent agent or at least by a teleological seeking for perfection.*" (Italics mine)[23]

Why not? Love, responsibility, justice, the idea of establishing a better life for everyone, expresses itself in various political systems manifesting the truth that "The unity of nature is not a slogan, but a principle to the truth of which all natural processes bear witness." To achieve this end, societies have evolved religious systems, but just as the notion of uniformity in scientistic thought did not lead to "truth," so dogmatic religion fails to be truly "catholic" and does not lead to "salvation."

The exclusive character of the rationality of both scientistic and dogmatic thinking is, to a high degree, responsible for our present spiritual malaise. The awe-inspiring developments in the biological and physical sciences are, however, the symbol of our "Exodus" from our former conceptions of the universe, and thus also from our own selves. Our changing apprehension of the universe is a further manifestation of the ontogenesis of the psyche.

Descartes brought the Cartesian doubt to its logical conclusion in the statement "I think therefore I am." It has been the dubious privilege of our time to extend the principle of doubt to its ultimate limits through the process of one-sided rationalization. Not only has doubt become our second nature, but in the end, we have come to doubt our doubting as well. The alienation of man from himself is the result of the circuitous dance around our unreasonable use of reason. Bertrand Russell in his superb way faced the issue squarely by commenting on Descartes' *Cogito*:

> "While [wrote Descartes] I wanted to think everything false, it must necessarily be that I who thought was something; and remarking that this truth, *I think, therefore I am*, was so solid and so certain that all the most extravagant suppositions of the sceptics were incapable of upsetting it, I judged that I could receive it without scruple as the first principle of the philosophy that I sought. . . ."

> "Thinking" is used by Descartes in a very wide sense. A thing that thinks, he says, is one that doubts, understands, conceives, affirms, denies, wills, imagines, and feels —for feeling, as it occurs in dreams, is a form of thinking. Since thought is the essence of mind, the mind must always think, even during sleep. . . .

> The method of critical doubt, though Descartes himself applied it only half-heartedly, was of great philosophical importance. It is clear, as a matter of logic, that it can only yield positive results if scepticism is to stop somewhere. If there is to be both logical and empirical knowledge, there must be two kinds of stopping points: indubitable facts, and indubitable principles of inference. Descartes' indubitable facts are his own thoughts — using "thought" in its widest possible sense. "I think" is his ultimate premise. Here the word "I" is really illegitimate; he ought to state his ultimate premises in the form "there are thoughts." The word "I" is grammatically convenient, but does not describe a datum. When he goes on to say "I am a *thing* which thinks,"

he is already using uncritically the apparatus of categories handed down by scholasticism. He nowhere proves that thoughts need a thinker, nor is there reason to believe this except in a grammatical sense. The decision, however, to regard thoughts rather than external objects as the prime empirical certainties was very important, and had a profound effect on all subsequent philosophy.[24]

The overextended Ego-philosophy of our time has resulted in a narcissistic and hedonistic culture. As a "natural" consequence, the rationalization of the experience of life as a whole divided into parts excluding each other, produced, apart from obvious political manifestations, a disastrous result: the alienation of man from himself. Descartes' *Cogito* was in philosophical terms contradicted by Kant's *a priori* categories of experience of thoughts, which have a basis other than the empirical one. This basically Platonic attitude, however, has been cast out in our time as "metaphysical nonsense" by logical positivists, e.g., A. J. Ayer. However, in the philosophy of science a renaissance has taken place which has not yet reached the majority of the teachers influencing society, and thus in particular the young. The young, just as the older generations, are in despair searching for a meaning in life. Hitherto society in its formally structured groups, such as Medieval guilds, provided meaning.

In our time, society has become more and more depersonalized through industrialization. This one-sided materialistic society sees persons primarily as consumers, customers for its cheapened merchandise. Industrialization, ruled by the computer and technology, cannot even provide the goods which a narcissistic culture has been educated to expect because of the scarcity of global resources. The Church, as an institution, has lost its efficacy to lead the searching individual to self-discovery. Today each one is condemned to seek his spiritual destiny by himself.

That modern man simply cannot believe anymore is symptomatic for the demands for an authentic *experience* and the rejection of a reliance on traditional *opinions.* Pope John Paul II claimed "the right to Truth" for the institutional Church, basing that claim on a tradition going back to St. Irenaeus. This claim to "the right to Truth" alienates modern man still more, not only from himself but from religious belief as well.

There is continuing in man's soul a revelation to which alone he feels destined to listen in a solemn dialogue between himself and his inner Christ. It is in this dialogue that man finds his way leading to the capacity for genuine love. It would be a genuine love where the human essence of man, the Thou, in mutuality relates itself to the other and where man does not enter a personal relationship in a kind of contractual form.

In contractual relationships the other, the "Thou," is seen rather as an "it" — an object, not a subject. A contract is negotiable, and if human relationship is consciously or unconsciously seen as such, another form of contract will be negotiated in due course, called divorce.

This kind of contractual relationship is implicit also in the form of a dehumanizing consumer oriented society where "Everyman" is understood to be an object for manipulation and exploitation by any devious means; or where a human laborer is considered in Labor/Management arrangements as an expendable object, an operator, who may, without scruple, be exchanged for a robot or replaced by automation. More and more, human values are being subverted, ruled by a crass materialism which essentially does not differ from Marxism.

This form of society is destroying man as man, curtailing his right to life, also in its racist tendencies. The extent to which this is true in the United States led to the following statement of the Right Reverend James Lyke, Auxiliary Bishop of Cleveland, Ohio. In an address to the Catholic

Press Association convention in Nashville, Tennessee on May 15, 1980, he said:

> I wish I could hear the clear, unequivocal and frequent condemnation against racism that I do against abortion.
>
> If I could spread over the 200 years of the enslavement of black people the same quantity, quality and equality of coverage that the Catholic press has given to abortion in the last 10 years, the average Catholic would certainly have an informed conscience on the issue of racism. More assuredly, however, the question of human dignity would have been consistently raised, and then today we may not have a problem with abortion.
>
> Let me add, that I know of at least one diocesan paper that has not yet printed the U.S. Bishops' pastoral on racism."[25]

There lies hope in the fact that not only the church's propaganda for their point of view is possible to be expressed in the West, but also Bishop Lyke's reminder. The hope for a possible change manifests itself in the fact that, after all, after 50 years of Hitler's clearly expressed denial of these rights to life, the Church is no longer as willfully silent as it was in 1933 in Europe. Abortion and euthanasia were dictated by the state as whims compelled on the basis of their right to truth.

Irenaeus spoke of the close relationship between God and the world in the following terms:

> Hence too His apostle Paul well says: *one God, the Father, who is above all and with all and in us all*; for "above all" is the Father, but "with all" is the Word, since it is through Him that everything was made by the Father, and "in us all" is the Spirit. . . .[26]

Irenaeus expresses God as wholeness in terms of both the Old and New Testaments. The sages in their Talmudic story [supra, p. 25] deal with the problem of the "right to Truth" in their own profound way, saying essentially the same thing at about the same time in history that Irenaeus was writing. The sages, however, upheld the right to truth for the individual. They even went so far as to say: "What did the Holy One, blessed be He, do in that hour? He laughed with joy. He replied saying, 'My sons have defeated me. My sons have defeated me.' "

Is the collective point of view necessarily more authentic than that of the individual based on personal experience? The Old Testament expressly states: "You shall not follow a multitude to do evil."[27]

To be sure, identification with an ideology produces a well-known state of inflation of the mind. The excesses of all totalitarian systems in repressing dissidents bear witness to this sad fact. No "truth" can be defended through the claim of exclusive possession. A defense based on such a claim is a contradiction in terms. A system which closes itself deliberately rationalizes the ideology which gave it birth, and thus betrays, like Judas' kiss, the spirit of Christ, of wholeness, of the pleroma. *Pleroma* in Greek means a "filling up," a "state of abundance," of "fullness."

The Gospel of Truth

THE GOSPEL OF TRUTH, a Gnostic writing contemporary with that of St. Irenaeus, states:

> . . . deficiency came into being because the Father was not known, therefore when the Father is known, from that moment on the deficiency will no longer exist. As with the ignorance of a person, when he comes to have knowledge his ignorance vanishes of itself, as the darkness vanishes when light appears, so also the deficiency vanishes in the perfection. So from that moment on the form is not apparent, but it will vanish in the fusion of Unity, for now their works lie scattered. In time *Unity* will perfect the spaces. It is within Unity that each one will attain himself; within knowledge he will purify himself from multiplicity into Unity, consuming matter *within himself* like fire, and darkness by light, death by life. (Italics mine)[28]

The author of the *Gospel of Truth* is believed by scholars to have been Valentinus, and it is presumed that Irenaeus was familiar with this school of thought and its writings.[29]

The concept of unity, the *pleroma* of the Gnostics, is an anticipation of the unity of modern science. "The unity of nature is not a slogan but a principal to the truth of which all natural processes bear witness."[30] For the Gnostics it signifies the fullness of the "upper world" with its "eternity, stability [and] completeness."[31] The *pleroma* is a spiritual world energized by the manifestation of spiritual power — a concept as mysterious to the non-initiate in ancient times as the higher mathematical world of the scientists is a mystery to the ordinary layman today. The *pleroma* is the spiritual realm whence come knowledge and maturity, just as in our world of modern science it is believed that DNA was present as an informing and directing agent at the very beginning in the fusion of the first elements.

Fred Hoyle wrote:

> The information content of a blizzard is essentially the same as that of a single snowflake. There is no hierarchy of structure, with one level of subtlety piled on another. It is the existence of such a hierarchy which characterizes biological systems. Each level in the hierarchy serves as the building block for the next level, apparently in an ever-expanding sequence. The fact that it can do so is determined by the physical laws, which *therefore seem to contain within themselves the information we have been seeking.*" (Italics mine)[32]

A scriptural parallel to this rarified manifestation of the ontogenesis of the psyche is found in Colossians 1:9-10 — "that you may be filled with the knowledge of His will in all spiritual wisdom and understanding . . . and increasing in the knowledge of God." Likewise, in Ephesians 3:18-19 is written: "that you may have power to comprehend with all the saints what is the breadth and length and height and depth, and to know the love of Christ which surpasses knowledge, that you may be filled with all the fullness of God."

For the Nobel Prize winner, Melvin Calvin, the fundamental conviction is that the universe is ordered:

> As I try to discern the origin of that conviction, I seem to find it in a basic notion discovered 2,000 or 3,000 years ago, and enunciated first in the Western world by the ancient Hebrews: namely, that the universe is governed by a single God, and is not the

product of the whims of many gods, each governing his own province according to his own laws. *This monotheistic view seems to be the historical basis of modern science....* (Italics mine)

For 2,000 years religious precepts have taught man must be his brother's keeper, but it remains for science to give example after example of the truth of this early philosophical concept.

There can be no ultimate right, no final understanding, no permanent solutions for the problems of mankind. For change is inherent in the structure of the molecules of which we are composed. This is perhaps the hardest truth, for it allows no rest.[33]

The ancient Hebrews gave spiritual expression in their vision on Mt. Sinai, anticipating as it were in their experience of reality, modern science, in the inspired concept of *hayah*, of "to be," of "becoming." Modern man knows that there are limits to the renewability of natural resources. Instead of using his energies therefore for adding and preserving of life, his main effort is directed toward annihilating it either by waste, the manufacturing of needless goods, or the production of atomic weapons.

The power potential of nuclear weaponry surpasses the human capacity to comprehend it, just as the *tremendum* of the Divine surpasses full human realization.

The nearly wholesale denial of the symbolic meaning of the Last Supper as it relates to Cain's eternal question — "Am I my brother's keeper?" — is demonstrated in the way civilization betrays the essential basis of life. In the problem of race relations, the hunger and despair of the "third world," the squalor of the "inner cities," and in the squandering of irreplaceable global resources, the enormity of our human failure is made manifest. Primitive man believed in the rebirth of gods and acted upon that belief. It is here, born of his intimate relation with and experience of nature, where the borders of his responsibilities lie. Pre-ice age figurines, 20,000 to 30,000 years old, apparently symbolizing fertility gods, show still the markings of red ochre, symbolic of the hope of rebirth. "The images often show the polish of long use and, at times the remains of red ochre, which indicates that they were often symbolically painted."[34]

The existence of the DNA molecule and the fusion of *four* basic elements in the primal life forms lead to the scientific conclusion that the impetus toward greater differentiation is an essential component in living things. It is this basic assumption which is the pathway and bridge from the initial beginnings to the renewal of life expressed symbolically in the use of red ochre. Scientific concepts now replace the magical use of red ochre as a symbol of the basic experience of man's participation in life's growth and renewal. Creation is continuous; the *hayah* is the active and efficacious agent and not a man-made god [supra, Preface, Gospel of Philip].

The *hayah* is the expression of true creative power and not an artificial human construct dogmatically promulgated as God. Though an individual may claim that an absolute criterion handed down by religious tradition is indeed his own, the fact remains that he must first experience this "truth" as it is manifested in his personal and unique symbols before it can have personal validity for his own growth and become more than empty words.

When an individual undertakes this "opus," it acquaints him with the "truth" of his unconscious motives; and it may inspire him not only to discover his own creativity, but it may also direct him to responsible social action, and thus assist in the creation of a truly humane society. Through self-examination the individual sees, at the very least, his own ignorance and withdraws projections from the general pool of social unawareness. If one thus relates himself to the origins of his own being, he contributes creatively not only to his own salvation, but also to the salvation of society as well.

Clement of Alexandria states that Adam "was not created

perfect in constitution, but suitable for acquiring virtue. . . . For God desires us to be saved by our own efforts."[35] And Isaiah says: "Wash yourselves, make yourselves clean."[36] Self-examination guides man to the "Exodus" of the soul's enslavement to unconscious and chaotic forces, and thus leads him toward freedom and salvation. Spinoza concludes his *Ethics* by saying:

> I have finished everything I wished to explain concerning the power of the mind over the emotions and concerning its freedom. From what has been said we see what is the strength of the wise man, and how much he surpasses the ignorant who is driven forward by lust alone. For the ignorant man is not only agitated by external causes in many ways, and never enjoys true peace of soul, but lives also ignorant, as it were, both of God and of things, and as soon as he ceases to suffer ceases also to be. On the other hand, the wise man, in so far as he is considered as such, is scarcely ever moved in his mind, but, being conscious by a certain eternal necessity of himself, of God, and of things, never ceases to be, and always enjoys true peace of soul. If the way which, as I have shown, leads hither seems very difficult, it can nevertheless be found. It must indeed be difficult since it is so seldom discovered, for if salvation lay ready to hand and could be discovered without great labor, how could it be possible that it should be neglected almost by everybody? But all noble things are as difficult as they are rare.[37]

The central message of the New Testament, indissolubly linked with the Old Testament dictum "choose life" and the *hayah* of Mt. Sinai, is found in I Corinthians 11:28: "Let a man examine himself, and so eat of the bread and drink of the cup." This process of self-examination only becomes truly efficacious if it is experienced through the symbols of the individual psyche. As each person is unique, the symbolic manifestations of that uniqueness cannot be explained by descriptive nouns or in collective assumptions about them. As in art, the interpretation needs to "fit" the individual situation in order to speak directly to his unique condition. Without this "opus" of self-examination, the collective ritual of the Eucharist not only continues to hold persons in bondage to the deeper layers of the psyche, but it ignores the additional warning: "Whoever shall eat this bread, and drink this cup of the Lord, unworthily, shall be guilty of the body and blood of the Lord."[38] The ecclesiastical practice of oral confession does not reach the depths of the individual psyche. At best, it deals with limited conscious concerns. Modern man's development has led to a deeper penetration of the levels of awareness, which has resulted in an inability to "believe" in the superficial or surface meaning of religious myth. This development has deprived modern man of the traditional "salvation by faith."

Self-examination of the depths of the personal psyche, when it becomes a true commitment to a meaningful life, is a kind of transubstantiation. That is to say, it transforms the attitudes of the mind in symbolical, mental terms. This transfiguration of our potentialities is very real when we experience through it our actual response of life. It is, in fact, a rebirth into another reality. This process of change in our responses to life is at the same time our becoming. The symbol for this experience is the Burning Bush which remains the same in the midst of change. Surely this is a way which is difficult to find, as Spinoza pointed out from his own philosophical perspective.

Spinoza, whom Bertrand Russell described as "the noblest and most loveable of the great philosophers,"[39] was excommunicated by the Jews on the one hand, and on the other left Spain in order to escape the Inquisition. His philosophy joins in a sense the modern philosophy of science which expresses the same essential truth, that finite things are defined by their boundaries, physical or logical, that is to say by what they are *not:* "All determination is negation." According to Spinoza, "There can be only one Being who is wholly positive, and He must be absolutely infinite."[40]

The same truth a modern philosopher calls The Tacit Dimension. "The laws of physics and chemistry include no conception of sentience [power of self-perception], and any system wholly determined by these laws must be insentient."[41] That is to say that the very fact that man is capable of feeling or perception contradicts these basic "insentient" laws as the basis of life. A modern physicist confirms Polanyi's point of view and calls it an "inner *forming activity* which is the cause of the growth of things, and of the development and differentiation of their various essential forms."[42] In biology Bernhard Rensch presumes "that already DNA and proteins have protopsychical characters" [supra, p. 46].

The philosophers, as well as the scientists, say essentially what the poet Goethe proclaims in the Homunculus poem of Faust Part II: "the artificial needs boundaries whilst for the natural the universe is just big enough." Goethe gave the name "Homunculus" to the creature which had been artificially created in a test tube [supra, p. 212]. Modern man tries desperately to break out of his artificial conditionings, realizing that the "universe is just big enough" for his unfolding. Philosophers, aware of mind and not only concerned with rationalistically conceived schemes of isolating, excluding thought, are returning to fundamentals. Science with its advanced thinkers, whose theories have been proven by experiment, does the same and both are at one with Irenaeus, the early Church Father, when he says: "There is one father above all things and *in all things*" [supra, p. 119].[43]

A development of the greatest significance has occurred in the physical sciences. Local laws of cause and effect are now realized not to be sufficient in themselves as explanations of reality.[44] The inclusiveness of the whole universe is the vital presupposition for understanding anything at all. Modern science *proves* experimentally that the open mind is not a metaphysical nonentity, but a necessity for the comprehension of Life as reality.

Dealing essentially, as modern science does, with patterns of organic energy, Max Planck, the father of quantum mechanics, writes: "Science does not mean an idle resting upon a body of certain knowledge; it means unresting endeavor and continually progressing development towards an aim which the poetic intuition may apprehend, but which the intellect can never fully grasp."[45]

As Keats' dictum, "Beauty is Truth," or Blake's "To See a World in a Grain of Sand," or Planck's poetic intuition, so is Niels Bohr's comparison of the expressions of nuclear science to poetry, and last but not least Heisenberg's saying: *"If harmony in a society depends on the common interpretation of the 'one,' of the unity behind the multitude of phenomena, the language of the poets may be more important than that of the scientists."*[46] All these statements are vital signposts on the way toward unity. The New Testament words, "to unite all things in [Christ],"[47] or the fundamental Old Testament insight preceding all these later developments of the psyche in the experience of Monotheism, or the depth psychological insights of integration, are manifesting the same truth each in its particular way.

Using the Buddhist name of Wu Li for patterns of organic energy, Gary Zukav points out that "20th century physics is the story of a journey from intellectual entrenchment to intellectual openness, despite the conservative prove-it-to-me nature of individual physicists."[48]

In 1964 J. S. Bell, a physicist of the European Organization of Nuclear Research in Switzerland, published the so-called "Bell Theorem." According to the theorem, all separate parts of the universe are connected to one another in an intimate and immediate way. "Some physicists are convinced that it is the most important single work, perhaps, in the history of physics."[49]

Bell's theorem is a mathematical proof . . . that if the statistical predictions of quantum theory are correct, then some of our commonsense ideas about the world are profoundly mistaken," and "the principle of local causes *must* be false."[50] Experiment after experiment has shown that the predictions of quantum mechanics are always correct.[51] The quantum theory has never failed! "Therefore, according to Bell's theorem, the principle of local causes *must* be false."[52] Again, and most importantly, Bell's theorem implies that decay reaction which occurs at a certain time is *not* a matter of chance. Like everything else, it is dependent upon something which is happening elsewhere. In the words of H. P. Stapp:

> . . . the conversion of potentialities into actualities cannot proceed on the basis of locally available information. If one accepts the usual ideas about how information propagates through space and time, then Bell's theorem shows that the macroscopic responses cannot be independent of far-away causes. This problem is neither resolved nor alleviated by saying that the response is determined by "pure chance." Bell's theorem proves precisely that the determination of the macroscopic response must be "nonchance," at least to the extent of allowing some sort of dependence of this response upon the far-away cause.[53]

Bell's theorem expresses in its own way the same thing that religious thinkers from all over the world and throughout history have been saying from a different perspective. The deep interrelationship between the propensity to "pass over" from one state to another and the symbolic content of the Last Supper are both expressions of the ontogenesis of the psyche. They share this characteristic with the events in science. The following Gnostic text lifts this to the height of anticipatory insight into human existence:

> Since the deficiency came into being because the Father was not known, therefore when the Father is

known, from that moment on the deficiency will no longer exist. . . . So from that moment on the form is not apparent, but it will *vanish in the fusion of Unity*. In time Unity will perfect the spaces. It is within Unity that each one will attain himself; within knowledge he will purify himself from multiplicity into Unity, consuming matter within himself like fire, and darkness by light, death by life.[54]

When man examines himself against the background of unity, of wholeness, and no longer sees himself from a mechanistic, rationalized and analytical perspective, he will come to an expression of the Unity within himself. This knowledge will "purify him" and transform darkness by light, and death by life. In this context, St. Paul's concern for the "and so eat the bread and drink this cup" takes on an awesome significance, freeing man from bondage to the dogma which speaks neither to the actuality of the human condition nor to its uniqueness. Above all, an understanding of "examine yourself" will free man from his enslavement to materialism. It will, in fact, transform meaningless materialism into animated and meaningful *materiality*. In Biblical terms, "the Word became flesh" incarnated itself into matter at the very beginning of life; the Word — the *hayah* — became audible, and the silence was broken.

This process of self-examination is clearly manifested in the symbol of the Burning Bush, in the transforming power of fire which transmutes and purifies the soulless, non-human aspects of materialism into mindful materiality. The same ontogenetic development of the psyche expresses itself in the manifestations toward Unity, mentioned above. It also illuminates Jacob's dream of the ladder reaching from earth to heaven, which may now be seen as an anticipatory psychic recognition of the developments of modern science, particularly in the fields of physics and biology which have begun to comprehend the interrelatedness and synchronicity of the total universe.

Synchronicity

Synchronicity is no more baffling or mysterious than the discontinuities of physics. It is only the ingrained belief in the sovereign power of causality that creates intellectual difficulties and makes it appear unthinkable that causeless events exist or could ever occur. But if they do, then we must regard them as *creative acts*, as the continuous creation of a pattern that exists from all eternity, repeats itself sporadically, and is not derivable from any known antecedents. We must of course guard against thinking of every event whose cause is unknown as "causeless." This . . . is admissible only when a cause is not even thinkable. But thinkability is itself an idea that needs the most rigorous criticism. Had the atom corresponded to the original philosophical conception of it, its fissionability would be unthinkable. But once it proves to be a measurable quantity, its nonfissionability becomes unthinkable. Meaningful coincidences are thinkable as pure change. But the more they multiply and the greater and more exact the correspondence is, the more their probability sinks and their unthinkability increases, until they can no longer be regarded as pure chance but, for lack of a causal explanation, have to be thought of as meaningful arrangements. As I have already said, however, their "inexplicability" is not due to the fact that the cause is unknown, but to the fact that a cause is not even thinkable in intellectual terms. This is necessarily the case when space and time lose their meaning or have become relative, for under those circumstances a causality which presupposes space and time for its continuance can no longer be said to exist and becomes altogether unthinkable.

For these reasons, it seems to me necessary to introduce, alongside space, time, and causality, a category which not only enables us to understand synchronistic phenomena as a special class of natural events, but also takes the contingent partly as a universal factor existing from all eternity, and partly as the sum of countless individual acts of creation occurring in time.[55]

To BE SURE, science is able to test and validate its theories through observation and experimentation. Psychic experiences, however, pose a powerful challenge to both science and religion because they are always individual and therefore unique. Religion dogmatically presents its assumptions as "facts" to be accepted by belief. Max Planck, the father of quantum mechanics who opened vistas into the inner workings of matter, spoke to both science and religion when he said: ". . . a positivism which rejects any transcendental idea is as one-sided as a metaphysics which scorns individual experience."[56]

Ultimately, what quantum mechanics proves is that there are "patterns of organic energy." The idea of organic patterns is as difficult for the ordinary mind to conceive as a reality as it was difficult for our most primitive ancestors in the dimmest past to conceive of the power of speech. Noam Chomsky maintains that the child, though needing to learn the meaning of words, has the innate capacity to form sentences. In other words, the human being is innately capable of bringing abstract mental formations into a meaningful organic whole, a pattern. To discover that words and sentences could be meaningful and complete in themselves, and prove to be effective in relation to life with one's neighbor, must have been an awesome experience for our ancestors. Today, we have developed speech effectively as a means for propaganda, and through it we try to reach the multitude. But somehow, perfecting the power of speech has not improved our ability to communicate truly between one individual and another. Not much has changed in this respect from the days of the Egyptian sage who 4,500 years ago exclaimed: "To whom do I speak today?" [supra, p. 242].

Today a billion-dollar electronic religion industry utilizes the deep-seated human need for communication by exploiting it for political ends. Tragically, the audience is treated through advertising gimmicks as if they were, in their need for relationship, customers for merchandise.

The radical changes of our time and the ensuing anxieties, which such changes produce, are met with frivolous platitudes. The word *religion* is etymologically based on *religare,* "to bind" or "to relate"; but this urgent need for relationship is addressed through the electronic media by wordy actors. Because the electronic machine cannot satisfy the need for relationship or cure human loneliness, despair and cynicism are widespread. The Word is prostituted and becomes merely empty rhetoric. Instead of genuine relationships, the participants of "religious" mass movements pathetically fall victim to a shallow social partyism. Rather than becoming members of a "communion," the misled and anxiety-ridden seekers become a group for the realization of political goals clothed in dogmatically conceived pseudo-moral terms. It is no wonder, therefore, that the so-called religious revival does nothing to allay the "age of anxiety" nor does it point a direction toward salvation. The Word is profaned and secularized.

The powerful primal experience of the creative force of the Word was incorporated into the Bible through the natural process of psychic development. The third verse of this holy book begins with "And God *said.*"[57] In the New Testament, the Gospel of John begins: "In the beginning was the Word, and the Word was with God, and the Word was

God."[58] The innate capacity to form sentences is a manifestation of the *hayah,* the awareness of which stands in direct relation to the level which the ontogenesis of the psyche has reached at a particular moment in the life of each person.

Irenaeus, the Church father, whose teachings form a vital part of the basis of Christian doctrine, said: "... *the Word is throughout in all things,*" echoing the Old Testament and in particular John 1:14: ". . . the Word became flesh."

Enuma Elish, The Babylonian Creation Myth

IT IS noteworthy in this context to remember that the oldest extant Creation myth, the Babylonian Genesis, *Enuma Elish,* shows the extraordinary significance of the Word. Here the hero Marduk has to prove his prowess through the creation and destruction of a garment by the power of his word:

> Thy destiny, O lord, shall be supreme among the gods.
> Command to destroy and to create, (and) they shall be!
> By the word of thy mouth, let the garment be destroyed;
> Command again, and let the garment be whole!
> He commanded with his mouth, and the garment was destroyed.
> He commanded again, and the garment was restored.[59]

Kingu, the brother of the hero Marduk, who had been chosen by their mother as her spouse, was killed. He was guilty of the "sin" of dependency which necessitates the battle. The illegitimate acquisition by Kingu of the propensity for using the Word as power from the mother is seen in this myth as "original sin":

> She gave him the tablet of destinies, she fastened (it) upon his breast, (saying):
> As for thee, thy command shall not be changed, (the word of thy mouth) shall be dependable![60]

The psyche, in its own process of becoming, must break free of the entanglement with the parental images. Mankind, according to this myth, was created from the blood of Kingu mixed with the dust from the ground. The ancient poets anticipated what we presume to have "discovered" today, namely that dependency on a parent figure (Freud's Oedipus Complex) does not lead to the freedom of the mind. These ancient poets also used the figure of Kingu's blood to represent the inherent tendency of the human being to remain inert, to stay in a state of immature dependency. The resounding theme of the New Testament is:

> If any one comes to me and does not hate his own father and mother and wife and children and brothers and sisters, yes, even his own life, he cannot be my disciple. Whoever does not bear his own cross and come after me, cannot be my disciple. . . .[61]

It is essentially the same as the call to Abraham: "get thee out . . . from thy kindred,"[62] and this important call is repeated in Matthew:

> Do not think that I have come to bring peace on earth;
> I have not come to bring peace, but a sword.
> For I have come to set a man against his father . . .[63]

Originating from an age presumably as far back historically as the *Enuma Elish*, a most revealing archaeological discovery has come to light. At Ebla, a Northwestern town in Syria, archaeologists have unearthed some 30,000 tablets which have been dated about 2,500 B.C.

Surely the most stunning place-name yielded by the Ebla tablets is *é-da-barki,* "the Temple of the Word." (The sign transliterated *é* means "house, temple"; *dā-bār* means "word.") We immediately recognize that here the Word is deified. The Canaanite background to the opening of John's Gospel, "In the beginning was the Word" may be seen at Ebla. A key term in Hebrew (more than 1,400 Biblical occurrences) is *dabar,* "word." This term enables one to interpret the Eblaite toponym, (a toponym is a geographical place name), *é-da-barki* as "Temple of the Word." Similarly a theological toponym like *é-b-a-ri-umki* can be interpreted as "Temple of the Creator," and *ba-ra-gú* as "the Voice has created." The opening verses of Genesis, it will be recalled, ascribe creation to God's word, that is, to his voice: And God said, "Let there be light," and there was light (Genesis 1:3). See also Psalms 33:6: "By Yahweh's word *(dābār)* were the heavens made, and by the breath of his mouth all their host."[64]

The feeling that the Word, in the Biblical sense, is an independent power can be illustrated by a few of the many possible samples:

>   *Numbers 22:8:*   *And he said to them, "Lodge here this night, and I will bring back word to you, as the Lord speaks to me."*
>
>   *Numbers 22:28:*   *Then the Lord opened the mouth of the ass, and she said to Balaam . . .*
>
>   *Numbers 22:38:*   *"The word that God puts in my mouth, that I must speak."*

Isaiah 55:11:   *"So shall my word be that goes forth from my mouth; it shall not return to me empty, but it shall accomplish that which I purpose, and prosper in the thing for which I sent it."*

John 1:14:   *And the Word became flesh and dwelt among us, full of grace and truth.*

The sanctity of the "Word" is reflected in the discoveries at Ebla, in the *Enuma Elish*, in the sayings of the Egyptian sage [supra, p. 310], in Genesis, "And God said . . . ," and in John's "the Word became flesh." There is portrayed in recurring images the divine *hayah* — the becoming.

The process of becoming manifested in the Word may seem as abstract as the mathematical language of modern science; however, it must be remembered that it was the language of mathematics which produced the atom bomb, and that the order to explode the bomb at Hiroshima was accomplished through the power of human speech.

It is in this context that a further aspect of the process of becoming manifests itself when we evaluate the use of atomic power.

> Real criticism — the criticism of ideas, of theories — arises I think only with language, and it seems to me that this is really one of the most important aspects of language. I want here to draw attention to that little step between thinking a certain thought in one's head as it were, and speaking it out. As long as the thought is not formulated, it is more or less part of ourselves. Only if it is formulated in language does it become an object . . . toward which we can adopt a critical attitude. . . .
>
> I would say that everything speaks in favour of the view that these two functions of language, the de-

scriptive and the argumentative functions, are the most characteristic aspects of *human language* as distinct from animal languages and other means of social communication.

I should like to add the following conjecture: it may be that this tension between *description* and *the need to criticize description* is the basis of the important intellectual problem which the invention of descriptive language puts before man, and this intellectual struggle stimulated the unprecedentedly fast growth of everything which follows — namely, the growth of language itself, of the brain, and of civilization.[65]

As mentioned earlier [supra, p. 226], the invention of tools and the need for their improvement is most probably linked with the development of the brain. Anthropologists generally agree that the earliest predecessors of man appeared about ten million years ago. Mary D. Leakey's discovery of footprints of creatures which walked with a two-legged gait three to five million years ago upsets the theory of many anthropologists that man's ancestors began walking upright in order to free their hands for tools.

Tool making has long been recognized as an ability unique to humans, and tools made of stone have long been used to date the antiquity of humanity. Now the date is being pushed back 500,000 years to at least 2½ million years ago. The reason: the discovery of 48 sharp stone flaked knives and three larger choppers in the Hardar of the Afra region of northeastern Ethiopia . . .[66]

If the dating holds up as it is expected to, these tools will be the oldest known human artifacts. They will, however, fall into a gap in the story of human evolution as we know it. The Afar region has yielded fossil hominids *(Austhralopithecus afarensis)* that roamed eastern Africa between approximately 3 and 4 million years ago.[67]

Many researchers feel that *Austhralopithecus afarensis* was on the direct line of human evolution, but it was a small-brained creature that probably was not capable of manufacturing tools. Hominids with larger brains have been dated back to two million years ago, as have stone tools, leaving a gap between three and two million years ago and historic times. "That is why this thing is exciting and intriguing," says Prof. Glynn Isaac:

> It opens the possibility that perhaps the first use of stone tools preceded the development of a significantly enlarged brain and were part of the behavior or way of life that helped to induce, or influence, the enlargement of the brain.

That is one possibility. The other, ". . . is that the trend toward brain enlargement began earlier than the oldest fossils we yet have. . ." Prof. Elwin L. Simons of Duke University . . . puts it this way: "The oldest documentation of stone tools is the beginning of archaeology; it's the beginning of cultural history."[68]

These archaeological findings give some credibility to the assumption that the development of tools assisted the development of the brain, and not the other way around. The behavior of *Marcipella spiralis,* which functions without a brain, is another example of the inborn *hayah* and its slow growth toward a "cultural history."

This process may also have assisted in the growth of language as well. The human psyche is a central participant in the spiral of becoming. Man's identification with the tools he invents is mirrored in mythologies, and particularly in art. An important symbol is in the Old Testament tradition in Genesis 9:13: "I set my *bow* in the cloud, and it shall be a sign of the covenant between me and the earth."

J. B. Harrod writes:

> The essence of the bow and arrow is a tacit herme-
> neutic; it may be seen as a description of the struc-
> ture, dynamics, and telos of the self, or human
> nature: filled with potential energy, a balanced ten-
> sion of opposites, tolerant of strain . . .
>
> This tacit hermeneutic has inspired cult, myth, and
> folklore across Europe and Asia, which speak of the
> bow as if they were alive, endowed with their own
> souls or spirits . . .
>
> In ancient Greek religion, the bow is an attribute
> or emblem of Apollo, Artemis and Herakles. Arte-
> mis is Toxia (She of the Bow), and in artistic repre-
> sentation the bow and arrow are part of her
> iconography . . .
>
> The very invention of the bow is associated with
> the gods . . .
>
> The subjects and styles of Mesolithic art [10,000 -
> 9,000 B.C.] sharply contrast with those of Paleolithic
> art. Rather than the ponderous art of the Paleolithic,
> whether the fertility figurines or the cave art, which
> depicts the majesty and solemnity of the animal
> world, with the human figure rare and usually
> masked, we now see two radically new kinds of art:
> linear, schematic art, utilizing geometric patterns —
> nets and chequers are characteristic — and biomor-
> phic designs . . . and an incredibly dynamic and
> graceful art in which human figures abound . . . The
> bow and arrow is everywhere in evidence . . .[69]

Tools as human creations thus represent a process of
self-invention (L. *in-venire,* "to come upon"). In other
words, it is the self which invents, and in so doing, assists in
the development of the brain. Through this growth, the
human being can become aware of the ontogenesis of the
psyche, and the whole process is closely integrated both in
the development and use of language. A telling illustration

of this phenomenon is the variant uses of the word for bow in the Old Testament.

In Genesis 9:13, the rain*bow* is characterized as a sign of God's mercy, and the same word is used for the war-*bow* in Psalms 7:12. The invention of the bow is a very early, perhaps primal tool necessary to hunters as a primary means of survival. No wonder then that the ancients identified themselves and their own powers for procreation of life with the bow as well. The Hebrew word for bow is *Kesheth* and is, in various rabbinical sources, a synonym for the penis.[70] The Babylonian Talmud, in an outspoken sexual context (Sota 36 b), says: "His bow regained its strength."[71] The bow is thus a manifold symbol also for continual birth and renewal.

If analytically approached, the invention of the bow by the hunter as a tool for survival can be seen in terms of causal relation. The poets, however, creatively present it as a sign of mercy in addition to its meaning as a power for war or as the procreative power of the penis, thus giving it an artistic symbolism which surpasses merely causal thinking. The bow thus becomes a synchronistic event of the psyche itself.

The penis both actually and symbolically is correlative to the bow as a tool for the procreation of life. The improvement of the bow in its utilitarian aspects as well as its being lifted to the position of a sacred attribute of the Divine is a slow process of transubstantiation; the material aspect becomes spiritual and materialism animated materiality. St. Augustine, commenting on the order which Abraham gave "his servant to place your hand under my thigh and swear by the God of heaven" (Genesis 24:2-3) comments that it is "rightly understood . . . as showing that Abraham well knew that the flesh in which the God of heaven was to come was the offspring of that very thigh . . ."[72]

The division between the conceptualization of experience and a reality apprehended in its wholeness cannot be kept open any longer. Heaven and Earth become one manifestation of the *one* God. The notion of heaven and hell, therefore, is seen as a clerical fantasy.

In Egypt corrupt priests sold new names or charms for high prices to the dying, so that when the deceased person confronted the judges in the underworld, according to the clerics' teaching, he could pretend to be somebody else.

> The judge, Osiris, is assisted by forty-two gods who sit with him in judgment on the dead. They are terrifying demons, each bearing a grotesque and horrible name, which the deceased claims that he knows. He therefore addresses them one after the other by name. They are such names as these: "Flame-Hugger-that-came-out-of-Troja" . . . "Bone-Breaker-that-came-out-of-Heracleopolis," "Blood-Eater-that-came-of-the-place-of-Execution." These and other equally edifying creations of priestly imagination the deceased calls upon, addressing to each god in turn a declaration of innocence of some particular sin.
>
> It is evident that these forty-two gods are an artificial creation. As was long ago noticed, they represent the forty or more nomes, or administrative districts, of Egypt. The priests doubtless built up this court of forty-two judges in order to control the character of the dead, from all quarters of the country.[73]

The threat of hell as a place of fire and brimstone as it is often depicted in our time has not proved effective to control the individual, leaving the ethical behavior of our society essentially unchanged. Such a threat neither produces change nor creates a new consciousness — a new awareness — which can speak to the individual in his own private and interior language and address him in these terms. In the face of the human predicament, however, at the Last Supper the Christ symbolically takes upon himself the burden, which in fact, can only be accomplished by each person in his most private sphere. In the recitation of the liturgy and by his symbolic participation in this sacrificial act, redemption is promised but not actually accomplished.

According to the Old Testament, it is Noah's ark which is the symbolic ship of salvation. In the New Testament the symbol of the ship also plays an important role: the disciples, tossed about by tumultuous waves on the sea of life, are saved by Christ.

> For the fathers it was the Church itself that was the ship of life here below, which in immense peril and yet in victorious security traverses the sea of the world.... No symbol was capable of conveying in a simpler or more convincing manner the fact that the Church finds herself between two eternal situations. She is even now, in the midst of the daemonic sea of the world, the only thing to which a man can cling and be certain of his salvation, and her ultimate entry into the haven of eternity is assured. . . .
>
> Hippolytus was the first of the Fathers to express the symbolism of this idea with something like a painter's sureness of touch. As a ship leaves no trace upon the changing waters, so also the Church which traverses the world after the manner of a ship; for she has left behind her on the shore all hopes that she otherwise might have had, and has pledged her life in advance to the heavens. And yet this same Church is already herself a kind of landing-place, a haven of salvation vouchsafed to us in advance, certain amid all uncertainties. This was a thought that inspired Ambrose. "The Church," he writes, "is a haven of salvation and with outstretched arms she calls imperilled seafarers into the bosom of her rest *(in gremium tranquillitatis),* for she shows herself as the landing-place in which we may put our trust." He who boards this ship leaves all old customs and conventions, indulgences of habit and weak-willed inclinations behind him; he is in a spiritual sense

what Secundus called the seaman — "a deserter from the land."[74]

Modern man's spiritual development is now beginning to be redirected into the concreteness of a mindful daily life. This growth can become efficacious if it is no longer projected on the one hand, into mindless external forms, i.e., brute materialism, and on the other hand, onto cheap promises of salvation presented in immature and simple answers to the complexity of modern life. Ecology, including a concern for life at every level, and the efforts toward a humanistic economy, are definite signs of this development.

David Bohm writes:

> *Parts are seen to be in immediate connection in which their dynamical relationship depend, in an irreducible way, on the state of the whole system (and indeed, on that of broader systems in which they are contained, extending ultimately and in principle to the entire universe). Thus one is led to a new notion of unbroken wholeness which denies the classical idea of analyzability of the world into separately and independently existent parts . . .*[75]

The Merkabah as Image of Wholeness

THE "scientific truth" is anticipated in Ezekiel's vision of the Merkabah (the seat of God) which became the root of a widespread mystical tradition:

As I looked, behold, a stormy wind came out of the north and a great cloud. . . . And from the midst of it came the likeness of *four* living creatures. And this was their appearance: they had the form of men, but *each had four faces* and each of them had four wings. . . . And the four had their faces and their wings thus: their wings touched one another; they went everyone straightforward, without turning as they went. As for the likeness of their faces, each had the face of a man in front; the four had the face of a lion on the right side, the four had the face of an ox on the left side, and the four had the face of an eagle at the back. . . . Now as I looked at the living creatures, I saw a wheel upon the earth beside the living creatures, one for each of *the four* of them. . . . When they went, they went in any *of their four directions,* without turning as they went. . . . And when the living creatures went, the wheels went beside them; and when the living creatures rose from the earth, the wheels rose. . . . And above the firmament over their heads there was the likeness of a throne, in appearance like sapphire; and seated above the likeness of a throne was a likeness as if it were of a human form. . . . I saw as it were . . . like the appearance of fire, and there was brightness round about him. Like the appearance of the bow that is in the cloud on the day of rain,

so was the appearance of the brightness round about.
Such was the appearance of the likeness of the glory
of the Lord.[76]

The Merkabah and the Last Supper are in their truest
sense mysteries, leading man into realms of the unknown.
As mysteries they were therefore jealously guarded in antiquity and only the initiated were allowed to participate in
them. So in Christianity today, only a baptized person is
allowed to receive the sacrament at the Holy Mass; he or she
must first be "reborn." The ontogenetic development of the
psyche however has given man "eyes to see it," i.e., to
approach the mystery of life in a new way. Approaches like
the philosophy of modern theoretical physics or genuine
experiences in depth psychology are manifestations of this
spiritual evolution. Biblical texts, as poetic visions, seem
primarily to assist the searching human being in the creation
of a new awareness and its application to life as a process of
wholeness.

Not only is the archetype of four an expression of wholeness symbolized in the Merkabah, but life as a process in
movement is represented as well. The four figures are
accompanied by wheels, the symbol of a moving process,
and thus the image as a whole appears to portray life in its
essence. As an artistic expression in its simultaneity it is
unthinkable; it can only be grasped intuitively in all its
grandeur.

For Pythagoras, the horizontal figure 8 (∞), namely, two
fours in a horizontal dimension "was the symbol of perfection, the symbol denoting that which is everlasting and at
rest."[77] In mathematics the same symbol expresses infinity
today. The ogdoad as a solid cube extends in all directions,
like the fluid movements of the Merkabah. The ontogenetic
process of the development of the psyche allows us to see in
the mystery of "eight" a basic truth, later incorporated into
Christian thought as the eight persons who boarded the
ark.[78]

In Plato's philosophy the soul is seen as:

". . . that which is self-moving" as the necessary condition for the stability of the "whole heavens and the entire world of *becoming."* At the same time he sees it as the nature . . . of the soul. Hence, the first principle of world and soul is identified. . . .

In the spiritual version of the *Phaedrus* two pictorial motifs interpenetrate: the horse-drawn chariot and the wings that carry it. The first motif has remarkable analogy in the *Katha Upanishad* of India. There the human body is the chariot[!!] The intellect *(buddhi)* guides it. The taut reins are the thinking organ *(manas).* The barely manageable steeds are the senses *(indriya).* The chariot is the body. The true soul, the self *(atman),* rides in such a hardly dirigible vehicle.[79]

In the *Katha Upanishad* there is a clear division between the vehicle, the body, and the various human functions which control it. In Jewish mysticism a clear distinction is made between the soul and God. There is however still another important variation of the central theme. The Indo-European chariot provides the archetype for the self-concept of these cultures. The chariot is a two-wheeled vehicle which connotes war and battle (e.g., Bhagavad Gita, whose hero is Arjuna, the charioteer on the field of battle). Ezekiel does not draw upon the same symbol; he uses the four-wheeled cart.

This vehicle was invented in the Transcaucasus area of the Near East about 3,000 B.C. and is perhaps associated with agricultural life, the nomadism of pastoralists. The two-wheeled chariot was introduced into the Near East by Indo-Europeans about 2,500 B.C.

Ezekiel's writings are dated about 600 B.C. His experience touches therefore exceedingly deep layers of the psyche. As an expression of the activity of the *hayah,* it is remarkable that the mystical tradition in Judaism makes a clear distinction between the soul and God and does not identify the actual experience of riding in a cart with the mystery of the becoming. *"The creator and His creature remain apart, and nowhere is an attempt made to bridge the gulf between them or to blur the distinction."*[80] The later mystics have lost their relation to this psychic energy.

> In this . . . stage the magical contents cease to represent a psychical reality and are gradually . . . replaced by a new devotional literature, at once stilted and lyrical. . . . The dangers of the ascent through the palaces of the Merkabah sphere are great, particularly for those who undertake the journey without the necessary preparation, let alone those who are unworthy of its object.[81]

The concern of the mystics about the "Perils of the Soul" so well known to primitive man and exemplified in Greek mythology, e.g., as the male Tartarus or the female Erinnyes of Hades is also manifested in the writings of St. Paul:

> Whoever . . . eats the bread or drinks the cup of the Lord in an unworthy manner will be guilty of profaning the body and blood of the Lord. Let a man examine himself, and so eat of the bread and drink of the cup. For any one who eats and drinks without discerning the body eats and drinks judgment upon himself.[82]

Twins

THE AWARENESS of the duality of existence and the responsible relation to the *hayah* are manifestations of the ontogenesis of the psyche. The principle of complementarity reigns supreme in the temples of science today, and it is also understood among the primitives like the Dogon of Nigeria, for whom "Twinship has been the rule . . . since the beginning of time.[83] The same situation is to be found, both actually and symbolically, in the Ougadougou district, village of Baloule, Upper Volta, Africa: "This shrine figure is used by the Mossi in connection with a cult dedicated to the generation of twin children."[84]

As with the Jacob-Esau twinship, touching the depth of human reality, so the Dogon cosmology mirrors,

> . . . their attitude to twins, a common enough theme in African ethnography. Throughout the continent twins are treated with the greatest respect or the greatest disrespect — worshipped or put to death. To the Dogon, twins are perfect births, echoes of a primordial world when twin births were the rule. . . .
>
> Twinship symbolizes the complementarity between all kinds of bonded pairs: friends, traders, husbands and wives, a man and his shadow, a man and his placenta. Even the rich and the poor, children of aristocrats and descendants of slaves, become twins once they have gone through circumcision and the ordeals of initiation together, thereby experiencing a new social state. . . .
>
> The Dogon universe, as a whole, issued from an

Figure 23.   Mossi Janus Twins.

infinity of smallness, created ... by *the Word of a single God,* called Amma. ... This infinite smallness developed and formed a vast womb, called the Egg of the World, which was divided into two parts and contained two placentas, which eventually gave birth to twin couples, pairs of mixed twins, living and animated beings, prototypes of man who *possessed the creative Word.* ... Each human being, from the first, was endowed with two souls of different sex, or rather with two different principles corresponding to two distinct persons. In the man, the female soul was located in the foreskin and in the woman the male soul was the clitoris. ... An incestuous act in creation had destroyed order based on the principle of twin or androgynous births; and order was only restored by the creation of human beings ... Twins express exchange, complementarity and equality as well as duality and order and, as such, they symbolize friendship and alliance . . . A child's body is one, but his spiritual being is two. And until his initiation rites, he remains spiritually, symbolically and physically "androgynous" — until puberty dual children retain their foreskins and clitorises; their "masculinity" and their "femininity" thereby remain equally potent. For a girl, the clitoris is a symbolic twin, a male makeshift with which she cannot reproduce herself and which also prevents her from mating with a man. She has it removed, since anyone trying to mate with an unexcised woman would be frustrated by opposition from an organ claiming to be his equal. Similarly, when a boy is circumcised, and his foreskin is transformed into a lizard, he loses both his femininity and his twin. . . .

Twins, as an ideal unit, also express the alliance and duality of friends, traders, joking-partners and husbands and wives. Each member of these dyads has in a sense found his other half. Most people are nevertheless born alone, and to compensate the Dogon for his misfortune, each child is linked to an animal who represents his unknown other half — his unborn twin. This animal twin himself has a twin, another tabooed animal and so on and so on; thus the aggregate of Dogon families is connected with the whole animal kingdom through the essential notion of twinness.[85]

The initiation rituals of the Dogon express within their context what on a higher level of organization depth psychology tries to achieve through the integration of complementarities, as they manifest themselves in actual behavior and/or in dreams, to help men or women to become balanced authentic personalities. On the religious plane the ontogenesis of the psyche is expressed also in symbols.

Both Ezekiel's vision of the Merkabah and the story of the Last Supper as ways to salvation are in their essences perhaps the most difficult paths to follow; and they may be the only true road to pursue in that they are both expressions of integrating parts into a whole. This is the same principle of complementarity referred to earlier in the story of the twins Jacob and Esau, in Jacob's way as a path to salvation, and in the Chinese symbol of Yin and Yang, the Taigitu, as well as the belief of the Dogons. In the *Book of Thomas the Contender* is a dialogue between the resurrected Jesus and his brother Judas Thomas, the Savior's twin who was thought to have direct insight into the nature of the Savior and his teaching. By "knowing himself" Thomas could also know the "depth of the All" from which the Savior came and to which he was going to return. The Savior said:

> I will reveal to you the things you have pondered in your mind. Now since it has been said that you are my twin and true companion, examine yourself that you may understand who you are, in what way you exist, and how you will come to be. Since you are called my brother, it is not fitting that you be ignorant of yourself. And I know that you have understood, because you had already understood that I am the knowledge of the truth. So while you accompany me, although you are uncomprehending, you have (in fact) already come to know, and you will be called the one who knows himself. For he who has not known himself has known nothing, but he who has known himself has at the same time already achieved knowledge about the Depth of the All. So then, you, my brother Thomas, have beheld what is obscure to men, that is, that against which they ignorantly stumble.[86]

In Indo-European Creation myths the mythologem, the archetypal pattern of the Twins is an ever-recurring theme.

As in Egyptian mythology Shu and Tefnut, the twins, were at the beginning of time; so in the Indo-European Creation myth. "We have here a virtually universal mythic theme, namely the twins, at the beginning of time, imbued with a typically Indo-European content, namely the complementarity of priests and kings."[87]

The decisive difference between the archetypal theme of the Twins, as an expression of complementarity on a mental level, and the Old Testament legend of the twins, Jacob and Esau, is that the latter is lifted onto a truly human level, expressing the ontogenesis of the psyche through *its very drama of integration towards wholeness, oneness.* The Old Testament legend shows a teleological direction while the Indo-European and Egyptian creation myths demonstrate rather a static mythologem, a symbolical illustration of a state of affairs in its primal order.

Furthermore we must not forget that Janus, the Roman god, is the god of the doors, of openings; he is the two-faced god who has both sides to his nature. It is moreover interesting to note that his temple was only open in wartime; in other words, in wartime one needed the other dimension, which one neglected at his peril, and brought, therefore, wars in peacetime. And in Revelation 3:8 it is said: "Behold, I have set before you an open door, which no one is able to shut."

The vision of the Merkabah anticipates in poetic terms what modern science has been slowly establishing from its own perspective. The harmony of the ever-flowing movement of the *hayah,* as a formative activity is apparently innate in life.

> Protagoras said: "Man is the measure of all things." Thus emphasizing that measure is not a reality external to man, existing independently of him . . . . Measure is a form of insight into the essence of everything, and . . . man's perception, following on ways indicated by such insights, will be clear and will

thus bring about generally orderly action and harmonious living . . . . But many who were in the habit
of looking at everything externally also applied this
way of what Protagoras said. Thus, they concluded
that measure was something arbitrary, and subject to
the capricious choice or taste of every individual. In
this way they of course overlooked the fact that
measure is a form of insight that has to fit the overall
reality in which man lives, as demonstrated by the
clarity of perception and harmony of action to which
it leads.[88]

As a poetic insight of wholeness, the Merkabah clearly
expresses in the symbolic human figures the four-dimensionality which science has now seen at the root of life.
Experiencing the world in bits and pieces rather than in
terms of its wholeness urges man to establish in reality what
is his driving motivation. In the long run, the imprisonment
of the true "measure of things" will shatter an atomistic
world view. It is the irony of our time that the atomistic
world view may well be shattered by atomic power.

As a forerunner of the today's so needed development of
the psyche may be considered the famous Indian seal "The
Lord of the Beasts" from about 2,000 B.C. He is seated with
crossed legs, i.e., in a meditative position, and wears a water
buffalo headdress and is surrounded by other beasts. It may
be, as some anthropologists believe, that the headdress is a
symbol of the bearer's belonging to a particular moiety, a
particular society or clan. However this may be, the seal
clearly depicts in any case a stage in the development of
consciousness. The Lord of the Beasts, symbolizing a particular level of awareness, is superceded by the dance of the god
Hevajra above an animal, as if he, like the four-faced Babylonian god who also has an animal underfoot, had mastered
the chaos. In other words, the Lord of the Beasts is also a mandala depicting a potential inner achievement of man, just as

Figure 24. Lord of the Beasts.

Adam's development in Genesis symbolizes a heightened state of awareness by having had to give names to the animals (Genesis 2:19).

We can observe the same essential meaning in rock art 20-30,000 years old. Prof. Anati writes:

> We can presume with some safety that the same kind of emotions and motivations that govern and sway us today informed the making of ancient rock art tens of millenia ago. Its study brings back to a conscious level archetypal elements of human experience that modern life has largely suppressed.[89]

The four-faced Babylonian god finds its parallel in Buddhist religion. The god Hevajra of the Mahayana Buddhism

Figure 25.   Hevajra, four-faced Buddhist god.

shows exactly the same archetypal features — he is also four-faced and has underfoot an animal. While the Babylonian god stems from about 1,800 B.C. the Buddhist figure is dated 800 A.D. The ontogenetic principle expresses itself as an artistic conception in a time span of about 2,600 years and is repeated in modern science's efforts, one thousand years later, to come to a unified, four-dimensional field theory in order to comprehend the unity of nature.

And as the dancing four-faced god Hevajra looks into the four directions of the universe, as does the Babylonian god, so do also the four giant faces on the famous Angkor Thom temple [supra, pp. 253, 262, and 338].[90]

The faces may represent realistically the faces of a king but they also allegorize his ever-presence as god. *As such he apprehends reality in its four basic dimensions, and expresses himself archetypically as enlightenment, each face in its distinct way enlightening a particular dimension and being enlightened by it in turn, consciousness and knowledge grow.*

Not only in the magnificent Babylonian figures of the god and his consort with four faces, the Merkabah, the vision of Ezekiel, the dancing Mahayana Buddhist god Hevajra, the four faces at the Angkor Thom temple in Cambodia, but also in "primitive" African art do we find four-dimensionality expressing the essence of everything.

The four-faced staff of Idoma may have different associations in the minds of the natives;[91] nevertheless, the archetypal four is represented as it is on the wooden head-dress looking out into the four dimensions and moving in unison at dances at festivals and funerals.[92]

> . . . walk before me, and be blameless.[93]

> You, therefore, must be perfect, as your heavenly Father is perfect.[94]

These exhortations from both the Old and New Testaments sound essentially the same note of wholeness. However,

Figure 26.   Angkor Thom Temple.

Figure 27. Four-faced Idoma Staff.

Figure 28. Ekpo Eyo, four-faced mask.

men and women of today can discern meaning in these admonitions only as *a way* toward integration of their essential "twinness" which includes both the reality of man's potential to be human and his propensity to be beast-like. This beast-like potential becomes an actuality in the ever-growing acts of violent terrorism in our time in which impotent groups of people vent their frustrations against whomever they feel to be at the root of their disappointment. In the U.S. lately, murders of black people were committed and in two cases the hearts of the victims were removed. The mind of these murderers showed an *abaissement du niveau mental*, a lowering of the mental state, into that of primitive man who ate parts of the bodies of their victims in order to acquire their strength.

God-Eating

FRAZER, in a well authenticated chapter entitled "Homeopathic Magic of a Flesh Diet," in Part V of his *Golden Bough*, gives innumerable examples of this custom. Captioning a special part Frazer wrote: "The flesh and blood, but especially the hearts of dead men [were] eaten or drunk for the sake of acquiring the good qualities of the dead."[95]

Anthropologists believe that the reports of the Franciscan Sahagùn and the Dominican Duran about human sacrifices by the Aztecs are accurate. Their accounts of buildings and temples coincide with archaeological evidence. They unearthed "in front of Huitzilopochtli's shrine . . . the sacrificial stone against which victims were laid back-down and spread-eagled prior to having their chests cut open and the hearts removed and offered to the sun to assure its daily reappearance."[96] Human sacrifice and cannibalism are closely interrelated as magical means for rebirth and the continuance of life.

Gruesome as these reports are, and as much as we would like not to "see" or understand, the hearts of the black victims *were* removed, and likewise, it is a fact that cannibalism was reported as a result of a plane crash in the Andes in 1972 where the eating of human flesh was a means of survival. The report of this incident was published in a book entitled *Alive*.[97] In just seven months 2,500,000 copies were printed, indicating that an enormous number of people have a deep-seated fascination for this gruesome subject.

Even the Bible shows clear traces of the ancient custom of man eating man. "What is to die, let it die; what is to be destroyed, let it be destroyed; and let those that are left devour the flesh of one another."[98] Further, Micah 3:2-3 says:

> . . . you who hate the good and love the evil,
> who tear the skin from off my people,
> and their flesh from off their bones;
> who eat the flesh of my people,
> and flay their skin from off them,
> and break their bones in pieces,
> and chop them up like meat in a kettle,
> like flesh in a cauldron.

Here the poets have unleashed archetypal symbols which reach deep into the psyche. Eating, as an assimilation, permeates the Bible: the eating of the apple in the Garden of Eden and Esau's eating of the red, and the drinking of the ashes of the Golden Calf. In Ezekiel 3:1-3 it is said: "And he said to me, 'Son of man, eat what is offered to you; eat this scroll, and go, speak to the house of Israel.' So I opened my mouth, and he gave me the scroll to eat. And he said to me, 'Son of man, eat this scroll that I give you and fill your stomach with it.' Then I ate it; and it was in my mouth as sweet as honey."

And last but not least, the eating of the bread and drinking the "blood" of Christ. Archaeologists unearthed in Nahariya, Israel, moulds which they believe to represent

Figure 29.   Astarte of the Horns, 1700 B.C.

possibly the goddess Astarte. The mould is dated 17th Century B.C. "Could it be that such moulds were used to bake in them cakes in the shape of Astarte, to be either eaten by the celebrants (perhaps as a precursor of the Holy Communion in which the Host, which is supposed actually to turn into the body of Christ, is eaten), or burnt on the altar? More data will be needed before this question can be answered, but the possibility that this was meant by the cakes in the image of the Queen of Heaven is an intriguing one."[99]

The Biblical reference to this "intriguing possibility" is Jeremiah 44:16-19:

"As for the word which you have spoken to us in the name of the Lord, we will not listen to you. But we will do everything that we have vowed, burn incense to the queen of heaven and pour out libations to her, as we did, both we and our fathers, our kings and our princes, in the cities of Judah and in the streets of Jerusalem; for then we had plenty of food, and prospered, and saw no evil. But since we left off burning incense to the queen of heaven and pouring out libations to her, we have lacked everything and have been consumed by the sword and by famine." And the women said: "When we burned incense to the queen of heaven and poured out libations to her, was it without our husbands' approval that *we made cakes for her bearing her image* and poured out libations to her." (Italics mine)

It is of importance also to note that these figurines have been found in every major excavation in Palestine and their prevalence extends from Middle Bronze Age, 2,000-1,500 B.C. to early Iron Age (II), 900-600 B.C. A parallel of god-eating is to be found in the Aztec culture, where the ritual certainly cannot be construed as being influenced by any other tradition. It is born and grew out of the deep recesses of the psyche, going back to the earliest beginnings of animated life. Customs of "god-eating" have a universal, biological character and are not confined to a particular tradition. Just as eating is an ever-recurring theme in both the Old and New Testaments, as through the eating, and the symbolic feeding of the masses, life is kept alive. Therefore it is not surprising that in the Aztec tradition we should find an important ritual of god-eating. Huitzilopochtli, to whom human hearts were offered, is himself symbolically eaten in this ritual. And here, as in the Biblical tradition, it is dough or cake which is the medium. A paste was made and moulded into the figure of the god Huitzlopachtli:

> And when the body of Uitzilopochtli was shapen, when they gave it form upon his feast day, when it was Panquetzaliztli, they made it of a dough of amaranth seed, a dough of fish amaranth seed, which is *chicalotl.* They ground it; they kneaded it well; they divided it into pieces; they put it into bowls. . . .
>
> And upon the next day the body of Uitzilopochtli died.
>
> And he who slew him was [the priest known as] Quetzalcoatl; and that with which he slew him was a dart tipped with flint, which was *plunged into his heart.*
>
> He died in the presence of Moctezuma and of the keeper of the god, with whom Uitzilopochtli could speak, to whom *he could make himself visible,* who could make offerings to him, and of four [priests who were high priests, and of *four*] leaders of the youths, front rank leaders. Before all of these died Uitzilopochtli.
>
> And when he died, thereupon they broke up his body, the amaranth seed dough. His heart was Moctezuma's portion.
>
> And the rest of his members, which were made like his bones, were disseminated among the people; there was a distribution. . . . And later they divided it among themselves, only going in order. Each year

they ate it. . . . And when they divided among themselves his body of amaranth seed dough, it was only
in very small [pieces]: only very small, tiny. *The
youths ate them.*

And of this which they ate, it was said: *"The god is
eaten."* And of those who ate it, it was said: *"They
keep the god."* (Italics mine)[100]

It is also of interest to note that in this dramatic presentation of the innermost process of becoming there appears
again like a universal song the so fundamental four: "and of
four leaders of the youths. . . ." However, the vital difference
of the level on which the drama is acted out, the drama of
becoming in which the "self-organizing and self-correcting
principle" of biology is manifesting itself in the realm of the
mind, is expressed in Hebrews 13:13-14: "Let us go forth to
him outside the camp, bearing abuse for him. For here we
have no lasting city, but seek the city which is to come."

The reference here is to the City of God, the "city which
hath foundations, whose builder and maker is God."[101] The
Holy Mass moves beyond mere biological need for survival,
beyond, that is, the "camp" which is a symbol for the secular
life. In the Christian ritual, it is no longer a play for mere
continuance, but a portrayal of the search for a new, a
spiritual life; it is the search for a life in the freedom to
become, unbounded by the narrow walls of the "camp," the
pre-determined forms, the boundaries of dogma. The ritual
itself as the quest for the "city which is to come" is an
expression of what Rudolf Otto calls the "numinosum."
"The numinosum as a term is the Holy *minus* the ethical, the
moral, and we wish to add at once, minus a rational aspect.
. . . The word is derived from the Latin *numen* and as it is a *sui
generis* category of experience it is like every primary and
basic datum not definable in a narrow sense."[102]

St. Augustine in *The City of God* maintains that the true
sacrifice consists in the interior surrender to God and in
every deed flowing from this surrender. Even the Old Testa-

ment sacrifices had their meaning only in such an interior act: "A visible sacrifice, therefore, is a sacrament or sacred sign of an invisible sacrifice." *("Sacrificium ergo visibile invisibilis sacrificii sacramentum, id est, sacrum signum est.[103])* For St. Augustine, the true sacrifice is the man "who dies to the world and lives for God."

For modern man, the numinous is an expression of unbroken wholeness, through which alone the individual and his society has a chance of survival. Samuel Pisar after his gruesome experiences as a young man in Auschwitz writes:

> The struggle for survival cannot be delegated to this or that providential leader. It can no more be left to a political platform or an economic program or diplomatic doctrine than to the expectation of a miracle; that is the road to bondage.
>
> The struggle for survival in freedom must begin with oneself.
>
> . . . It takes a state of mind where the government is perceived neither as a magnanimous Santa Claus nor as armed sentry on the other side of a barbed-wire fence. It takes an ability to understand the tragic and hypocritical and unpredictable dimension of history, to grasp and act upon appearances of mortal danger, however they may be disguised, before one smells the sulfur of exploding bombs or the stench of burning flesh. . . .
>
> . . . The return to a world of stability and security must begin at the very roots, with faith in the intelligence of man rather than in the dogmas of a party, a church, or a state; rules prescribed by an allegedly infallible authority give way under the first shock of brutality.[104]

The dualism reflected in St. Augustine's *City of God* in all probability was inspired by the passage from Hebrews quoted above. In the third verse of the same chapter, we read: "Remember those who are in prison, as though in prison with them; and those who are ill-treated, since you are in the body." As we read these ringing words of the author of the Epistle to the Hebrews, it is difficult to escape the same sense of dualism, or to fail to see the sharp relief they provide against the terrible human sacrifice of prisoners by the Aztecs.

It has been reported that "shortly before the arrival of the Spanish conquerors the number of victims sacrificed in Central Mexico annually reached 250,000."[105]

Our minds cringe when we read of these events of only 500 years ago. But in our own time, authorities representing the inmost core of Christianity in Germany determined to keep silent as the dark clouds of the greatest crime in history were gathering. It is as though the same motif of Aztec sacrifice to the gods was being repeated on a scale unprecedented in human history. Samuel Pisar, having survived the death camp at Auschwitz, and searching for the meaning of his own survival, wrote:

> During World War II, Pope Pius XII had a moral duty, under the precepts of his own faith, to speak through the powerful transmitters of the Vatican against the Nazi extermination of Europe's Jews ["to remember those who are in prison"]. As apostolic ambassador to Berlin, before the white clouds of smoke from the chimney of the Sistine Chapel announced his election as the Vicar of God on Earth, he had known the truth. Where was the fiery encyclical that might have created a crisis of conscience among the Catholics in the German nation and the German army?
>
> His Holiness was face to face with a challenge that history reserves only once every two hundred years: to pick up the cross on his back and to announce to the tortured skeletons behind the barbed-wire fences:

"I'm coming to join you; my place is in this world with you." That challenge he failed to meet, as he maintained a deafening diplomatic silence, the silence of a pope of indifference.[106]

We can recall, on the other hand, the prayer of Pope John XXIII [supra, p. 16]. Though he had intended to have this prayer read from all the Roman Catholic pulpits of the world, his successor, Paul VI, withheld the order, and had no intention of releasing it even at a later date. This prayer of Pope John XXIII is a magnificent echo of the symbolism of the Last Supper. Here was no betrayal, no Judas' kiss.[107] However, Pius XII negotiated and signed the concordat with the Nazis and did not "remember those who are in prison."[108]

On the one hand, the Last Supper is a feast celebrating the passover from bondage into the freedom of becoming in both a physical and symbolic sense;[109] and on the other hand, it is a powerful manifestation of the *hayah* itself, a *numinosum* in all its depths. Here, the ontogenetic process is revealed in all its grandeur.

For St. Augustine, the supreme human task is that of surrender to God, while for humanity today the quest involves learning how to surrender to life and at the same time, to become a responsible human being.

> What takes place in the celebration of the Eucharist is a continuation, a making-present, of the event of redemption. Hence it is an objective memorial: objective not merely in an external sign (however solemn the ceremony surrounding it), but objective in the sense that the very event celebrated thereby becomes present.[110]

Many minds and many centuries were required to create the beautiful and dramatic presentation of the eucharistic ritual. But the ritual in itself, therefore, is still an artifact. "The origin and historical development of the Canon is one of the most difficult problems of the entire history of the liturgy. Indeed it seems to be a problem that will never be satisfactorily solved."[111] The basis of the Last Supper is Matthew 26:26-28:

> Now as they were eating, Jesus took bread, and blessed, and broke it, and gave it to the disciples and said, "Take, eat; this is my body." And he took a cup, and when he had given thanks he gave it to them, saying, "Drink of it, all of you; for this is my blood of the covenant, which is poured out for many for the forgiveness of sins."

In Luke 22:19 there is added: "Do this in remembrance of me." And St. Paul in I Corinthians 11:24 adds also: "Do this in remembrance of me."

In the Roman Mass, the most sacred portion is the Consecration. And precisely because it is regarded as sacred, when the text was translated into the vernacular, it created discomfort for many orthodox Christian believers. The following is the translation of Parsch-Eckhoff, and is used here by reason of the imprimatur which it received.

> ... the day before he suffered he took bread into His holy and venerable hands, and with His eyes lifted up to heaven, unto Thee, God, His Almighty Father, giving thanks to Thee, He blessed, broke, and gave to His disciples, saying: Take ye, and eat ye all of this, *for this is my body.*
>
> In the like manner, after He had supped, taking also this excellent chalice into His holy and venerable hands; also giving thanks to Thee, He blessed, and gave it to His disciples, saying: Take, and drink ye all of this; *for this is the chalice of my blood of the new and eternal testament; the mystery of faith: which shall be shed for you and for many unto the remission of sins.* As often as ye shall do these things, ye shall do them in memory of Me.[112]

The sacred solemnity of the eucharistic consecration rests upon the equivalence of bread with body and wine with blood, making it a numinosum pregnant with creative meaning. It is a ritual which reverses the "natural" order by lifting the common elements of natural food to the level of divine human responsibility. It is on this level that the "Divine ambiguity" can find its resolution through man's surrender to life and the human being enacting his divine aspect, in the freedom of choice. In the natural order there is no choice; at best there is only evolution. Freedom of choice is the divine creative aspect in the working of the human mind which allows for participation in *conscientia*, "knowing with" [supra, p. 4], and thus for choosing.

In paganism, god-eating has exactly the opposite meaning. Man eats the god, whether friend or foe, in order to acquire strength from the flesh of the victim, but not for the purpose of becoming a creative participant in the process of life.

"An old man, who is in the relation of Kami to the deceased steps into the grave and cuts off all the fat adhering to the face, thighs, arms and stomach, and passes it round to be swallowed by the relations. The order in which they partake of the fat is as follows: The mother eats of her children, and the children of their mother; a man eats of his sister's husband and of his brother's wife; mother's brothers, mother's sisters, sister's children, mother's parents or daughter's children are also eaten of; but the father does not eat of his children, nor the children of their sire. The relations eat of the fat in order that they may be no longer sad. ... The aborigines said that the body was eaten with no desire to gratify or appease the appetite, but only as a symbol of respect and regret for the dead."[113]

The historical procedures for administration of the Eucharistic Host reflect the very gradual and reluctant acceptance of personal responsibility both by the Church and by the individual believer. In some cases, the bread was received from a basket and the participants fed themselves as a memorial act only. In the 1st century A.D., the Host was presented to each by the officiating priest. The Church authorities, however, had some doubt about allowing so much personal participation. "The custom of placing the sacred Host on the bare hands of men and *upon a cloth (dominicale) spread over the hand of the women,* was observed until after the beginning of the Middle Ages; as late as the ninth century, a council at Rome was legislating against this practice" (italics mine).[114]

Today, the normal practice is to place the Host directly into the mouth of the believer. By participating in this sacrificial ritual, in theory the recipient is lifted to the level of becoming, but in fact the recipient remains in the passive mode of reception only. "May this mingling and hallowing of the body and the blood of our Lord Jesus Christ avail us that receive it unto life everlasting."[115]

When Pope John Paul II administered the sacrament in Munich, Germany in November 1980, he abandoned the custom of placing the Host in the mouth, and presented the bread to the people. It is to be hoped that this symbolizes a step in growth toward personal responsibility and individual action, for only so shall the Western world experience a semblance of real redemption.

The depth of penetration of the ritual of the Holy Mass is strikingly illustrated by an early story which is perhaps apocryphal; St. Ambrose and other early Fathers believed in its authenticity.

After a quarrel with the emperor Valerian (A.D. 257), the martyr St. Laurence was, according to a poem by Prudentius, condemned to death: "You shall die by inches!" Then the emperor had a great gridiron made ready, and glowing coals put under it, that the martyr might be slowly burnt. Laurence was stripped and bound upon his iron bed over the slow fire, which roasted his flesh little by little. His face appeared to the Christians to be surrounded with a beautiful light, and his suffering body to give off a sweet smell; but the unbelievers neither saw this light nor perceived the smell.

The martyr felt not the torments of the persecutor, says St. Augustine, so passionate was his desire for Christ; and St. Ambrose observes that while his body burned in the material flames, the fire of divine love was far more active within his breast and made him regardless of the pain. Having suffered a long time he turned to the judge and said with a cheerful smile, "Let my body be turned; one side is broiled enough." When the executioner had turned him, he said: "It is cooked enough, you may eat." "St. Laurence has been one of the most venerated martyrs of the Roman Church since the fourth century, and he is named in the canon of the Mass."[116]

In Abraham's sacrifice of Isaac, so closely related to the Holy Mass, we meet in a legend surrounding it a similar poetic motif.

> [Abraham] noticed upon the mountain a pillar of fire reaching from earth to heaven, and a heavy cloud in which the glory of God was seen. Abraham said to Isaac: "My son, dost thou see on that mountain which we perceive at a distance that which I see upon it?" And Isaac answered, and said unto his father: "I see, and, lo, a pillar of fire and a cloud, and the glory of God seen upon the cloud." Abraham knew then that Isaac was accepted before the Lord for an offering. He asked Ishmael and Eliezer: "Do you also see that which we see upon the mountain?" They answered: "We see nothing more than like the other mountains," and Abraham knew that they were not accepted before the Lord to go with them.[117]

The way to Mt. Moria and the Stations of the Cross are symbolic and sacred precincts within the psyche to be arrived at by personal choice. "Thou shall love the Lord thy God with all thine heart, with all thy soul, and with all thy might."[118] Rashi comments: "With all your heart —with both your impulses."[119] The drama of Mt. Moria and the Last Supper is perhaps the most profound poetic demonstration of the transubstantiation of the human mind. Such a transubstantiation as the becoming of the psyche is, in a primitive stage, essentially mirrored in a pictorial representation of this basic theme.

This drawing from the *Florentine Codex* of Sahagún's "New Spain" clearly shows the primitive rite of cannibalism of the Aztecs as practiced long before the Spanish conquest.

The same theme is depicted in this 16th century illumination, but with a totally divergent purpose. Here the body is "cooked," not for cannibalistic purposes, but in order that through the fire there should be a process of change, of transubstantiation, until the dove (spirit) ascends from it.

Figure 30. The Florentine Codex of Sahagún.

Figure 31.   *Mercurius Senex*, from Trismosin "Splendor Solis," Ms 1582.

A third alchemical illumination shows the *prima materia* (the primal stuff) symbolized by the monster, Mercurius, "cooked" in order to produce the "Philosopher's Stone," the essence of wisdom. As the transformation of Mercurius, symbolizing the mental process, is the projection of an inner state onto the outer material, so it was hoped that the low grade metal (lead) might be transformed into gold. In this picture, the transforming process is demonstrated for a Bishop and a monk by an alchemist whose assistant keeps the fire burning. These three illustrations are reflections of stages in the psyche's process of becoming.

Figure 32. Maier. *Tripus Sureus*, Three Artists in the Library.

A supreme example of the human potential for transformation is depicted in the New Testament story of Jesus at the Wedding Feast at Cana in the 2nd Chapter of John. The drama here is a poetic prefiguration of the Last Supper, for to view this account as a miracle story is to mistake the form for the essence. In this case, the natural element, water, is transformed into the spiritual element, wine. "And when they wanted wine, the mother of Jesus saith unto him, They have no wine. Jesus saith unto her, *Woman* [he did not address her as mother] what have I to do with thee? mine hour is not yet come."[120]

In terms of the *hayah*, becoming, a man remains in the natural state of bondage to his mother until he has matured sufficiently to surrender to life, at which time he arrives at his own limited freedom. Jesus says: "Mine hour is not yet come" because the essential of the experiences of life is a timeless time, an endless becoming. The "mother," in this ontogenetic process, also gets the freedom to be herself, a woman in her own right, with all of the human strengths and weaknesses which are her own.

But above all else, this chapter portrays in a dramatic and vital way the message of the *hayah*: "I have not come to bring peace. . . ."

The Wedding at Cana stands symbolically for the natural human situation, but at the same time it stands for separation from the family. The formative cause — the inner Christ — of this apparent contradiction is the process of becoming in the psyche itself. This necessary development does not mean that feeling relationships — "honor thy father and thy mother" — need to be curtailed in any way. On the contrary, the openness which results enables a much freer and honest relationship with one's parents.

In the Wedding Feast story, the dramatic ambiguity reaches its height as serving the family in the proper way, which is symbolically expressed in the transformation of the water into wine, thus achieving freedom. The neglect of this basic human situation in our time has led not only to the breakdown of family life, but also to the bondage of subservience to narcissistic emptiness.

And again, as at the Last Supper, the symbolic motif of the passover is reflected in this same chapter. "And the Jew's passover was at hand."[121]

There is portrayed as well the demonic power of shallow materialism. "And [he] found in the temple those that sold oxen and sheep and doves, and the changers of money."[122] What he found, like Judas' kiss of betrayal, is a poetic symbol of the betrayal of the spirit — the betrayal of the mind on the way to freedom and fulfillment. "And said to them that *sold doves*, 'Take these things hence; make not my Father's house an house of merchandise.' "[123] And making a whip of cords, he drove them all, with the sheep and oxen, out of the temple; and he poured out the coins of the money-changers and overturned their tables.[124]

The dove, as the symbol of the spirit, is singled out. In the Gospels, the dove descends upon Jesus and can certainly neither be bought or sold like a piece of merchandise which the religion industry of today, presenting itself as the representative of the "good shepherd," arrogates to its own system of delivery.[125]

There is a significant precursor of this development in Zechariah 11. In this compact chapter laden with images, there is a trenchant demonstration of the essences of both the Wedding at Cana, and of the Last Supper. Here the poets have given us a true record of the actual psyche in its contradictory aspects, those of acceptance and rejection. When the voice of the Lord speaks, it is a manifestation of the *hayah*, the *numinosum* in all its mystery. In Zechariah we read: "Thus said the Lord my God: 'Become shepherd of the flock doomed to slaughter.' Those who buy them slay them and go unpunished and those who sell them say, 'Blessed be the Lord, I have become rich'; and their own shepherds have no pity on them. . . . 'Lo, I will cause men to fall each into the hand of his shepherd —and each one into the hand of his king; and they shall crush the earth, and I will deliver none from their hand.' "[126]

The confusion of our time bears witness to this truth. A consumer society, under the various guises of dictatorship, conditioned by materialism, be it capitalism, or communism, threatens "to crush the earth." The psyche's effort to cope with the human condition results in despair and cynicism: ". . . 'I will not be your shepherd. What is to die, let it die; what is to be destroyed, let it be destroyed; and let those that are left devour the flesh of one another.' And I took my staff Grace and I broke it, annulling the covenant which I had made with all the peoples. . . . Then I said to them: 'If it seems right to you, give me my wages; but if not, keep them.' And they weighed out as my wages *thirty shekels of silver.* . . . I took the thirty shekels of silver and cast them into the treasury in the house of the Lord. Then I broke my second staff Union, annulling the brotherhood between Judah and Israel."[127]

In the Last Supper the same archetypal motif plays a pivotal role. There is a lengthy discourse about who will enact the betrayal of Christ and in what form it will take place. Above all, we are meeting in exactly the same context as in Zechariah the figure of thirty shekels of silver and the returning of the money to the temple. The betrayal is of no avail, Judas hangs himself and in Zechariah it is said:

> *Woe to my worthless shepherd, who deserts the flock!*
> *May the sword smite his arm and his right eye!*
> *Let his arm be wholly withered, his right eye utterly blinded!*[128]

The Odyssey

IN THE GREAT DRAMA of the psyche's becoming, of the slow and painful way to the freedom from the shackles of our own bestialities and misunderstandings, the symbol of the shepherd plays an important role. In Zechariah as well as in the Last Supper an essential meaning of man's growth towards a free and responsible being turns, as if in a ritualistic dance, around the central question: "Am I my brother's keeper?" In Homer's *Odyssey* the worthless shepherds are described:

> Kyklopês have no muster and no meeting,
> no consultation or old tribal ways,
> but each one dwells in his own mountain cave
> dealing out rough justice to wife and child,
> indifferent to what the others do.[129]

In this Homeric statement, man is described symbolically in his isolation, and therefore in his depravity as well, echoing the Old Testament question of man at the beginning of his journey into self-discovery, "Am I my brother's keeper?"[130] Homer's poetic expression shows the inner face of man today as though in a surrealist painting, depicting the source of neglected human values, and the consequent denial of human rights.

In the present "age of anxiety," the anguish of modern man is artistically represented in Munch's famous painting "The Scream." Human anxiety today is a consequence of the absence of feeling and the denial of the essence of love. Modern society is not far removed from the Cyclopes' cannabalistic mentality of Polyphemus. When we reflect on the fact that the Nazis "cooked" their victims in great ovens, we are reminded of the patron saint of cooks and restaurateurs, St. Laurence, whose emblem is an iron grill. More recently, *Le Matin* for January 12, 1978 reported of a demonstration in Marseilles that there were demonstrators wearing T-shirts imprinted with the words "If you are hungry put a Jew into your oven." And in order to satisfy their greed for material things, nations are preparing the super-incinerator, atomic warfare.

Cain's question is eternal and above all other questions provides weight and meaning for the process of becoming human. Dietrich Bonhoeffer attempted to be "his brother's keeper" when he confronted the Nazis, and in so doing addressed this ultimate question of human existence. In the utter isolation of his prison cell, constantly facing the prospect of death, he came to realize how superfluous is the *Deus ex machina* as the god who rescues us as a matter of course:

Religious people speak of God when human perception is (often just from laziness) at an end, or human resources fail: it is in fact always the Deus ex machina they call to their aid, either for the so-called solving of insoluble problems or as support in human failure — always, that is to say, helping out human weakness or on the borders of human exist-

ence. Of necessity, that can only go on until men can,
by their own strength, push those borders a little
further, so that God becomes superfluous as a Deus
ex machina.[131]

Likewise, Samuel Pisar wrote of his experience with the
modern Cyclopes: "The struggle for survival cannot be
delegated to this or that providential leader. . . . The struggle
for survival in freedom must begin with oneself."[132] Because
each of these men were being confronted with the ultimate
concerns of existence, the question of God as the "Good
Shepherd" was not for them an issue.

The archetypal basis of the psyche's effort to overcome
mindless brutality is symbolized in the Chafadsche tablet,
which is Babylonian in origin and dates from the second half
of the third millennium B.C. Prof. Henry Frankfort describes
this relief as a forerunner of Polyphemus, and concludes on
the basis of the way this god is dressed that:

> This demon is not a newcomer but belonged to the
> well-established figures of Babylonian mythology,
> although no representations of it have been found
> before now. Its main characteristics are the rays
> which emanate from its head, and the fact that it is a
> Cyclops. . . . The artist . . . has been careful to indicate
> with clear engraving one large eye on the forehead of
> the demon.
>
> Now we are, of course, reminded at once of the
> Cyclops of Greek mythology, and it is important to
> remember that Homer's Polyphemus does not
> embody the complete Greek tradition concerning
> these creatures. The great poet has vividly portrayed
> an uncouth ogre, but Hesiod knew of Cyclopean
> sons of Uranus and Gaia, subterranean demons who
> forged thunderbolts for their liberator Zeus. Even
> Virgil (*Aen.* VIII, 246ff.) speaks of Cyclopean assis-
> tants of Vulcan in Etna. Not only the single eye placed

Figure 33. Chafadsche Monster, 3000 B.C., terracotta relief plaque showing a god killing a cyclopic demon.

on the forehead connects our relief, therefore, with Greek mythology; the Cyclops is, in both cases, a being imbued with dangerous powers over fire and its forces.

We published (ILN July 22, 1933, p. 124) evidence that the myth of Herakles and the Hydra derives from Babylonian beliefs connected with the god of fertility. Here we have another instance of the oriental origin of certain motives which the Greeks borrowed from the East. To state this fact does not diminish in any way our appreciation for the originality of the Greek mind. But it only reminds us of the fact that the Greeks were late arrivals in an ancient and highly developed civilised world, where they found much that could be used to express what, till then, they had not formulated. At the same time, it illustrates once more how our own civilisation is, through Hellas, inseparably linked with the Ancient Near East.[133]

In this tablet, the complexity of the archetypal symbol of the shepherd, so basic to the nomadic societies of the ancient world, is expressed on still another level. *Twelve* rays are shown emanating from the head of the Chafadsche monster; Odysseus brought *twelve* friends with him in *twelve* ships, and *twelve* women have "taken to immorality" at the end of the Odyssey. There were *twelve* Hebrew tribes; at the Last Supper, Jesus was with the *twelve* disciples. When seen in conjunction with the *twelve* signs of the Zodiac, the *twelve* months of the year with the rising and the setting of the sun, this symbolic number may connote wholeness. In Fourth Ezra, the monsters have *twelve* wings and in the apocalypse of Baruch there are *twelve* different waters.

According to Greek mythology, the Mother Earth gave birth to "three wild one-eyed Cyclopes" among the other giants. The word *Cyclops* means "ring-eyed." The mythic description of Odysseus searing the eye of the drunken Cyclops appears to have been combined with an Hellenic allegory of how the sun Titan is blinded every evening by his enemies, and is restored to sight the following dawn.[134]

According to the legend, after he had invaded the cave of the Cyclops, Odysseus and his men were discovered. The Cyclops asked of Odysseus his name. Odysseus replied that his name is "Nobody" in order to escape being also devoured as some of his friends were. Escape from the cave was accomplished by inducing Polyphemus to drunkenness, and as he lay in a drunken stupor, Odysseus with a heated wooden bar:

> . . . bored that great eye socket
> while blood ran out around the red hot bar.
> Eyelid and lash were seared; the pierced ball
> hissed broiling, and the roots popped.[135]

These are variations on a theme: the one-eyed Chafadsche monster of Babylon; the one-eyed Polyphemus of the Greeks; ". . . let his right eye be utterly blinded" from the Old Testament;[136] and "if your right eye causes you to sin, pluck it out and throw it away" from the New Testament.[137] In Greek mythology the poets made Oedipus blind himself because he had offended an essential law of human relationship — he had committed incest. Mythic structure in relation to the ontogenesis of the psyche reveals that both Odysseus and Polyphemus are also poetic symbols, *dramatis personae*, forged in the minds of countless generations, as are both of the Biblical references to the right eye.

The perennial forces of darkness seem unconquerable, yet always in the midst of the symbols of the dark there is to be found the symbol of rebirth, of self-correction. We have already referred to the Greek myth of the blinding and recovering of sight by the sun Titan. In Egyptian mythology, "the eye of the sky-god, in its guise as the moon, is injured, but is then restored."[138] The same archetypal theme is lifted into the metaphysical realm in an old Jewish legend:

Seven days before the rising of the moon the spirit of gentleness prepares to do battle with Semael and his hordes on account of the waning of the moon. The hairy man [Esau?] becomes embroiled with the smooth man [Jacob?] over the beauty of the moon, and Michael and Gabriel join issue with the accusers. But at the end of the seventh day Gabriel weakens their power and the High Priest Michael takes Semael, who is on the side of the hairy man and who looks like a ram, and offers him as a kind of sacrifice on the altar which is built as a penance at the beginning of each month. Then the supreme will is appeased, the moon grows big and full and the power of the ram is consumed in the fire of the Almighty. At the time, however, that the moon is waning, the ram is born again, and again grows in strength, and so it will continue until the Last Day, when it is said: "The shining of the moon will be as the shining of the sun."[139]

The reference to the Akedah and the "fire of the Almighty" notwithstanding, the perspective of this legend is clearly pagan — the opposites collide, rise, fall back, and rise again; the circle turns back upon itself forever and forever until the Last Day. This is a true picture of the human existential problem, insoluble by itself, save for the awareness of personal choice enlightened by the *hayah,* the inner Christ.

Though the archetypal basis of the psyche's effort to overcome mindless brutality is symbolized in the Chafadsche tablet and its antecedent mythology, man's flight from any encounter with his own primitive behavior and lack of regard for human values is symbolized in Polyphemus. Yet, out of the depths of this primitivity is born a hope that the inner conflict may be "religiously" resolved. The 23rd Psalm gives voice to such a hope:

> *The Lord is my shepherd,*
> *I shall not want . . .*
> *Even though I walk through*
> *the valley of the shadow of death,*
> *I fear no evil . . .*

Out of the multitude who were victims of the one-eyed totalitarian monster, there were many like Bonhoeffer and Pisar to whom the true God was revealed, not as an external agent, but as the shepherd-Lord within themselves. This is also the essential truth revealed in the great epic drama of Jacob and Esau.

Writing half a millennium after Homer, Aeschylus puts these words into his tragedy, *Agamemnon:*

> Zeus: whatever he may be, if this name
> pleases him in invocation,

thus I call upon him.
I ponder everything
yet I cannot find a way,
only Zeus, to cast this dead weight of
ignorance finally from out my brain . . .

Zeus who guided men to think,
who has laid it down that *wisdom
comes alone through suffering.*[140]

The ultimate is revealed in man at the very base of his being, in the chthonic realm of the primal creation experience, where brute animality resides. To speak of mankind springing from the dust of the earth is symbolic of the *prima materia,* the primal matter reaching back to the very origin of life at the moment of its creation. Science today speaks of "star dust" as the possible origin of it all. The Babylonian myth, the *Enuma Elish,* says man was created from the blood of Kingu, the symbol of dependency.[141] Just as man is dependent upon the *prima materia,* so is he dependent upon the mother. This dependence is phylogenetically overcome through the evolvement of language — the Word — through which relationship can be established. The word plays in both Babylonian mythology and in the Judaeo-Christian tradition a pivotal role. In the *Enuma Elish,* Kingu got from his mother the "tablet of destiny" through which he established his reality, unlike Marduk who had proven to own this power out of himself through his own words. The New Testament according to John begins: "In the beginning was the word . . . the same was in the beginning with God."[142] And in the Old Testament we read: "And God *said* . . ."[143] Just as the Word so the act of seeing is a creative experience in that another aspect of reality emerges. On a physical level for every baby seeing and the uttering of words are primal experiences. The Old Testament says man is created from "the dust of the earth," but God breathes life unto him, and thus in so "becoming" man manifests the *hayah,* and therefore is not, as in the Babylonian myth, imprisoned by a dependent nature.

The same theme is reiterated in the New Testament in the story of Jesus giving sight to a man born blind. Jesus mixed dust and spittle to form clay to place on the eyes of the blind one. Then, cured of his blindness, the man is made alive because he now can "see." It is significant that the question then addressed to Jesus is: "Rabbi, who sinned, this man or his parents, that he was born blind?" Jesus replied: " 'It was not that the man sinned, or his parents, but that the works of God might be made manifest in him. . . . As long as I am in the world, I am the light of the world.' As he said this, he spat on the ground and made clay of the spittle and anointed the man's eyes with the clay."[144]

Though biological being as such may be traced back at least three and a half million years, the three passages quoted above reflect the emergence of mind and human understanding.

Not only do we find the symbol of the shepherd closely connected with the idea of "seeing" in the Biblical context, but it appears in *The Odyssey* of Homer as well as in *The Iliad*. These, of course, are presumed by scholars to be a long verbal tradition of storytelling finally committed to writing.

The mastering of the one-eyed monster depicted on the Chafadsche tablet and of Odysseus in tricking Polyphemus both symbolize developmental stages in the ontogenesis of the psyche. The awesome scene of Odysseus' invading the sheepfold of the one-eyed Cyclops depicts the mindless, worthless shepherd Polyphemus as a cannibal. As such he ate up some of Odysseus' most trusted friends.

The Old Testament speaks of the worthless shepherd whose "arm be wholly withered, his right eye utterly blinded" (Zechariah 11:12). But the New Testament lifts the archetypal motif of the Good Shepherd to the level of personal responsibility as it responds to the question "Am I my brother's keeper?"

You have heard that it was said, "you shall not commit adultery." But I say to you that everyone who looks at a woman lustfully has already committed adultery with her in his heart. If your right *eye causes you to sin, pluck it out* and throw it away; it is better that you lose one of your members than that your whole body be thrown into hell. And if your right hand causes you to sin, cut if off and throw it away; it is better that you lose one of your members than that your whole body go into hell.[145]

In our own time, Martin Buber has written a work entitled *I and Thou,* in which he distinguishes clearly between the treatment of a person as a Thou and as an It. To address another as Thou is to acknowledge the spiritual essence of that person. To treat another person as an It is to behave as though the other were merely a physical being, a thing. True love, therefore, exists in the relationship between one Thou and another Thou. A merely sexual relationship is manifested primarily in sensual communication wherein each person treats the other as an object, an It. Such are the worthless shepherds to each other.

We have seen in the basic, primitive behavior of Polyphemus, who had no sense of human values, a matching brutality on the part of Odysseus. In this instance, the figure of Odysseus is a symbol of man on the voyage to self-discovery. Here he enacts the barbarity of his own inner monster, and as a true trickster, he tells Polyphemus, appropriately, that his name is Nobody. As a nobody, as a non-person, he was unable to face and "see" the beast within his own nature.

In contrast to the "worthless" shepherd, the "institutionalized" shepherd is called "good shepherd" because the latter promises that the individual will be relieved of any need for authentic personal choice and action.

> *He makes me lie down in green pastures.*
> *He leads me beside still waters;*
> *He restores my soul.*

> *He leads me in paths of righteousness*
> *for his name's sake.*[146]

The aim of modern society is to hold men in slavery to their *wants,* and to this end it will imprison and torture dissenters, and sacrifice men in war. The *needs,* on the other hand, which Pope John XXIII acknowledged as basic human *rights,* are neglected.[147] Whole societies are now conditioned to focus on wants rather than on needs, and through the medium of commercial advertising, and through phony religious systems, an ever-increasing spiral of material want is stimulated in the common mind. The masses of modern society are lured by material greed as though by the Sirens of Homer's *Odyssey.*

> Listen with care
> to this, now, and a god will arm your mind.
> Square in your ship's path are Seirênês, crying
> beauty to bewitch men coasting by;
> woe to the innocent who hears that sound!
> He will not see his lady nor his children
> in joy, crowding about him, home from sea;
> the Seirênês will sing his mind away
> on their sweet meadow lolling. There are bones
> of dead men rotting in a pile beside them
> and flayed skins shrivel around the spot.[148]

Odysseus on his voyage of self-discovery passes the island of the Sirens. But instead of being personality enough to withstand the lure of the temptations of the Sirens out of his own inner *maturity* of choice, his *inner weakness* in the form of a female goddess, Circe, advises him. In Greek mythology it is Circe — the witch of the dark — who turns men into swine, i.e., they become lustful and greedy in their animality.

> Scarce had they drunk when she flew after them
> with her long stick and shut them in a pigsty —
> bodies, voices, heads, and bristles, all
> swinish now, though minds were still unchanged.[149]

Paradoxically, however, it is this same goddess, personifying the human weakness so difficult to control, who points the way to further psychic growth. Sex without love transforms any male or for that matter any female human being into "swine." This is an ever-recurring human experience, in which both male and female are prone to elicit the animal characteristics of the other sex. Much of the advertising in a consumer-oriented society is based on the recognition of this psychological fact. These ads do not address human *needs* but call out *wants,* because they contain innuendos to primitive sexuality.

In Jeremiah 2:18-19, we find a similar message which says that weakness can provide guidance for growth:

> *And now what do you gain by going to Egypt,*
> *to drink the waters of the Nile?*
> *Or what do you gain by going to Assyria,*
> *to drink the waters of the Euphrates?*
> *Your wickedness will chasten you*
> *and your apostasy will reprove you.*

The theme is struck again in II Corinthians 12:9:

> My grace is sufficient for you,
> for my power is made perfect *in weakness.*

In the deepest recesses of our undeveloped humanity there reveals itself spiritually, or psychologically, what biological science in the work of Eigen and Schuster has rationally proven in the principle of Hypercycle [supra, p. 61]. In both the inner structure of matter and in the inner structure of mind are the same governing principles at work as manifestations of the *hayah.* The principle of self-correction appears to be active on all levels.

Circe had advised Odysseus as to how not to fall victim to the lures of his own temptations. He reports this counsel to his shipmates:

> ... Seirênês
> weaving a haunting song over the sea
> we are to shun, she said ...
> yet she urged that I
> alone should listen to their song. Therefore
> you are to tie me up, tight as splint,
> erect along the mast, lashed to the mast,
> and if I shout to be untied,
> take more turns of the rope to muffle me.[150]

Nor was this imagery lost on the early Fathers of the Church. Relating this story to the mystery of Christ crucified, the mast becomes the Cross. Hugh Rahner writes: "The companions of Odysseus are types of human weakness, and it was only a single man who sailed past the Sirens' isle with his ears open to hear, for by *divine command* this man had been tied to the mast. Let us listen . . . to Clement as he gives a Christian meaning to the symbolism of the myth:

'Sail past their music and leave it behind thee, for it will bring about thy death. But if thou wilt, thou canst be the victor over the powers of destruction; tied to the wood, thou art made free of perdition. Thy helmsman will be God's Logos and the Holy Pneuma will waft thee into the port of heavens.' "[151]

Another Church father, Ambrose, writes: "And so we see that the cross is like a mast in the ship of the Church. Amidst the pleasant but deadly shipwrecks of this world this ship alone suffers no harm. Whosoever in this ship suffers himself to be bound to the mast of the cross, need have no more fear of the sweetly flattering tempest of unchaste desire. For it was for this reason that Christ, the Lord, hung upon the Cross: that he might save the entire human race from the shipwreck of the world."[152]

If we review these several adventures of Odysseus, what do we see of the ontogenesis of the psyche at this stage of human development?

Odysseus' journeying may be seen perhaps as the psyche's

voyage in search for genuine love. The drama of the Odyssey opens so to speak, with Odysseus' encounter with Polyphemus, a creature devoid of feeling for others or for any human value. Let me repeat:

> Kyklopês have no muster and no meeting,
> no consultations or old tribal ways,
> but each one dwells in his own mountain cave
> dealing out rough justice to wife and child
> indifferent to what the others do.

In the drama Odysseus is sailing past the Sirens who are possibly the representatives of mindless, merely sensual sexuality, without love. Such a superficial attitude makes objects of either male or female human beings and leads to the death of a mindful, authentic personality. "There are the bones of dead men rotting in a pile beside them and flayed skins shrivel around the spot." If man on his mental journey is to progress he needs to grow into a proper relationship with whatever "Circe" as seductress may represent in a given situation. Otherwise "Circe" is ruling from behind, from the deep layers of the unconscious, like a dogma. This dogma ruling as it does — socially sanctified, universally accepted in the tenor of advertising — produces a multi-billion dollar sex industry on the one hand and a denial to apply money for desperate human needs on the other.

The Odyssey was composed about 900 B.C. and shows Odysseus bound to the mast of his ship because he was not able to control himself from within. This is an illustration of a lack of psychological maturity and a state of bondage in the psyche.

Very early in the New Testament account of the life of Jesus, he is confronted by temptation. After being baptized by John (though he was presumed to be without sin), "Jesus was led up by the Spirit into the wilderness to be tempted by the Devil."[153] As in the Exodus account, the Israelites wandered for *forty* years in the wilderness, so Jesus fasted for *forty* days. The Church utilizes this symbolism in the Christian calendar by setting aside *forty* days of Lent in preparation for Easter, and specifies *forty* days from Easter to the Ascension. In a similar fashion, the Israelites in the wilderness were assailed by fiery serpents and were instructed to face the metal serpent which Moses fashioned and held up before them in order not to die: "And the Lord said unto Moses, Make thee a fiery serpent, and set it upon a pole: and it shall come to pass, that every one that is bitten, when he looketh upon it, shall live."[154]

So also was Jesus tempted by Satan in the wilderness, and assailed by wild beasts in Mark 1:12-13. Here Jesus faced the devil, his Sirens, and overcame these temptations out of his own inner strength, thus becoming fully alive. Here in the New Testament is symbolized the beginning of the journey of the soul in which Jesus demonstrates the freedom of his own being. Yet in the end he is nailed to a cross, ostensibly to free the human race from the darkness at the depths of the human psyche.

The same theme is developed in the story of Jacob and Esau, though without the ship's mast or a *deus ex machina* intervening in Jacob's challenge to become fully himself. Both Jacob and Odysseus resorted to trickery in the journey to freedom: Jacob when he presented himself as his hairy elder brother so that his *blind* father would give him the blessing intended for the older son; Odysseus as he blinded the drunken Polyphemus and escaped under the belly of the Ram. Jacob, however, did not escape the essential encounter with himself. In the darkness by the ford of Jabbok he met his own Polyphemus, and wrestling with this "man" until daybreak, *earned* his new name: Israel. He could face the encounter within himself only after a long time of preparation through serving the "hard way" and not through vicarious sacrifices, trying to enlist the help of the *deus ex machina*.

While the Odyssey described the story of the search for love by the psyche, the Old Testament epic, the Jacob-Esau story, began with love. "And Jacob loved Rachel; and said: I will serve thee seven years for Rachel thy younger daughter."[155]

The "way" of Jacob was intensely personal, a true meeting with himself through manifold demonstrations of his own character as trickster and cheater and his capability of genuine love. Through the integration of a variety of experiences he reached a state of wholeness as an expression of the *hayah*.

The poetic insight which produced the legendary drama of Jacob and Esau with Jacob as the *dramatis persona,* as a prototype of the ontogenesis of the psyche, is indeed remarkable. Here was a small cluster of nomadic tribesmen, developing out of their own experience and the creative imagination of their storytellers, an intricate tale describing the spiritual growth of mankind against the backdrop of everyday life.

It would be unrealistic for us to assume that the Greek poets or the Biblical compilers intended to reveal the same truths which we find by means of a structural hermeneutic. The ancients have superbly symbolized the dark side of the psyche in these epic dramas, showing us the inherently brutal animality of which man is capable. It is as if the poets are perhaps personifying as mediums the attempts of the psyche itself, in its own surge for growth, to impress itself upon the minds of human beings for the sake of their own choosing.

The actors in these stories are the *dramatis personae* which we invest with meaning commensurate with the stage of growth and development of the psyche at a given time. Quite logically, therefore, the Old Testament poets had Jacob utter so profoundly: "For truly to see your face is like seeing the face of God."[156]

Seen in a broader context, we can detect that Jacob in wrestling with himself may possibly reflect the need to reconcile the conflict between basic loyalties. In our contemporary situation, such conflicts are a stormy sea upon which modern humanity is tossed. A few examples come immediately to mind: national loyalties versus the need for world community; natural science versus religious belief; self-interest versus community concern; profit motive versus social purpose of industry; or nearer home, the conflicts of loyalties in the relationships between the sexes, e.g., one man between two women or vice versa.

As a basic poetic demonstration of the depth of these conflicts Homer superbly painted their dynamic nature in most powerful pictures:

> And all this time
> in travail, sobbing, gaining on the current,
> we rowed into the strait — Skylla to port
> and on our starboard beam Charybdis, dire
> gorge of the salt sea tide. By heaven! when she
> vomited, all the sea was like a cauldron
> seething over intense fire, when the mixture
> suddenly heaves and rises . . .
> Then Skylla made her strike,
> whisking six of my best men from the ship.
> I happened to glance aft at ship and oarsmen
> and caught sight of their arms and legs, dangling
> high overhead. Voices came down to me
> in anguish, calling my name for the last time.[157]

The gloom and despair which permeates society today to a high degree results from the anxieties produced as man is faced with equally untenable alternatives. Contemporary man fears to be crushed either by the Scylla of the one position or the Charybdis of another. Modern man is up against a cultural development where he himself has become the center again. And what is this fundamental change? The absolute validity of the law of nature has become relative. This fact then shifts the emphasis from an "objective" world view to a more human one. By looking at "facts" man felt secure and rational, even in his religious outlook, but his "indubitable" facts have become a mystery again, because he himself is involved. The turmoil societies all over the world are undergoing is the outward manifestation of the inner development of man.

In the encounter of the soul's battle with herself, Homer in his *Iliad* uses the symbol which plays such an important part in Jacob's fight with Esau.

> Diomedes
> bent for a stone and picked it up — a boulder
> no two men now alive could lift, though he
> could heft it easily. This mass he hurled
> and struck Aineías *on the hip*, just where
> the hipbone shifts in what they call the bone-cup . . .
> Aineías would have perished there
> but for the quickness of the daughter of Zeus,
> his mother, Aphrodítê . . . Then from the battle
> heavenward she lifted her dear son.[158]

Since paleolithic times, in animal sacrifices meant to ensure the continuance of the species and to assuage the spirit of the victim, the thigh played a very important role. The thighbones have been collected and deposited in holy places to form the center of Greek sacrificial practice: the burning thighbones on the altar.[159]

The thigh is, after all, not only the "hinge" on which movement depends, it is also in the Old Testament a term synonymous with the sexual organ [supra, p. 129].

In Jacob's fight with "a man" on the brook of Jabbok, he was also injured *on the hip;* unaided and not lifted "heavenward" he stayed on earth, but limped away "because of his thigh."[160] "When the man saw that he did not prevail against Jacob, he touched the hollow of his *thigh;* and Jacob's thigh was put out of joint as he wrestled with him."[161]

Homer used the symbol of the thigh in still another, yet very important context. Odysseus returning home is recognized by his old nurse:

> This was the scar the old nurse recognized;
> she traced it under her spread hands . . .[162]

Hunting a boar, Odysseus was wounded at the beginning of his voyage:

> [The boar] hooked aslant with one white tusk
> and ripped out flesh above the knee . . .[163]

It is as if Homer had handed the torch of description of human development 500 years later to Aeschylus, who in his epos *Agamemnon* addresses squarely the vexed problem of conflict of loyalties.

> *The elder lord spoke aloud before them:*
> *"My fate is angry if I disobey these,*
> *but angry if I slaughter*
> *this child, the beauty of my house,*
> *with maiden blood shed staining*
> *these father's hands beside the altar.*
> *What of these things goes now without disaster?*
> *How shall I fail my ships*
> *and lose my faith of battle?*
> *For them to urge such sacrifice of innocent blood*
> *angrily, for their wrath is great — it is right.*
> *May all be well yet."*
> *But when necessity's yoke was put upon him*
> *he changed, and from the heart the breath came*
>   *bitter*
> *and sacrilegious, utterly infidel*
> *to warp a will now to be stopped at nothing.*
> *The sickening in men's minds, tough,*
> *reckless in fresh cruelty brings daring. He endured*
>   *then*
>   *to sacrifice his daughter*
> *to stay the strength of war waged for a woman,*
> *first offering for the ship's sake.*[164]

Aeschylus describes not only Agamemnon's sacrifice of his own daughter, Iphigenia, but also the ancient cannibalism symbolized by Polyphemus:

> Behold there the witness to my faith.
> The small children wail for their own death
> and the flesh roasted that their father fed upon.[165]

Further along,

> Thyestes' feast upon the flesh of his own children I
> understand in terror of the thought, and fear is on
> me hearing truth and *no tale fabricated*.[166]

Commenting on the ancient works, St. Ambrose writes: "All this is but the imagining of poets, having no substance in truth and being nothing but empty fable and smoke."[167]

Are today's societies really basically so different from the pagan forerunners? Here as there human considerations are sacrificed the world over, surrendered, yielded to assumed necessities, to the yoke of political, economic or religious dogmas. The Minoan culture (3,000 - 1,000 B.C.) from which both Homer and Aeschylus apparently derived their inspiration for description and critique, in fact performed, as we do in our ways, human sacrifices.

> Blood sacrifice, common at Minoan festivals and funerals, normally centered on animals. . . . Evidence of a similar rite turned up during the author's excavation of a Cretan temple, but this time the victim was human. The skeleton of an 18-year old male lay in fetal position on a low platform. The right heel is so close to the thigh that Greek anthropologists believe the youth was bound before being killed with the knife. The rare bronze blade bears the finely incised outline of a *boarlike* beast.[168]

The symbolism of the Sirens and the poetic description of the essential meaning of the Scylla and Charybdis are just as real from the psychological point of view as the actual human sacrifices are historically real. Today there is a growing awareness on the part of many people the world over that they are being tempted and sacrificed by secular and religious powers beyond their control, and it is precisely in this *awareness* that the corrective antidote is manifest, as the *hayah* makes itself felt. Such inner awareness provides an authentic basis for faith. Faith in the power of self-correction and real meaning in life.

But only the individual, by responsibly relating himself to the conditions of his environment, can at least withdraw his own misunderstandings from the general pool of social confusion and thus creatively contribute to the growth of a responsible society. The individual is thus able to adhere to the injunction, "You shall not follow a multitude to do evil,"[169] and to realize that Romans 13, which states that the authority is in any case right because it was put in by God, is more than questionable. Are we fulfilling the task of responsibility untruthfully by seeking the real authority expressing itself as *hayah?* Both the secular and religious authorities fall prey to their own Sirens. Faced with conflicts of loyalty, certain religious authorities assume that by silence they can escape the encounter with their Scylla and Charybdis. We have experienced the disastrous results of this silence in the past. Present global tensions and brutalities are also the clearly defined symptoms of such an abdication of a truthful response. "For whoever would save his life will lose it; and whoever loses his life for my sake, he will save it. For what does it profit a man if he gains the whole world and loses or forfeits himself?"[170]

The Self

IN OUR TIME it is difficult to know this "Self" which is in danger of being lost. In the not-too-distant past, it was possible to identify the "Self" through membership in particular guilds, or by means of a strong identification with a particular group. But now, partly as a result of higher education, and partly through an overweening rationalism, we have come to believe that we can discard belief in Self. It is now replaced with skepticism which doubts even itself. The "Self" of the past was defined by artificial borders, and thus could not be universal or "catholic."

The ontogenesis of the psyche seems to give birth to a new understanding and experience of "Self." If the experience of this new Self is not straight-jacketed by some form of "totalitarianism," it is felt in a variety of different ways, depending upon the unique nature of each individual's being. This Self may be found in dream symbols or in artistic manifestations as a circle, an inner eye, a mandala, a fountain or stream, or it may appear personified in a whole range of figures varying from a hermaphrodite to the Christ. But in all these varied symbols and images, two essential qualities may be discerned: the quality of wholeness in which all opposing forces are reconciled, and at the same time, an intrinsic openness — rounded, unified, yet open precisely as the universe seems to be. That which is flat, dimensional, and delimited by space and time gives way to a rounded and harmoniously revolving whole. Such a Self is not an idealized abstraction, but is experienced in actuality, seeing the interrelatedness of events and of life as a profound *process*. No longer hindered by artificial boundaries, nor imprisoned by rationalistically defined dogmas, the way is open to faith. Because this is a rich experience, it is now superfluous to define it any longer in terms of some rationalistic exclusivism.

In his *Phaedrus* Plato provides a most trenchant delineation of this vexing problem:

> All soul is immortal, for that which is ever in motion is immortal. But that which while imparting motion is itself moved by something else can cease to be in motion, and therefore can cease to live; it is only that which moves itself that never intermits its motion, inasmuch as it cannot abandon its own nature; moreover this self-mover is the source and first principle of motion of all other things that are moved. Now a first principle cannot come into being, for while anything that comes to be must come from a first principle, the latter itself cannot come to be from anything whatsoever; if it did, it would cease any longer to be a first principle. Furthermore, since it does not come into being, it must be imperishable, for assuredly if a first principle were to be destroyed, nothing could come to be out of it, nor could anything bring the principle itself back into existence, seeing that a first principle is needed for anything to come into being.
>
> The self-mover, then, is the first principle of motion, and as it is as impossible that it should be destroyed as that it should come into being; were it otherwise, the whole universe, the whole of that which comes to be, would collapse into immobility, and never find another source of motion to bring it back into being.
>
> And now that we have seen that that which is moved by itself is immortal, we shall feel no scruple in affirming that precisely that is the essence and definition of soul, to wit, self-motion. Any body that has an external source of motion is soulless, but a

body deriving its motion from a source within itself is animated or *besouled,* which implies that the nature of soul is what has been said.[171]

Thus, Plato likens the nature of the soul as does the Old Testament concept of the soul: the Merkabah, "a body deriving its motion from the nature of the soul." The *hayah,* the integration of complementary forces, is compared to "the union of powers in a team of winged steeds and their winged charioteer." "Now all the gods' steeds and all their charioteers are good, and of good stock, but with other beings it is not wholly so. With us men, in the first place, it is a pair of steeds that the charioteer controls; moreover one of them is noble and good, and of good stock, while the other has the opposite character, and his stock is opposite. Hence the task of our charioteer is difficult and troublesome."[172]

In Plato's *Phaedrus* it is the task of the "charioteer" to handle the duality of life. This development in the ontogenesis of the psyche is also mirrored in the Camunian Rock Art, which consists of drawings dating between 8,000 to 16 B.C., i.e., the Roman conquest. They were discovered on rocks in the Camonica Valley in Italy near Switzerland about 1930. "During the whole length of period III, (3,000 - 1,000 B.C.) the subjects most commonly represented are weapons and symbols. Human figures are somewhat rare and the animals appear only slightly more frequently than in period II (4,000 - 3,000 B.C.). A change occurs in this quantitative relation of the figures during period III-D (1,400 - 1,200 B.C.): one notes a proportional diminution of weapons and symbols and a sharp increase in human representations." And from this period, significantly enough, a drawing depicts "A scene of praying figures in front of a two-wheeled chariot, probably being pulled by horses."[173]

Both in Plato's imagery and in the Camunian Rock Art, we find the symbol of the two-wheeled chariot. The Indo-European two-wheeled chariot in this context is the symbol for the archetype of self-concept. In Ezekiel's vision of the

Figure 34.   Two-wheeled chariot, ca. 2000 B.C. (Copyright 1983 by
        Centro Camuno di Studi Preistorici, 25044 Capo di Ponte,
        Italy).

Merkabah, however, it is not the chariot, but the four-
wheeled cart which is given. The four-wheeled cart is an
earlier invention which appears to have come from the Near
Eastern Transcaucasus area about 3,500 B.C. It is assumed
that the two-wheeled chariot was introduced by Indo-
Europeans into the Near East about 2,500 B.C.[174]

A four-wheeled cart appears at a later date, about 850
B.C., in the Camunian Rock Art. It would appear that there
is no religious significance in this instance. The Ezekiel
vision, on the other hand, archetypically using the four-
wheeled cart and transfiguring it, lifts it out of the secular
into a four-dimensional spiritual sphere.

As a supreme example of archetypal art the passage in
Ezekiel, as we shall see later, depicts what also modern
physics, congruent with the level of awareness of the present

time, tries to express: the interrelatedness of events in a four-dimensional field of experience [supra, p. 274]. From the point of view of the ontogenesis of the psyche, it is another telling example of the eternal quest for the Self.

Prof. Bohm expresses his scientific "mythopoetic" insight succinctly, writing:

Relativity theory calls for this way of looking at the atomic particles, which constitute all matter, including of course human beings, with their brains, nervous systems, and the observing instruments that they have built and that they use in their laboratories. So, approaching the question in different ways, relativity and quantum theory agree, in that they both imply the need to look at the world as an *undivided whole,* in which all parts of the universe including the observer and his instruments, merge and unite into a totality. In this totality, the atomic form of insight is a simplification and abstraction, valid only in some limited context.

The new form of insight can perhaps best be called *Undivided Wholeness in Flowing Movement.* This view implies that flow is, in some sense, prior to that of the "things" that can be seen to form and dissolve in this flow. One can perhaps illustrate what is meant here by considering the "stream of consciousness." This flux of awareness is not precisely definable, and yet it is evidently prior to the definable forms of thoughts and ideas which can be seen to form and dissolve like ripples, waves and vortices in a flowing stream. As happens with such patterns of movement in a stream, some thoughts recur and persist in a more or less stable way, while others are evanescent.[175]

In Ezekiel the poet speaks thus:

And from the midst of it [the fire] came the likeness

of four living creatures. And this was their appearance: they had the form of men, but each had four faces and each of them had four wings. . . (1:5)

Now, as I looked at the living creatures, I saw a wheel upon the earth beside the living creatures, one for each of the four of them. (1:15)

And when the living creatures went, *they went in any of their four directions* without turning as they went. The four wheels had rims and they had spokes; and their rims were full of eyes round about. And when the living creatures went, the wheels went beside them; and when the living creatures rose from the earth, the wheels rose. Wherever the spirit would go, they went, and the wheels rose along with them; for the spirit of the living creatures was in the wheels. (1:19)

The Camunian Rock Art, because it presents to us a continuum of human development, is of particular value in our considerations. Marija Gimbutas writes:

The changes in style and subject matter detected in rock art are consequential phenomena and happened together with other changes of a material and ideological nature that have modified and influenced the human group. . . . the evolution of art does not in fact follow a strictly linear development. Each phase of development was more a reflection of contemporary influences than a progression built upon the artistic style of past generations.[176]

However, both the conclusions drawn from the analysis of the Camunian rock carvings and the numerous pertinent ethnological parallels, seem to indicate that "art for art" never existed in prehistoric Valcamonica, that the carvings were aimed at magico-religious functions and that their execution was considered as part of the activities vital to the group in ensuring successful economic and social outcomes, and good relationships with the occult forces of the "beyond."[177]

In the transition phase between periods III and IV the human figure again became the main subject after having occupied a figurative role of secondary importance for two thousand years. This factor also indicates profound changes in the social structure and in the mentality of the ancient Camunians.[178]

Throughout the records of human history, no matter where we look, whether it be at the primitive rock art of the Val Camonica, in the poetic works of Homer and Aeschylus, in the philosophical writings of Plato, in the Hebraic-Christian Bible, or other sacred writings, in the painting, sculpture and art of every culture — in all these manifestations reveals itself as supreme the *hayah,* life's process of becoming — becoming. Gradually a more persistent theme comes to the fore: the human being's active participation in the process of becoming—the ontogenesis of the psyche. Reliance on "the good shepherd" is transformed into self-responsibility with all of the attendant complexities this requires. As mentioned before, the Old Testament reminds: "And now what do you gain by going to Egypt, to drink the waters of the Nile? Or what do you gain by going to Assyria, to drink the waters of the Euphrates? Your wickedness will chasten you, and your apostasy will reprove you."[179] The realization of imperfection is the way towards becoming. So the New Testament in John 14:6 says: "I am the way, the truth and the life; no man cometh unto the Father, but by me."

The essence of "The Way" is expressed in Ephesians 1:10, "that in the dispensation of the fulness of times he might gather together in one all things in Christ, both which are in heaven, and which are on earth; even in him." The holy, that is wholeness, is essentially related to being, and is not primarily determined by moral values. "The Way" transcends the

discriminating intellect. Dogmatic formulas which delineate
right and wrong limit the individual person to the realm of
the judging ego, and inhibit the experience of what Rudolph
Otto has called the *numinosum*. As the mind of modern man
reaches back 15 or 20 billion years to the earliest beginnings,
it comes to the level of greatest depth where there is only
silence and timeless awe. Here, the mind reaches the
paradox of creative nothingness.

According to an ancient Chinese poet:

> *If you wish to know the origin of Yüanshih, [an
> incarnation of Yin and Yang], you must pass beyond
> the confines of Heaven and Earth, because he lives
> beyond the limits of the worlds. You must ascend
> and ascend until you reach the sphere of nothingness
> and of being, in the plains of the luminous shadows.*[180]

In the Jacob-Esau motif of the Old Testament and in the
Christ figure of the New, the opposites coincide and are
integrated, and "The Way" is no longer confined to mystical
unreality, but becomes existentially real as "Divine Ambiguity." At the beginning of life, the history of becoming
also began, and it is therefore a history of salvation, salvation
from every form of containment which would restrain it.
Moses and the Christ are both personifications of this becoming, and the Exodus and the Last Supper are the historical
symbols of this process. "The Way" is the dramatic representation of the ontogenesis of the psyche which leads to the
experience of the *numinosum*. For those who experience
it, the numinous is felt to be both Divine and awe-ful, awe-
inspiring. Because the origin of this experience is ambiguous, the psychological response is to acknowledge that *"It is
a fearful thing to fall into the hands of the living God."*[181]

The anxieties which are generated by the drive toward
becoming cause the individual to become ever more
entrenched in the familiar, thereby aggravating the conflicts
inherent in the process itself. In saying "I have not come to

bring peace, but a sword," Jesus but reflected one of the awesome dimensions in the painful process of growth.[182] In order to give rational justification to his resistance to change, man makes gods of his foibles, and in turn is devoured by them. Hence, according to an ancient Gnostic text: "God is a man-eater." But even this shocking Gnostic text is a demonstration of the ontogenetic process of becoming, for the full text reads: *"God is a man-eater. For this reason men are [sacrificed] to him. Before men were sacrificed animals were being sacrificed, since those to whom they were sacrificed were not gods."*[183]

Totalitarianism

IDENTIFICATION or obsession with religious or political ideologies, with commercial enterprises or the cult of success in any mundane endeavor, or with the projections upon members of the opposite sex, all prohibit differentiation between essential needs and superficial wants. And because of this tragic fact, entrenchment into inadequate, pseudo-realities gets stronger and deeper, and man is unable to live by his own gyroscope-conscience, tossed between the Scylla and Charybdis of his own unredeemed being.

When the New Testament presents the statement "that he might gather all things together in Christ" as "The Way" to wholeness, it is not a metaphysical speculation, but has a logic of its own. A structural hermeneutic is based on *analogical* thought, and provides a system of concepts imbedded in images, depicting a synchronistic totality. "Symbols are not an artefact of the human mind but are indeed something anterior to any agency of the latter. They are, therefore, in their basic forms operative in every religion and their use must be reckoned as part of the archetypal pattern of man's search after God."[184]

The quest for God in these rationalistic times, however, is

particularly complicated by the bifurcation of soul and body. But the experience of unity and wholeness, which so many long for in our time, is now a distinct possibility due to the ontogenesis of the psyche on the one hand, and the corresponding development in the natural sciences on the other. Despite the fact that the modern psyche has been projected onto gross materialism and into the political ideologies of the totalitarian state, these have begun to lose their power through the growing awareness that they are false gods — that they are "man-eaters."

The innate shallowness of sheer materialism is undergoing an essential change both in the sciences and in economics. The totalitarian state also demonstrates its weakness when only by torture and imprisonment is it able to deal with internal dissension for its survival. Technology, which has become a tool for the depersonalization of the individual, has also become a self-defeating agent, as its awesome potential destructive power confronts man with a momentous choice, and thereby establishes him as a moral agent in his own right. To achieve the full freedom of personal being, modern man must now respond to the momentous decision which Moses put before Israel: "I call heaven and earth to witness against you this day, that I have set before you life and death, blessing and curse; therefore choose life, that you and your descendants may live."[185]

It is not an abstract god in the heavens who makes the choice for him; it is man himself who is, in our situation of "passing over" into a new era, his own redeemer. Or, failing in that existential task, he will become his own destroyer. Today, the nuclear bomb is the symbol of both the destructive and the redeeming power because it is not only man-made, but at the same time it puts into human hands the decision to "live or die" — "to be or not to be."

For many it is a fearful process. For some, perhaps, too difficult to bear — to be confronted not only with the complexities of the "real" world, but still more with the *only* real world, which is him or herself. It is all the more difficult to be confronted with the inescapable reality of the Self when the institutions which have provided moral guidance in the past are undergoing a gradual dissolution as fewer and fewer people find in them any real help for their dilemma. Yet, it is still the Bible in which the figures of Moses and Christ speak to the situation of our time.

The abiding problem for humanity is expressed at the beginning of the Bible in Cain's question: "Am I my brother's keeper?" It is the problem of to be or not to be a good shepherd. This very process has an *Urbild* expressing the *hayah,* not in metaphysical terms, but addressing the individual most directly. Luke 13:24 provides specific and convincing guidance: "Strive to enter by the narrow door; for many, I tell you, will seek to enter and will not be able." Each person is a "narrow door" in his uniqueness and in the constellation of problems which are his alone. To face and deal with this personal constellation is to meet the inner Christ — not Christ as the symbol of perfection, but Christ as "the way" of becoming.

> Truly, truly, I say to you, he who dares not enter the sheepfold by the door but climbs by another way, that man is a thief and a robber; but he who enters by the door is the shepherd of the sheep. To him the gatekeeper opens; the sheep hear his voice, and he calls his own sheep by name and leads them out.[186]
>
> I am the door; if any one enters by me, he will be saved and find pasture . . . I am the good shepherd.[187]

Seen not literally, these statements become symbols of the most profound nature. The individual who tries to climb into the intricacies of being either by intellectual, that is, dogmatic, antics is not authentic but an impersonating imposter. He usurps pseudo-knowledge and presents it by way of imitation as his own. He is a thief and a robber. To enter by the door — the "narrow gate" — is to deal with the realities of one's own being, and thus the "sheep" therein are truly "known" by him. As an integrated person, consciousness about himself therefore "enlightens" other aspects of his being, and the continuance of psychic growth is possible. In this context Matthew 7:13 is an analogical expression which amplifies this central theme:

> *Enter by the narrow gate; for the gate is wide and the way is easy, that leads to destruction, and those who enter by it are many. For the gate is narrow and the way is hard, that leads to life, and those who find it are few.*

Those who enter by the "wide gate" are, of course, the masses who uncritically follow the path of least resistance. The figure of the gate is directly related to that of the "good shepherd" and to the "sheepfold." The sheepfold is a telling symbol which immediately speaks to everyone's mind of fellowship and closeness and of peaceful sheep cuddled near to each other in connectedness. The symbol has therefore a strong power of appeal to undiscerning masses. And even in these times when the pastoral imagery is no longer directly familiar to the majority, the passive nature of the flock of sheep is retained in the common mind. While such imagery accurately reflects the herd instinct, few persons stop to reflect that such an approach to religious organization is precisely the opposite of the real need of both the individual and society.

The continued use of this symbol of the sheepfold serves the purpose of the electronic religion industry which wishes to maintain control through the promulgation of dogma and blind obedience to their leaders. Given the susceptibility to mass psychology which is common in our time, meaningless "religious" moral rhetoric makes it a simple matter to sway people for a blind following.

In the long term, the fostering of such images and attitudes results in a Belsen or an Auschwitz, or in our own time, in the passive acceptance of preparation for a world-wide nuclear holocaust. Stalin's Russia, Hitler's Germany, and repressive, brutal regimes the world over are symptoms of this approach to social order — and the narcissistic terror promoted by all autocratic states is the end result. Such is not the meaning of the "good shepherd" whose task it is to lead persons into the process of their own becoming.

Institutions are the representatives of the masses from whom they acquire their power. Broadly speaking, this power is exercised through the use of dogma, giving the individual an artificial, rationally conceived construction of identity. Yet the true identity of each can be authentically discovered only by entering through the "narrow gate"; that is, through the unique entrance of each one to personal being. Not only so, but genuine relationship exists only when truly authentic personalities meet; not in the coming together of those who simply conform to artificially constructed models.

Communism reveals in its very name the deep human need for communion; and yet in actuality, the communist philosophy imposes the precise opposite upon its party members and upon the population of any state under its control. It succeeds by denying the possibility of any graceful pluralism in values and in understanding. Even as this is true of secular states, it is also true of religious institutions. Recognition of the conflict between institutions and personal growth is surely one of the reasons that so many have turned away in despair from the support of those institutions which have traditionally provided guidance and leadership for the welfare of the whole.

The neglect based on monotheism in Christianity to realize the pluralistic "natural" state of the psyche has led to a repression of what found its expression in the Greek Pantheon. This problem found its manifestation in Ephesians 1:10: ". . . to unite all things in him, things in heaven and things on earth." The perversion of this Judaeo-Christian concept of monotheism found in our time is its political expression in the monolithic structure of Communism and

Fascism. What monstrous bestialities were committed in that name of the "One God"!

A further powerful cause for disillusionment with both Church and State has been the utter failure of "spiritual" leaders to speak out before state control became excessive. This has resulted in an abstention from voting in secular affairs and a dropping away from religious institutions in many democratic societies. The problem was particularly evident in the cooperation of the Roman Catholic Church with the Nazi state in Germany when a Thanksgiving *Te Deum* was offered upon the occasion of the signing of a concordat between the two in 1933. Such a performance made a farce of interpreting the saying of Jesus: "Render unto Caesar the things that are Caesar's, and unto God the things that are God's." In this instance, the guardians of the "spiritual life" transferred their sacred responsibility to the state, which shortly thereafter subverted this spiritual trust for purposes of its own. In the Church's surrender of moral authority to the state, the activities of the state were thereby given sanctification, so that even the Evangelicals accepted "the education of the young through the national socialistic state and the Hitler Youth as the very representatives of the idea of the totalitarian state. . . . Whoever is not a member of the Hitler Youth . . . cannot be a member of the evangelical youth work" (translation mine).[188] From education to justice, from art to the manufacturing of pure Aryans in special mating institutions to which specifically selected men and women went for this purpose, Hitler and the state were the sole arbiters.

A photo taken at the time of the *Te Deum* of Thanksgiving shows the Catholic Youth like sheep with their Nazi counterparts, the Hitler Youth, with Church banners and Swastika Flags mingled together, while their elders filled to overflowing the pews of the Hedwigs Cathedral in Berlin. A short time later, under the direction of Von Schirach, the Hitler Youth and the religious youth organizations of Germany were united, and these young people were assigned the

Figure 35. *Te deum* celebrated in the Hedwigs Kirsche, Berlin (from *Die Zeit*, 11/2/81).

task of informing the authorities of any suspicious behavior on the part of their parents. Thus, the youth population of Germany was identified with the state and with Hitler, whom Heidegger described as the "future" and the "law" of Germany.

A photo from *The New York Times* in June of 1981 reflects a similar and dangerous trend in the United States, as several thousand youth, according to the accompanying story, representing a number of "religious" educational institutions, paraded in New York City with placards bearing such slogans as "Christian Youth Are Patriotic." The regimentation and paramilitary stance of such organized efforts reveal the fact that the temptation to identify religious concerns with the secular power is always close to the surface of the collective mind.

Figure 36.   John Sotomayor/NYT Pictures.

The German experience under Hitler has left the world a legacy of understanding how such measures as those cited above result in a population fashioned by state-imposed structures and values. Conditioned to measure the meaning of existence according to the state dogmas of race and opportunism, a numbness of feeling resulted. The masses in general could not realize any sense of guilt because their own conscience was put out of action. With the personal conscience stilled, complete dependence upon the Leviathan-state was established, and a fear of Polyphemus became the overriding consideration for daily existence. Thus paradoxically, the criminal and perverter who personified this demonic state of affairs, Hitler, was adored as the savior. In a vicious circle, indoctrination through education produced artificial values and artificial personalities; and these in turn further tightened the indoctrination process, effectively blocking the potential in each person to enter the "door"; and man was prevented from knowing himself to be himself.

As Rembrandt in his famous etching "The Magic Mirror" was enlightened as to his own inner nature through himself, so in the apocryphal Acts of John man, by entering through the narrow gate, learns himself through *Him-Self*.

> *I am a lamp to you.*
> . . .
> *I am a mirror to you*
> *who know me. Amen.*
> *I am a door to you*
> *Who knock on me. Amen.*
> *I am a way to you*
> *[the] traveler. [Amen.]*[189]

The vitality of the structure of the Biblical myth is not revealed in the relative isolation of academic analysis; it is a part of the journey into personal awareness of what it means to the human. This truth is impressively confirmed poetically in The Acts of John in the idea that man meets Him when he meets himself. Or in the words of Pope John XXIII:

> If we could find a way of getting mankind to sit down and read the Bible as a newly published book, *a narrative of man searching for himself*, it would become very popular in places where people have forgotten it.[189]

As man searches for meaning, it is often the case that formal beliefs reveal themselves as idols. The decline of such idols in our time is counteracted by the electronic religion industry which attempts to force the erection of new idols. Through a rational, exclusive point of view, in terms of structural analysis, everything is "justified." But then life necessarily loses contact with its divine source because it is seen in terms of an alleged historicity.

CHAPTER 7

Integration

The Book of Daniel

TRYING to interpret the Book of Daniel, some critics
fastened their attention onto the historical allusions,
which are, however, as stated, not correct. Within the
context of the Bible as a true record of the ontogenesis of the
psyche, historical "facts" are not of primal importance any-
how. The import and significance of *Daniel* is to be found,
for example, in the presentation of the archetypal "four."
Daniel can also be seen as a striking example of the demoli-
tion of idols; and the figure of Daniel, the *dramatis persona*,
illustrates such a dramatic development.

In his monumental *Introduction to the Old Testament*,
R. H. Pfeiffer says that "the historicity of the Book of Daniel
is an article of faith, not an objective scientific truth,"[1] and
again: ". . . was Daniel a historical character . . . [or] a
legendary character like Job, or Jonah in the belly of the
fish?" Further on: "In dating an apocalypse such as Daniel,
the period in which the seer is said to have received the
revelations, is entirely irrelevant."[2]

Despite strenuous efforts, scholars have generally concluded that Daniel was "grievously in error [and yet] the
book serves us most usefully, for it is of the greatest importance to the church that the whole wearisome business of

'Biblical arithmetic' and eschatological calculation should
have been tried so sincerely and found to be a false path."[3]

The name Daniel means "God (or El) has judged," or "My
judge is God."[4] In Ezekiel 14:14 the name Daniel appears in
conjunction with two other "saved" figures, Noah and Job.
These three are not historical persons but psychic representations on various levels of development, depicting the ontogenesis of the psyche. The legend of Daniel does not describe
historical events, but is nonetheless a most meaningful and
artistic demonstration of man's essential being, illustrative
of all the contradictions and turmoil to which the human
psyche is subject. At the same time it describes the human
encounter with the penetrating divine force of the *hayah,*
simultaneously immanent and transcendent. When this
power penetrates life, the human response is to experience it
as "divine ambiguity" and dread-ful, because it is rationally
incomprehensible; it speaks, by using the Word and thus
creating the world, and yet it is silent in the moments of
greatest human need.

In the Greek version of the Sermon on the Mount, this
unnamed power — this unknown God — is designated by
the word *teleios,* which means "full grown, mature, having
reached the appointed end *(telos)* of its development."[5] In
other words a fully integrated state, a state of wholeness.

> Be ye therefore perfect, even as your
> Father which is in heaven is perfect.[6]

Albright and Mann in their commentary to this all important passage say: " 'Be true as your heavenly father is true'.
The Greek word *teleios* in this context does not refer to
moral perfection, but 'truth, sincerity.' "

The whole tenor of the Sermon on the Mount was an
exhortation for the disciples. It was "directed to the inner
circle of the disciples and not to the whole people," as *the
way* toward perfection, not by submitting to evil, but by
learning of its nature. Therefore the verb *teleioō* does not
describe a completed state, but rather a process of becom-

ing, a manifestation of the *hayah*. It is an expression of a striving toward an ideal, which cannot be dogmatically fixed.

I John says:

> If we love one another, God dwelleth in us, and his love is *perfected* in us.[7]

And again in John it is written:

> In this is love *perfected* with us, that we may have confidence for the day of judgment because *as he is so are we* in this world. (Italics mine)[8]

The Book of Daniel is characterized by strife and the absence of love. In this, Daniel shows us the true picture of the brutal and loveless aspect of man in the process of becoming. An older Biblical theme, the Burning Bush, becomes in Daniel the fiery furnace into which Daniel and his friends are thrown: "... and behold, the bush burned with fire, and the bush was not consumed."[9]

According to Daniel 3:1, "King Nebuchadnezzar made an image of gold, whose height was sixty cubits and its breadth six cubits." And further on:

> ... if you do not worship [the image which I have made] you shall immediately be cast into a burning fiery furnace; and who is the god that will deliver you out of my hands? .... Then King Nebuchadnezzar was astonished and rose up in haste. He said to his counselors, "Did we not cast three men bound into the fire?" They answered the King, "True, O king." He answered, "But I see four men loose, walking in the midst of the fire, and they are not hurt; and the appearance of the fourth is like *a son of the gods*." (Italics mine)[10]

The archetypal motif of the missing fourth dimension is also stressed by Plato who opens his *Timaeus* by saying: "One, two, three, but where, my dear Timaeus, is the fourth . . . ?"[11] Are we not finding here in the question of the quaternity, a common background of both Hebrew and Greek civilizations? Are we not finding the poet's vision about Daniel and his friends in the furnace a beautiful image embodying justice itself as the principle of order and harmony, an archetypal pattern for wholeness?

Another powerful symbol demonstrating the process of becoming human is that of Daniel in the lion's den. By coming to terms with the potential bestiality within himself, man is therefore no longer in danger of being destroyed by these forces. Though such a symbol of integration may seem only to apply to the individual situation, it is nevertheless a symbolic action representing the universal process. Many generations have felt the power and dramatic impact of the legend of Daniel as imaginations have been kindled by this artistic expression of an essential truth of the way toward becoming. In Christian mythology, the same truth is to be found in the figure of St. Francis of Assisi and his relationship with the animals.

The basic truth revealed in the Book of Daniel is of vital importance in our time when the bestial treatment of human beings, man against man, is rampant. It cannot be overstressed. In the Daniel legend the reality of faith is most clearly demonstrated as an intimately experienced and direct relationship with Being:

> ". . . Any man who makes petition to any god or man for thirty days, except to you, O king, shall be cast into the den of lions". . . . The king said to Daniel, "May your god whom you serve continually, deliver you!" And a stone was brought and laid upon the mouth of the den, and the king sealed it. . . . Then, at the break of day, the king arose and went in haste to the den of lions. When he came near to the den where Daniel

was, he cried out in a tone of anguish and said to
Daniel, "O Daniel, servant of the living God, has
your god, whom you serve continually, been able to
deliver you from the lions?" Then Daniel said to the
king, "O king, live for ever! My God sent his angel
and shut the lions' mouths, and they have not hurt
me. . . ."[12]

Here it is appropriate to repeat the statement of Bonhoeffer, who, as a theologian found himself in "the lion's
den": "Religious people speak of God when human perception is (often just from laziness) at an end, or human
resources fail: it is always the *Deus ex machina* they call to
their help, either for the so-called solving of insoluble problems or as support in human failure — always, that is to say,
helping our human weakness or on the borders of human
existence. Of necessity, that can only go on until men can, by
their own strength, push those borders a little further, so
that God becomes superfluous as a *Deus ex machina*."

To be sure, in the end Bonhoeffer was devoured by Hitler,
the monster, but though he was killed, he kindled a light for
our own time, so that survival might be possible without
calling on idols and false gods which embody the spiritual
dangers of our day.

Thus, the legend of Daniel is a mythopoetic anticipation
of the need to understand life in terms of complementarities
and not to be caught in the dualistic bifurcation of soul vs.
body, good vs. evil, etc.

Earlier we referred to the Golden Calf. This too is a model
which enables man to enter life and reality as a whole person
without mental reservation, when the beast (the Calf) is
truly integrated rather than adored as an idol in some dis-
guise. When men are confined by a definite system of dogmatic thought, philosophical, political or religious, they
therefore are worshipping idols. When worship of such idols
is refused, on the other hand, the inherent brutality of modern dictators is revealed to be no different than the brutality
of the ancient world portrayed in the story of Daniel.

On the spiral of becoming, the story of Daniel represents a higher level of the ontogenesis of the psyche than the idolatry of the Golden Calf. The story of Daniel portrays an attempted enforcement of an adoration of an idol, while in the legend of the Golden Calf, there is a spontaneous dance around the idol. Such spontaneity had its roots perhaps in Egyptian mythology. Osiris, the corn God, and Mithras, the god of nature, were both worshipped as a calf or a bull, and each spring these animals were sacrificed in resurrection ceremonies. By participating in these rituals, the worshippers re-established their sense of unity with the natural order.

Thus, the legends of both Daniel and the Golden Calf demonstrate the need to overcome man's preconditionings paradoxically of being both contained within nature and being at the same time divorced from one's true individual nature, one's being. Such a realization is vital for each person if he is to proceed on his way to becoming fully human.

What we are here describing is what we have called "Jacob's way" — the way of integration which leads to a state of wholeness. These legends reveal the essential meaning of *teleioō*, perfecting. To experience *teleioō* in turn leads to an understanding of the *hayah*, and establishes unity between nature and personal growth toward maturity. Here, where the living dialogue takes place, each person responds, or refuses to listen and respond. If one refuses to react, the living encounter with the natural side is deserted, and becomes a source of danger like Polyphemus.

The monstrous battles in World War I in Flanders and its cemeteries demonstrate the dance around the golden calf of money and industrial supremacy. The ecstasy of the destruction of Guernica by the Nazis, Auschwitz and Hiroshima and the crescendo of a possible global Auschwitz, are the witnesses to man's identification with Polyphemus. The blind monstrosity of the Cyclops in his cannibalism is the grotesque mirror picture of 20th century man, blinded through his soulless technology and the resulting destruction of man as man.

The image of the shepherd is now carrying the mask of death because the singular, the unique man in his multidimensionality has become emptied by the creation of the insatiable demands of a computerized consumer society in which human needs are neglected. A blinded Polyphemus now roams the inner cities, destroying the possibility of intimacy and love.

Picasso's "Guernica" portrays the barbarism of Nazi Germany, and gives mythological expression to brutal and bestial inhumanity of man to man. The poet who produced the Book of Daniel was engaged in essentially the same task.

The so-called "Eclipse of God" in our time has surely been a result of such practices and structurally interpreting Daniel as factual history and the inane exercise of "Biblical Arithmetics." Such one-sided rationalism and exclusiveness prevents man from "understanding the nature of reality in general and of consciousness in particular as a coherent whole, which is never static or complete, but which is an unending process of movement and unfolding."[13]

The ontogenesis of the psyche and its way "naturally" expresses itself also in science. David Bohm's statement quoted above and the scientific axiom of complementarity affirm the principle of integration — "Jacob's way" — and thus rationally open the possibility of faith in the meaningful continuance of life. The issue of "belief" is not under consideration here, for the reality of "the way" is a discovery, not an invention. By "invention" one generally means the combining of supposedly known parts in a particular way. The formation of religious dogma, for example, is an invention — an artifact. But by "dis-covery" one means literally *"un*covering" or "coming upon" that which pre-exists or is already there.

A discovery in this sense, one may say, has been "revealed" and thus Being is illuminated. The Gnostic saying in the preface of this book addressed the religious dilemma of today eighteen centuries ago:

> [*For in the beginning*] *God created man.*
> [*But now men*] *create God. That is the*
> *way it is in the world — men create gods and*
> *worship their creation. It would be*
> *fitting for the gods to worship men!*

Security lies in a living acceptance of complementarity, not in theory, pseudo-religious or psychological. When it is only theoretical, it is an intellectual game played with reality. A living acceptance involves the total person as in the ritual of the Last Supper, if it is, in fact, efficacious. Under such conditions it asserts a truth, but only through an authentic relationship with that which it tries to articulate. The same authentic relationship is symbolized in the drinking of the ashes of the Golden Calf as in the eating and drinking of the Eucharistic elements. In the King James translation of the Bible, the story is told in this way in Exodus 32:1-2, 24, 20:

> And when the people saw that Moses delayed to come down out of the mount, the people gathered themselves together unto Aaron, and said unto him, Up, make us gods, which shall go before us; for as for this Moses, the man that brought us up out of the land of Egypt, we wot not what is become of him. . . . And I said unto them, whosoever hath any gold, let them break it off. So they gave it me: then *I cast it into the fire, and there came out this calf.* . . . And he took the calf which they had made, and burnt it in the fire, and ground it to powder and strewed it upon the water, and *made the children of Israel drink of it.*[14]

In this Biblical narrative, God was active, not only on the mountaintop delivering the Ten Commandments as laws of social behaviour, but also on the plain below. The Golden

Calf, which was made as an idol, was revealed in its true nature when it was fully and physically assimilated. In this account we have a vibrant, vital and necessary dimension of life which leads to an experience of unity — the unity of all that is. The poets here anticipated the Resurrection as a rite of transformation, and in creating a symbol of this magnitude, demonstrate that the human psyche at this point had achieved a new and vastly significant stage in the ontogenesis of the psyche.

The Jacob-Esau legend in Genesis 25 is a majestic precursor of the story of the Golden Calf in Exodus 32.[15] In the continuance of the dramatic display of the process of integration, the *hayah* as the essence of "to be," is expressed. The same vital message was enacted on a world-wide scale in the use of Red Ochre, which in symbolic terms makes life possible and assures its continuance. In these dramatizations is mirrored a spiritual, divine development of the highest order, immersed at the same time in the basics of biological life.

In the ontogenetic development of the psyche from the patriarchal symbol of Jacob to the impersonal ritual of the Golden Calf, from the figure of Daniel to the personalization of Jesus, the principle of *teleioō* or the movement toward perfecting is revealed. According to modern science, this principle is manifested in the Hypercycle, thus proving scientifically the truth which had been anticipated in spiritual legends and writings centuries ago.

In more recent times, Nietzsche poetically took up the theme of the movement towards perfecting in his *Zarathustra*. Starting with the proposition that God as constructed by man is dead, he proceeds to give poetic expression to man as he really is. In his chapter entitled "The Gift-Giving Virtue," Zarathustra says:

> Remain faithful to the earth, my brothers, with the power of your virtue. Let your gift-giving love and your knowledge serve the meaning of the earth. Thus

I beg and beseech you. Do not let them fly away from earthly things and beat with their wings against eternal walls. Alas, there has always been so much virtue that has flown away. Lead back to the earth the virtue that flew away, as I do — back to the body, back to life, that it may give the earth a meaning, a human meaning.[16]

And further, denounced as an atheist, Nietzsche wrote:

Now I bid you lose me and *find yourselves*; and only when you have all denied me will I return to you . . . One repays a teacher badly if one always remains nothing but a pupil . . . You say you believe in Zarathustra? But what matters Zarathustra? You are my believers — but what matters all believers? You had *not yet sought* yourselves: and you found me. Thus do all believers; therefore all faith amounts to so little. (Italics mine)

But even more importantly:

You revere me; but what if your reverence tumbles one day? Beware lest a statue slay you.[17]

The idols in Akhenaton's temple tumbled to the ground; Daniel and his friends refused to give reverence to the idol made by men. Both are instances of supreme examples of man's voyage to self-discovery. In these examples of the archetypal truth, the *hayah* has its roots.

Man is a rope, tied between beast and overman — a rope over an abyss. A dangerous across, a dangerous-on-the-way, a dangerous looking-back, a dangerous shuddering and stopping.[18]

In the meeting of man with himself, there is essentially a discovery of his being "on the way," an experience of the transformation of his being.

And that is the great noon when man stands in the

middle of his way between beast and overman and celebrates his way to the evening as his highest hope: for it is the way to a new morning.

Then will he who goes under bless himself for being one who goes over and beyond; and the sun of his knowledge will stand at high noon for him.

'Dead are all gods: now we want the overman to live' — on that great noon, let this be our last will.

Thus spoke Zarathustra.[19]

On this "great noon" when man has become truly his own, the idols and the false gods will "be dead." Here we have a poetic expression for the hope of rebirth and transformation, laying the same stress on the individual himself, as did the *Book of Daniel.* Zarathustra's "Only when you have denied me will I return to you" is an echo of the words of Jesus in John 16:7: *"Nevertheless I tell you the truth: it is to your advantage that I go away, for if I do not go away, the Counselor [the Paraclete] will not come to you; but if I go, I will send him to you."*

In John it is said also: "If you love me, you will keep my commandments. And I will pray the Father, and he will give you another Counselor, to be with you for ever, even the Spirit of truth, whom the world cannot receive, because it neither sees him, nor knows him; you know him, for he dwells with you, and will be in you."[20]

In both of the Biblical Testaments, and in other sacred books of mankind, there are guiding principles to lead the human race into its full humanity. And at the same time, they reflect and mirror the biological background of the ontogenetic principle in poetic imagery.

A powerful illustration of the psyche's confrontation with itself occurs in the encounter between Nebuchadnezzar and Daniel, both of whom in this context are personified symbolic aspects of the human psyche. The second chapter of the *Book of Daniel* clearly reveals that Nebuchadnezzar is lacking in self-understanding, for he does not know his own dream. Daniel, representing a higher state of awareness, not only "knows" the actual dream, but is able to interpret its meaning. The same archetypal truth is affirmed by Nietzsche in *Zarathustra*. When man does not know himself, he constructs and adores idols; as they inevitably tumble down, man is in danger of being slain by their fall — his life is meaningless.

The essential truth which Nietzsche was expressing when he says "Man is a rope tied between beast and overman," was perverted by the Nazis as they considered themselves to be the "overman," the sole possessors of knowledge and truth. On the contrary, they lived on the level of the "beast," raising this idolatrous perversion to the level of state doctrine, and presumed racial superiority, proclaiming themselves to be instruments of the "spirit." Even the churches succumbed to the perversion, by entering into a concordat with the Nazi beast, or by remaining silent in the face of, not the "transvaluation," but the destruction of value. When this nationalized idol tumbled to the dust, the very humanity of man was slain.

It appears that Fascists by any name, in any state, draw the world into their underworld with them. In our time, the hopelessness of a culture ruled by the laws of a consumer society has created a sense of loss for a purposeful human existence. Only the amassing of money seems to provide a purpose for life. The use of drugs abounds from the highest echelons of society to the lonely junkie in Harlem, from the laboratory scientist to the lost, sad and aimless teenager, or the religious fanatic. In the face of such emptiness, the idolatrous fantasy of the comic book Superman has captured the imagination of thousands of youngsters as they attempt to compensate for their own sense of powerlessness. The Superman figure reveals the fallacy of the technological age, unable to provide work for masses of the population, not to mention the destruction of the context for a meaningful human existence.

When the *Book of Daniel* is examined, not from the perspective of "Biblical Arithmetics" but with a structural hermeneutical approach, it is evident that some of the characteristics of contemporary society are reflected. Modern industrialized society does indeed demonstrate an arrogance similar to that of Nebuchadnezzar in that it seems to believe that the industrial dominion reaches to the very heavens. The humble truth that only in returning to our "roots" can the true meaning of humanity be found is lost in the industrial expansionism.

> The visions of my head as I lay in bed were these: I saw, and behold a tree in the midst of the earth; and its height was great. The tree grew and became strong, and its top reached to heaven, and it was visible to the end of the whole earth. Its leaves were fair and its fruit abundant, and in it was food for all. The beasts of the field found shade under it, and the birds of the air dwelt in its branches, and all flesh was fed from it . . .
>
> The tree you saw, which grew and became strong, so that its top reached to heaven, and it was visible to the end of the whole earth; whose leaves were fair and its fruit abundant, and in which was food for all; under which beasts of the field found shade, and in whose branches the birds of the air dwelt — *it is you* . . .
>
> And whereas the king saw a watcher, a holy one, coming down from heaven and saying, "Hew down the tree and destroy it, but leave the stumps of its roots in the earth, bound with a band of iron and bronze, in the tender grass of the field; and let him be wet with the dew of heaven; and let his lot be with the beasts of the field, till seven times pass over him; this is the interpretation, O king: . . . that you shall be driven from among men, and your dwelling shall be with the beasts of the field; you shall be made to eat

grass like an ox, and you shall be wet with the dew of heaven. . . . And as it was commanded to leave the stump of the roots of the tree, your kingdom shall be sure for you from the time you know that Heaven rules. Therefore, O king, let my counsel be acceptable to you; break off your sins by practicing righteousness, and your iniquities by showing mercy to the oppressed, that there may perhaps be a lengthening of your tranquillity."[21]

Pope John XXIII thought of the Bible as a "narrative of man searching for himself." The dream of Nebuchadnezzar about the tree extending to the heavens is a perfect example of the Pope's viewpoint, for the text clearly and unmistakably states: "the tree you saw . . . *it is you.*" Individual megalomania is often presented in dreams in symbols similar to the tree which grew into the heavens.

The struggle of imperfect human beings toward perfectibility is an intensely personal affair. It cannot be achieved by rote learning of the correct doctrinal answers. The restoration of a human being's self respect and dignity presupposes the recognition not only of the *hayah* (the "to be," the "I am that I am"), but also the recognition that *"I* am the way" — that is, *I myself* am the way. Nietzsche uses the same meaning in yet another symbol when he says that "man is a rope tied between beast and the overman." Seen in this basic context, the Old Testament saying "thine own wickedness will correct thee" gains profound significance. The story of Daniel, therefore, is a prototypical example of the Bible "as a narrative of man searching for himself."

The stories and visions of Daniel form a unity, a true picture of the human being with his potentialities for growth, with his inner conflicts and tensions. As a stage setting for his story, the poet made reference to public events and persons, though they were anachronistic and fictional in their application. It is comprehensible that some scholars and commentators have seen the *Book of Daniel* as a "pious fraud." It is possible that these tales may have been incorporated into local traditions as the people attempted to come to terms with the political realities of their time.

Transformed as they are through the artistic imagination, these legends represent the basic elements of the psyche, particularly since archetypal motifs play such a dominant role. There are four kingdoms, even as the realm of science is ruled by the four dimensions of reality. There are four beasts, symbolizing not only bestiality as such, but representing also the four corners of the world even as the four winds do the same in Babylonian mythology:

> Daniel said, "I saw in my vision by night, and behold, the four winds of heaven were stirring up the great sea. And four great beasts came up out of the sea, different from one another. The first was like a lion and had an eagle's wings. Then as I looked its wings were plucked off, and it was lifted up from the ground and made to stand upon two feet like a man; and the mind of a man was given to it. And behold, another beast, a second one, like a bear. It was raised up on one side; it had three ribs in its mouth between its teeth; and it was told, 'Arise, devour much flesh.' After this I looked, and lo, another, like a leopard, with four wings of a bird on its back; and the beast had four heads; and dominion was given to it. After this I saw in the night visions, and behold, a fourth beast, terrible and dreadful and exceedingly strong; and it had great iron teeth; it devoured and broke in pieces, and stamped the residue with its feet. It was different from all the beasts that were before it; and it had ten horns. I considered the horns, and behold, there came up among them another horn, a little one, before which three of the first horns were plucked up by the roots; and behold, in this horn *were eyes like the eyes of a man*, and a mouth speaking great things. ... I looked then because of the sound of the great

words which the horn was speaking. And as I looked, the beast was slain, and its body destroyed and given over to be burned with fire. As for the rest of the beasts, their dominion was taken away, but their lives prolonged for a season and a time.

> I saw in the night visions,
> and behold, with the clouds of heaven
> *there came one like a son of man*
> and he came to the Ancient of Days
> and was presented before him." (Italics mine)[22]

In the same way, out of the depths of the psyche, we see in the Book of Ezekiel, the use of the same symbols and the same terms, as the poet portrays his own vision of man becoming man:

> As I looked, behold, a stormy wind came out of the north, and a great cloud, with brightness round about it, and fire flashing forth continually, and in the midst of the fire, as it were gleaming bronze. And from the midst of it came the likeness of four living creatures. And this was their appearance: they had the form of men, but each had four faces, and each of them had four wings. . . . As for the likeness of their faces, each had the face of a man in front; the four had the face of a lion on the right side, the four had the face of an ox on the left side, and the four had the face of an eagle at the back. . . . And above the firmament over their heads there was the likeness of a throne, in appearance like sapphire; and seated about the likeness of a throne was a likeness as it were of a human form.[23]

> And he said to me, *"Son of man,* stand upon your feet, and I will speak with you." And when he spoke to me, the Spirit entered into me and set me upon my feet; and I heard him speaking to me. And he said to

me, "Son of man, I send you to the people of Israel, to a nation of rebels. . . ."[24]

As the four-faced humans in Ezekiel were born out of the deeper layers of the mind, so also were the four-faced Babylonian god and his consort, the four-faced goddess. Though the Babylonian figures were presumed to be divine, Ezekiel saw in his vision four *human* faces. Further, in Ezekiel's vision, "the son of man" (e.g., man) is *instructed* to speak out against the misunderstandings of the "corporate personality" — that is, the collective sense of the people of Israel. When we come to *Daniel*, the psychic advance allows the poet to have his chief protagonist speak out of his *own* "knowing" as an individual.

Etymological study bears out this development. "That the human figure is a mere symbol and no reality is clear from the use of *k* before *bar 'enāš* (. . . literally, "in the likeness of a son of mankind"), just as *k* is used before 'aryēh, (k^e' aryēh." "in the likeness of a lion") in vs. 4. . . . Daniel does not see a real human being any more than he sees a real lion. . . . ."[25]

"The author of Daniel 7 who, though quite at home in the Old Testament, displayed great originality and ability in the selection and use of traditional materials. . . . Montgomery, pp. 323-324, aptly observes: 'We must allow [the chapter] its own originality and do justice to the simply but finely limned features of the drama without thinking that every detail is a painful borrowing on the part of a second-hand *littérateur.*' "[26]

And furthermore in Ezekiel the animal faces were attached to the human. In Daniel the animals were detached and different, each one in its own way. The psyche in Daniel had reached a state of relationship to the animal which the Book of Ezekiel did not portray. Psycho*logically*, therefore, Daniel could cope with the animal, the lion in himself, and was therefore not destroyed by it, as were the courtiers and their family.[27]

The sages of the Talmud sensed the inherent dynamic of

the *Book of Daniel* as an enactment of "man's search for himself" and found a deep connection with Abraham: "Daniel is the promised Messiah, and the miracles wrought for David, as well as God's granting his request were not due to his own merits, but to those of Abraham."[28] Abraham, may I recall, overcame his own "bestiality" and did not kill his son Isaac, but sacrificed instead the ram, as a symbol of his own brutality.[29]

Above all, Abraham followed the inner command to "go from your country and your kindred and your father's house to the land that I will show you."[30] And then, as Abraham began the voyage to himself, what he was shown at the very beginning was: "Lift up your eyes and look from the place where you are, northward and southward and eastward and westward; for all the land which you see I will give to you."[31] What he saw, in fact, was the inner land in its four dimensions, namely the essence of the *SELF*.

From the amoeba and its production of oxygen, to the refinements of the human mind as a potential source of direction and understanding, the *hayah* reveals itself as ever-present on both the inner and the outer levels of reality.

The Book of Revelation

Is it not written in your law, "I said,
you are gods?"

THE *HAYAH,* existing from the beginning, expressing itself in the present and reaching into the endless future, is superbly allegorized in the Book of Revelation, summing up, as it were, the essence of this remarkable writing:

> I am the Alpha and the Omega,
> the first and the last,
> the beginning and the end....[33]

and further in Revelation:

> I am the root and the offspring of David,
> the bright morning star.[34]

This is essentially the same theme that was expressed by Plato in the Laws: "God, who, as the old saw has it, holds in his hands beginning, end and middle of all that is. . . ."[35]

Significantly, the Book of Revelation *opens* by expressing the same theme with which it ends: "Fear not, I am the first and the last, and the *living* one. . . ."[36]

The Book of Revelation repeats what, taken as a whole, the Old and New Testaments portray. In Chapter 44 of Isaiah, the poets magnificently describe the essence of what is later unfolded in Revelation. This chapter from Isaiah is pregnant with meaning, calling upon the symbol of Jacob as the center of its meaning. Here, Jacob is the archetype of man's voyage to himself as he integrates the two eternal antagonists of the human psyche. Isaiah portrays it thus:

> But now hear, O Jacob my servant,
> Israel whom I have chosen!
> Thus says the Lord who made you,
> who formed you from the womb
> and will help you.[37]

> This one will say, "I am the Lord's,"
> another will call himself by the
> name of Jacob, and another will write
> on his hand, "The Lord's,"
> and surname himself by the name of
> Israel. Thus says the Lord, the King
> of Israel and his Redeemer, the Lord
> of hosts: "I am the first and I am the last;
> besides me there is no God. . . ."[38]

A structural hermeneutic reveals that the *in*-formed creative imagination of the poets provides but variations on a theme. Such an approach does not lose itself in subjectivity nor does it alienate man from his fundamental roots. The essence, the underlying issue of man's growth toward maturity and responsible action is enfolded in Genesis 3:5: ". . . you will be like God, knowing good and evil."

The same motif is essentially expressed in the Babylonian creation myth *Gilgamesh*. Gilgamesh's "brother" who was specially created to help him, is at one with the animals and feeds himself like them. He is in this respect like Esau of the Old Testament, who was also depicted as "a man of the fields."[39] In order to entice him away from his oneness with the animals, a woman is sent to seduce him into the human way. After having made love to her for a full seven days and nights, Enkidu goes first back to his animals, but they shy away from him. A differentiation has taken place on the way to becoming. Enkidu as an exponent of part of the psyche, just as Adam and Eve, has experienced a new level of distinguishing consciousness. And just like the Old Testament text so the *Gilgamesh* epos extols: "Comely thou art, e'en *like to a god. . . .*"40

It is here, as in the Judaeo-Christian tradition, that the sexual act is a decisive factor in helping the psyche to reach a higher level of development. The translator of the *Gilgamesh* epos uses the word *hetaera* in describing the female. She was not a whore. In Greek tradition a *hetaera* introduced the immature man into the art of how to make love; these women were fully accepted in society. In the psychic drama of reconciling vitally related parts — Gilgamesh and Enkidu — the self-organizing and self-correcting principal is symbolically at work. The *hayah* expresses itself also in the sphere of non-Biblical mythology.

For the *Gilgamesh* epos states that the Old and New Testaments are records of the unfolding of this awesome Truth. In a great vision the poets dramatically used the symbol of eating as assimilation and transfiguration, as with the Eucharist, to portray the human condition. Adam and Eve, according to the text, were not expelled from the "Garden of Eden" because their state of unawareness transfigured into awareness: ". . . then the eyes of both were opened, and they knew that they were naked."41

For untold thousands of years man "tilled the ground from which he was taken" and "lived in toil" . . . "and ate of the ground." This saying is a poetic record of historical fact. However, in Genesis 3:20, "The man called his wife's name Eve, *because she was the mother of all living*." (The Revised Standard Version states here in a footnote: "The name in Hebrew resembles the word for *living*.")

The name Eve is the personification of the primal water out of which everything has its origin, not only present-day scientific theories but also mythologies from ever so many different cultures. "The mother of all living" in Genesis 3:20 is also mentioned in a different form: "And God said:

'Let the waters bring forth swarms of living creatures. . . .' "[42]
After all, the primal habitat of the human foetus, the "waters"
of the womb, is an actual life experience. And the chemistry of the blood which every human being carries, is basically the same as that of seawater [supra, p. 57]. Seawater
is considered to be actually and symbolically "the mother
of all living creatures." The primal waters are the "chicken
broth" of the biologists, a mixture of simple organic com-
pounds in water. Sir Francis Crick together with Leslie
Orgel, following the Swedish scientist Arrhenius, holds
it possible that an earlier highly sophisticated civilization, far out in space, is the origin of it all on our planet.[43]
These creatures shot billions of years ago, so the theory
goes, with a phallus-like rocket *panspermia* — meaning
"sperm everywhere" — to the earth, where the spores fell
into the primal water and thus established life. It is fascinat-
ing to see how such brilliant rationalizers of biological facts
like DNA and DNR and their complementary nature, are
the media for the archetypal background of creation. This
"tacit dimension" of the mind informs their thinking, which
results in a mythopoetic statement dressed up in scientific
terms of a miraculous conception.

And John M. Allegro maintains:

> If rain in the desert lands was the source of life, then
> the moisture from the heaven must be only a more
> abundant kind of spermatozoa. If the male organ
> ejaculated this precious fluid and made life in the
> woman, then the above skies the source of nature's
> semen must be a mighty penis, as the earth which
> bore its offspring was the womb. It followed there-
> fore that to induce the heavenly phallus to complete
> its orgasm, man must stimulate it by sexual means,
> by singing, dancing, orgiastic displays and, above all,
> by the performance of the copulatory act itself. . . .
> The heavenly penis was not only the source of life
> giving semen, it was the origin of knowledge. The
> seed of God was the Word of God.[44]

The language of the scientist, Sir Francis Crick, and that of the theologian-biologist, Teilhard de Chardin, refer both to the same unnameable archetypal background. Sir Francis Crick said: "An honest man, armed with all the knowledge available to us now, could only state that in some sense, the origin of life appears at the moment to be almost *a miracle* [italics mine], so many are the conditions which would have had to have been satisfied to get it going."[45] And Teilhard de Chardin in search of himself, his own individuality, writes: ". . . it was concealed beneath the innumerable strands which form the web of chance, the very stuff of which the universe and my own small individuality are woven. Yet it was *the same mystery* without a doubt: I recognized it. Our mind is perplexed when we try to plumb the depth of the world beneath us. But it reels still more when we try to number the favourable chances which must conjoin at every moment if the least of living things is to survive and succeed."[46]

The ontogenesis of the psyche toward its own becoming is vividly expressed in Genesis 3:22-24:

> *Then the Lord God said: "Behold, the man has become like one of us, knowing good and evil; and now, lest he put forth his hand and take also of the tree of life, and eat, and live forever—therefore the Lord God sent him forth from the Garden of Eden, to till the ground from which he was taken!" He drove out the man; and at the east of the garden of Eden he placed the cherubim, and a flaming sword which turned every way, to guard the way to the tree of life.* (Italics mine)

Man's mind grew from a state of mindless immortality toward potentially responsible action. The poetic dramatization of man's becoming is expressed in terms of expulsion, which on a higher level of differentiation is shown in Abraham's leaving his kindred and in Jesus' saying unless you cut the ties to your childish dependencies "you cannot follow me."

Jesus, most dramatically, focuses the essence of both Old and New Testaments in a single thrust when he says: *"Is it not written in your law, 'I said you are gods'? . . . know and understand that the Father is in me and I am in the Father."*[47] Significantly this is the same chapter of John in which Jesus speaks to the image of the sheepfold: "I am the good shepherd,"[48] and "I am the door of the sheep."[49]

This whole set of Biblical themes is based on Psalms 82 and Genesis 3:22, "the man has become like one of us, knowing good and evil. . . ."

> They have neither knowledge nor understanding,
> they walk about in darkness;
> *all the foundations of the earth are shaken.*
> *I say, you are gods,*
> sons of the Most High, all of you;
> nevertheless you shall die like men,
> and fall like any prince.[50]

Truly, "there is nothing new under the sun" in human social behavior. As it was in the past, so it remains today. The Psalmist profoundly introduces this statement:

> God has taken his place in the divine council;
> in the midst of the gods he holds judgment:
> "How long will you judge unjustly and
> show partiality to the wicked?
> Give justice to the weak and the fatherless;
> maintain the right of the afflicted and the
> destitute. Rescue the weak and the needy;
> deliver them from the hand of the wicked."[51]

The eternal question "Am I my brother's keeper?" is addressed by the Old Testament in Psalm 82, and in the New Testament in John 10:34. The breakdown of family relationships and social unrest the world over show clearly that "the foundations of the earth are shaken." Love finds its expression not only in the realm of interpersonal relationships, but in social and international relationships as well. It is specifically in the social context that the references of both the Psalmist and John's Gospel refer to men as "gods."

On a cosmic scale, as in the individual situation, the drama is experienced in the constant flux of complementary opposites. Just as the psyche is dependent for balance upon the relation of its positive and negative aspects, the male and female opposites, so in the Book of Revelation, both "angels" and "beasts" are the poetic representations of the realities of the psyche.

> A careful study of these apocalyptic visions will reveal their artificial character; they are not records of actual experiences, but are literary productions, using sources and conforming to traditional patterns.[52]

Thus, the responsibility ultimately lies on the shoulders of the individual, since in his psyche he bears the primal source of "traditional patterns." The psyche is the actualization of the *hayah* with all of its ambiguities. But because society is necessarily "a community of interdependent individuals" what society understands as "the will of God" is often the special interest of a particular group, lacking the balanced quality of the *hayah*. The Talmudic story [supra, p. 25] is an example of such a state of affairs where the common will results in the excommunication of the dissenter.

When, in these times of rapid change, an individual is prompted by the evolution of the psyche to rise to a new level of being, the bearer of this condition often feels *his own* cherished values are threatened. The change is often resisted; and the inner experience of the "shaking of the foundations" is projected onto the *whole world* as though the world itself were on the verge of complete disaster. The agglomeration of individuals thus resisting change, perceive their position as "moral," whereas in fact "they walk about in darkness." It is such a response as this which has brought the world to the threshhold of nuclear annihilation. To call this anthropomorphic, self-centered attitude "the will of God" is to create an idol in the image of human imperfection which they in return expect to serve their own ends. Recognition of this human tendency is poignantly expressed as early as 250 A.D. in the Gospel according to Philip:

> [For in the beginning] God created man [But now men] create God. That is the way it is in the world — men make gods and worship their creation. It would be fitting for the gods to worship men!

Modern man lives in fear of this condition which he himself has created, producing an "age of anxiety," seeking always to rationalize his resistance to change by naming it "the will of God." What is made manifest in the apocalyptic writings of Revelation (*apokalypsis* is Greek for "uncovering or revealing") is, in fact, the *hayah*, rather than a prophetic revelation of doomsday.

The Book of Revelation is, if you will, a "manual for perfecting," designed to lead to maturity by integrating what is inherent in man. The incorporation of "angels" and "beasts" demonstrates the process by which the individual can arrive at inner peace, and thereby contribute a sense of peace to the society in which he lives. When such growth comes to pass, the *hayah* is accepted as something "given" and there arises a sense of stewardship in providing for "the earth a human meaning" and a faith that existence itself is meaningful. Integrating the apparent opposites of angel and beast is essentially "Jacob's way," allowing the tension to ease so the true self can function.

Anticipating the conclusion of the Book of Revelation, Isaiah 6 expresses romantically and poetically this "apocalyptic" potential of the human being:

> The wolf shall dwell with the lamb,
> and the leopard shall lie down with the kid,
> and the calf and the lion and the fatling together,
> and a little child shall lead them.[53]

The last chapter of the Book of Revelation begins:

> Then he showed me the river of the water
> of life, bright as crystal, flowing from
> the throne of *God and of the Lamb*, through
> the middle of the street.[54]

The vision in Ezekiel 47:1 describes "the water of life" as flowing from "the threshold of the temple" in an archetypal fashion toward the four corners of the world, as if the tabernacle would be the center, the navel of the world. The vision in Revelation describes "the throne of God *and* the Lamb." In her commentary on Revelation, Dr. Ford writes: "... one finds an element in the vision which is only barely hinted at in the visions of the Old Testament prophets. This is the Lamb on the right hand of the throne. Ezekiel thought he saw one who had "the appearance of a man."[55] Daniel had seen "one like a son of man" coming to the throne of God and receiving power, honor and dominion.[56] "John, instead of a similar apparition, sees a Lamb. In Jewish mystical and apocalyptic literature animals represent men, men represent angels, and often precious stones or light or fire indicate the presence of God. This gives one a clue to the identity of the Lamb. He must be human."[57]

Dr. Ford, with other scholars, holds that the first three chapters of Revelation are late additions by a Jewish Christian disciple. In any case, to whatever source these chapters may be attributed, Revelation 1:13 reads: "... I saw seven golden lampstands, and in the midst of the lampstands *one like a son of man*." The apocalyptic writings of Ezekiel, Daniel and Revelation all clearly express the ontogenesis of the psyche as it is torn between the opposites in order to achieve integration. Here the figure of the Lamb is a supreme symbol which combines the *hayah* and the human — the angel and the beast.

The whole tenor of the first chapter is archetypal in character. It makes use of symbols freely taken from external events; here, the number seven. But the external reference is not important. These symbols are used to communicate as backdrop scenery against which the basic idea is displayed. To take an example from the conscious level, we see in Aeschylus' play *Seven Against Thebes* the seven hills of Rome and the seven days of the week in which the archetypal seven was previously used. In Revelation, we find the archetypal seven not only in the seven lampstands, but also in the seven seals,[58] the seven trumpets,[59] and the seven plagues,[60] in each case depicting a state of wholeness or completeness. "Originally, however, Revelation 4-11 in its oral, not written, form would be assigned to the time of the Baptist and therefore to an era prior to Jesus' public ministry. Revelation 12-22 would be dated in the mid-sixties as the Roman War gathered momentum. . . . Thus, the original apocalypse, comprising 4-22, with some additions in the last chapter, was an almost entirely Jewish and/or Jewish Christian work."[61]

The foregoing structural analysis, though it is interesting in itself, overlooks the clues to the very essence of the matter which are provided by a structural hermeneutic, namely the ontogenesis of the psyche. The lamb is mentioned in Isaiah, but in Revelation is elevated to the very throne of God — a sure sign of the heightened awareness of the significance of the symbol itself. The four-faced Babylonian god [supra, p. 253] holds his left foot on a lamb-like creature with horns indicating that the mental development of man had by this time (2,500 B.C.) become concerned with the same problem. The consort of the god [supra, 262], holding a vase with overflowing water is, in the later stages of the psyche, integrated into the concept of the *one* God.

Still another aspect may be seen in the Babylonian figure. The male lamb under the foot of the god is in the position of submission to the conqueror. Thus it seems to anticipate the later development reflected in Isaiah and Revelation where the essential quality of the "beast" is lifted into the realm of awareness. The all-embracing quality of the "monster" in the human mind is described as originating both from the sea and the land. In Revelation 13, one monster comes out of the sea while the other rises from the earth and "it had two horns like a lamb."[62] The monster from the earth assisted the monster from the sea by demanding from the earth dwellers that they,

> ... make an image for the beast ... so that the image of the beast should even speak, and to cause those who will not worship the image of the beast to be slain. Also it causes all, both small and great, both rich and poor, both free and slave, *to be marked on the right hand or the forehead, so that no one can buy or sell* unless he has the mark, that is, the name of the beast or the number of its name. This calls for wisdom: let him who has understanding reckon the number of the beast, for it is a human number, its number is six hundred and sixty six.[63]

We have met the same motif earlier in Isaiah 44:5: "and another will write on his hand 'The Lord's.'" In the same context a few lines later it is written: "besides me there is no god."[64] Just as Nebuchadnezzer in Daniel 3:5 demanded the worship of an image of himself, so in Revelation man is confronted with the unconscious beastlike mentality of his mind. Using structural analysis, scholarly ingenuity has attempted to decipher the meaning of 666 and find in it some correspondence to an historical person or an historical event. It is true, of course, that history may have provided a medium for the poetic communication of the condition of the inner man.

Buying and selling has become the essence of our time. The monster of our time is the rationalization that by artificially created demands, economic expansion will continue to grow like Nebuchadnezzar's dream of the tree, into the heavens. With such a fantasy have modern societies created the idol of materialism, demanding that citizens should honor it, even to the point of sacrificing themselves for it. So one is tempted to join together the number 666 with the modern idol, and as Daniel answered the king, to say to the contemporary world "it is you."[65]

In short, the symbolism of the monster is a projection of our human condition. As in Job, meaning and peace of mind were dependent upon the integration of the Behemoth into awareness as an *aspect* of the human condition rather than the totality of human nature.

From a variety of sources we see the archetypal man described through the creative imagination, combining and integrating later that which was primarily split in the action of creation. In the Babylonian creation myth, *Enuma Elish*, e.g., Marduk split Tiamat, the primal monster [supra, p. 128] thus establishing Heaven and Earth. In the Old Testament, the poets expressed the split in this way: "Let the waters under the heavens be gathered together into one place and let the dry land appear. And it was so."[66] And in Genesis 2:21 Eve was differentiated from Adam, only later in Genesis 2:24 to "become one flesh" again.

In our time physics split the atom, which was considered indivisible. This action created a different experience of reality and the need for global integration. The process of integration, the realization that *contraria sunt complementa* [supra, p. 256], is in the Old Testament expressed as Adam Kadmon, reaching from heaven to earth, in Indian mythology as Purusha and as Pan 'Ku in Chinese thought as the original "atoms." In more modern times Nietzsche expressed the same mental "reality" as "superman" [supra, p. 93]. In the New Testament tradition, the Book of Revelation provides us with a grandiose picture of integration, of an "angel" combining land and sea. The text in Revelation reads thus:

Then I saw another mighty angel coming down from heaven, wrapped in a cloud, with a rainbow over his head, and his face was like the sun, and his legs like pillars of fire. He had a little scroll open in his hand. *And he set his right foot on the sea, and his left foot on the land.* . . . And the angel whom I saw standing on sea and land lifted up his right hand to heaven and swore by him who lives for ever and ever, who created heaven and what is in it, and the earth and what is in it, and the sea and what is in it, *that there should be no more delay,* but . . . that the mystery of God . . . should be fulfilled. Then the voice which I had heard from heaven spoke to me again, saying: "Go, take the scroll which is open in the hand of the angel who is standing on the sea and on the land." So I went to the angel and told him to give me the little scroll; and he said to me, "*Take it and eat;* it will be bitter to your stomach, but sweet as honey in your mouth." And I took the little scroll from the hand of the angel and ate it; it was sweet as honey in my mouth, but when I had eaten it my stomach was made bitter.[67]

Here is truly a majestic picture of the integration of the opposites of land and sea, man standing with one foot on each, thus uniting them as the complementary opposites were united in the Jacob-Esau poem. Here too the symbol of "eating" is repeated as a vital aspect of the total drama. The eating of the apple played a major role in Eve's entering into relationship with Adam; Esau ate the meal prepared by Jacob, his brother; the Israelites drank the waters mixed with the ashes of the golden calf; and climactically, in the Last Supper, the bread and wine are consumed. So in this outstanding example, the Biblical narrative presents us with an exact symbolic record of the ontogenesis of the psyche.

This essential development is expressed in that in Ezekiel

it is God who speaks directly to the poet. In Revelation, however, it is an angel as mediator:

> But you, son of man, hear what I say to you; be not rebellious like that rebellious house; open your mouth, and *eat what I give you.* And when I looked, behold, a hand was stretched out to me, and, lo a written scroll was in it; and he spread it before me; and it had writing on the front and on the back, and there were written on it words of lamentation and mourning and woe. And he said to me, "Son of man, eat what is offered to you; *eat this scroll,* and go, speak to the house of Israel." So I opened my mouth, and he gave me the scroll to eat. And he said to me, "Son of man, eat this scroll that I give you and fill your stomach with it." Then I ate it; and it was in my mouth as sweet as honey.[68]

In Revelation, the contents of the scroll held by the angel have become human "lamentations and woe": "And when I had eaten it my stomach was made bitter." Even today the symbol is still in use: "You will have to eat your words!" has the connotation of bitterness. In Ezekiel's account, such a reaction has not yet entered the human stage. As the psyche evolved toward a truly human state, however, it reached its final development in the example of Jesus, who prayed, "My father, if it be possible, let this cup pass from me; nevertheless, not as I will, but as thou wilt."[69] But he was not spared the bitter experience: *Eli, Eli, la'ma sabach-tha-ni?* that is "My God, my God, why hast thou forsaken me?"

The awesome dynamics in the symbol of eating as it represents assimilation and integration appears in the 19th Chapter of Revelation:

> Then I saw an angel standing in the sun, and with a loud voice he called to all the birds that fly in mid-heaven, "Come gather for *the great supper of God,* to eat the flesh of kings, the flesh of captains, the flesh

of mighty men, the flesh of horses and their riders, and the flesh of all men, both free and slave, both small and great." And I saw the beast and the kings of the earth with their armies gathered to make war against him who sits upon the horse and against his army. And the beast was captured, and with it the false prophet who in its presence had worked the signs by which he deceived those who had received the mark of the beast and those who worshiped its image. These two were thrown alive into the lake of fire that burns with brimstone. And the rest were slain by the sword of him who sits upon the horse, the sword that issues from his mouth; and all the birds were gorged with their flesh.[71]

Once again, as in the Old Testament, we meet the theme of cannibalism in the midst of "man's search for himself." As if to accentuate the never-ending process of the growth of the psyche — the sense of never arriving at a state of static completeness — of forever being on the way of *teleioō,* of "perfecting" — the "revealing" book speaks of the true human condition of man's mind in relation to the beast:

The beast that you saw *was, and is not, and is to ascend* from the bottomless pit and go to perdition; and the dwellers on earth whose names have not been written in the book of life from the foundation of the world, will marvel to behold the beast, because *it was and is not and is to come.*[72]

The essential and existential problem from which man yearns to be redeemed is his never-ending confrontation with the chaos he feels, eternally locked in combat with the inner beast from which there is no escape. Like the proverbial leopard who never changes his spots, man carries with him a Mr. or Mrs. Hyde. By becoming aware of this specific and unique aspect of himself, however, and by facing it, as Jesus did in the desert of his own being, it is possible for man to prevent his falling victim to the temptations of inner chaos or forming idols which rule him through their dogmatic ways.

The Biblical poets, and the author(s) of Revelation in particular have given us a spectacular presentation of the inner drama of the *hayah,* and have presented mankind with a truly illustrated "narrative of man searching for himself."

One such dramatic illustration is found in the 10th chapter of Revelation, where the mighty angel descends from heaven enveloped in a cloud with a rainbow around his head.[73] This sums up, as it were, the way of human salvation. In the Old Testament, the rainbow is a sign of the covenant, that man will never again have to face a flood —that chaos will not overtake him.[74] The validity of this covenant is to be found when man cooperates in dealing with the problem: by means of awareness he becomes related to the flood, and the rainbow then connects the two spheres of existence — the heavenly and the earthly. Thus, in this chapter of Revelation, we see that the symbol of integration plays a central role.

We meet the same problem in Greek mythology. We are not told by Homer whether or not Odysseus had to eat the plant moly,[75] but Rahner writes:

> Closely following the Homeric text, Heraclitus now develops the allegory of moly, *"Phronesis"* he writes — insight illuminated by reason, that is — is most appropriately represented by moly. This is a gift which can only be given to human beings, and to very few human beings at that. The most essential thing about moly is that its root is black and its flower milk-white. Now the first steps towards insight, which is a kind of simultaneous comprehension of all that is good, are rough, unpleasant and difficult, but when a man has bravely and patiently surmounted the trials of these beginnings, then, as he progresses, the flower opens to him, as in a gentle light.[76]

It was this plant which enabled Odysseus to conquer the tempting, seductive Circe whom he had to face on his way to self-fulfillment, on his journey to become human. A similar motif is to be found in the story of Rachel, the love for whom Jacob longed and labored fourteen years. In order to fulfill her womanhood as a mother, Rachel bargained for the mandrake — the "love apple." Of this fruit, J. C. Trevor says: "although considered edible by the natives, the somewhat poisonous fruit produces a purgative effect."[77] Perhaps Rachel, seeking creativity in the fruit of motherhood, experienced from eating the mandrake what Revelation describes as the "stomach was made bitter." Heraclitus, a classical exponent of Greek culture, allegorized the process of "becoming" when he spoke of "rough, unpleasant and difficult trials."

Odysseus was aided on his journey to self-discovery by Hermes, the psychopompos who in Greek thought was the guide of the soul through the darkness of the netherland, or we might say, through the unconsciousness of becoming. At the hand of Hermes, Odysseus receives the strange plant:

> He bent down glittering for the magic plant
> and pulled it up, black root and milky flower
> a *molü* in the language of the gods —
> fatigue and pain for mortals to uproot;
> but gods do this, and everything, with ease.[78]

This plant, the *molü*, appears as the symbolic integration of light and darkness (black root/white flower). Here is a repetition of the Chinese Yin and Yang, the Taigitu, symbolizing the same integration. Through the symbolic integration of the plant received from Hermes, Odysseus is enabled to overcome the powerful and unholy drug administered by Circe for the purpose of luring men to their doom, transforming them into swine. As "the witch of the dark" Circe is the godlike representative of loveless sex.

What champion, of what country, can you be?

> Where are your kinsmen and your city?
> Are you not sluggish with my wine? Ah, wonder!
> Never a mortal man that drank this cup
> but when it passed his lips he had succumbed.
> Hale must your heart be and your tempered will.[79]

The darkness of Circe's magic is rendered ineffective as Odysseus becomes aware of the basic life-principle of the complementarity of opposites. The *molü* allows Odysseus to join with Circe in the bed of loveless sex, compelled by her magic, but of his own free choice.

In the Genesis story, Rachel eats of the love apple, the mandrake; she had previously tried through a subterfuge to fulfill Jacob's sexual desires and her own womanhood. "Then she said, 'Here is my maid Bilhah; go in to her, that she may bear upon my knees, and even I may have children through her.' "[80] The same sequence is observed in Jacob's relation to Leah, Rachel's sister — here the psyche's complementary symbol. "Leah saw that she had ceased bearing children, she took her maid Zilpah and gave her to Jacob as a wife."[81] Here, the Biblical text presents loveless sex as a description of the psyche in a non-creative state. Genesis presents this state of affairs as the eternal conflict within the psyche and offers this resolution:

> With mighty wrestlings I have wrestled
> with my sister and *have prevailed*.[82]

> [And Rachel] conceived and bore a son, and
> said, "God has taken away my reproach."[83]

This Biblical account unmistakably displays the ontogenesis of the psyche and manifests the *hayah* as its underlying force. Significantly, the Biblical account of Jacob's wrestling with himself at the ford of Jabbok describes the conclusion in the same terms:

> . . . for you have striven with God and
> with men, and *have prevailed*.[84]

In the laws of Hammurabi is described the historical and juridical background to these so vital stories in the Bible, depicting the psyche's urge toward genuine creativity — childbearing. These very laws are demonstrating the persistent urge of the psyche for its own fulfillment. We find allusion to this rather peculiar custom in the Laws of Hammurabi in a section dealing with a man who marries a *naditu*-priestess. This is a special class of women who may have been whores or nuns, but it is at least clear that whatever their sexual condition they were not legally allowed to have children. Here we find:

> 144. If a man married a *naditu* and that *naditu* has given a female slave to her husband and she (the slave) has then produced children: if that man then decided to marry a *šugitu* (a secondary wife), they may not allow that man (to do so); he may not marry the *šugitu*.

> 145. If a man married a *naditu* and she did not provide him with children and he decides to marry a *šugitu*, that man may marry a *šugitu*, bringing her into his house — with that *šugitu* to rank in no way with the *naditu*.

> 146. If a man married a *naditu* and she gave a female slave to her husband and she (the slave) has then borne children: if later that female slave has claimed equality with her mistress because she bore children, her mistress may not sell her, (but) she may mark her with the slave-mark and count her among slaves.

> 147. If she did not bear children her mistress may sell her.

Frymer-Kensky describes the custom as it prevailed in Near Eastern law: "Apart from the insights that this section gives us into the relationship between Sarah and Hagar, these provisions also indicate the reason behind this apparently peculiar custom. A woman was expected to bear children for her husband. If she could not do so, whether prohibited by law as the *naditu* in Hammurabi, or otherwise incapable, he might marry another. Possibly to forestall this, the woman might give her own personal slave to her husband to bear the children for her."[85]

Whores and nuns, *naditu*, are complementary opposites and the law as a rationalization of the human condition insists on an authentic relation between husband and wife.

In this peculiar and particular play of opposites there is revealed on the social plane that there is not only a Dr. Jekyll and Mr. Hyde in each person; there is also a female Dr. Jekyll and Ms. Hyde, the latter being that dimension of the personality which is hidden behind the façade of respectability.

What modern science has discovered to be true of the complementarity of opposites in the physical world, is true in the realm of the mind as well. But as each person searches for himself, this truth of complementarity cannot be apprehended merely as a rational discovery, but must penetrate the whole person, emotional as well as rational, and thus be related to the uniqueness of each individual. The essential character of the *hayah* is contradicted when Biblical study is confined by a structural analysis to an historical framework, or when it rests upon the assumptions of religious dogma, or upon psychological clichés. Such an approach falsifies the actual dynamic reality of Being which reaches backward as a whole into the darkness of the past and forward into the shades of an unknowable future. The awareness of the extension of the mind has now become a vast reservoir of ideas out of which new scientific discoveries are being made. Crude materialism has now become the banal correlative to an expanding consciousness, and is the negative aspect of it.

Faithful to its apocalyptic character, the Book of Revelation uncovers a universal and archetypal situation which has, therefore, the same validity in our day that it had in times past. In dramatic images, it reveals the essence of the human predicament projected onto the heavens of truth and hope. As is the case with dreams, the visions in Revelation do not show a clearly defined progression. The individual can recognize the actuality of the "progressive" development in his own mind as whatever the "dragon," the Ms. or Mr. Hyde, loses power over the Self. Such power decreases in direct proportion to the awareness of its existence and its control. This growth process in awareness is not like a mathematical progression, rationally definable, but rather like the figure of a spiral, in which the movement leads away from the center, only to return on the other side at a higher level. The events in the Book of Revelation reflect such a spiral development.

Integration

HUMAN HISTORY extends backward in time for millions of years, and likewise does the human mind. The symbol for the underlying chaos, the *Urgrund* out of which the human psyche has arisen, is the beast. The important role which animal figures have played throughout all human history and cultures demonstrates the affinity of the human psyche to the bestial, the animal world. These biological roots of our psychic origins, however, do not belittle the immensity of the contribution man has made to his own development. Rather this is an affirmation that the *hayah* is also active on the subhuman levels of creation. This misuse of the Book of Revelation as a set of predictions to foretell the events of history is utterly trivial and banal. The enormous change which has taken place in our time is probably no more disruptive than the periods of radical change in times past, but then, as now, such change has resulted in a sense of fear and the advent of a doomsday mentality. Anticipation of the "second coming of Christ" is as much a fantasy in our day as was it in earlier times, and in all cases, it is a result of the growth of the human psyche into new dimensions of awareness, and the consequent desire to be released from the ensuing creative tensions.

In the Musée de Cluny of Paris, there is a tapestry showing a woman seated and holding a Unicorn in her lap. To her right, a lion supports a staff bearing a coat of arms. The damsel of the tapestry appears to have come to terms with the beast, and she is holding a mirror in which the Unicorn is able to see itself. "So Moses made a bronze serpent, and set it on a pole; and if a serpent bit any man, he would look at the bronze serpent and live."[86] In this case, the monster — the Unicorn — is also being made self-aware as the lady enables it to look at its own image. In the Middle Ages, the Unicorn was the subject of many stories. The Unicorn is a

Figure 37.   Tapestry, 1600 A.D., Musée de Cluny, Paris.

fabulous mysterious beast of great strength and the symbol may have its origin in Isaiah 34:7.[87]

In both the Christian and earlier Greek legends, the spirit of the beast was often seen in close conjunction with the feminine. Artemis, for example, was none too graceful a mother goddess.[88] At Ephesus, the capital of the Roman province of Asia, statues of Artemis have been unearthed depicting the black goddess with multiple breasts symbolizing fertility (some believe to see in them another symbol of fertility — eggs) and adorned with the figures of various ferocious beasts on her body. It may well be that the bestial figures are not only a representation of her powers of nature as goddess of the hunt and as a complement to her "giving" nurturing capacity; but also that she integrates the Circe-like animal aspects of her nature.

In such symbols, the opposites are united and in that union the essence of wholeness is expressed. We have seen this earlier in *The Odyssey* which vividly portrays the stages of movement toward wholeness in the encounter with the beast cyclops, Polyphemus. Or again, the same theme was echoed in the remarkable clay tablet from Chadfadsche. The encounter of the human being with the opposites within himself is beautifully described also by Plato in reference to the charioteer with two steeds: "one of them is noble . . . and of good stock, while the other has the opposite character."[89] Hence the task for steering oneself through life is troublesome. As the Old Testament says: "You shall love the Lord with *all* your heart" — that is, with the whole of your personality. Without such integration there is no truly responsible choice; and responsible choice is the essence of being human.

Figurines dating back to pre-ice age times, 25,000 to 30,000 years ago, have also been unearthed, indicating that the mother goddess had been venerated from the earliest times.[90]

A grand and dramatic presentation of this very human existential problem as it effects both the individual in his

Figure 38.   Artemis of Ephesus, 1st century A.D.

personal life and society is expounded in the 12th Chapter of Revelation:

And a great portent appeared in heaven, a woman clothed with the sun, with the moon under her feet, and on her head a crown of twelve stars; she was with child and she cried out in her pangs of birth, in anguish for delivery. And another portent appeared in heaven; behold a great red dragon, with seven heads and ten horns, and seven diadems upon his heads. His tail swept down a third of the the stars of heaven, and cast them to the earth. And the dragon stood before the woman who was about to bear a child, that he might devour her child when she brought it forth; she brought forth a male child, one who is to rule all the nations with a rod of iron, but her child was caught up to God and to his throne, and the woman fled into the wilderness, where she has a place prepared by God, in which to be nourished for one thousand two hundred and sixty days.

Now war arose in heaven, Michael and his angels fighting against the dragon; and the dragon and his angels fought, but they were defeated and there was no longer any place for them in heaven. And the great dragon was thrown down, that ancient serpent, who is called the Devil and Satan, the deceiver of the whole world — he was thrown down to the earth, and his angels were thrown down with him. And I heard a loud voice in heaven, saying, "Now the salvation and the power and the kingdom of our God and the authority of his Christ have come, for the accuser of our brethren has been thrown down, who accuses them day and night before our God. And they have conquered him by the blood of the Lamb and by the word of their testimony, for they loved not their lives even unto death. Rejoice then, O heaven and you that dwell therein! But woe to you, O earth and sea, for the devil has come down to you in great wrath, because he knows that his time is short!"

And when the dragon saw that he had been thrown down to the earth, he pursued the woman who had borne the male child. But the woman was given the two wings of the great eagle that she might fly from the serpent into the wilderness, to the place where she is to be nourished for a time, and times, and half a time. The serpent poured water like a river out of his mouth after the woman, to sweep her away with the flood. But the earth came to the help of the woman, and the earth opened its mouth and swallowed the river which the dragon had poured from his mouth. Then the dragon was angry with the woman, and went off to make war on the rest of her offspring, on those who keep the commandments of God and bear testimony to Jesus. And he stood on the sand of the sea.

The figure of the woman "clothed with the sun, with the moon under her feet and on her head a crown of twelve stars," pursued by the dragon, is a mythopoetic and archetypal image. The sun, moon, and twelve stars echo the twelve signs of the zodiac, conveying a cosmic image. The moon under her feet as though it were a foundation perhaps derives its meaning from the waxing and waning within a *period* of four weeks.

In the fairly recent past, the nonsentient universe of physics and chemistry, approaching life purely from a rational attitude, was thought to be the whole basis from which to judge life. In the world of science, devoid of emotion and feeling, imagery such as that found in Revelation has no power to convince the rational mind that there is an equally if not actually more powerful foundation, the root for one's comprehension of life. Yet today, we see that the poets anticipated in visionary statements what modern science now understands in terms of the interrelationships within the context of the whole. "Ultimately, the entire universe (with all its 'particles,' including those constituting human beings, their laboratories, observing instruments, etc.) has to be understood as a single undivided whole, in which analysis into separately and independently existent parts has no fundamental status."[91]

In the dynamics of a *living* process, the inherent tension is informed by the *hayah,* for without this creative tension, what we know as *life* would not be alive. In the realm of mental and spiritual life, as in the physical, there is also an expression of imperfection, of process and becoming. In neither realm is there a fixed, completed wholeness or perfection. It is only in the realm of rational thought that the concept of perfection has meaning; for the rational, analytical process approaches the world through the notion of physical causation, and treats the universe as a machine.

The female figure pursued by the dragon in Revelation has a parallel in the Greek myth of Iris being forced to flee with her son, Horus, before the serpent Typhon. Graves describes Typhon:

> Typhon [was] the largest monster ever born. From the thighs downward he was nothing but coiled serpents, and his arms which, when he spread them out, reached a hundred leagues in either direction, had countless serpents' heads instead of hands. His brutish ass-head touched the stars, his vast wings darkened the sun, fire flashed from his eyes, and flaming rocks hurtled from his mouth. When he came rushing towards Olympus, the gods fled in terror . . .[92]

Howard Wallace writes:

> The Pueblo Indians of the Southwest, the Mayans and Aztecs of ancient Mexico, and Kwakiutl of British Columbia all have similar dragon monsters in their mythology. The ancient Egyptians believed that there was an eternal struggle between Re, the

Sun-God, and Apophis, the dragon or serpent,
which tried daily to overcome it. ... The Ras
Shamarah texts, found in Syria at the ancient site of
Ugarit nearly twenty years ago, record Canaanite
myths of the period 1700 - 1400 B.C. The section of
one text tells of the fight of Anath and the dragon.
... "I have destroyed the underworld dragon,
beloved of El."[93]

The figure of the dragon appears in a variety of forms. In
Chapter 9 of Revelation it is presented as a swarm of locusts
arising from a bottomless pit in a cloud so thick that it
darkened the sun like smoke from a furnace. The locusts
were then directed to torture those who did *not* have the
"seal *of God* upon their foreheads."

> . . . they were allowed to torture them for five
> months, but not to kill them, and their torture was
> like the torture of a scorpion, when it stings a man.
> And in those days men will seek death and will not
> find it; they will long to die, and death flies from
> them. In appearance the locusts were like horses
> arrayed for battle; on their heads were what looked
> like crowns of gold; their faces were like *human
> faces.* . . . And this was how I saw the horses in my
> vision: the riders wore breastplates the color of fire
> and of sapphire and of sulphur, and the heads of the
> horses were like lions' heads, and fire and smoke and
> sulphur issued from their mouths. By these three
> plagues a third of mankind was killed, by the fire and
> smoke and sulphur issuing from their mouths. . . .
> The rest of mankind, who were not killed by these
> plagues, did not repent of the works of their hands
> nor give up worshiping demons and idols of gold and
> silver and bronze and stone and wood, which cannot
> either see or hear or walk; nor did they repent of their
> murders or their sorceries or their immorality or
> their thefts.[94]

In Biblical terms, the sign on the forehead is a symbol of both, of crime and of protection for the criminal: ". . . the Lord put a mark upon Cain, lest any who came upon him should kill him."[95] And within the context of man's existential question "Am I my brother's keeper?" — at the very beginning of the Bible is the "narrative of man searching for himself":

> The Lord said to Cain, "Why are you angry, and why has your countenance fallen? If you do well, will you not be accepted? And if you do not do well, sin is couching at the door; its desire is for you, *but you must master it.*"[96]

As an indication of human potential for "perfecting," a sign was given to those who had become aware that society had failed.

> And the Lord said to him, "Go through the city, through Jerusalem, and put a mark upon the foreheads of the men who sigh and groan over all the abominations that are committed in it."[97]

This mark, then, symbolizes man's ability "by virtue of the developing personality and within a limited freedom — to choose."[98]

In the traditional Ash Wednesday ritual, the ashes on the forehead carries the same meaning, as well as the implication that the recipient follows "the way" of the Christ. In Indian mythology, the marking of the forehead with red dye symbolizes a guiding point for the life force, the Kundalini. Kundalini Yoga is a total system for psychic growth through various stages of awareness, beginning on the lowest levels and working upward to ever higher awareness.

On the journey of becoming man experiences enlightening moments. This experience is often accompanied by seemingly destructive forces which are therefore resisted. Chapter 9 of Revelation starts with a dream-like image of a great star falling like a meteor and making an impact on the earth. An "angel" releases the destructive forces from the pit created by the impact of a star. The locusts with the stinging power of scorpions are the symbol of destructive force. As new perceptions and awareness enter the psychic realm, the impact is as that of a star falling from heaven. When the ideas resulting from heightened awareness enter the public arena, no matter whether they be scientific, political, or religio-philosophical, their sting arouses the opposition of the entrenched and therefore idolatrous institutions of power. Inertia opposes the creative response, blocking the evolution toward a new understanding. Verse 20 of Chapter 9 indicates that the only survivors were those who clung to the "old negative ways."

This is the same eternal conflict between creativity and inertia that is demonstrated in John 10. Because Jesus put forward an authentic way and represented a heightened awareness toward human relationship which was expressed in terms of "miracles," the crowd did not accept him. Inertia ruled them; and they tried to destroy Jesus just as the "locust riders" of Revelation left only those alive who adhered to the "old" ways. It was on the occasion of this rejection that Jesus sought to remind the people of their true human essence: "Is it not written in your law, 'I said, you are gods'?"[99] In the same context also the close relationship of the *hayah* to Being, that is, to becoming and to perfecting is revealed: ". . . that you may know and understand that the Father is in me and I am in the Father."[100] The same truth is described in "My Father is working still, and I am working."[101]

The impressive figure of the pregnant woman pursued by the dragon is a mythopoetic and archetypal image of the *hayah* at work in the deeply human dimension. The creative moments in human existence, particularly for serious artists, have their tensions and destructive aspects. The image of "giving birth" reflects such a creative moment when inertia, the suppressive tendency, is *revealed* both in the personal and a social context. The question raised in Revelation, "Who is like the beast, and who can fight against it?" is a rationalization for the tendency to stand still and do nothing.[102] Even when this inhibiting force is defeated in the course of a personal or a social revolution, the "monster" is not subdued forever. True to an ordinary human situation this devil has to be fought time and time again. Revelation depicts the "Devil" in chains, imprisoned for a thousand years, but in experience, he can be free again the next day. The eternal dance around the center and hub of human existence is the integration of the awareness of the duality of existence. Neither the positive nor the negative can be established as a forever.

Near the end of the book, Revelation reflects this truth in dramatic terms:

> Then I saw an angel coming down from heaven, holding in his hand the key of the bottomless pit and a great chain. And he seized the dragon, that ancient serpent, who is the Devil and Satan, and bound him for a thousand years, and threw him into the pit, and shut it and sealed it over him, that he should deceive the nations no more, till the thousand years were ended. *After that he must be loosed a little while.*[103]

At the *beginning* of the Book of Revelation, we are told that John saw "one like a son of man" who held "in his right hand seven stars, from his *mouth issued a sharp two-edged sword,* and his face was like the sun shining in full strength."[104] The words of Jesus in Matthew 10:34 express the need for men to be freed from the bondage of unconscious forces: "Do not think that I have come to bring peace on earth; I have not come to bring peace, but *a sword."* The text from Revelation quoted immediately above is surely the visual representation of these words from Matthew.

The text of Revelation then continues: "When I saw him, I fell at his feet as though dead. But he laid his right hand upon me saying, 'Fear not, I am the first and the last, and the living one; I died, and behold I am alive forevermore, and I have the keys of Death and Hades."[105] The *hayah* as a manifestation of the ontogenesis of the psyche is expressed in lines of great beauty and significance in the Syrian apocryphal text of Thomas the Apostle:

> Thou didst become the Messiah, and didst put on the first man. Thou art the power, and the wisdom, and the knowledge, and the will, and the rest of Thy Father in whom Thou art concealed in glory, and in whom Thou art revealed in Thy *creative agency;* and Ye are one with two names. And Thou didst manifest Thyself as a feeble (being), and those who saw Thee, thought of Thee, that Thou wast a man who had need of help.[106]

Is it not written in your law, "I said, you are gods?"[107]

The war against the "dragon" is an ever-present reality of human existence, and grows out of the chaos at the biological base of life. The beast, "that old serpent," is not destroyed in any of the encounters described in the Bible. The imagery of Revelation 12 describes the essence of chaos: "The serpent poured water like a river out of his mouth after the woman to sweep her away with the flood." This is the theme, of course, of the flood of Noah and the "fiery" serpents which pursued the Israelites in the desert of their becoming. Thus, it remains the integration of this duality of existence which can give direction not only to one's own life, but the life of society as well. The war in heaven described in Revelation 12 is remarkably illustrated in the decorative detail of an ancient manuscript.[108] Here the futility of attempting to kill the beast is represented by shooting arrows at the beast, only to find that they are turned back against the archer.

The theme of symbolic integration of the monster Leviathan was exemplified in our time as the Jews riding the death trains to Auschwitz sang the song of eating it at the

Figure 39. Detail from *The Dragon Expelled from Heaven,* Tuscan School, 14th century A.D.

messianic banquet. The slow turning of the spiral of becoming which is the ontogenesis of the psyche as it moves towards individual choice is also mirrored in the Song of Moses and the dance of the Israelites celebrating their victory over the "monster" of confinement in Egypt. From the perspective of a structural hermeneutic, the "right hand and the sword" motif of Revelation 1:16 and the Song of Moses: "I will sing to the Lord, for he has triumphed gloriously; the horse and his rider he has thrown into the sea,"[109] as well as the words of Jesus in Matthew: "I have not come to bring peace, but a sword,"[110] are connected with the messianic hope. Here, the hand and the sword symbolize separation or distinction, as the individual is enabled to distinguish his own containment in bondage as that of which he has heretofore been unconscious. According to the image contained in

Revelation, it is futile to attempt to chain the devil ejected from heaven and confine him forever in the pit, for he returns to plague mankind as a swarm of stinging locusts, as the retributive horses of the apocrypha and the rampaging beast "with horns like a lamb and he spake as a dragon."

In our time, the "monster" is released as rapid changes in contemporary society are resisted by the institutions of power. In a social context, the principle of the complementarity of values is observed as opposing factions referring to one another as the bearers of monstrous evil. This monstrous situation, where the balance of terror shall produce peace or where terrorist acts by activists shall satisfy human needs is in fact our contemporary "flood."

Needs cannot be satisfied by social action addressed solely to relieve human *wants*. The perfecting of an imperfect society can only be accomplished by each individual within himself, and such a process of integration is an intensely personal affair. The existential need to become — to move toward wholeness — cannot be met by institutional doctrines, which because of their very institutional character are inauthentic, or by political systems. In his Christmas Homily of 1978, Pope John Paul II highlighted this problem with the following statement:

> I am addressing this message to every human being, to man in his humanity. Christmas is the feast of man. A human being is born. He is one of the millions and millions of people who have been born, are being born and will be born on earth. A human being, one item in the vast range of statistics. It was not without reason that Jesus came into the world when a census was being held, when a Roman emperor wanted to know the number of subjects in his territory. *A human being is an object to be counted, something to be considered under the aspect of quantity, one of many millions.* Yet at the same time he is a single being, unique and unrepeat-

able. .... If our human statistics, human categories, human political, economic and social systems, and mere human possibilities fail to ensure that man can be born, live and act as one who is unique, unrepeatable, then all this is ensured by God.[111]

A human being is *never an object to be counted* because personhood cannot be made into a statistical unit. The most that can be done in the interest of collective information is to count citizens or individuals.

"Poverty is in the person as well as in the purse; its abolition demands the restoration of a human being's self-respect and dignity as well as meeting his or her material needs."[112]

"Enlightened" capitalism for its own self-preservation, hopes that the materialistic god of free trade will transform communistic materialism; and Communism returns the compliment. Raising the living standard of untold millions the world over is a laudable idea; but one must question whether the appropriate method is the exploitation of the natural resources of the poorer nations, and / or low wages.

Contemporary society is confronted by the anger and wrath of youth in revolt. Though the causes of this revolt are complex, surely a major source of the problem lies in the destruction of a meaningful future for humanity by a society obsessed with the notion of technological "progress." Many young people seek to lose themselves by means of drugs and alcohol, unable to find meaningful employment. Yet, simultaneously in New York, for example, vast condominiums are being built, some of which are priced as high as twenty four million dollars. There "are already 17,000 applicants from all over the world" waiting for their completion.[113] Consider the account of a twelve-year-old girl speaking despairingly to her mother: "They tell us in our physics class that the next habitat of man will be in space, but they also tell us that atomic waste will also have to be dumped out there. Are they already fouling up the space that the youth will have to occupy tomorrow?"

Edward: There was a door
And I could not open it. I could not touch the handle.
Why could I not walk out of my prison?
What is hell? Hell is oneself,
Hell is alone, the other figures in it
Merely projections. There is nothing to escape from
and nothing to escape to. One is always alone.
Lavinia: Edward, what *are* you talking about?
Talking to yourself. Could you bear, for a moment,
To think about *me?*[114]

If we juxtapose a 24-million dollar condominium in New York with the anxious question of a twelve-year-old child, we see the meaningless future, despair and emptiness of our time staring us in the face. In former times there were a few monarchs who spent millions of dollars to build elaborate palaces. In our day, the "millions" are human beings who starve. "About half a billion individuals are still crippled by hunger, and a billion more should have a more varied diet, according to nutritionists."[115]

At the time of the French Revolution when Marie Antoinette was told the people had no bread, it is reported that she responded: "Then let them eat cake." Such historical "facts" are symptomatic of our human confusion and manifest the failure of both the individual and society to enter through the "narrow door." In the Bible, the saying of Jesus, "Is it not said, 'Ye are gods,'" as well as the source of this saying in Psalm 82, are both set in a social context, asking in effect, "could you bear, for a moment, to think about me." In our time this refers to the millions, nay, billions, to whom our attention must be turned if the world is to survive. It has been through the functioning of the religions of mankind that the "heavens have been kept open" for the flights of fantasy of redeeming angels and good fairies. But today the heavens have become a sky devoid of fantasy, a cold emptiness full of silence. Such is the image presented to modern man as he searches for the meaning of his existence. Instead of fantasizing about angels in space man knows as *fact* that satellites with deadly weapons are encircling him — another manifestation of the symbolic iron curtain.

Despite the intrinsic beauty of space exploration, it only serves to intensify the feeling of individual loneliness and meaninglessness as one sees personal existence against the vast scheme of the cosmos. Faced with this reality, modern humanity cannot respond authentically to St. Paul's injunction: "Set your mind on things that are above, not on things that are on the earth. For you have died, and your life is hid with Christ in God."[116]

Epictetus (50-130 A.D.), a Greek stoic philosopher and contemporary of Paul who indeed may have known the apostle, saw life from a different perspective. He writes:

> . . . *you are a being of primary importance; you are a fragment of God; you have within you a part of Him. Why, then, are you ignorant of your own kinship? Why do you not know the source from which you have sprung? Will you not bear in mind, whenever you eat, who you are that eat, and whom you are nourishing? . . . that you are nourishing God?*[117]

Lewis Mumford poignantly writes:

> When at last it emerges into recorded history, organic duration reverses the mechanical, externalized time that is measured by calendars and clocks. Not how long you live, but how much you have lived, how much meaning your life has absorbed and passed on, is what matters. The humblest human mind encompasses and transfigures more conscious experience in a single day than our entire solar system embraced in its first three billion years, before life appeared.
>
> For man to feel belittled, as so many now do, by the vastness of the universe or the interminable corridors of time is precisely like his being frightened by

his own shadow. It is only through the light of consciousness that the universe becomes visible, and should that light disappear, only nothingness would remain. Except on the lighted stage of human consciousness, the mighty cosmos is but a mindless nonentity. Only through human words and symbols, registering human thought, can the universe disclosed by astronomy be rescued from its everlasting vacuity. Without that lighted stage, without the human drama played upon it, the whole theater of the heavens, which so deeply moves the human soul, exalting and dismaying it, would dissolve again into its own existential nothingness, like Prospero's dream world.[118]

The sensitivity of the poetic recognition that hell is "to be alone" and "is oneself" has now become an awareness of sociologists and advanced economists. Indeed, the economic recovery of the world cannot be accomplished without the development of the poorest nations — the "third world." New industry must be created commensurable with the real needs of billions of men and women in the exploited and therefore impoverished world. The vision of achieving such a distant goal is augmented by scientific realities already in existence, namely continuing development of microcomputers and responsible bioengineering. The computer terminal has the potential for redressing the basic destroyer of family life, that is the bifurcation of life at work and life at home, wherever feasible. Through the ready accessibility of stored and organized knowledge, when combined with the insights of the "life sciences" such as the discoveries of the DNA molecule, man can become a coworker with the divine process of becoming. In the growth and expansion of the human mind from the immediate present backward fifteen billion years and forward into an infinite future, man can be enabled "to walk out of his prison."

Gandhi's ideal of village-centered industry, linked with

the vast store of accumulated knowledge by means of the minicomputer, may, and indeed must to the degree possible, be realized. Such a development can also free mankind from the dangers of a computerized society. It is one thing to create a rural industry, near to the soil and local rites and customs, and quite another thing to computerize an urban society in which the individual becomes "an object to be counted" and statistically manipulated.

Computers are modern facilitators not only of information, but also in particular of dogmas destroying man as man if he is not aware of them. It is possible for man to be "mentally computerized" and thus be led into the desert of his own being, accepting such a condition as "freedom" . . . freedom from personal responsibility, that is — "It's the computer's fault!"

> . . . it is highly misleading to assert, as many people have, that computer intelligence is limited because a computer can do only what it is programmed to do. In many cases the programmer does not know what his program can do until it is run on a computer.[119]

Removing man with his human intelligence still more from the scene of authentic experience, the computer replaces it by an artificial intelligence. The computer has become "a laboratory in which to develop new ways of thinking about thinking."[120]

Only through awareness is man able to disassociate himself from such external control. If the individual *knows himself* and is aware of the dangers inherent in the development of computers, he can have a limited control over his own life, and thus be able to "walk out of his prison." Otherwise one can be manipulated by the authorities who, as in the past by dogmas be they religious or political, will find an immoral way to deny human freedom. The knowledge explosion will then explode all knowledge brought about by the electronic flood. Man would then become his own destroyer; and the hope for a humanistic economy would then reveal itself as an empty fallacy.

The enrichment of man's life through the acquisition of scientific knowledge needs to be complemented through the enrichment of the individual's authentic awareness of his own psychic depths and its endless resources. As scientific knowledge has brought about innumerable changes in modern life, so also openness by the individual to the inner world can bring about changes, and through them hope and meaning. The ontogenesis of the psyche is then both the field and the manifestation of the *hayah,* the *I AM THAT I AM.*

Notes

A NOTE TO THE READER

1. Jacob Bronowski, *The Ascent of Man* (Boston: Little, Brown & Co., 1973), p. 374.

2. The Gospel of Philip 2.3, trans. Wesley W. Isenberg, in *The Nag Hammadi Library: In English,* ed. James M. Robinson (San Francisco: Harper & Row, 1977), p. 143.

CHAPTER 1

3. Rainer Maria Rilke, *Das Stunden-Buch, Das Buch vom monschischen Leben* (Leipzig: Insel Verlag, 1924), p. 25. Translation mine.

4. Siegfried Morenz, *Egyptian Religion* (Ithaca: Cornell Univ. Press, 1973), p. 65.

5. B. Guttman, *Das Recht der Dschagga* (Munich: C. H. Beck'sche Verlagsbuchhandlung, 1926), p. 726. Translation mine.

6. Dietrich Bonhoeffer, *Letters and Papers from Prison* (Glasgow: Fontana Books, 1959), p. 93.

7. 2 Corinthians 12:9. The Revised Standard Version will be referred to unless a different version is specifically cited.

8. Bonhoeffer, op. cit., p. 91.

9. Heinrich Zimmer, *Philosophies of India,* Bollingen Series 26 (New York: Pantheon Books, 1951), p. 300. Italics mine.

10. Edward T. C. Werner, *Myths and Legends of China* (London: S. Harrap, 1922), p. 129.

11. *Edda,* "Das Wafthrudnirlied," trans. Felix Genzmer (Düsseldorf/ Köln: Eugen Diederichs Verlag, 1956), p. 86. Translation mine.

12. Talmud, *Der Babylonische Talmud,* trans. Lazarus Goldschmidt, Synhedrin Fol. 38 a & b (Berlin: Verlag Biblion, 1929). Translation mine.

13. Martin Heidegger, *Freiburger Studentenzeitung,* no. 1, 1933. Translation mine.

14. Klaus Scholder, *Die Kirchen und das dritte Reich* (Berlin: Propyläen Verlag, 1977), p. 340.

15. Hannah Arendt, *Eichman in Jerusalem; a Report on the Banality of Evil* (New York: Viking Press, 1963), p. 182.

16. Albert Speer, *Spandau: the Secret Diaries,* trans. Richard and Clara Winston (New York: Macmillan, 1976), p. 16.

17. Charles S. Macfarland, *The New Church and the New Germany* (New York: Macmillan & Co., 1934), pp. 198-99, 204.

18. Barmen Declaration, in Arthur C. Cochrane, *The Church's Confession under Hitler* (Philadelphia: Westminster Press, 1962), p. 241.

19. "Pacem in Terris," in *The Papal Encyclicals,* ed. Claudia Carlen (n.p.: McGrath Publishing Co., 1981), 5:112. Italics mine.

20. Max Picard, *The World of Silence,* trans. Stanley Godman, Gateway Editions (Chicago: Henry Regnery, 1952), p. 14.

21. *The Guardian,* February 6, 1983, p. 1.

22. Georg Denzler, *Die Zeit,* 10 September 1982, pp. 9 & 10, quoting Max Pribilla, *Deutsche Schicksalsfrage* (1950). Translation mine.

23. "Nostra Aetate," in *Documents of Vatican II,* ed. Walter M. Abbott (New York: Herder & Herder, Association Press, 1966), p. 660-61.

24. Augustine *On Original Sin* ch. 46, trans. P. Holmes, in *Basic Writings of St. Augustine,* ed. Whitney J. Oates, 2 vols. (New York: Random House, 1948), 1:653.

25. Ibid., ch. 47, 1:650-51.

26. Francis X. Murphy, C.S.S.R., "Of Sex and the Catholic Church," *Atlantic Monthly,* February 1981, p. 54.

27. Heinrich Zimmer, *Kunstform und Yoga* (Berlin: Frankfurter Verlagsanstalt, 1925), p. 97. Translation mine.

28. "Nostra Aetate," op. cit., p. 739.

29. "Redemptor Hominis," in *The Papal Encyclicals*, op. cit., 5:255.

30. F. E. Cartus, "Vatican II & the Jews," *Commentary*, January 1965, p. 21; and Friedrich Heer, *Gottes erste Liebe; 2000 Jahre Judentum und Christentum: Genesis des österreichischen Katholiken Adolf Hitler* (Munich: Bechtle Verlag, 1967), Preface. Translation mine.

31. See also David L. Miller, *Christs* (New York: Seabury Press, 1981), p. 34ff.

32. Helmut Schmidt, *Die Zeit*, November 9, 1978, n. pag.

33. *Evangelische Kommentare*, 11 (1978), p. 675ff.

34. Matthew 23:13-16.

35. Walter Burkert, *Structure and History in Greek Mythology and Ritual* (Berkeley: University of California Press, 1979), p. 67.

36. Ibid., p. 70.

37. Alban Butler, "St Sebastian, January 20," in *Lives of the Saints*, ed. Herbert Thurston, 4 vols. (New York: Kennedy, 1956), 1:128-30.

38. Psalms 82:6.

39. Gunter Weisenborn, *Der Lautlose Aufstand*, 4th Ed. (Frankfort/Main: Verlag Roderberg, 1974 und 1981), p. 128.

40. Matthew 13:20-21.

41. James H. Breasted, *The Dawn of Conscience* (New York: Charles Scribner's Sons, 1954), pp. 178-79.

42. Karol Cardinal Wojtyla, "The Acting Person," in *Analecta Husserliane*, 10 (Dordrecht, Holland: D. Reidel, 1979), p. 105. Italics mine.

43. Idem, *Sign of Contradiction* (New York: Seabury Press, 1979), p. 119. Italics mine.

44. Murphy, op. cit., p. 53.

45. Talmud, op. cit., Baba Mecia 4, Fol. 59 a & b.

46. André Dupont-Sommer, *The Dead Sea Scrolls; a Preliminary Survey*, trans. E. Margaret Rowley (Oxford: Blackwell, 1952), pp. 98-100. Solomon Zeitlin, from his vantage point, does not agree with Dupont-Sommer's and other scholars' interpretations of the actual texts; see his "The Propaganda of the Hebrew Scrolls and the Falsification of History," *Jewish Quarterly Review* 46 (October 1955): 116ff.

47. Rudolf Bultman, *Theology of the New Testament*, trans. Kendrick Grobel (New York: Charles Scribner's Sons, 1951), 1:31.

48. Bonhoeffer, op. cit., p. 124.

49. Noam Chomsky, *Problems of Knowledge and Freedom* (New York: Vintage Books, 1971), pp. 4, 6, 10.

50. Ibid., p. 10.

51. Werner Heisenberg, *Natural Law and the Structure of Matter* (London: Rebel Press, 1970), p. 44.

52. Augustine, "Question 46, On the Ideas," in *Eighty-Three Different Questions*, trans. David L. Mosher (Washington, D.C.: Catholic Univ. of America Press, 1982), pp. 80-81.

53. Chomsky, op. cit., p. 18.

54. John Keats, "Ode on a Grecian Urn," in *Romantic and Victorian Poetry*, ed. William Frost (New York: Prentice-Hall, 1955), p. 232.

55. Heisenberg, op. cit., p. 45.

56. Dirac, quoted by C. A. Coulson, "The Longing for Truth," in *Question*, ed. H. Westman (London: Hammond & Hammond, 1953), 6, no. 1: 31.

57. James D. Watson, *Double Helix* (New York: Atheneum, 1969), p. 131. Italics mine.

58. Fred Hoyle, *Ten Faces of the Universe* (London: Heineman Educational Books, 1977) p. 50. Italics mine.

59. Bronowski, op. cit., p. 340.

60. Alexander Marshack, *Ice Age Art* (New York: American Museum of Natural History, 1978), pp. 6-7.

61. Bart Jordan, "Ice Age Art and Science," *Parabola* 3 (September 1978): 90, 94.

62. Hoyle, op. cit., pp. 126, 128.

63. PBS, "Whisper from Space," *Nova*, Philip Morrison, narrator (transcript) (WGBH Educational Foundation), p. 16.

64. Ibid., p. 17.

65. W. Brandt, "Arts & Science," *NYU Bulletin* (Spring 1967).

66. Colossians 3:3.

67. Francis Crick, *Of Molecules and Men* (Olympia: Univ. of Washington Press, 1966), pp. 13-14.

68. Daniel Goleman, "Holographic Memory, Karl Pribram Interviewed," *Psychology Today*, February 1979, pp. 71ff.

69. Ibid., passim.

70. Bertrand Russell, *History of Western Philosophy* (London: Allen & Unwin, 1948), p. 606.

71. John Keorian, "On the Origin of Life," *Science*, 19 February 1960, p. 480.

72. Melvin Calvin, *Chemical Evolution* (New York: Oxford Univ. Press, 1969), pp. 104-105.

73. Bernhard Rensch, *The Evolution of Brain Achievements* (New York: Appleton-Century Crofts, 1967), p. 28ff.

74. Sheila Ostrander and Lynn Schroeder, eds., *Psychic Discoveries Behind the Iron Curtain* (New York: Bantam Books, 1971), p. 203ff.

75. Claude Alvin Villee and Vincent Gaston Dethier, *Biological Principles and Processes* (Philadelphia: W. B. Saunders, 1971), p. 322. Italics mine.

76. Robert Graves, "In No Direction," in *Images of Tomorrow*, ed. J. F. A. Heath-Stubbs (London: SCM Press, 1953).

CHAPTER 2

1. David Bohm, in a contribution to "Physics and Beyond," New Ideas of Order, presented by Paul Buckley, Radio Canada International, 1978.

2. John Scott Haldane, *The Philosophy of a Biologist*, 2nd ed. (London: Oxford Univ. Press, 1936), pp. 138-40.

3. Kenneth B. Miller, "The Photosynthetic Membrane," *Scientific American*, October 1979, p. 102.

4. Preston E. Cloud, "Atmospheric and Hydrospheric Evolution on the Primitive Earth," *Science*, 17 May 1968, p. 734.

5. "The Proton Pump," *Time*, 15 March 1976, p. 76.

6. E. Wreschner, *Ochre in Prehistoric Contexts* (n.p.: Israel Prehistoric Society, 1975), p. v.

7. Ibid., p. vii.

8. Ibid., p. viii.

9. U.S. Bureau of Ethnology, *Report*, 1882-1883, p. 54.

10. Ralph S. Solecki, *Shanidar; the First Flower People* (New York: Alfred A. Knopf, 1971), pp. 225-26.

11. James Mellaart, *Earliest Civilizations of the Near East* (London: Thames & Hudson, 1965), p. 20.

12. Ibid., p. 26.

13. Jacquetta Hawkes and Sir Leonard Woolley, *Prehistory and the Beginnings of Civilization* (New York: Harper & Row, 1963), p. 208.

14. Solecki, op. cit.

15. Robert Graves, *The Greek Myths*, 2 vols. (New York: Penquin, 1977), 1:304.

16. Gilgamesh, *The Epic of Gilgamish*, Tablet 11, trans. R. Campbell Thompson (London: Luzac & Co., 1928), pp. 55-56.

17. Alfred William Howitt, *Native Tribes of South East Australia* (New York: Macmillan & Co., 1904).

18. Karl Polanyi, *The Great Transformation: the Political and Economic Origins of Our Time* (Boston: Beacon Press, 1957), p. 59.

19. Manfred Eigen and Peter Schuster, "The Hypercycle: A Principle of Natural Self-Organization," *Naturwissenschaften*, 64 Jahrgang, November 1977, pp. 547-48; 65 Jahrgang, January 1978, p. 7-41, and July 1978, p. 341-369.

20. Ibid.

21. Carl Gustav Jung, *Psychology and Alchemy*, Vol. XII of *The Collected Works* (London: Routledge & Kegan Paul, 1953), p. 224. Italics mine.

22. Bronowski, op. cit., p. 123.

23. Jeremiah 2:19. Italics mine.

24. *The World Book Encyclopedia*, 1980 ed., s.v. "Australia."

25. Isaiah 1:18.

26. Matthew 27:28-29, 31.

27. "The Tasadays," *National Geographic*, August 1972, p. 243.

28. H. Westman, *The Springs of Creativity* (New York: Atheneum, 1961), p. 170.

29. Ibid.

30. Numbers 19:2.

31. Numbers 19:9.

32. Plutarch *Moralia*, vol. 5, "Isis and Osiris," 1. 363, 31, trans. F. C. Babbitt, Loeb Classical Library (Cambridge: Harvard Univ. Press, 1936), p. 75.

33. Diodorus Siculus *Bibliotheca Historica* 1. 88.4, trans. C. H. Oldfather (New York: G. P. Putnam, 1933), p. 301.

34. Hebrews 11:8.

35. Chaim Bermant and Michael Weitzman, *Ebla* (New York: Times Books, 1979), p. 2.

36. Thomas L. Thompson, *The Historicity of the Patriarchal Narrative* (Berlin, New York: W. De Gruyter, 1974) and John Van Seters, *Abraham in History and Tradition* (New Haven: Yale Univ. Press, 1975).

37. Westman, *Springs*, p. 111.

38. A. Eisenlohr, *Der Grosse Papyrus Harris* (Leipzig: J. C. Hinrichs Buchhandlung, 1872), p. 75.

39. Donald B. Redford, "The Razed Temple of Akhenaten," *Scientific American*, December 1978, p. 146. Italics mine.

40. Genesis 15:8-12, 17-18 (King James Version). Italics mine.

41. Wilhelm von Humboldt, *The Limits of State Action* (Cambridge: Univ. Press, 1969), pp. 76, 63, 28.

42. Luke 14:26.

43. Genesis 32:29.

44. Augustine, *On the Trinity*, trans. A. W. Haddan, in *Basic Writings* 2:734-735.

45. Allogenes 61. 15, Introd. Antoinette Clark Wire, trans. John D. Turner and Orval S. Wintermute, in *The Nag Hammadi Library*, p. 449. Italics mine.

46. Burkert, op. cit., pp. 87, 92, 93.

47. Morenz, op. cit., p. 144.

48. Ibid., p. 145.

49. Ibid., p. 163.
50. Genesis 17:15-16.
51. Genesis 18:1, 2, 9, 10. Italics mine.
52. Matthew 1:20-21, 24.
53. Exodus 2:6.
54. "Pacem in Terris," (Part 1, Order between Men) in *The Papal Encyclicals*, 5:108-12.
55. Bronowski, op. cit., p. 411.
56. Fritjof Capra, *Tao of Physics* (Boulder, Colo.: Shambhala Publications, 1975), p. 107.
57. Bonhoeffer, op. cit., p. 93.

CHAPTER 3

1. *The New York Times*, 3 October 1979, 2, 4:3. Italics mine.
2. Micah 7:2-4, 5-6.
3. Breasted, op. cit., p. 201.
4. Ibid., p. 202.
5. Genesis 14:18-20.
6. The Gospel of Thomas 2. 32, introd. Helmut Koester, trans. Thomas O. Lambdin, in *The Nag Hammadi Library*, p. 118.
7. Exodus 2:3 (King James Version).
8. Louis Ginzberg, *The Legends of the Jews*, trans. Henrietta Szold, 7 vols. (Philadelphia: The Jewish Publication Society of America, 1913), 5:209.
9. Matthew 2:13.
10. Genesis 21:10.
11. Genesis 22:2.
12. *Enuma Elish*, Tablet 1, 35-40, in *The Babylonian Genesis*, ed. Alexander Heidel, 2nd ed. (Chicago: Univ. of Chicago Press, 1951), p. 19.
13. *Atrahasis Epic*, in *Bibliotheca Orientalis* 13 (Mai-Juli 1956).
14. Ezekiel 5:9-10.
15. Matthew 10:21, 22 (King James Version).
16. Manfred Eigen and others, "The Origin of Genetic Information," *Scientific American*, April 1981, p. 92. Italics mine.
17. Romans 7:19 (King James Version).
18. Numbers 22-24.
19. Numbers 24:13.
20. Numbers 22:21-22.
21. Numbers 22:28, 31, 32.
22. *The Interpreter's Dictionary of the Bible* (New York: Abingdon Press, 1962), s.v. "Satan," by T. H. Gaster, 4:224-25.
23. Matthew 4:1.
24. Numbers 23:19.
25. Friedrich Nietzsche, *Thus Spoke Zarathustra*, in *The Portable Nietzsche*, ed. & trans. Walter Kaufman (New York: Viking Press, 1954), p. 369.
26. Jonah 2:5-6.
27. Jonah 2:8 (King James Version).
28. Acts 9:9.
29. Acts 9:3.

30. Acts 9:18.
31. Acts 17:23.
32. Ibid.
33. Acts 17:27-28.
34. Deuteronomy 27:15.
35. Deuteronomy 30:11-14. Italics mine.
36. Genesis 1:3.
37. Romans 13:1-7.
38. Acts 17:23, 28.
39. Eduard Nordon, *Agnostos Theos* (Stuttgart: B. G. Teubner, 1956).
40. Romans 13:1-2.
41. Karl Barth, *Epistle to the Romans* trans. Edwyn C. Hoskyns, 6th ed. (London: Oxford Univ. Press, 1953), p. 484.
42. Matthew 27:46.
43. Genesis 14:17.
44. Psalms 110:4.
45. Genesis 22:1-2.
46. Ginzberg, op. cit., 1:283.
47. Ibid., p. 278.
48. Ibid., p. 285.
49. Deuteronomy 6:5 (King James Version). Italics mine.
50. Genesis 14:18.
51. Hebrews 7:1-3.
52. Psalms 110:2-4.
53. Breasted, op. cit., p. 142 and Morenz, op. cit., p. 273.
54. Morenz, op. cit., pp. 12, 114.
55. Hebrews 6:13, 19-20.
56. M. de Jonge and A. S. Van der Woude, "11Q Melchizedek and the New Testament," in *New Testament Studies* 12 (1965): 303.
57. Ginzberg, op. cit., 1:233.
58. Ibid., 5:117.
59. Ibid., p. 126.
60. Harold Rosenberg, *Barnett Newman* (New York: Henry N. Abrams, 1978), p. 56.
61. "M. P. Rsukanov, Director of the State Museums of the Kremlin," *Realités*, November-December 1979, p. 38.
62. *The New Testament Apocrypha*, ed. Wilhelm Schneemelker, Eng. trans. ed. R.McL. Wilson, 2 vols. (Philadelphia: Westminster Press, 1963-65), 2:193.
63. Ibid., p. 241.
64. Ibid., pp. 467-69.
65. Nahum M. Sarna, in reply to a comment on a review by him of Van Seter's "Abraham in History and Tradition," *Biblical Archaeology Review* 4 (March 1978): 52.
66. Morenz, op. cit., p. 114.
67. Julius Stone, *Human Law and Human Justice* (Stanford: Stanford Univ. Press, 1965), pp. 10-11, chs. 1 & 2. Italics mine.
68. Hugh Lloyd-Jones, *The Justice of Zeus* (Berkeley: Univ. of California Press, 1971), p. 166.
69. Ibid., p. 87.
70. Ibid., p. 44.
71. Ibid., p. 131.

72. Giorgio del Vecchio, *Justice: an Historical and Philosophical Essay*, 1st Eng. ed. (Edinburgh: The Univ. Press, 1952), p. 6.

73. Hesiod *Theogony* 886-900.

74. Graves, op. cit., p. 46.

75. Genesis 14:18-19.

76. Hebrews 5:5-6.

77. Karl R. Popper and John C. Eccles, *The Self and its Brain* New York: Springer International, 1977), p. 558.

78. Apocalypse of Peter 7. 3, Introd. James Brashler, trans. Roger A. Bullard, ed. Fredrik Wisse, in *The Nag Hammadi Library*, p. 343. Italics mine.

79. Ibid., p. 5.

80. Ibid., p. 343.

81. Bronowski, op. cit., p. 340.

82. The Gospel of Philip 2. 3, op. cit., p. 137.

83. Melchizedek 9. 1, in *The Nag Hammadi Library*, p. 400. Italics mine.

84. The Gospel of Thomas 2. 32, op. cit., p. 118. Italics mine.

85. Genesis 15:12.

86. Genesis 15:1, 7-11, 12, 17-18.

87. Ginzberg, op. cit., 1:233.

88. Ibid., 5:117.

89. Matthew 10:34-39.

90. *The Gospel According to Thomas*, log 55 and 56, Coptic text est. and trans. A. Guillaumont et al. (Leiden: E. J. Brill; New York: Harper & Bros. 1959), p. 31.

91. Hugh G. Evelyn-White, *The Sayings of Jesus, from Oxrhynchus* (Cambridge: Univ. Press, 1920), p. 36.

92. Augustine *De Vera Religione* 29. 72, in *Augustine*, trans. John H. S. Burleigh (Philadelphia: Westminster Press, 1953), p. 262.

93. Hippolytus, quoting "Monöimus," in *Philosophumena*, "The Refutation of All Heresies," 8. 8, The Ante-Nicene Fathers, 5 (Buffalo: The Christian Literature Co., 1886), p. 122.

94. *The Gospel According to Thomas*, Coptic Text, op. cit., p. 41.

95. Genesis 15:8.

96. Charles G. Leland, *The Algonquin Legends of New England* (Boston: Houghton, Mifflin, 1898), pp. 1-2, 106. Italics mine.

97. Westman, op. cit., pp. 115ff.

98. Job 2:10. Italics mine.

99. Job, Vol. 15 of *The Anchor Bible*, introd., trans. and notes by Marvin H. Pope (New York: Doubleday, 1965), p. 268.

100. Westman, op. cit., p. 122.

101. Job 29:14 (King James Version).

102. Westman, op. cit., pp. 121-22.

103. Ginzberg, op. cit., 1:121.

104. Karl Barth, *A Shorter Commentary on Romans*, trans. D. H. van Daalen (Richmond, Va.: John Knox Press, 1960), p. 39.

105. James George Frazer, *Folklore in the Old Testament*, 3 vols. (London: Macmillan, 1919), 1:393.

106. Deuteronomy 27: 12-13.

107. Joshua 8:33.

108. Deuteronomy 30:19. Italics mine.

109. Deuteronomy 30:6.

110. Deuteronomy 10:16 (King James Version).

111. Romans 2:29 (King James Version).

112. John 15:5 (King James Version).

113. John 15:16 (King James Version).

114. *Laws and Customs of Israel*, trans. Gerald Friedlaender, 4 vols. (London: Shapiro, Vallentine & Co., 1927), 2:183.

115. Genesis 22:1-14, as shown in *The Springs of Creativity*, op. cit., pp. 101ff.

116. *Enuma Elish*, Tablet 4, 137, op. cit., p. 42.

117. Popper and Eccles, op. cit., p. 120.

118. Gershom Scholem, "Jerusalem: Farben und ihre Symbolik in der jüdischen Uberlieferung und Mystik," *Eranos* 41 (1972):40.

119. R. David Freedman, "Put Your Hand Under My Thigh," *Biblical Archaeology Review* 2. (June 1976):3-4.

120. Exodus 4:1-5.

121. Deuteronomy 25:8-9.

122. James Henry Breasted, *Ancient Records of Egypt*, 5 vols. (New York: Russell & Russell, 1962) 4:29, 31.

123. Exodus 4:10, 16.

124. Genesis 15:8.

125. Numbers 20:8, 11-12. Italics mine.

126. Westman, op. cit., p. 189.

127. Thorleif Boman, *Hebrew Thought Compared with Greek* (London: SCM Press, 1960), p. 58.

128. Marie Luise Von Franz, *Patterns of Creativity Mirrored in Creation Myths* (Zürich: Spring Publications, 1978), p. 168. Italics mine.

129. Ibid., pp. 190-91. Italics mine.

130. Psalms 29:3-4.

131. Jeremiah 23:28-29.

132. Isaiah 55:11.

133. Boman, op. cit., p. 65.

134. Frederick L. Moriarty, S. J., "Word as Power in the Ancient Near East," in *A Light Unto My Path: Old Testament Studies in Honor of Jacob M. Meyers*, ed. Howard N. Bream et al. (Philadelphia: Temple Univ. Press, 1974), p. 349.

135. Boman, op. cit., p. 184.

136. Morenz, op. cit., p. 9.

137. Ibid., p. 164.

138. Von Franz, op. cit., p. 145. Italics mine.

139. Jacob Leveen, *The Hebrew Bible in Art*, The Schweich Lectures of the British Academy, 1939 (London: Oxford Univ. Press, 1944).

140. Westman, op. cit., p. 74.

141. Ralph Cohen, "The Mystery MBI People: Does the Exodus Tradition in the Bible Preserve the Memory of Their Entry into Canaan?" *Biblical Archaeology Review* 9 (July/August 1983): 29.

142. Breasted, *The Dawn of Conscience*, p. 349; and G. W. Ahlström, "Where Did the Israelites Live?" *Journal of Near-Eastern Studies* 41 (April 1982): 134.

143. Moshe Greenberg, *The Hab/Piru*, American Oriental Series, 39 (New Haven: American Oriental Society, 1955), pp. 96, 89, 9.

144. Edward F. Campbell, "The Amarna Letters and the Amarna Period," in *Biblical Archaeologist Reader, 3* (New York: Doubleday Anchor Books, 1970), pp. 67-68.

145. George E. Mendenhall, "The Hebrew Conquest of Palestine," ibid., pp. 105-106.

146. Genesis 12:1.

147. Matthew 10:37-38.

148. Matthew, Vol. 26 *The Anchor Bible*, introd., trans. and notes by W. F. Allbright and C. S. Mann (New York: Doubleday, 1971), p. xix-xx, cviii.

149. Genesis 32:29.

150. Westman, op. cit., pp. 138ff.

151. Matthew, Vol. 26 of *The Anchor Bible, p. lv.*

152. Exodus 3:13.

153. Exodus 3:2.

154. Bronowski, op. cit., p. 142.

155. Ibid., p. 187.

156. Martin Buber, *Moses* (New York: Harper Bros., 1958), p. 39.

157. George H. Forsyth and Kurt Weitzmann, "Saving the Mt. Sinai Mosaics," *Biblical Archaeoogy Review* 4 (November/December 1978): 22.

158. Ibid., p. 31.

159. Matthew, Vol. 26 of *The Anchor Bible*, p. cviii.

160. Exodus 3:13-14.

161. John 14:6.

162. Boman, op. cit., p. 39.

163. *Philosophical Works of Descartes*, quoted by Chomsky, op. cit., p. 28.

164. Chomsky, op. cit., p. 10, 18.

165. O. S. Rankin, "The Development of the Biblical Thought about God," in *Theological Word Book of the Bible*, ed. Alan Richardson (New York: Macmillan, 1950), p. 96.

166. Martin Buber, *Eclipse of God* (London: Victor Gollancz, Ltd., 1953), pp. 83-84.

167. Giovanni Pettinato and Alfonso Archi, "Epigraphic Evidence from Ebla: a Summary," *Biblical Archaeology* 43 (Fall 1980): 201.

168. Ibid., p. 205.

169. Boman, op. cit., p. 31.

170. Ibid., pp. 45-49.

171. Ibid., p. 20.

172. Exodus 32:24.

173. Exodus 32:35. Italics mine.

174. Westman, op. cit., pp. 138ff.

175. Amihai Mazar, *Biblical Archaeology Review*, September-October, 1983.

176. Westman, op. cit., p. 156.

177. Deuteronomy 30:14.

178. Deuteronomy 30:19. Italics mine.

179. John 11:52. Paraphrased.

180. Exodus 20:4.

181. *Code of Hammurabi*, in *Sources of Ancient and Primitive Law*, ed. Albert Kocourek and John H. Wigmore, Evolution of Law Series, 2 vols. (Boston: Little, Brown, 1915), 1: 387.

182. *The Interpreter's Dictionary of the Bible*, s.v. "Moses," by R. F. Johnson, 3:441.

183. Exodus 21:24.

184. *Code of Hammurabi* 197, in *Sources of Ancient and Primitive Law*, p. 428.

185. Matthew 5:38.

186. Matthew 5:17.

187. *Code of Hammurabi* 215-220, pp. 431-32.

188. Wojtyla, op. cit., p. 106.

189. Genesis 17:1.
190. Exodus 6:2-3.
191. Ginzberg, op. cit., 2:319.
192. David Biale, "The God with Breasts: El Shaddai in the Bible," *History of Religions* 21 (February 1982):256.
193. Westman, op. cit., p. 208.
194. Exodus 13:21-22.
195. Luke 14:26.
196. Genesis 17:1.
197. Matthew 5:48.
198. Leviticus 19:2.
199. Leviticus 20:9.
200. 1 Peter 1:13-16.
201. Matthew 6:9-13.
202. Pirke Aboth, *Ethics of the Talmud: Sayings of the Fathers*, ed., introd. and trans. R. Travers Herford (New York: Schocken Books, 1962).
203. Speer, op. cit., p. 16.

CHAPTER 4

1. Matthew, Vol. 26 of *The Anchor Bible*, p. 71.
2. Westman, op. cit., p. 190.
3. Isaiah 2:2-3, 4-5. Italics mine.
4. Genesis 25:26.
5. Robert Graves and Raphael Patai, *Hebrew Myths* (New York: Doubleday, 1964), p. 229.
6. Genesis 28:12, 16-17.
7. Westman, op. cit., p. 189.
8. *Enuma Elish*, Tablet I, 156-57.
9. Luke 14:26-27.
10. Genesis 25:29-32. Italics mine.
11. Ginzberg, op. cit., 1:319.
12. Rachel Hachlili, "Ancient Burial Customs Preserved in Jericho Hills," *Biblical Archaeology Review* 5 (July/August 1979): 34.
13. L. Y. Rahmani, "Ancient Jerusalem's Funerary Customs and Tombs," pt. 1, *Biblical Archaeologist* 44 (Summer 1981): 175.
14. Ibid., pt. 2, *Biblical Archaeologist* 44 (Fall 1981):230. Italics mine.
15. Andrew M. T. Moore, "A Pre-Neolithic Farmers' Village on the Euphrates," *Scientific American* 241 (August 1979): 62.
16. Alexander Marshack, "The Art and Symbols of Ice Age Man," *Human Nature*, September 1978, p. 41. Italics mine.
17. Mircea Eliade, *Rites and Symbols of Initiation; the Mysteries of Birth and Rebirth*, trans. Willard R. Trask (New York: Harper & Row, 1958), p. 8.
18. L. G. Freeman and J. Gonzáles Echegaray, "El Juyo: A 14,000 Year Old Sanctuary from Northern Spain," *History of Religions* 21 (August 1981): 15, 18.
19. Mircea Eliade, *The Forge and the Crucible*, trans. Stephen Corrin (New York: Harper Bros., 1962), p. 166.
20. John Canaday, "The Greek Who Bore Gifts to All Mankind," *Smithsonian*, July 1982, p. 55. Italics mine.
21. Plato *Republic* 9, 588 b-d, trans. Allan Bloom (New York: Basic Books, 1968).

22. Revelation 13:4.

23. Daniel 7:7-8:13. Italics mine.

24. Genesis 3:5.

25. *Art of the Huichol Indians*, ed. Kathleen Berrin (San Francisco: The Fine Arts Museums of San Francisco; New York: Harry N. Abrams, 1978), pp. 160, 23. Italics mine.

26. Ibid., p. 18, quoting Carl Lumholz, *Symbolism of the Huichol Indians*.

27. Mircea Eliade, *The Two and the One* (Chicago: Univ. of Chicago Press, 1979), p. 91.

28. Hiram W. Woodward, "Borobudar and the Mirrorlike Mind," *Archaeology* 34 (November-December 1981): 44, 46.

29. Zimmer, *Kunstform und Yoga*, p. 94 and plates 11-14.

30. *Time*, December 7, 1981, p. 93.

31. *The Gospel According to Thomas* log. 22:22-30, pp. 17-18.

32. Ibid., log. 82, p. 45.

33. Bronowski, op. cit., p. 142.

34. Exodus 3:2.

35. Ginzberg, op. cit., 1:319.

36. Heinrich Zimmer, *Zum Streit um die "Christusmythe"* (Berlin: Reuther & Reichard, 1910).

37. *The Interpreter's Dictionary of the Bible*, s.v. "Resurrection in the New Testament," by J. A. T. Robinson, 4:48.

38. Emil Brunner, *The Misunderstanding of the Church*, trans. Harold Knight (Philadelphia: Westminster Press, 1953), p. 48.

39. Colossians 3:2.

40. Hugh J. Schonfield, *The Passover Plot* (New York: Bernard Geis Associates, 1965), pp. 162ff.

41. Morton Smith, *Jesus the Magician* (New York: Harper & Row, 1978), pp. 5, 8.

42. Genesis 30:37-39.

43. Exodus 7:10-12.

44. Donald Wismer, *The Islamic Jesus; an Annotated Bibliography of Sources in English and French* (New York: Garland Publishing Co., 1977), p. 77.

45. 1 Corinthians 11:25.

46. Isaiah 2:3.

47. Isaiah 9:8.

48. Isaiah 9:2.

49. Isaiah 9:6.

50. Westman, op. cit., p. 138ff.

51. Diana L. Eck, "India's Tirthas: 'Crossings' in Sacred Geography," *History of Religions* 20 (May 1981): 323-44.

52. Ibid., p. 331.

53. Ibid., p. 328.

54. Genesis 32:22, 24.

55. Eck, p. 336.

56. Ibid., p. 339.

57. Ibid., p. 340-41.

58. Ibid., p. 342.

59. Confucius Ta Hsueh, *The Sacred Books of Confucius*, ed. and trans. Ch'hu Chai and Winberg Chai (New Hyde Park, N.Y.: University Books, 1965), p. 295.

60. Ibid., p. 296.

61. Genesis 3:22-23 (King James Version)

62. Kenneth W. Mann, review of *The Springs of Creativity* by H. Westman, in *Journal of Religion and Health* 1 (January 1962): 188.

63. Westman, op. cit., pp. 101ff.

64. Ginzberg, op. cit., 1:59.

65. 1 Corinthians 15:49 (King James Version).

66. Zohar, Fol. 144b, trans. Harry Sperling and Maurice Simon (London: Soncino Press, 1932) 2:65.

67. Joshua 6:5.

68. Ludwig Wittgenstein, *Philosophical Remarks* (Oxford: Basil Blackwell, 1975), p. 181.

69. Genesis 3:7.

70. Marshack, *Ice Age Art.*

71. James Mellaart, *Çatal Hüjük, A Neolithic Town in Anatolia* (New York: McGraw-Hill, 1967), p. 148.

72. John 1:46.

73. Matthew 8:20.

74. Matthew 8:19-20.

75. Matthew 8:23-26.

76. Matthew 8:28, 31-32.

77. Philippians 2:12. Italics mine.

78. Albert Rosenfeld, "Sociobiology Stirs a Controversy Over the Limits of Science," *Smithsonian*, September 1980, p. 73.

79. J. B. Haldane, *The Inequality of Man* (London: Chatto and Windus, 1932).

80. Popper and Eccles, op. cit., p. 98.

81. Goethe *Faust* 2,2 (Berlin: Verlag Th. Knaur, 1927), pp. 297-300. Translation mine.

82. Genesis 25:22

83. Exodus 13:12.

84. Exodus 34:19.

85. Genesis 27.

86. Genesis 32:22, 24, 26-29. Italics mine.

87. Genesis 32:30.

88. Genesis 33:10 (King James Version)

89. See also Westman, op. cit., pp. 138ff.

90. Exodus 33:18.

91. Exodus 33:20.

92. Westman, op. cit., pp. 48ff.; Exodus 32:20.

93. Leviticus 19:17. Italics mine.

94. Deuteronomy 23:7. Italics mine.

95. Deuteronomy 6:5 (King James Version).

96. Matthew 22:37. Italics mine.

97. Matthew 5:39, 48 (King James Version).

98. Matthew 5:41, 39.

99. Jeremiah 2:19 (King James Version).

100. Isaiah 45:7 (King James Version).

101. Amos 3:6 (King James Version).

102. Job 2:10.

103. Job, Vol. 15 of *The Anchor Bible*, p. 265.

104. Job 40:14-15.

105. Job Vol. 15 of *The Anchor Bible*, p. 268.

106. Westman, op cit., pp. 121-22.

CHAPTER 5

1. Rainer Maria Rilke, *Sonnette An Orpheus,* Second Series, No. 12, Translation mine.
2. 1 Corinthians 11:28.
3. Nikolaas Tinbergen, *The Study of Instinct* (Oxford: Clarendon Press, 1951), p. 76.
4. Sir Alister Hardy, *The Living Stream* (London: Collins, 1965), p. 230.
5. Ibid., p. 254.
6. *Atrahasis Epic,* op. cit.
7. Morenz, op. cit., p. 158.
8. PBS, "Termites and Telescopes," *Nova,* J. Bronowski Memorial Lecture, 1979.
9. Popper and Eccles, op. cit., p. 167.
10. Calvin, op. cit., p. 144.
11. *The Book of the Dead, the Papyrus of Ani,* trans. E. A. Wallis Budge (New York: Dover, 1967), p. cxviii.
12. Morenz, op. cit., p. 23.
13. Ibid., p. 33.
14. Ibid., p. 51.
15. Hermes Trismegistus. *Thrice-Greatest Hermes; Studies in Hellenistic Theosophy and Gnosis,* trans. G. R. S. Mead, 2 vols. (London: The Theosophical Publishing Society, 1906), 1:44-45.
16. Ibid., p. 50.
17. Ibid., p. 19.
18. Morenz, op. cit., p. 64.
19. Deuteronomy 30:11-13.
20. *Gilgamesh,* 11, 188-89, op. cit., p. 53.
21. *Atrahasis Epic,* op. cit.
22. Ibid., p. 96.
23. Bronowski, op. cit., p. 411.
24. Jeremiah 31:33, 29-30.
25. Breasted, op. cit., p. 142.
26. Ibid., p. 144.
27. Diodorus Siculus *Bibliotheca Historica* 1. 70.1, op. cit., p. 241.
28. Lance Morrow, "Wondering If Children Are Necessary, Time Essay," *Time,* 5 March 1979, p. 42.
29. Hebrews 8:9.
30. Jeremiah 31:33-34. Italics mine.
31. Pirke Aboth, 2.4, op. cit., p. 43.
32. Hebrews 10:31.
33. Deuteronomy 5:4-5.
34. Psalms 42:1-3.
35. Thorkild Jacobsen, *The Treasures of Darkness* (New Haven: Yale Univ. Press, 1978), p. 119.
36. Ibid., p. 120.
37. George Every, *Christian Mythology* (Feltham: Hamlyn, 1970), p. 29.
38. Genesis 6:18-19.
39. Genesis 8:18-19 (King James Version).
40. Genesis 9:12.
41. Genesis 9:15.

42. Malcolm W. Browne, "Scientists See a Loophole in the Fatal Law of Physics," *New York Times,* 29 May 1979, p. Cl.

43. Ibid.

44. Hebrews 6:19-20.

45. Jonah 2:8 (King James Version).

46. Murphy, op. cit., p. 52.

47. Jonah 1:1-2:8.

48. Mark 4:37, 39.

49. Mark 4:40.

50. David L. Miller, *The New Polytheism* (New York: Harper & Row, 1974), p. 59.

51. The Gospel of Philip 2.3, op. cit., p. 138.

52. Jeremiah 31:26-30, 34. Italics mine.

53. Breasted, op. cit., pp. 172-73.

54. Leviticus 16:6-10, 14, 15-22.

55. Burkert, op. cit., p. 65.

56. Leviticus 16:21.

56. Ginzberg, op. cit., 5:123.

58. Heinrich Karl Brugsch, *Religion and Mythologie der Alten Aegypter,* 2.Ausgabe (Leipzig: J. C. Hinrichs'sche Buchhandlung, 1891), p. 333. Translation mine.

59. Numbers 21:6-9.

60. 2 Kings 18:4.

61. Ditlef Nielsen, *Die Altarabische Mondreligion und die Mosaische Uberlieferung* (Strassburg: Verlag von Karl J. Truebner, 1904), pp. 190-91. Translation mine.

62. Job 40:14-15, 19. Italics mine.

63. Ginzberg, op. cit., 1:150.

64. Burkert, op. cit., pp. xi, 3.

65. *Enuma Elish* 4, 37, op. cit., p. 38-39; Westman, op. cit., p. 187ff.

66. Ibid., pp. 21-22.

67. Niels Bohr, *Collected Works,* ed. J. Rud Nielsen, 4 vols. (Amsterdam, N.Y.: North Holland Publishing Co., 1977), 4:26-27.

68. Idem, *Essays 1958-1962 on Atomic Physics and Human Knowledge* (New York: John Wiley & Sons, 1967), p. 2.

69. *I Ging, das Buch der Wandlung,* trans. Richard Wilhelm (Jena, Diederichs Verlag, 1924), p. 49. English translation mine.

70. Westman, op. cit., p. 187.

71. Bohr, *Essays,* p. 7.

72. Gertrude Stein, "Sacred Emily," in *Geography and Plays* (Boston: Four Seas Co., 1922), p. 187.

73. Exodus 14:16.

74. Genesis 1:6-8.

75. Numbers 20:8, 10-12.

76. Psalms 147:15ff.

77. Ezekiel 1:5-6.

78. *The Babylonian Genesis,* p. 85.

79. Frankfort, op. cit.; see also E. Douglas Van Buren, *The Flowing Vase and the God with Streams* (Berlin: Hans Schoeltz & Co., 1933).

80. Ginzberg, op. cit., 3:52.

81. Genesis 2:10.

82. Numbers 20:1-2.

83. Ginzberg, op. cit., 3:308.

84. *The Dura-Europos Synagog; a Re-Evaluation (1932-1972),* ed. Joseph Gutmann (Missoula, Mont.: American Academy of Religion, Society of Biblical Literature, 1973), p. 8.

85. Psalms 147:18.

86. Genesis 1:2.

87. Brian Lewis, *The Sargon Legend: A Study of the Akkadian Text and the Tale of the Hero Who Was Exposed At Birth* (Cambridge, Mass.: American Schools of Oriental Research, 1980). See also Exodus 2:1-10.

88. Oscar Wilde, "Salome," in *The Plays of Oscar Wilde* (New York: Modern Library, 1980), pp. 12, 39.

89. H. W. and D. J. Janson, *History of Art* (Englewood Cliffs, N.J.: Prentice Hall; New York: Abrams, 1967), p. 310.

90. Matthew 14:17.

91. Matthew 14:23.

92. Matthew 14:22, 24 (King James Version).

93. John 6:15-21 (King James Version).

94. Hugh Rahner, *Greek Myths and Christian Mystery* (New York: Biblio and Tannen, 1971), p. 346.

95. Ginzberg, op. cit., 3:49.

96. René Huyghe, *Art and the Spirit of Man,* trans. Norbert Guterman (New York: Abrams, 1962), p. 406.

97. Pierre Teilhard de Chardin, *The Divine Milieu* (New York: Harper Brothers, 1960), pp. 48, 49-50.

98. Calvin, op. cit., p. 121.

99. Aubrey Menen, *Venice* (Amsterdam, N.Y.: Time and Life Books, 1976), pp. 13, 16.

100. Revelation 9:18-19.

101. Black Elk, *Black Elk Speaks; Being the Life Story of a Holy Man of the Oglala Sioux,* as told to John G. Neihardt (Lincoln: Univ. of Nebraska Press, 1961), pp. 167, 179.

102. 2 Enoch 30:8.

103. Gilles Quispel, "The Gnostic Anthropos and the Jewish Tradition," *Eranos* 22 (1954): 217.

104. Hans Küng, "Toward a New Consensus in Catholic (and Ecumenical) Theology," in "Consensus in Theology? A dialogue with Hans Küng and Edward Schillebeeckx," *Journal of Ecumenical Studies* 17 (Winter 1980): 5.

105. Fred Pratt Green, "Is There a Purpose?" in *Images of Tomorrow* ed. J.F.A. Heath-Stubbs (London: SCM Press, 1953).

CHAPTER 6

1. William Blake, "Auguries of Innocence," in *The Poetry and Prose of William Blake* (New York: Doubleday, 1970), p. 481.

2. John 7:34.

3. Acts of John 95, 24ff., in *The New Testament Apocrypha,* p. 230.

4. Donald M. MacKinnon, "Sacrament and Common Meal," in *Studies of the Gospels,* ed. D. E. Nineham (Oxford: Blackwell, 1957), p. 205.

5. Translation mine.

6. Talmud, op. cit., Baba Bathra, Fol. 75.

7. *The Interpreter's Dictionary of the Bible,* s.v. "Sacrifices," by T. H. Gaster, 4:158.

8. Ibid., p. 151. Italics mine.

9. "A Time to Speak," *Christianity and Crisis*, 1 March 1982, p. 56.

10. Breasted, op. cit., p. 174.

11. Laurens Van Der Post, *A Bar of Shadow* (London: Hogarth Press, 1954), p. 16.

12. Hans Küng, "Why I Remain a Catholic," in *Journal of Ecumenical Studies* 17:165.

13. *The Apocrypha*, Revised Standard Version of the Old Testament (New York: Thomas Nelson, 1957).

14. Don Cupitt, *Times Literary Supplement*, 25 April 1980, p. 458.

15. Bonhoeffer, op. cit., p. 122.

16. Peter Brian Medawar and Jean S. Medawar, *The Life Science* (London: Wildwood House, Ltd., 1977), p. 173.

17. John 9:41.

18. Frederick Henry Heinemann, *Existentialism and the Modern Predicament* (New York: Harper, 1953), p. 192.

19. Ibid.

20. Ibid., p. 197.

21. Ibid., p. 201.

22. Talmud, op. cit., Synhedrin, Fol. 38a.

23. *The Origin of Life on Earth*, ed. A. I. Oparin, Proc. of the International Symposium Sponsored by the Union of Biochemistry, August 1957 (New York: Pergamon Press, 1959), pp. 385-86. Italics mine.

24. Bertrand Russell, op. cit., p. 586ff.

25. "When the Poor Evangelize the Church," *Origins*, NC Documentary Service, 5 June 1980, p. 36.

26. Irenaeus *Proof of the Apostolic Preaching*, trans. and annotated by Joseph P. Smith, Ancient Christian Writers, no. 16 (Westminster, Md.: Newman Press, 1952), p. 50.

27. Exodus 23:2.

28. The Gospel of Truth 1. 3, in *The Nag Hammadi Library*, op. cit., p. 41. Italics mine.

29. Hans Jonas, *The Gnostic Religion*, 2nd ed. (Boston: Beacon Press, 1970), p. 40.

30. Medawar and Medawar, op. cit., p. 173.

31. *The Interpreter's Dictionary of the Bible*, s.v. "Pleroma," by C. F. D. Moule, 3:827.

32. Hoyle, op. cit., p. 164. Italics mine.

33. Calvin, op. cit., p. 258.

34. Marshack, "The Art and Symbols of Ice Age Man," op. cit., p. 41.

35. John Norman Davidson Kelly, *Early Christian Doctrines* (New York: Harper, 1958), p. 179.

36. Isaiah 1:16.

37. Spinoza *Ethics*, ed. James Gutman (New York: Hafner Publishing Co., 1957), p. 280.

38. 1 Corinthians 11:27 (King James Version).

39. Russell, op. cit., p. 592.

40. Ibid., p. 594.

41. Michael Polanyi, *The Tacit Dimension* (New York: Doubleday, 1961), p. 37.

42. David Bohm, *Wholeness and the Implicate Order* (London: Routledge & Kegan Paul, 1980), p. 12.

43. Irenaeus, op. cit., p. 50.

44. Hoyle, op. cit., p. 122.

45. Max Planck, *The Philosophy of Physics* (New York: Norton, 1936), p. 83.

46. Heisenberg, op. cit., p. 45.

47. Ephesians 1:10.

48. G. Zukav, *The Dancing Wu Li Masters; An Overview of the New Physics* (New York: William Morrow & Co., 1979), p. 329.

49. Ibid., p. 298.

50. Ibid., p. 305, 320.

51. Some experiments of late proved in some instances their own premises. Bell's theorem was exposed to criticism and experiments based on Albert Einstein's, Boris Podolsky's, and Nathan Rosen's exclusive beliefs in classical physics, cf. *Science News*, 22 August 1981, p. 117.

52. Zukav, op. cit., p. 320.

53. Ibid., p. 316.

54. The Gospel of Truth 1, 3, op. cit., p. 41. Italics mine.

55. Carl Gustav Jung, *The Structure and Dynamics of the Psyche*, vol. VIII of *The Collected Works*, (London: Routledge & Kegan Paul, 1960), pp. 518-19.

56. Planck, op. cit., p. 114.

57. Genesis 1:3.

58. John 1:1.

59. *Enuma Elish*, Tablet 4. 21-27, op. cit., p. 37.

60. Ibid., 1. 156-57, p. 24.

61. Luke 14:26-27.

62. Genesis 12:1 (King James Version).

63. Matthew 10:34-35.

64. Mitchell Dahood, S.J., "Are the Ebla Tablets Relevant to Biblical Research?" *Biblical Archaeology Review* 6 (September/October 1980): 56.

65. Popper and Eccles, op. cit., pp. 451, 456.

66. "Oldest Tool Kit Yet," *Science News*, 7 February 1981, p. 83.

67. Ibid., p. 84.

68. Ibid.

69. James B. Harrod, "The Bow: A Techno-Mythic Hermeneutic — Ancient Greece and the Mesolythic," *Journal of the American Academy of Religion* 49 (1981): 427, 429, 438-39.

70. Genesis 49:24.

71. In private correspondence, Professor Gershom Scholem has drawn my attention also to Palestinian Talmud, Hovayoth Ch. 2,5: Midrash Breshith Rabba, Ch. 98, 201, ed. Theodor Albek, p. 1270.

72. Augustine *On Original Sin*, ch. 32, in *Basic Writings*, 1:643.

73. Breasted, op. cit., pp. 256-57.

74. Rahner, op. cit., pp. 345-46.

75. David Bohm and B. Hiley, "On the Intuitive Understanding of Nonlocality as Implied by Quantum Theory," preprint, Birkbeck College, University of London, 1974. See also David Bohm, *Wholeness and the Implicate Order*.

76. Ezekiel 1:4-6, 8-10, 15, 17, 19, 26-28.

77. Rahner, op. cit., p. 74.

78. Ibid., p. 75.

79. Paul Friedlander, *Plato*, trans. Hans Meyerhoff (New York: Harper & Row, 1964), Vol. 1, pp. 192-93.

80. Gershom Scholem, *Major Trends in Jewish Mysticism*, rev. ed. (New York: Schocken Books, 1946), p. 56.

81. Ibid., p. 51.

82. 1 Corinthians 11:27-29.

83. Robert Brain, *The Last Primitive Peoples* (New York: Crown Publishers, 1976), p. 196.

84. Maude Southwell Wahlman, *Traditional Art of West Africa: Selections from the Victor DuBois Collection.* Exhibition at Colby College, August-October 1980 (Waterville, Me.: Colby College Museum, 1980), pp. 56-57.

85. Brain, op. cit., pp. 196-202.

86. The Book of Thomas the Contender 2. 138, in *The Nag Hammadi Library*, pp. 188ff.

87. Bruce Lincoln, *Priests, Warriors and Cattle; A Study in the Ecology of Religions* (Berkeley: Univ. of California Press, 1981), p. 82.

88. Bohm, *Wholeness and the Implicate Order,* op. cit., p. 22.

89. Emmanuel Anati. "Saving the World's Rock Art," in *Archaeology*, 36 (March/April 1983): 30.

90. B. P. Groslier, *Hinterindien* (Baden Baden: Holle Verlag, 1980). pp. 192-93.

91. William Bascom, *African Arts* (Berkeley: Lovie Museum, 1967), p. 79.

92. Ekpo Eyo, *Two Thousand Years of Nigerian Art* (Lagos: Federal Department of Antiquities, 1977), p. 184.

93. Genesis 17:1.

94. Matthew 5:48.

95. James George Frazer, *The Golden Bough*, 12 vols. (London: Macmillan, 1936), 8:148.

96. Alfred Meyer, "Temple of the Aztecs," *Science '80*, November 1980, p. 69.

97. Piers Paul Read, *Alive* (New York: Avon Books, 1974).

98. Zechariah 11:9.

99. Raphael Patai, *The Hebrew Goddess* (New York: KTAV Publishing House, 1967), p. 98.

100. Bernardino de Sahagún, *General History of the Things of New Spain*, Florentine Codex, Book 3 (Santa Fe, N.M.: School of American Research, Univ. of Utah, 1978), pp. 5ff. Italics mine.

101. Hebrews 11:10.

102. Rudolf Otto, *Das Heilige*, 35th ed, Sonderausgabe 1963 (Munich: C. H. Beck, 1963), p. 6. Translation mine.

103. Augustine, quoted in Joseph A. Jungman, S. J., *The Mass* (Collegeville, Minn.: The Liturgical Press, 1976), p. 56.

104. Samuel Pisar, *Of Blood and Hope* (Boston: Little, Brown, 1979), p. 310.

105. Meyer, op. cit., p. 70.

106. Pisar, op. cit., pp. 288-89.

107. Matthew 26:49.

108. Hebrews 13:3.

109. Exodus 12:14.

110. Jungman, op. cit., p. 104.

111. Pius Parsch, *The Liturgy of the Mass*, trans. Frederic C. Eckhoff (St. Louis: B. Herder Book Co., 1947), p. 186.

112. Ibid., p. 234.

113. Howitt, op. cit., p. 458.

114. Parsch, op. cit., p. 308. Italics mine.

115. Ibid., p. 288.

116. "St. Laurence, August 10," in Butler, op. cit., 3:297-98.

117. Westman, op. cit., p. 112, quoting Ginzberg, op. cit., 1:278.

118. Deuteronomy 6:5 (King James Version).

119. Rashi, *Kommentar zum Pentateuch*, trans. Selig Bamberger (Hamburg: Verlag Georg Kramer, 1928), p. 469.

120. John 2:2-4 (King James Version).
121. John 2:13 (King James Version).
122. John 2:14 (King James Version).
123. John 2:16 (King James Version).
124. John 2:15 (King James Version).
125. Matthew 3:16, Mark 1:10, Luke 3:22, John 1:32.
126. Zechariah 11:4-5, 6.
127. Zechariah 11:9-10, 12-14.
128. Zechariah 11:17.
129. Homer *Odyssey*, Bk. 9, trans. Robert Fitzgerald (New York: Doubleday & Co., Anchor Books, 1963), p. 148.
130. Genesis 4:9.
131. Bonhoeffer, op. cit., p. 93.
132. Pisar, op. cit., p. 310.
133. Henry Frankfort, "Religion in Babylonia 4000 Years Ago," *Illustrated London News*, 5 September, 1936, p. 390.
134. Graves, op. cit., pp. 31, 153.
135. Homer, op. cit., p. 156.
136. Zechariah 11:17.
137. Matthew 5:29.
138. Morenz, op. cit., p. 83.
139. Micha bin Gorion, *Die Sagen der Juden*, Die Erzvater (Frankfurt / Main: Rütten and Loening, 1914), p. 356. Translation mine.
140. Aeschylus *Agamemnon*, ll. 160-66, 176-78, trans. Richard Lattimore, in *The Complete Greek Tragedies*, ed. David Grene and Richard Lattimore (Chicago: Univ. of Chicago Press, 1942), pp. 39-40.
141. *Enuma Elish*, 6.33, op. cit., p. 47.
142. John 1:1-2 (King James Version).
143. Genesis 1:3.
144. John 9:3, 5-6.
145. Matthew 5:27-30.
146. Psalms 23:2-3.
147. "Pacem in Terris," op. cit., 5:108-10.
148. Homer, op. cit., p. 210.
149. Ibid., bk. 10, p. 172.
150. Ibid., p. 214.
151. Rahner, op. cit., p. 376. Italics mine.
152. Ibid., p. 383.
153. Matthew 4:1.
154. Numbers 21:8 (King James Version).
155. Genesis 29:18.
156. Genesis 33:10; and Westman, op. cit., p. 156.
157. Homer, op. cit., pp. 217-18.
158. Homer *Iliad*, trans. Robert Fitzgerald (New York: Anchor Books, 1975), p. 119.
159. Burkert, op. cit., p. 55.
160. Genesis 32:31.
161. Genesis 32:25.
162. Homer *Odyssey*, Bk. 19, op. cit., p. 368.

163. Ibid., p. 367.

164. Aeschylus *Agamemnon*, ll. 205-225, op. cit., p. 41.

165. Ibid., ll. 1095-1097, p. 69.

166. Ibid., ll. 1242-45, p. 74.

167. Rahner, op. cit., p. 380.

168. *National Geographic*, February 1981, p. 207. Italics mine.

169. Exodus 23:2.

170. Luke 9:24-25.

171. Plato *Phaedrus*, ll. 245ff., in *Collected Dialogues of Plato*, trans. R. Hackforth, Bollingen Series, 71 (Princeton, N.J.: Princeton Univ. Press, 1961), pp. 492-93.

172. Ibid., ll. 246ff., p. 493.

173. Emmanuel Anati, *Evolution and Style in Camunian Rock Art*, trans. Larryn Diamond (Capo di Ponte: Centro Camuno di Studi Preistorici, 1976), p. 111.

174. Marija Gimbutas, "The Beginnings of the Bronze Age in Europe and the Indo-Europeans: 3500-2500 B.C.," *Journal of Indo-European Studies* 1 (1973): 163-214.

175. David Bohm, op. cit., pp. 10-11.

176. Gimbutas, op. cit., p. 15.

177. Ibid., pp. 53-54.

178. Ibid., p. 111.

179. Jeremiah 2:18-19.

180. E. T. C. Werner, *Myths and Legends of China* (London: S. Harrap & Co., 1922), p. 129

181. Hebrews 10:31.

182. Matthew 10:34.

183. The Gospel of Philip 2. 3, op. cit., p. 138.

184. Rahner, op. cit., p. 14.

185. Deuteronomy 30:19.

186. John 10:1-3.

187. John 10:9, 11.

188. Scholder, op. cit., p. 736. Translation mine.

189. Acts of John 96. 28ff., op. cit., pp. 230-31.

190. Curtis Bill Pepper, *An Artist and the Pope* (New York: Grosset & Dunlap, 1968), pp. 192-93. Italics mine.

CHAPTER 7

1. Robert Henry Pfeiffer, *Introduction to the Old Testament* (London: A. & C. Black, Ltd., 1948), pp. 754-55.

2. Ibid., p. 764.

3. *The Interpreter's Dictionary of the Bible*, s.v. "Daniel," by S. B. Frost, 1:768.

4. Daniel, vol. 23 of *The Anchor Bible*, trans. Louis F. Hartman and Alexander A. Di Lella (New York: Doubleday, 1978), p. 7.

5. *The Interpreter's Dictionary of the Bible*, s.v. "Perfection," by J. Y. Campbell, 3:730. See also *Theological Dictionary of the New Testament*, ed. Gerhard Friedrich, 8:167, and G. Abbott, *Manual Greek Lexicon of the New Testament*, 3rd ed. (Edinburgh: T. & T. Clark, 1937), p. 42, as well as Matthew, vol. 26 of *The Anchor Bible*, op. cit., pp. 71, 49.

6. Matthew 5:48 (King James Version).

7. 1 John 4:12 (King James Version).

8. 1 John 4:17. Italics mine.

9. Exodus 3:2 (King James Version).

10. Daniel 3:15, 24. Italics mine.

11. Plato *Timaeus*, l. 17a, in *Collected Dialogues of Plato*, op. cit., p. 1153.

12. Daniel 6:12, 16-17, 19-22.

13. Bohm, op. cit., p. ix.

14. H. Westman, The Golden Calf (London: Guild of Pastoral Psychology, 1941, repr. 1945); *Springs*, pp. 48ff. Italics mine.

15. Idem, *The Old Testament and Analytical Psychology, The Problem of the Shadow: Jacob-Esau* (London: Guild of Pastoral Psychology, 1939); *Springs*, pp. 138ff.

16. Nietzsche, op. cit., pp. 188-90.

17. Ibid., p. 190.

18. Ibid., p. 126.

19. Ibid., p. 190-91.

20. John 14:15-17.

21. Daniel 4:10-12, 20-22, 23-24, 25, 26-27. Italics mine.

22. Daniel 7:2-8, 11-12. Italics mine.

23. Ezekiel 1:4, 10, 26.

24. Ezekiel 2:1-3.

25. Daniel, vol. 23 of *The Anchor Bible*, p. 219.

26. Ibid., p. 101n.

27. Daniel 6:24.

28. Talmud, op. cit., Berakot, Fol. 7b.

29. Westman, *Springs*, pp. 101ff.

30. Genesis 12:1.

31. Genesis 13:14-15.

32. John 10:34.

33. Revelation 22:13.

34. Revelation 22:16.

35. Plato *Laws*, ll. 715-16a, in *Collected Dialogues of Plato*, pp. 1306-1307.

36. Revelation 1:17-18.

37. Isaiah 44:1-2.

38. Isaiah 44:5-6.

39. Genesis 25:23.

40. *Gilgamesh* 1, 4, op. cit., p. 13.

41. Genesis 3:7.

42. Genesis 1:20.

43. Francis Crick, *Life Itself: Its Origin and Nature* (New York: Simon & Schuster, 1981), p. 15.

44. John M. Allegro, *The Sacred Mushroom and the Cross* (New York: Bantam Books, 1971) pp. xi-xii.

45. Crick, op. cit., p. 88.

46. Teilhard de Chardin, op. cit., p. 49. Italics mine.

47. John 10:34, 38.

48. John 10:11.

49. John 10:7.

50. Psalms 82:5-7.

51. Psalms 82:1-4.
52. *The Interpreter's Dictionary of the Bible*, s.v. "Apocalypticism," by M. Rist, 1:158.
53. Isaiah 11:6.
54. Revelation 22:1.
55. Ezekiel 1:26 (King James Version).
56. Daniel 7:13.
57. Revelation, vol. 38 of *The Anchor Bible*, trans. and commentary by J. Massyngberde Ford (Garden City, N.Y.: Doubleday, 1975), p. 51.
58. Revelation 6:1.
59. Revelation 8:2.
60. Revelation 15:6.
61. Revelation, vol. 38 of *The Anchor Bible*, p. 4.
62. Revelation 13:11.
63. Revelation 13:14, 15-18.
64. Isaiah 44:6.
65. Daniel 4:22.
66. Genesis 1:9.
67. Revelation 10:1-2, 5-10.
68. Ezekiel 2:8-10; 3:1-3.
69. Matthew 26:39.
70. Matthew 27:46.
71. Revelation 19:17-21.
72. Revelation 17:8.
73. Revelation 10:1.
74. Genesis 9:17.
75. Homer *Odyssey*, bk. 10, l. 318, p. 174.
76. Rahner, op. cit., p. 194.
77. *The Interpreter's Dictionary of the Bible*, s.v. "Mandrake," by J. V. Trever, 3:256-57.
78. Homer, op. cit., l. 311ff., p. 174.
79. Ibid., p. 175.
80. Genesis 30:3.
81. Genesis 30:9.
82. Genesis 30:8.
83. Genesis 30:23.
84. Genesis 32:28.
85. Tikva Frymer-Kensky, "Patriarchal Family Relationships and Near Eastern Law," *Biblical Archaeologist* 44 (Fall 1981): 211.
86. Numbers 21:9.
87. *The Interpreter's Dictionary of the Bible*, s.v. "Unicorn," by E. M. Good, 4:734.
88. Graves, op. cit., pp. 177, 235, 264ff.
89. Plato *Phaedrus* ll. 246ff., op. cit., p. 493.
90. Alexander Marshack, *Roots of Civilization* (New York: McGraw-Hill, 1972).
91. Bohm, op. cit., p. 174.
92. Graves, op. cit., p. 134.
93. Howard Wallace, "Leviathan and the Beast in Revelation," in *Biblical Archaeologist Reader*, 1 (New York: Doubleday Anchor Books, 1961), p. 290.
94. Revelation 9:4-7, 17-18, 20-21.

95. Genesis 4:15.

96. Genesis 4:6-7.

97. Ezekiel 9:4.

98. Westman, op. cit., p. 91.

99. John 10:34.

100. John 10:38.

101. John 5:17.

102. Revelation 13:4.

103. Revelation 20:1-4.

104. Revelation 1:13, 16.

105. Revelation 1:17-18.

106. *The Acts of Thomas*, ed. A. F. J. Klijn (Leiden: E. J. Brill, 1962), p. 70.

107. John 10:34.

108. British Library, MS. Catalogue 3535413.

109. Exodus 15:1.;

110. Matthew 10:34.

111. "Urbi et Orbi," 25 December 1978, in *L'Osservatore romano*, Weekly Edition in English, 1 January 1979, p. 1. Italics mine.

112. Shirley Williams, *Politics is for People* (New York: Penquin Books, 1981), p. 205.

113. J. D. Reed, *Time*, 27 July 1981, p. 77.

114. T. S. Eliot, *The Cocktail Party* (New York: Harcourt, Brace & Co., 1950), act 1, sc. 3, p. 98.

115. Ann Crittendon, *New York Times*, 17 August 1981, p. 1, col. 4. See also Nancy Amidei, *Christianity and Crisis*, 28 December 1981, p. 451.

116. Colossians 3:2-3.

117. Joseph Klausner, *From Jesus to Paul* (London: Allen and Unwin, 1942), p. 77.

118. Lewis Mumford, *The Myth of the Machine*, Vol. 1 (New York: Harcourt, Brace & World, 1966), p. 33.

119. David L. Waltz, "Artificial Intelligence," *Scientific American*, October 1982, p. 120.

120. Ibid., p. 118.